Popular Music & Society

Third Edition

BRIAN LONGHURST AND
DANIJELA BOGDANOVIĆ

polity

First edition published in 1995 by Polity Press
Second edition published in 2007 by Polity Press
This edition first published in 2014

Polity Press
65 Bridge Street
Cambridge CB2 1UR, UK

Polity Press
350 Main Street
Malden, MA 02148, USA

ISBN-13: 978-07456-5364-8
ISBN-13: 978-07456-5365-5 (pb)

A catalogue record for this book is available from the British Library.

Typeset in 9.5 on 12 pt Utopia by
Servis Filmsetting Ltd, Stockport, Cheshire
Printed and bound in Great Britain by Clays Ltd, St Ives plc

For further information on Polity, visit our website: www.politybooks.com

Popular Music & Society

Third Edition

PO44525

Contents

Figures

Tables

Boxes

Acknowledgements

Brian Longhurst

Those who have helped on the two previous editions of this book will still see their influence. Thanks in particular are due to Nick Abercrombie, Celia Lury, Scott Lash, Eamonn Carrabine and Dan Laughey and for the encouragement of my former Salford colleagues Derek B. Scott and Sheila Whiteley. Danijela Bogdanović's exemplary work meant that a third edition could exist at all.

All at Polity Press have been very helpful, as were the comments from the publisher's readers; special thanks to Pam Thomas on the first edition and Andrea Drugan on the second.

At points this book argues that music is very important to members of society in emotional ways that almost cannot be put into words. That argument in part stems from my own feelings about music and personal life. Thanks to my cousin, Terry Boiston, who educated me in Elvis Presley and Otis Redding, leaving me with continuing attachments.

More than ever, my biggest debts are to those I love most. Thanks to mum and dad who always had music around and respected my own musical tastes, which can't always have been easy. I would like to thank my dad in particular, whose musical creativity I have not appreciated enough for all the times he plated 'The Old Music Master' for me in the back room at Shakespeare Road when I was a child. James and Tim inspire with knowledge, discussion and fun. Above all, thanks to Bernadette, who puts on the music that I would not hear otherwise, listened to a significant part of my record collection one night in the very, very early days, and most importantly is always there for me. Seeing Bonnie Prince Billy and Harem Scarem in Ardross in April 2006 with Bernadette, James and Tim was very special.

Danijela Bogdanović

I am indebted to Brian Longhurst for inviting me to contribute to the third edition of *Popular Music and Society*. Although developing an established text can be taxing, working alongside Brian has been a rewarding, valuable and stimulating experience. I hope that our diverse cultural references, coupled with our wide-ranging taste in music, contributed positively to the arguments presented herewith.

The University of Salford has provided the space, facilities and resources that allowed me to pursue many of the text preparation tasks. Alison Adam offered flexibility and supported my work on this edition, which took place alongside our joint endeavours on VOME project. My colleagues Michael Dowd and Eileen Wattam commented astutely in our daily conversations about music, with Michael guiding me through the maze of music streaming services and Eileen sharing her own experiences as a performer.

Many others, including all the musicians who took part in my PhD research on popular music masculinities, have been supportive of my efforts; however, my gratitude extends to the following people in particular:

Laurence – for love, resilience, patience and encouragement; for access to his impeccable record collection and for sharing his feelings and thoughts about music; for widening my musical taste; and for reminding me that musical exclusivity can easily become a form of 'fascism'.

Andrew – for keeping alive the Sound of Young Scotland; for being a seeker of new and exciting words, images and sounds; for our musically themed days and nights in Glasgow, Edinburgh and Manchester; for pointing me in the direction of valuable resources; and for sharing his precious copies of *Plan B* magazine.

Steven – for demystifying many things 'digital' without losing the sight of the human; for sharing his experiences of writing, recording and performing music; and for a memorable evening of wine and stargazing at the Old Observatory House, Edinburgh.

Simon – for never failing to remind me that good music existed before 1977, for François and Scott, for continually providing inspiration with his own recordings, films and art.

Craig – for matters of music and the heart, for Elliott and Sufjan. For hand claps and harmonies.

The authors and publishers wish to thank the following for permission to use copyright material:

American Sociological Review and David Berger for table 1.1, from David Berger and Richard A. Peterson, 'Cycles in symbol production: the case of popular music', *American Sociological Review*, 40 (1975).

Berg Publishers for figure 9.1, from D. Muggleton, *Inside Subculture* (2000).

British Phonographic Industry Ltd for material in tables IN1, IN2, IN3, 7.1 and 7.2 and figure 1.4.

Cambridge University Press for box 9.1 from Tia DeNora, *Music in Everyday Life* (2000).

Charly records for box 3.3 from the sleeve notes for *Jimmy Reed Upside Your Head* (1980), by Cliff White, courtesy of Charly Records.

Jonathan Cape and Hill & Wang for figure 5.4, an excerpt from *Mythologies* by Roland Barthes, trans. Annette Lavers. Translation copyright © 1972 by Jonathan Cape Ltd. Reprinted by permission of Jonathan Cape and of Hill & Wang, a division of Farrar, Straus & Giroux, LLC.

Constable Publishers Ltd for figures 1.9, 1.10, 1.11 and 1.12, from R. Wallis and K. Malm, *Big Musics from Small Peoples* (1984).

Faber & Faber Ltd for box 2.1, from J. Savage, *England's Dreaming: Sex Pistols and Punk Rock* (1991), reprinted by permission of Faber & Faber Inc., an affiliate of Farrar, Straus & Giroux, LLC.

The Guardian for material in box 3.1 by Olivia Mace, box 3.5 by Suzanne Moore, box 4.4 by Alexandra Topping, and box 8.1 by Steven Wells. Copyright *The Guardian*.

HarperCollins Publishers Ltd and Hill & Wang for box 5.1, an excerpt from *Image/Music/Text* by Roland Barthes, trans. Stephen Heath. English translation copyright © 1977 by Stephen Heath. Reprinted by permission of HarperCollins and of Hill & Wang, a division of Farrar, Straus & Giroux, LLC.

Hutchinson & Co. for figure 7.1, from S. Hall and T. Jefferson (eds), *Resistance Through Rituals: Youth Subcultures in Post-War Britain* (1976).

The International Federation of the Phonographic Industry for figure 1.5, from *World Sales 1989* (1990).

International Music Publications Ltd for the lyrics quoted in figure 5.6, from 'Material Girl' by Peter Brown and Robert Rans as recorded by Madonna.

Lawrence & Wishart for box 6.3, from E. Carrabine and B. Longhurst, 'Mosaics of Omnivorousness: Middle-Class Youth and Popular Culture', in *New Formations* 38: *Hating Tradition Properly: the Legacy of the Frankfurt School in Cultural Studies* (1999).

Manchester University Press and the authors for box 4.2, from D. Hatch and S. Millward, *From Blues to Rock: An Analytical History of Pop Music* (1987).

The Open University for figure 7.2, from R. Middleton and J. Muncie, 'Pop culture, pop music and post-war youth: countercultures', Unit 20 of the Open University course on Popular Culture.

Open University Press and the authors for figures 5.4 and 5.5, from R. Middleton, *Studying Popular Music* (1990); table 5.1, from D. Laing, *One Chord Wonders: Power and Meaning in Punk Rock* (1985); and box 3.2, from D. Bradley, *Understanding Rock 'n' Roll: Popular Music in Britain 1955–1964* (1992).

Oxford University Press for box 2.2, from M. Bayton, *Frock Rock: Women Performing Popular Music* (1998), and box 5.3, from R. Middleton, *'Introduction' to Reading Pop: Approaches to Textual Analysis in Popular Music* (2000), by permission of Oxford University Press.

Penguin Books Ltd for box 7.1, from David Robins and Philip Cohen, *Knuckle Sandwich: Growing up in the Working-Class City* (1978), copyright © David Robins and Philip Cohen, 1978.

Pluto Press for box 2.5, from S. Steward and S. Garratt, *Signed, Sealed and Delivered: True Life Stories of Women in Pop* (1984).

Polity Press for figures IN.1 and IN.2, from D. Held, *Introduction to Critical Theory: Horkheimer to Habermas* (1980); and box 6.2, from S. Thornton, *Club Cultures: Music, Media and Subcultural Capital* (1996).

Routledge Publishers for figure 1.2, from J. Bishop, 'Building international empires of sound: concentrations of power and property in the "global" music market', in *Popular Music and Society* 28 (2005); figure 1.3, from Paul Bagguley, 'Post-Fordism and enterprise culture: flexibility, autonomy and changes in economic organization', in R. Keat and N. Abercrombie (eds), *Enterprise Culture* (1991); figure 5.6, from Barbara Bradby, 'Like a virgin-mother? Materialism and maternalism in the songs of Madonna', from *Cultural Studies* 6 (1992); figure 5.7, from E. Ann Kaplan, *Rocking Around the Clock: Music Television, Postmodernism, and Consumer Culture* (1987); figure 6.1, from P. Bourdieu, *Distinction* (1984); and box 8.3, from H. Jenkins, *Textual Poachers: Television Fans and Participatory Culture* (1992).

S. T. Publishing for box 1.2, from George Marshall, *The Two Tone Story* (1990).

Sage Publications for figures 9.2, 9.3 and 10.4, from N. Abercrombie and B. Longhurst, *Audiences* (1998), copyright © N. Abercrombie and B. Longhurst, 1998.

Serpent's Tail for box 4.3, from D. Toop, *Rap Attack 3* (1999).

Sony/ATV Music Publishers for box 5.1, from Lana Del Rey, 'Video Games' (Grant/ Parker) and for lyric reprint from Oasis, 'Some Might Say' (Gallagher).

Souvenir Press for box 3.1, from C. Gillet, *The Sound of the City: The Rise of Rock and Roll* (1983).

University of Massachusetts Press for figure 2.3, from *On Becoming a Rock Musician* by H. Stith Bennett, copyright © 1980 by University of Massachusetts Press.

University of Minnesota Press for figures 5.8, 5.10 and 5.11, copyright © University of Minnesota Press.

Virago Press and Random House, Inc., for box 4.1, from M. Angelou, *Singin' and Swingin' and Gettin' Merry Like Christmas*, copyright © by Maya Angelou 1976, published by Random House 1976 and Virago Press 1985.

Preface

This book is written for undergraduate students. It aims to provide an introduction to the area of popular music and society that will be useful to those taking courses in the areas of the sociology of culture, cultural studies, communication studies and media studies. It should also be of interest to those more general readers wanting an overview of contemporary developments in the sociological study of popular music. Our aim has partly been to locate the analysis of popular music in the context of more general debates about culture, its analysis and effects.

The book gives accounts of the main theories in the area of popular music and reviews the most important substantive studies which have appeared in this field. It also includes a significant amount of empirical data where relevant. In addition to words on the page, the book uses three main devices to convey information and illustrate the accounts and theories.

Figures, which often summarize whole arguments or the most salient parts of them, are used in a number of places. These summaries are represented in diagrams or lists of points. We have created some of the figures ourselves and others are drawn from other acknowledged sources. Our view is that a clear diagram is often a useful way of conveying the sense of an argument and can help in the understanding of the overall structure or main themes. It is a device which is under-employed in sociology.

There are also a number of tables in the book. In the main, these contain quantitative data and are distinguished from figures on that basis. The data given most often refer to the United Kingdom, though figures are also provided for world record sales, and so on. Salient points to be drawn from the tables are discussed in the text of the book. However, the data may also be of use in student project work and essays, where other issues may be important.

The third device is the box. Boxes have been used to set off material which goes beyond the main flow of the text but which illustrates key points. The boxes also contain some of the less sociological writing on popular music, which can be very informative and provoke thought on the nature of contemporary music. Our hope is that these boxes might encourage the reader to seek out such literature, which contains some of the most pleasurable writing on pop music. There is also a fair amount of quotation from important sources, which is used in a direct way in the main text of the book.

The book is written in the belief that the pleasures of pop music and its analysis can be combined. It is a common experience for anyone teaching a course on the media to be approached at some point by a student who says that their pleasures in television or film have been ruined by the analysis carried out on them (see Carrabine and Longhurst 1997 for discussion and empirical investigation). Those of us who teach such courses can often recall such feelings when we were first introduced to the study of media. Our (perhaps inadequate) response is to suggest that the pleasures of analysis can lead to new enjoyments of the media texts themselves. In our view, this is a part of the 'sociological imagination' and something to be welcomed. We hope that the arguments and studies reviewed here contribute to such analytic pleasures. Certainly, working through the material did not detract from our pleasure in pop music and often stimulated us to explore new areas in a different frame of mind or dig out (again) old, and almost forgotten, records, CDs and tapes. We hope some of this comes through in the text.

We use 'popular music' as an overall term. There is much debate about the meanings of terms such as pop and rock which is examined at several places in the book, and we do not want to begin with extensive consideration of this issue. We ask the reader to go along with us in adopting a relatively broad and open categorization of popular music – at least at the beginning.

More detail on the contents of each chapter can be found at the end of the Introduction, where the logic of the arrangement of the chapters should be apparent from the discussions and criticism of general theories contained therein.

In preparing this third edition, we have taken the opportunity to update all the chapters with data and the most important studies that have been carried out since the last edition was published. In addition, we have sought to address the key aspects of what may be termed the 'digital revolution' in production, content and consumption.

Introduction: Constraints and Creativity – Arguments and Framework

Not long after the publication of the first edition of this book, Brian Longhurst was invited to give a talk to a meeting of the Stephen Sondheim Society. The organizer of this group, which consisted of enthusiasts for the musicals of the American composer, had read the book and thought that a presentation of its broad themes would be of interest. Brian duly gave the talk, which outlined some of the main ideas of the book. This seemed to go quite well, and we had an interesting exchange of ideas. At one point a particularly lively discussion was generated by a question from the audience, which went something along the lines of: 'Why study the musicals of Sondheim at all? After all, they are simply great works of art.' There were different views expressed in the audience in response. The question is both very significant and in many respects common. Another version would be whether it is possible to write about a form such as music at all. Not very surprisingly, we think that a sociological approach (that is significantly informed by cultural and media studies) is useful and that it is therefore possible to write about music in context in interesting and informative ways. The content of the book is, we hope, a demonstration of that value. However, to illuminate why this is so, more needs to be said by way of introduction to locate our approach in the field of studies of popular music in particular and other media in general, and to indicate our general response to the Sondheim Society questioner.

In broad terms, there are two main ways in which popular music has been written about academically, journalistically and by enthusiasts: in a critical mode and in a celebratory mode. Each of these modes has a 'political' and an 'aesthetic' dimension, which are sometimes linked together or conflated. The critical mode is against popular music (or indeed popular culture) in two main ways, therefore. For example, it can be seen as a form of commercial activity that is about selling forms of music for profit, or it is seen as having regressive ideas about 'race' or 'gender' in it. Moreover, in the 'aesthetic' mode, the music can be seen as 'rubbish', poor art, trite, and so on. This sort of critique has been developed in very sophisticated ways by authors such as Adorno, and this is considered at some length below, but it is also familiar in other forms of writing.

The celebratory mode is, in effect, the mirror image of the critical. The music is appreciated because it expresses values that criticize dominant political powers or enables the expression of ideas that seek social and cultural change; it may also be seen as innovative and doing new things in musical terms and is thus to be valued aesthetically. These positions are common and apply to other media as well. However, in our view they are limited, especially as starting positions for searching engagement with a form such as popular music. They are limited, as they remain stuck on a terrain of debate that constrains innovation. In a book about audiences, Nick Abercrombie and Brian Longhurst made a similar sort of argument about audience research, maintaining that it was constrained by a research agenda that focused on whether people in the audience were incorporated by or resisted media messages (see Abercrombie and Longhurst 1998 and chapter 9 below). Eamonn Carrabine and Brian Longhurst made a similar argument about research on youth subcultures (Carrabine and Longhurst 1999).

For reasons that we hope will become clear as this book progresses, we do not want to inhabit this ground, not least because we do not think that a better understanding of the complexities of music in society can be produced from such bases. We therefore seek neither to criticize popular music nor to celebrate it per se. Rather, we seek to analyse it on the basis of the interrogation of the now extensive research on it. In our view, this does not mean that we can't develop a critical or indeed celebratory argument about some forms of music, but it is likely that there will be contradictory elements to these arguments. We are as much 'fans' of some forms of popular music as the next person. However, one thing of which our reading has convinced us is that forms of popular culture such as popular music are full of contradictions. Thus, we may greatly like the music of Miles Davis (the African-American trumpeter), and find his social location in the changing nature of American society from the 1920s to 1990s intriguing, while deploring his reported violence to women and attitudes to some of his collaborators. In the end, it makes little sense to us to attempt to resolve those contradictions: we live them as human beings, researchers, students and fans.

On this basis, the aims of this Introduction are both to introduce significant sociologically informed, general accounts of the nature and place of popular music in society and to criticize these accounts in moving towards a framework to be used in the subsequent presentation of the material in the book. Three bodies of literature are considered. First, the work of Adorno on the culture industry and popular music; second, the Weberian examination of rationalization; and, third, contemporary approaches based on audience research, which seek to move away from some of the themes central to these earlier accounts. The first two of these approaches can be seen as 'critical' and the third has been argued to be more celebratory. In this Introduction, most space is devoted to the first two approaches, as they will not be treated at length elsewhere, though issues they raise are examined in a number of other places. Key aspects of the third body of literature are considered in more detail in chapters 7, 8 and 9 (and see also, for a summary, Abercrombie and Longhurst 1998).

Commodification and standardization: Adorno and popular music

The British sociologist and pop writer Simon Frith draws attention to the key importance of Theodor Adorno's work on music in the following way:

> Adorno's is the most systematic and most searing analysis of mass culture and the most challenging for anyone claiming even a scrap of value for the products that come churning out of the music industry. His argument . . . is that modern capital is burdened by the problem of overproduction. Markets can only be stimulated by creating needs . . . needs which are the result of capital rather than human logic and therefore, inevitably, false. The culture industry is the central agency in contemporary capitalism for the production and satisfaction of false needs. (Frith 1983: 44–5)

This book takes up Frith's argument that Adorno's analysis is a challenge to those who seek to recognize some value in pop music. However, our suggestion is that the generality of Adorno's work also represents a challenge of a rather different kind to those who want to engage in the systematic and specific analysis of the place of pop music in society. We shall explain why Adorno's arguments represent such a challenge to analysis in a short while. However, before this is possible, it is necessary to examine his position in more detail.

Adorno (1903–69) was a member of the Frankfurt School of theorists and writers, founded at the University of Frankfurt in 1923, who developed critical theory as an attempt to further social change from within a broadly Marxist understanding of the structure of society. Along with other figures, such as Max Horkheimer (1895–1971), Herbert Marcuse (1898–1979) and, most recently, Jürgen Habermas (1929–), Adorno criticized capitalism's control over social life and the subsequent inequalities this causes. In his work with Horkheimer, he maintained that the culture industry was central to capitalist domination (Adorno and Horkheimer 1977).

In contemporary capitalist societies, the culture industry produces forms of culture which are commodities. Culture is something that is produced to be bought and sold on a market, to generate more money. It possesses exchange value, and the companies that produce culture do so to make a profit from it. According to the Frankfurt School writers, such commodification had become increasingly widespread, penetrating all aspects of cultural production and social life. This led to a standardization of the products of the culture industries, which in turn induced passivity in those who consume the culture industry products. Held explains:

> The main characteristics of the culture industry reflect the difficult problem it faces. It must at once both sustain interest and ensure that the attention it attracts is insufficient to bring its produce into disrepute. Thus, commercial entertainment aims at an attentive but passive, relaxed and uncritical reception, which it induces through the production of 'patterned and pre-digested' cultural entities. (1980: 94)

For Adorno, popular music is a part of the culture industry. An important claim that he makes about popular music is that it is standardized. In his view, the whole product is standardized, including types of songs, songs themselves and parts of songs. Thus, if Adorno had been writing about popular music today, instead of in the 1930s, 1940s and 1950s, he might argue, first, that popular music is divided into a number of standardized types – heavy metal, country, folk, blues, soul, urban, dance, rock, and so on – which are immediately recognizable to the audience. Second, he might maintain that the music and songs within these types are themselves standardized into a small number of different structures. Therefore, a musicological analysis would show that one heavy metal track is very much like another in its essential structure and form (Walser 1993). There are a small number of components to such tracks which, on Adorno's account, are interchangeable. As he says, 'the beginning of the chorus is replaceable by the beginning of innumerable other choruses' (1990: 303).

In Adorno's account, the parts of a piece of popular music are interchangeable. Gendron explains such 'part interchangeability' through the example of a mass-produced car: Thus, 'virtually any mechanical part from any 1956 Cadillac Eldorado (e.g., a carburettor) can be substituted for any other 1956 Eldorado without disturbing the functional unity of the overall mechanism' (1986: 20). Or, to take another example suggested by Gendron, the speakers from one stereo system can be replaced by others and the system will normally still work. Part interchangeability is very important to rationalized industrial systems, although manufacturers often try to ensure that, in order to keep the market demand for their parts buoyant, only their own parts can be used in their products. Hence, it is possible to substitute a particular part from one Ford Fiesta for that in another Fiesta, but not to place that part into a Renault Clio. Nevertheless, certain parts are more likely to be interchangeable, such as the tyres.

Adorno calls the type of variation that exists between such standardized products 'pseudo-individualization'. Such variations do not alter the basic structure of the product, as they represent only surface changes. For example, the addition of racing stripes to a Ford Fiesta may affect its appearance to the taste of its owner, but they will not alter its performance. Adorno suggests that the variations in popular music are of this type. The details of the popular song may be changed, but the essential structure or form remains the same. Goodwin gives an example of how these ideas of part interchangeability and pseudo-individualization might be applied to the contemporary music scene:

> [P]op songs often utilize the same or very similar drum patterns, chord progressions, song structures, and lyrics while being distinguished by marketing techniques (the construction of 'personalities' involved in selling, say, New Kids on The Block, the makeup once worn by the rock band Kiss), performance quirks (Michael Jackson's 'hiccup', Madonna's 'controversial' videos) or rhetorical gestures (Pete Townsend's 'windmill' swing at his guitar, Chuck Berry's 'duckwalk'). (1992: 76)

Adorno's analysis of popular music is built upon a comparison between popular music and 'serious' music. He argues that it is possible to distinguish standardized popular music from 'serious' music, where the detail of a section of music takes on meaning only in relation to the piece as a whole and standardization does not exist in the way that it does in popular music. Adorno's argument about 'serious' music rests on the valuation of an intimate relation between the specific parts and the overall nature of the piece of music as a whole, giving the piece its own particular distinctiveness and individuality. Great works of music, such as those of Beethoven, are distinctive and original. The parts of the piece come together to form a whole which is not simply the sum of the parts. It is an artistic creation, which uses the parts to create an overall meaning. The substitution into the piece of a different part would seriously affect the meaning of the whole piece.

According to Jay (1973: 182), the distinction drawn by Adorno between these types of music relates to issues of the market and the context in which music is produced and consumed. It is not that Adorno was a conservative who simply liked classical music because it was better in an unexplained way. As Jay argues: 'The real dichotomy, Adorno contended, was not between "light" and serious "music" – he was never a defender of traditional cultural standards for their own sake – but rather between music that was market-oriented and music that was not.' The main features of popular and serious music as distinguished by Adorno are summarized in figure IN.1.

The Frankfurt School argued that the principles of mass production applied to the production of culture as well as the production of goods such as motor-cars. In this view, popular music would be produced in an industrial way. However, Adorno's analysis ran into a specific problem at this point, as much pop music is not written on a production line but rather in what he called a handicraft fashion. Thus, the writing of a piece of standardized popular music might be carried out by a lone individual

'Serious' music	'Popular' music
Every part/detail depends 'for its musical sense on the concrete totality and never on a mere enforcement of a musical scheme'	Musical compositions follow familiar patterns/frameworks: they are stylized
	Little originality is introduced
Themes and details are highly interwoven with the whole	Structure of the whole does not depend upon details – whole is not altered by individual detail
Themes are carefully developed	Melodic structure is highly rigid and is frequently repeated
Details cannot be changed without altering scheme the whole – details almost contain/anticipate the whole	Harmonic structure embodies a set ('The most primitive harmonic facts are emphasized')
	Complications have no effect on structure of work – they do not develop themes
Consistency is maintained between formal structure and content (themes)	Stress is on combination of individual 'effects' – on sound, colour, tone, beat, rhythm
If standard schemes are employed (e.g. for (the dance) they still maintain a key role in the whole	Improvisations become 'normalized' boys can only 'swing it' in a narrow framework)
	Details are substitutable (they 'serve their function as cogs in machines')
Emphasizes norms of high technical competence	Affirms conventional norms of what constitutes intelligibility in music while appearing novel and original

Figure IN.1 The structure of production and consumption of 'serious' and 'popular' music
Source: Held 1980: 101

sitting at home with a pen and paper who would not be constrained by the discipline of producing standardized parts for a production line. For Adorno, this showed the remnants of an earlier form of production which was not subject to capitalist work patterns. Despite this, he maintained that the popular music industry was industrialized in other very important ways – most notably, in its promotion and distribution.

According to Adorno, the listener to industrialized popular music is caught up in a standardized and routinized set of responses. He argues that the listener is distracted and inattentive. In this sense, pop music is a part of the everyday background of contemporary social life. For example, we do not listen to it in the way that musical experts think that we should listen to a Beethoven symphony – that is, by sitting down and giving it all our attention (see, for example, Plotkin 2003) and seeing how the parts relate to the whole in creating the kind of meaning that Beethoven intended to communicate. In Adorno's view, the pleasure derived from popular music is superficial and false. Thus, the listener may be what he calls 'rhythmically obedi- ent'. He or she is a 'slave to the rhythm', following the standardized beat of the song and becoming overpowered or conditioned by it. For Adorno, individuals who enjoy these pleasures are corrupted by immersion and are open to the domination of the industrialized, capitalist system. Another type of pleasure, which Adorno calls 'emo- tional', is, in his view, also dangerous. Feelings of emotion brought on by the popular song are false or immature rather than deep or penetrating. There is no comparison between such feelings and the sorts of emotion that can be generated and expressed by the best forms of serious music. The distinctions that Adorno draws between the audience responses to serious and popular music are summarized in figure IN.2.

Adorno's argument implies that the production, textual form and audience recep- tion of popular music are all standardized, revealing a similar essential structure. Industrial production in capitalist societies gives rise to a standardized product which is used in superficial ways by members of the audience, who desire or express a wish for such industrial products because of their familiarity. Such a system reinforces the domination of society by those who control the industrial apparatus – the capital- ist or bourgeois class – as the vast majority of the population is passive and falsely happy having been manipulated by the culture industry, which feeds them products that they think they want. The different aspects of Adorno's thesis are summarized in figure IN.3.

It has already been suggested that Adorno's approach attempts to characterize the nature, production and consumption of popular music. Adorno wanted to develop a critique of this along the lines of a critical theory derived from Marx. As such, the theory covers a lot of ground and seeks to mount a critical attack on much contem- porary music and culture, which would show how it was implicated in the oppression of the working class in capitalist society. Some of the problems with this account are examined in the next section.

Adorno and pop: key criticisms

In considering the criticisms that can be made of Adorno's thesis, it is important to recognize that his formulations seem to have some applicability to contemporary music. Thus, there does seem to be a great deal of standardization of pop music around different forms, and the commodity status of the product seems increas- ingly prevalent. However, a number of points can and have been made against the sort of approach outlined by Adorno. The more specific of these are considered first, followed by some more general considerations.

Gendron suggests that Adorno confuses what he calls functional and textual artefacts. An example of a functional artefact is a washing machine and of a textual artefact a compact disc. Gendron points to a key difference between text and func- tional artefact when he says: 'A text (whether written or oral) is a universal, whereas a functional artefact is a particular. However, to be marketed and possessed, every uni- versal text must be embodied in some functional artefact (paper, vinyl discs)' (1986: 27). Thus, when a person buys a compact disc, he or she is actually buying a combina-

'*Serious*' music	'*Popular*' music
To understand a piece of serious music one must experience the whole of it	The whole has little influence on reception and reaction to parts – stronger reactions to part than whole
The whole has strong impact on reaction to details	The music is standardized into easily recognizable types, which are pre-accepted/known prior to reception
Themes and details can only be comprehended in the context of the whole	Little effort is required to follow music – audience already has models under which musical experiences can be subsumed
The sense of the music cannot be grasped by recognition alone, i.e. by identifying music with another 'identical' piece	Little emphasis on the whole as musical event – what matters is style, rhythm (the movement of the foot on the floor)
Effort and concentration are required to follow music	Leads back to familiar experiences (themes and details can be understood out of context because listener can automatically supply framework)
Its aesthetic disrupts the continuum of everyday life and encourages recollection	A sense of the music is grasped by recognition – leading to acceptance
	Pleasure, fun gained through listening are 'transferred' to the musical object, which becomes invested with qualities that stem from mechanism of identification
	The most successful, best music is identified with the most often repeated
	Music has 'soporific effect' on social consciousness
	It reinforces a sense of continuity in everyday living – while its reified structure enforces forgetfulness
	Renders 'unnecessary the process of thinking'

Figure IN.2 Differences between 'serious' and 'popular' music in responses encouraged/demands made upon listener
Source: Held 1980: 103

tion of functional and textual artefacts. The universal artefact, according to Gendron, is the recording that appears on the disc, which is a product of the recording process, mixing, and so on (dimensions of the recording process are considered at greater length in chapter 2). However, before it can be sold, this universal artefact needs to be 'embodied' in a functional artefact (even if it is embodied in a computer file). The

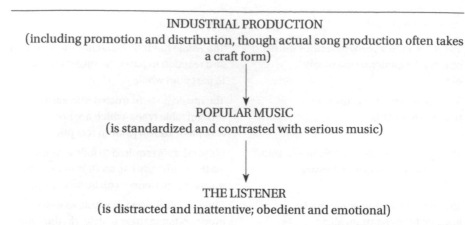

Figure IN.3 Adorno's account of popular music

extent to which both these dimensions are industrialized should be investigated, but it cannot be assumed that they are equally industrialized and rationalized in the same sorts of way. Thus, the universal artefacts that are the product of the music industry may be produced under industrialized conditions, whereas the actual recordings may not be, as was pointed out above, and recognized by Adorno when he talked of the handicraft nature of much song-writing. However, there are problems with this conceptualization of handicraft, as it does not in itself actually examine the nature of song production or the nature and extent of the technology that is used in the process. This suggests that sociological analysis of the production of music needs to pay attention to two different levels: the more macro-level structure of the pop music industry and the more micro-level of the social production of pop music itself, which takes place in the context of this organization of the music industry but which is not simply determined by it.

Furthermore, Gendron argues that the part interchangeability of the functional artefact is largely a consequence of its being produced on an assembly line: 'In this system of production, every whole (e.g. the automobile) is assembled out of qualitatively different parts, each of which is taken at random from qualitatively indistinguishable batches' (1986: 26). However, in Gendron's view, the increased use of technology in the production of music actually *expands* the degree of variation possible. For example, this may be seen in the marketing of music in a number of different formats, which leads to greater availability of different forms. Further, the importance of the relatively cheap cassette tape increased the variety of available music, which can also be copied by those who have bought the original tape, as does the widespread availability of music to download from artists' websites, and so on (see Kusek and Leonhard 2005).

Middleton makes a related point when he suggests that Adorno pays insufficient attention to the 'specificity of cultural goods', which he explains by quoting from Simon Frith that 'music can never be just a product (an exchange value), even in its rawest commodity form; the artistic value of records has an unavoidable complicating effect on their production' (1990: 38). In addition to not recognizing the specificity and variations in the nature of cultural production, Adorno does not pay enough attention to the struggles which take place between different cultural producers (Middleton 1990) and to the competitive market relations which prevail in the different sectors of the music industry. Thus, in speaking of the culture industry, there is a tendency to neglect variations between different sections of that industry and the precise patterns of relations between different companies.

Another of the key problems in Adorno's approach is that he does not allow for enough diversity in the structure and form of popular music texts (Middleton 1990). Adorno wrote a good proportion of his work on popular music in the late 1930s and early 1940s. At this point, it may have seemed that the products of the popular music section of the culture industry were standardized. However, it is more difficult to sustain this thesis in the light of the current variation in pop music styles, though we may still wish to take seriously as matters for empirical investigation the extent to which this is true rather than superficial variation. There is a problem here, however, in that it is not always easy to decide what is fundamental, and what superficial, textual variation is. This distinction might conceivably work for the very standardized songs produced from Tin Pan Alley in the 1930s, but it is not so easily applicable to some more recent forms or to free-form jazz. The further elucidation and consideration of this point depends upon analysis of the structure of musical texts themselves and the tools that can be used in this exercise (see chapter 5).

In a similar way, Adorno's account of the reception of pop music is very unspecific. He makes a number of generalizations which are not backed up by evidence of a substantive kind. Before his suggestions can be accepted, it would be necessary to consider the different ways in which people actually relate to popular music. Thus, it might be difficult to argue that people respond to Madonna and Frank Zappa in similar ways. What is more, Adorno does not consider in enough detail the different sorts of pleasure that are a part of the consumption of popular music. Some forms of music may be valued because they are exceptionally good to dance to; others may invite contemplation – and so on. These pleasures are not all as superficial as Adorno seems to think.

These more specific criticisms can be related to the general nature and basis of Adorno's account in terms of four areas.

1 *Immanent method* Middleton (1990) suggests that many of the problems of Adorno's approach stem from his initial focus on a particular type of music. In his view, Adorno generalizes from within the Western tradition of 'serious' music and compares other forms against this. These are then seen to be of less value. A more proper procedure, rather than implicitly or explicitly comparing different forms of music against the ideal of aspects of the Western classical tradition, would be to proceed in a non-judgemental way. This involves the suspension of critical judgement about value. A similar point is made by Gendron (1986).

2 *Historical and social location* Adorno's approach is too constrained by his own historical and social location, of being a highly educated, musically literate German intellectual of the mid-twentieth century. Owing to his lack of reflection on the effects this may have, his approach has many difficulties in coping with social and historical change in music-making, as he continued to value a particular and very specific form of music. However, as Gendron (1986) points

out, and as has been noted several times above, there are senses in which Adorno's theory does seem to explain features of contemporary pop music. The extent to which this is the case – for example, in the kind of superficial variation identified by Goodwin (1992) – and the extent to which his theory also illuminates aspects of contemporary pop need consideration. A different view of this issue has been addressed by Robinson (1994), who argues that Adorno's understanding of jazz was critically affected by the way in which it was interpreted in Weimar Germany in the 1920s and 1930s. For a variety of reasons, particular and distinctive forms of jazz, which were different from American jazz, developed at this point. While Robinson shows how this affected Adorno's analysis, he does not answer the question of why Adorno failed to take account of the different understandings of jazz that became available to him in later years.

3 *Innovation* In a way related to these other general points, Adorno pays insufficient attention to the dynamic and changing nature of music. Popular music has developed considerably since he formulated his ideas, and consideration needs to be given to the issue of whether musical innovation and the development of new technologies actually alter aspects of musical production in quite significant ways.

4 *Analysis* As Adorno's account is so general, it constrains detailed analysis of the specific nature of musical production, textual variation and consumption. Our suggestion is that, as well as problematizing pleasure, Adorno's critical account militates against sociological exploration and analysis. In the terms set out at the start of this Introduction, critique overpowers analysis. Before the relevance of such a theory can be determined, there needs to be investigation of the changing nature of the music industry, the ways in which music is actually produced in different places and times, the specific political effects of music in different contexts, the extent of textual variation between forms of pop music, and the different ways in which music is consumed and produces pleasure. We are now much more able to consider these issues, as there has been plenty of research carried out since Adorno's time, some of which is reported in this book. However, as a general theory, we have to ask if Adorno's account allows the kind of detailed analysis which is necessary for the proper evaluation of pop music in society.

Having made these points against Adorno, we want to consider the relevance of work on rationalization, influenced by Max Weber, to the contemporary study of music.

Rationalization and McDonaldization

A different and potentially illuminating approach to the place of music and culture in society derives from the approach of the German sociologist Max Weber (1864–1920) and in subsequent writers influenced by his work. Weber's sociology is based around a typology of different types of social action: rational action towards a goal, rational action towards a value, affective action and traditional action. One of the central themes of his work is that Western societies are becoming increasingly rationalized as forms of rational action become more central. An example of this form of action and social organization is a bureaucracy. Weber's ideal type of this form of organization consisted of elements such as a clear hierarchy of positions, a division of labour, writ-

---

- efficiency
- calculability
- predictability
- control

Figure IN.4 Dimensions of McDonaldization
Source: Ritzer 1993

ten documentation, promotion and recruitment on merit, government by rules, and impersonal relations between bureaucracy members and clients. Bureaucracies were becoming increasingly common, and in important ways society was bureaucratized and rationalized. This was not necessarily a bad thing in Weber's mind, though his work did also have a pessimistic tone and he talked of becoming imprisoned in the 'iron cage' of bureaucracy.

Moreover, this would seem to be even more likely, and depressing perhaps, if many other areas of social life were being organized along the lines identified by Weber. A contemporary argument that this is clearly the case has been made by the American sociologist George Ritzer (1993). Ritzer suggests that the dominant form of organization of social life is not bureaucracy as identified by Weber but the similar type of rationalization exemplified by the McDonald's fast-food restaurant chain. Ritzer argues that a large number of other social enterprises are being organized along lines similar to the fast-food restaurant, and he calls this 'the McDonaldization of society'. Thus, sport, education and medical care, to take just three of the examples examined by Ritzer, increasingly exhibit features similar to McDonald's. The main dimensions of this sort of organization are efficiency, calculability, predictability and control. They aim to deliver their goods in an efficient way, eliminating wasteful operations in the working practices of staff and not keeping the customer waiting for long periods. Every aspect of the production and delivery of the good is measured and calculated. Hence, the burgers and rolls in McDonald's restaurants are of a precise size and are cooked for an exactly measured period of time. The products and surroundings in McDonaldized organizations are standardized and predictable. The idea is that a hamburger will look and taste the same in New York, London, Paris or Moscow (despite the planned variation of the type discussed by the two main characters played by John Travolta and Samuel L. Jackson in Quentin Tarantino's film *Pulp Fiction*). Finally, the processes in organizations like McDonald's are controlled with clear lines of management.

Ritzer suggests, rather like Weber, that, despite the rationalization processes involved in McDonaldization, such organizations can be irrational and inefficient. For example, we may have to queue for a relatively long time for a hamburger and may find the lack of variation in the quality boring and unexciting. Further, other types of organization develop which attempt to produce experiences that are not routinized and predictable in the McDonaldized fashion.

An important aspect of Ritzer's argument is his suggestion that our leisure time has become rationalized. Hence, it is not only the production of goods and the places where we consume them that are rationalized, but also our time and our wider leisure activities. The places where we might have escaped from office or state bureaucracies in earlier times have themselves become organized along the rationalized, McDonaldized model.

It has been argued that these processes of rationalization are applicable to pop music. Weber (1958) identifies the particular nature of the rational structure of Western music, and his argument suggests that 'The value of musical rationalization is the transformation of the process of musical production into a calculable affair operating with known means, effective instruments, and understandable rules. Constantly running counter to this is the drive for expressive flexibility' (Martindale and Riedel 1958: li). As Goodwin explains: 'It is suggested that just as capitalist societies need increasingly to rationalize production to bring order to the creation of commodities, so Western music also creates a network of rules for music making. Thus a universal notational system and precise measurement of tonal and rhythmic differences comes to define what music is' (1992: 76).

Goodwin finds evidence that the development of new forms of technology and their application to music involve the rationalization of the nature and production of musical texts along Weberian lines. He identifies three dimensions to this: 'harmonic rationalization, temporal rationalization, and timbral conformity': 'Harmonic rationalization occurs partly, for instance, through the elimination of microtonality that is involved in many modern synthesizers. This has implications for the globalization of music because many non-Western musics depend on microtones that are difficult to achieve on Western synthesizers' (1992: 83). Thus, there is a limiting of the range of tones that we might expect to hear in music. Temporal rationalization occurs through technology such as the drum machine, which can produce a precise number of beats per second, thus structuring the overall nature of a piece of music. Timbral conformity occurs through the ways in which the sounds from synthesizers are often pre-set at the factory, which means that 'the new machines produce the same sounds whoever plays them, whenever and wherever they are played' (ibid.: 84).

On a Weberian interpretation, production in the music industry might increasingly be organized along rational lines. Thus, different aspects of a piece of music may be constructed in different places and brought together for completion if they have been recorded at the same rate of beats per minute. This increases the importance of the beat, which structures the whole piece of music. Moreover, tracks can be constructed from a limited range of sounds in a rapid fashion by people skilled with computers rather than musical instruments. A further discussion of the use of new technologies in this process can be found in chapter 2.

In addition, the delivery of the musical product increasingly takes place in large leisure stores and supermarkets such as Tesco that used to sell only groceries, as well as online (from suppliers such as Amazon and iTunes). In supermarkets or shops such as HMV in the centre of Manchester, the music is lined up in tidy boxes and packets, self-selected by the customer and taken to a till to be paid for. There are relatively few staff in evidence and they mainly interact with customers only to take their money. By contrast, record shops more frequently used to be places where the potential purchaser could ask advice from the expert salesperson who would allow the customer to listen to several records of his or her own choice before deciding on a purchase – or not, as the case may have been. Such modes of interaction would now be expected only in the increasingly marginalized specialist shops. According to the BPI's figures and analysis (BPI Yearbook 2012), music retailing has undergone a considerable change in recent years. The number of independent record shops in the UK dropped from 900 at the beginning of the twenty-first century to fewer than

Table IN.1 *Key permanent music retail outlets*

	2009	2010	2011
HMV	273	269	244
Independent Specialists	293	281	295
Tesco	830	877	892
Sainsbury's	547	557	570
Asda	371	389	514
Morrisons	417	436	470

Source: Millward Brown

Table IN.2 *Other music outlets 2011 (on a seasonal and 'event' basis)*

Co-op	3,000
Tesco Express	1,236
Blockbuster	604
M&S	600
Sainsbury's Local	439
Game	380
BP	368
Wilkinson	364
WHSmith	353
Waterstones	300
Matalan	200
BHS	180
Debenhams	124
Disney	57

Source: Millward Brown

300 in 2011, some retailers such as WH Smith and Boots no longer stock music, while others such as Borders, Woolworths and Music Zone have stopped trading altogether. Some shops stock music selectively during festive seasons – for example, in the run-up to Christmas or Valentine's Day. In contrast, digital retailing is on the increase, with over seventy legal digital services operating in the UK in 2011. Tables IN.1 and IN.2 offer evidence of the increasing importance of the McDonaldized-type chains and supermarkets, while table IN.3 shows that, despite an ongoing increase in overall digital retailing, pop remains the dominant selling music genre at such outlets.

Potential purchasers of such music are quite likely to work in organizations structured along McDonaldized lines, such as call centres. In Douglas Coupland's novel *Generation X* (1992), for example, the young characters have had a series of McJobs in the past, and, at the beginning of the movie version of *Wayne's World*, Wayne describes his career in terms of lots of jobs which entail wearing a name badge and a hairnet. In themselves, the consumers of music might be affected by these same processes of rationalization.

Table IN.3 *Retailers' genre profile, 2011 (% across)*

	Pop	Rock	R&B	MOR/Easy	Dance	Hip Hop	Classical	Folk	Country	Jazz	Blues	Soul	Other
Internet (Home Delivery)	**27.0**	**32.1**	**4.5**	**7.8**	**4.0**	**1.8**	**5.6**	**2.5**	**2.1**	**2.3**	**1.4**	**1.4**	**7.5**
Amazon	26.1	31.3	4.4	9.0	4.1	1.8	6.0	2.9	2.6	3.0	1.6	1.7	5.6
Play.com	32.1	39.0	5.9	6.0	3.3	1.4	2.8	1.1	1.6	0.7	0.9	1.3	3.8
HMV	29.9	35.8	6.1	4.8	5.2	3.4	4.7	1.0	1.0	1.4	0.9	1.0	4.8
Tesco	51.0	23.4	5.5	5.9	1.6	0.8	4.6	0.5	0.1	0.6	0.8	0.5	4.7
Music Specialists	**27.4**	**37.0**	**5.9**	**5.9**	**4.2**	**2.8**	**4.4**	**1.3**	**1.5**	**1.4**	**1.6**	**1.1**	**5.5**
HMV	28.8	35.8	6.3	6.2	4.0	2.9	4.4	1.1	1.4	1.2	1.6	1.0	5.2
Other Music Specialists	13.1	50.0	2.0	3.2	6.5	1.5	3.4	3.5	1.5	3.5	1.7	1.7	8.4
Supermarkets	**48.4**	**15.6**	**8.4**	**12.4**	**3.4**	**0.8**	**2.5**	**0.6**	**1.1**	**0.9**	**1.1**	**0.8**	**4.1**
Tesco	49.4	14.3	7.7	14.1	2.9	0.7	2.1	0.6	0.9	0.9	1.5	0.4	4.5
Asda	47.4	17.4	10.0	9.8	4.3	1.2	1.7	0.8	1.2	0.5	0.8	1.0	4.0
Sainsbury's	47.7	16.0	6.6	12.4	1.9	0.6	5.8	0.4	1.6	1.5	1.0	0.7	3.9
Morrisons	49.3	14.6	9.0	13.8	4.5	0.3	1.8	0.5	0.6	0.7	0.6	1.5	2.9

Source: BPI Yearbook 2012

Base: physical music expenditure

Rationalization and McDonaldization: some criticisms

Since Ritzer's analysis was first published in 1993, it has been subject to much discussion and analysis. Ritzer himself updated the book (see Ritzer 2004), while other authors have applied his analysis to a range of different areas of social life (see, for example, Ritzer 2002a) and there have been general and specific criticisms of his work (see, for example, Alfino et al. 1998). Ritzer has defended the overall outlines of his argument. He concedes that there is some evidence of countervailing tendencies to the success of McDonald's, which he labels de-McDonaldization. Thus, he recognizes that the economic strength of McDonald's in the USA is under pressure (though it is still globally successful), that it has become a 'negative symbol' (Ritzer 2002b: 256) for a range of protesting groups, and that it is difficult for any corporation to 'stay on top indefinitely' (ibid.: 257). While these may create difficulties for McDonald's, in Ritzer's view these are separable from the overall process of McDonaldization. What matters is the process of rationalization that has been given this label rather than McDonalds per se.

Ritzer then examines the threats to this process of rationalization. He considers that there are examples of new and successful small and local businesses. But these are either of relatively minor significance or, if successful, will become subject to rationalizing pressures. Further, while there are examples of McDonaldized businesses that produce a high-quality product (Ritzer examines Starbucks Coffee Company), these are successful because of the focus on just one product or a limited product range. Moreover, large companies may be producing an increasing range of goods (such as styles of trainers) but the processes of production are still McDonaldized. Thus, while suggesting that his analysis has to confront such issues, Ritzer remains confident of its overall thrust. However, some problems for the thesis remain.

As will be examined in more detail in chapter 2, it is not clear that rationalization is the only process at work in the production of contemporary popular music. Thus, some writers have argued that there will always be dimensions that are not rationalized and that musical production will escape from this kind of straitjacket. Frith captures several aspects of this notion:

> The industrialization of music hasn't stopped people from using it to express private joys or public griefs; it has given us new means to do so, new ways of having an impact, new ideas of what music can be. Street music is certainly an industrial noise now, but it's a human noise too so it is perhaps fitting to conclude that the most exciting and political music of the early 1990s should be the hip-hop sounds of young urban black bands like Public Enemy, groups that are heavily dependent on both the latest technology and street credibility. (1992: 74)

Goodwin suggests that rap and hip-hop music, while using technologies that might imply rationalization, have broken with conventionalized forms. He argues that 'what is really striking about the recent development of popular music is its progressive shift away from conventional tonality and structural conformity.' Furthermore, 'extremely avant-garde sounding recordings that thoroughly challenge the conventions of tonality and song structure have routinely charted' (1992: 92–3). Moreover, music producers using such technologies often experiment with them to produce new sounds that were not envisaged by the makers.

In addition, the consumers of this sort of music might try to escape from the structures of rationalization in which they are forced to work. The characters in *Generation X* seek escape from their McJobs, and Wayne and Garth in *Wayne's World* develop their own forms of creativity by running their own cable-access television programme and in their appropriation of heavy metal music.

As with the account offered by Adorno, the arguments about rationalization seem overgeneralized, again implying the need for a more specific and empirically based understanding and theorization of the precise nature of musical production, products and consumption. While general theories can provoke thought and may capture significant aspects of contemporary practice, they need to be evaluated in the context of the application of the theory to a range of different cases. This may often lead to a reformulation of the theory with more specific reference. The argument here is not about theory per se, but about the attempt to stretch a theory to cover all cases in different contexts.

Audience power and creativity

The two general accounts considered in this Introduction so far have stressed themes of commodification, standardization and rationalization. In different ways, they are critical and pessimistic accounts of contemporary culture and popular music. Both theories continue to have influence upon interpretations and understandings of popular music. However, in recent years a number of writers have sought to understand the limits to the influence of mass culture and rationalization. This has often entailed a move away from consideration of what culture does to its audience towards an evaluation of the ways in which audiences use the products of the culture industries in their own lives. The contours of these developments have now been traced by a number of different authors (for example, McGuigan 1992), who show the way in which the sort of critique of the culture industries put forward by Adorno and Horkheimer was superseded by the theory of hegemony associated with the work of the Italian Marxist writer Antonio Gramsci (1891–1937). Hegemony is explained by Abercrombie in the following terms:

> In such a view, popular culture cannot be seen as a simple imposition of dominant ideology on subordinate classes. While cultural relations have to be understood in terms of the antagonistic relationships between the bourgeoisie and the working classes, bourgeois culture is not simply dominant. One cannot speak of domination here but rather the struggle for hegemony – that is, moral, cultural and political leadership. For Gramsci, the bourgeoisie can achieve hegemony only to the extent that it can accommodate subordinate class values. The establishment of hegemony is thus a case of negotiation between dominant and subordinate values. (1990: 201)

Such an approach entails the attempt to understand how members of society negotiate with the products of the culture industries. These developments are reviewed at length in chapters 7, 8 and 9 of this book. However, one of the key suggestions of more recent versions of this sort of approach is that audiences have power to negotiate with the texts of media products. Based partly in these theories of hegemony, the works of Hall (1980) and Morley (1980) argued that audiences could accept the dominant messages in media texts, could oppose them, or could develop a negotiated reading on them (see further Abercrombie and Longhurst 1998: 9–28). In adopting a particular variation of this approach, Fiske has argued against the common belief that the capitalist cultural industries produce only an apparent variety of products whose variety is finally illusory for they all promote the same capitalist ideology. Their skill in sugar coating the pill is so great that the people are not aware of the ideological practice in which they are engaging as they consume and enjoy the cultural commodity. I do not believe that 'the people' are 'cultural dopes'; they are not a passive, helpless mass incapable of discrimination and thus at the economic, cultural, and political mercy of the barons of the industry. (1987: 309)

This leads Fiske to consider how audience members use media texts in different ways in their lives. For example, he writes of Madonna in the following way:

The meanings of the Madonna look, as of the Madonna videos, cannot be precisely specified. But that is precisely the point, the pleasure that they give is not the pleasure of what they say, but of their assertion of the right and the power of a severely subordinated subculture to make their own statements, their own meanings. Madonna's invitation to her girl fans to play with the conventions of patriarchy shows them that they are not necessarily subject to those conventions but can exercise some control over their relationship to patriarchy and thus over the sense of their identity. (Ibid.: 233)

Fiske's subsequent work received a somewhat hostile reception, one criticism being that it leads to a simple celebration of popular culture and suggests that opposition to domination can be found in all its forms. It may be that, in attempting to focus attention on the different ways in which products of the culture industries can be used, Fiske (and others like him) has played down the dimensions of the culture industry identified by Adorno. However, this does not mean that the implications of this work should be ignored, and the ideas of activity and creativity on the part of the audience need to be considered in empirical terms alongside those of commodification, standardization and rationalization.

In recent years Web 2.0 has been facilitating quite a rapid expansion of what came to be known as participatory culture, which extends the above identified negotiation of media texts and thus audiences' roles of consumers to that of contributors and producers. Jenkins and his colleagues (2009: 9) identified affiliations, expressions, collaborative problem-solving and circulations as significant forms of participatory culture which play an important part in education, civic engagement, workplace and various forms of cultural expression. In terms of popular music audiences, the activities associated with each of the forms may include:

affiliations – membership of online communities based on a particular artist and their music;
expressions – producing new musical content such as digital sampling, mash-ups, fan videos;
collaborative problem-solving – working with other fans on Wikipedia articles or collaborative blogs dedicated to a particular artist or a band;
circulations – blogging, podcasting.

The above forms of participatory culture signal a degree of levelling out of production and consumption roles, where: 'We are moving away from a world in which some produce and many consume media, toward one in which everyone has a more active stake in the culture that is produced' (Jenkins et al. 2009: 12).

Axel Bruns coined the term 'produsage' for this new form of engagement, where:

Produsers engage not in a traditional form of content production, but are instead involved in *produsage* – **the collaborative and continuous building and extending of existing content in pursuit of further improvement**. Participants in such activities are not producers in a conventional, industrial sense, as that term implies a distinction between producers and consumers which no longer exists; the artefacts of their work are not products existing as discrete, complete packages; and their activities are not a form of production because they proceed based on a set of preconditions and principles that are markedly at odds with the conventional industrial model. (http://produsage.org/produsage)

Consumers are not just increasingly creating their own content but also interacting with other consumers, producers and content, frequently in non-traditional contexts. For example, because of an expansion in mobile devices such as smart phones, we can now view YouTube videos or comment on somebody's blog post while going about our daily tasks, and alongside other activities. This shifting context may play a part in the way we interpret cultural processes and artefacts, including popular music. Gauntlett (2011: 8) (see also chapter 5) argues that such online connections and collaborations extend into offline worlds, resulting in an important shift from 'sit back and be told culture' to 'making and doing culture'.

A framework for analysis

The implication of the discussion in this Introduction so far is that there is a need to pay detailed analytical attention to the different dimensions of research on production, the nature of the product and its consumption. The field of popular music studies (in the wider context of the study of a range of media) has developed in precisely these ways. To reflect this and to structure such consideration in this book, we have organized the discussion according to a scheme of production, text and audience. In its essentials this scheme is very simple. It argues that any cultural object, such as a book, play, film, television programme or record, should be thought of as a text. These texts do not come into existence spontaneously but result from production processes that involve various different institutions. In some cases, such production may be relatively simple. Thus, when writing a lecture, we may sit down at a computer or with a pen and paper and write a text which is then delivered orally to an audience sitting in a room. In other cases, production is exceedingly complex. Thus, a recording will be the outcome of an elaborate set of procedures involving different people and social processes, including musicians, recording engineers, record producers, playing instruments, interaction in a recording studio, the manufacture of CDs in a factory, and so on. Such cultural objects are not only produced, they are also consumed, or read, by an audience or audiences, and it is necessary to study the processes that occur here. This scheme can be represented diagrammatically as in figure IN.5.

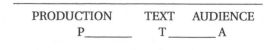

PRODUCTION	TEXT	AUDIENCE
P_____	T_____	A

Figure IN.5 Production, text and audience scheme

This scheme leads to at least five sets of issues or questions that need to be examined in sociological analysis. First, there is a set of concerns raised by the consideration of what is meant by production and producers. Here, it is important to examine the way in which producers such as musicians or novelists are located within a range of contextualizing social institutions. For example, musicians may be contracted to a multinational corporation with interests in many different fields, or they might publish material on their own website or write music for their own interest and never have it published or performed. It can be suggested that most cultural production takes place within an economic context where the profit motive is paramount, and this will have effects, however mediated, on the text.

Second, there is the question of precisely how production takes place. It is important to examine not just who produces, and the wider economic and institutional contexts for such production, but the actual nature of the processes themselves. Therefore, it will be necessary to consider whether people collaborate in the production of the text and whether one organization, or group, has the power to prevent another group or individual from developing ideas: for example, is one institution – such as the state – attempting to prevent another – such as a rock group – from recording certain songs? Furthermore, it is important to examine whether there are conflicts within a company or group involved in cultural production.

Third, there is a range of issues raised by the description of the cultural object as a text. One consequence of this depiction is that a text such as a pop record is thought to have a structure, which can be examined through analysis. In chapter 5 of this book a number of different concepts used in the analysis of texts are identified. It is also important to recognize that, at least partly because of the way in which they are structured, there can be different interpretations of texts and the meanings they contain.

Griffiths, in an insightful and polemical survey of the study of popular music as music, has identified three positions that have been adopted, which have tended to operate in the critical mode. For Griffiths, the 'high analysis of low music' can be typologized into 'earnest onlooking', that pursued by 'street fighting men' and the approach of 'the managers'. The earliest stage is the first and really begins the serious study of popular music (if not its sociology). This approach is 'serious and lacking irony, morally purposeful, slightly awkward in relation to the object of study' (Griffiths 1999: 398). With the next group, 'popular music literature really takes off' (ibid.: 400). This approach is strongly influenced by sociology and cultural studies and is heavily politically engaged in its discussion of popular music. As will be considered in chapter 5 and elsewhere, the work of Middleton (1990) was central in this move. As Griffiths argues:

> *Studying Popular Music* stands at the cusp of where an engaged literature of the left, outward-looking and able firmly to articulate its intent, turns in to the text itself. The book's method, which is effectively to try to wrap every literature in the language of critique, endlessly deferred, seems to me its most enduring display, and right now its most important legacy and challenge. (1999: 407)

The final group of writers – termed the 'managers' – engage in the theory of popular music, which appears very complex. As Griffiths suggests, this sort of approach 'appears characteristically where an observation concerning technique which is, be honest, *dead easy*, suddenly requires a load of graphs' (1999: 409). Whether or not this

PRODUCTION	TEXT	AUDIENCE
Takes place in a wider economic and institutional context	Is structured	Reads the text in a social context

Figure IN.6 Developed production, text and audience scheme

is 'dead easy' is debatable (especially for those of us without musicological training), but there is a shift from the politics and influences of the second type of approach.

Fourth, returning to the production, text and audience scheme, there are issues deriving from the idea of an audience and what is meant by this term. Thus, the particular make-up of the audience for any particular text should be investigated, and we may want to think about the way in which a text or set of texts is used by different social groups. For example, do contemporary heavy metal fans listen to Black Sabbath or Led Zeppelin differently from rock fans from the late 1960s and early 1970s? Also, it is important to consider the ways in which texts produce certain identifications for us when we watch, read or listen to them. For example, when some people listen to guitar-based music, they pretend to be playing the electric guitar themselves, thus in some way identifying with the guitar player. This is similar to identifying with the hero of a narrative, and it is no accident that players such as Eric Clapton and Jimi Hendrix were known as guitar heroes.

Fifth, it is important to study how it is that a text is consumed. This may involve examination of whether music is listened to on an iPhone, an iPod, a small stereo or a system costing thousands of pounds, as these may alter the ways in which the text is understood and the forms of pleasure that are derived from it. Does an individual listen to a text on his or her own in the bedroom or dance to it in a club? The detail of social context can have a great effect on meaning and form of appropriation of a text. These different aspects can be mapped onto the basic production, text and audience scheme, as shown in figure IN.6.

Popular music can be examined in the context of such a production, text and audience scheme, and the development of the field that is surveyed in this book reflects this. In what follows, this framework is adopted to structure the presentation of material. In chapter 1, the wider institutional and economic context of popular music production is looked at. This includes a discussion of the patterns of ownership in the pop music industry, an examination of the nature of the markets for the products of that industry, details of the income derived from rights in the industry, the effects of digitization, and consideration of the ways in which 'globalization' of the music industry is occurring.

In chapter 2, on the social production of music, more 'micro-' and detailed aspects of musical production are examined, among them the subcultures of musicians, the social backgrounds of pop musicians and the detail of more 'amateur' musical production in local contexts. The chapter includes discussion of the changing division of labour in the popular music production process and the effects of technological change on these processes.

In chapters 3, 4, 5 and 6, attention moves from the production of texts to issues raised by the nature of texts themselves. Chapter 3 considers a range of material and issues deriving from the history of popular music, its political orientation and connections with sexuality.

Chapter 4 develops the discussion of these matters through an analysis of 'black' music. This includes examination of the problems of attributing music to different racial groups and three case studies, of the genres of blues and soul, ska and reggae, and rap and hip-hop. Again, these involve consideration of some of the different dimensions of the debate around fragmentation in contemporary culture.

Chapter 5 focuses on the structure of texts and how they convey meanings. It begins with a look at the limits of musicology in the study of popular music and then some different aspects of musical meaning. This involves the introduction of some key terms from structuralism and semiotics. The chapter continues with an examination of the debate on the relative importance of words in the creation and communication of musical meaning before analysing the debates on music and visuals, particularly through music video.

Chapter 6 investigates a range of issues that derive from the fact that popular music is performed. Drawing on the work of Judith Butler and Pierre Bourdieu, a number of different aspects of dance are examined, as are processes and meanings of collecting. There is also a study here of processes of distinction in popular music and how taste operates.

Chapters 7, 8 and 9 consider different dimensions of the audience for popular music. Chapter 7 looks first at some of the most important recent accounts of text/audience relations and then some data on the trends in consumption of different musical texts by different parts of the audience. This is followed by a description of some of the main contours of the examination of music as it is used and developed by different subcultural groups. Chapter 8 outlines the literature on fans and summarizes the most important accounts that have been produced on the attachment of fans to individual groups and artists and some of the recent theorizations of fan activity in general. This involves consideration of some theorizations of celebrity. This is followed by an examination of the debates on the increasing difficulty of defining the relations between production and consumption in the sphere of popular music, returning in conclusion to some of the issues raised by the studies of local music-making described in chapter 2. These issues are further explored in chapter 9 via a discussion of recent work that has developed the idea of subculture in new ways in the light of the sort of issues considered in chapter 8. Chapter 9 also observes the ideas of scene and the idea that cultural tastes have become more omnivorous. It concludes with a look at different aspects of audience and everyday life.

The production, text and audience scheme thus structures the presentation of the material to be analysed in this book. There are a number of different sociological dimensions to the analysis which run through the application of this scheme. Thus, attention is paid at different points to dimensions of class, gender, race, age and place. Any sociological analysis worth its salt has to do this. The utilization of these dimensions as threads running through the book does mean that there is no chapter entitled 'Women and Pop', for example, and no chapter on young people and music – and so on. However, examinations of both of these dimensions (and the others) will be found in various different places. As we have suggested, our approach is sociological, drawing on media and cultural studies. This means that the emphasis is less on the musicological, though key aspects of this are discussed in the book.

There we also examine a number of specific concepts and issues which are important in contemporary cultural studies and the sociology of culture. These have to do with, for example, the value that is placed on particular pieces of music and the struggle which takes place between different social groups around music. The salience of these issues is identified as they are introduced in particular contexts, so as to avoid overburdening the discussion at this introductory stage.

Summary

This chapter has considered:

- the differences between critical, celebratory and analytical approaches;
- Adorno's account of popular music and criticisms that can be made of it;
- the Weberian account of rationalization and its development through the thesis of McDonaldization by Ritzer;
- some criticisms of the rationalization idea;
- work which has moved beyond Gramsci's account of hegemony to emphasize audience power and creativity;
- the production, text and audience framework for the analysis of culture and the issues it raises;
- the structure of the remainder of the book.

PART I

PRODUCTION

In Part I, 'Production', we focus on the music industry, its various parts and its main participants. In order to outline and discuss the industry's economic organization, structure and ownership, as well as the roles, practices and meanings created and maintained within it, we examine it through its main streams: the music publishing stream, the recording stream and the live performance stream (Hull et al. 2011). The discussion is not linear as there are many overlaps between the three streams, with roles and participants interacting in order to produce, distribute and perform music. Chapter 1 focuses on the music publishing stream as well as some aspects of live performance stream, while chapter 2 extends the discussion to practices as well as traditional and emerging roles of people involved in music-making and performance. Revisiting and reviewing the industry's structure and parts played by its various participants is particularly pertinent at this time of rapid technological change, which has resulted in new structures, functions, positions and meanings.

1 The Pop Music Industry

Since the publication of the second edition of this book in 2007, the music industry has been undergoing a momentous transformation. An uptake and popularization of the new digital technologies, coupled with the emergence and extensive adoption of social networking and other social media, has resulted in a new dynamic that extends to every aspect of the industry, from the ways in which music is produced, through marketing and selling strategies, to modes of consumption. Subsequently, many of the traditional music industry structures and roles are being contested, negotiated and redefined. While aiming to capture the key characteristics of the shifting and changing musical environments, this chapter will address the following main areas, habitually associated with the music industry:

1 economic structure and organization;
2 music industry products;
3 rights.

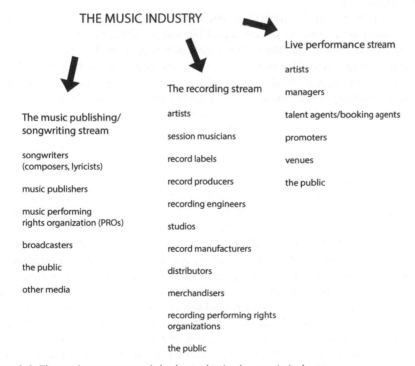

THE MUSIC INDUSTRY

Live performance stream

artists

managers

The recording stream

talent agents/booking agents

artists

promoters

**The music publishing/
songwriting stream**

session musicians

venues

record labels

the public

songwriters
(composers, lyricists)

record producers

music publishers

recording engineers

music performing
rights organization (PROs)

studios

broadcasters

record manufacturers

the public

distributors

other media

merchandisers

recording performing rights
organizations

the public

Figure 1.1 The main streams and the key roles in the music industry

The economic structure of the pop music industry

As was explained in the Introduction, all pop music is produced within a social context, and a great deal of it is produced from within an industry attempting to generate profits. This being the case, how is the pop music industry currently structured?

The music industry is one of the most concentrated industries. For a number of years, and until recently, the popular music industry was dominated by four major companies: Universal Music Group, Sony Music Entertainment, Warner Music Group and EMI Group (Wikström 2009: 71). Together they controlled more than 85 per cent of the market. Universal is the largest of the four, with approximately 31.9 per cent of the global recorded music market, but is closely followed by Sony, with a 25 per cent share, while Warner has a 20.3 per cent share and EMI has 9.4 per cent (Rayna and Striukova 2009). All except Warner have also been parts of larger companies; Universal's parent company is Vivendi, Sony operates within Sony Corporation, and EMI was purchased in 2007 by a private equity partnership, Terra Firma. Universal, Warner and EMI have been operating as both record companies and music publishers, the latter business arm representing an important income stream during the times of falling record sales. In June 2012 EMI Publishing was sold to a consortium led by Sony/ATV Music Publishing, while in September 2012 an announcement about Universal's £1.2 billion takeover of EMI was made. The takeover came with the condition that Universal 'offloads' the Parlophone label (except for The Beatles), EMI France, EMI Classics, Mute and 50 per cent of EMI's stake in the Now That's What I call Music compilation brand. Despite this, Universal will still own about 30 per cent of EMI's existing operations.

The aforementioned Sony/ATV Music Publishing, a stand-alone music publishing company renowned for ownership of 180 songs written by The Beatles, and Live Nation Entertainment, the largest live music company, formed in 2005 and expanded through a merger with Ticketmaster in 2010, represent important actors within the current music industry's landscape. In addition to producing concerts, owning, leasing and operating music venues, at the time of writing Live Nation is branching out into the recording industry by continuing to develop Live Nation Artists, thus extending its primary role of the promoter (who does not own the copyright of the artist's recordings) to that of a record company or a record label 'who "signs" artists as a "record label" but predominantly takes the role of a promoter, rather than "owner of music"' (Wikström 2009: 140). Launched in 2007, Live Nation Artists adopted a 360-degree business model, where record sales are just one of the several income streams (ibid.: 139), with others including merchandise sales, management of fan sites and tour revenues. Some of the globally established artists such as Madonna, Jay-Z and U2 have signed deals with Live Nation. Despite a wide range of interests and a broad range of businesses (see horizontal and vertical integration), by and large since the Second World War the record companies' main business has been selling records. However, over the past decade the music industry has been seeking new streams of income to complement decreasing record sales and income generated through ownership of rights. In so doing it has turned to the live music sector, where there has been an increase in opportunities for making profit, with key implications of incorporation of live performance in the 360-degree record deal discussed later in this chapter.

Despite the ongoing changes in production, dissemination and consumption of music, the music industry is still one of the most concentrated industries (Rayna and Striukova 2009). Concentration refers to the fact the ownership of an area of production is held in the hands of a small number of companies, and it can be discussed across an economy as a whole or in terms of specific sectors. It is often expressed by what economists call the *concentration ratio* – 'the extent to which the largest firms contribute to activity in an industry' (Mahajan 2006: 25). Mergers and demergers, takeovers, regulation and deregulation, restructurings, and new products and technologies can all lead to changes in the concentration ratio in a particular industry. On the figures given by Bishop (2005), the concentration ratio for the music industry would be over 75 per cent, while Rayna and Striukova (2009) give a figure of 85 per cent.

The music industry has been concentrated for much of its existence (Negus 1992). However, it is important to recognize that concentration ratios and the precise nature of the relationship between companies vary historically. For example, in their classic discussion of 'cycles in symbol production' in the American pop music industry, Peterson and Berger (1990) demonstrate significant variation in the four- and eight-firm concentration ratios between 1948 and 1973, as is shown in table 1.1. The American industry was most concentrated in the early 1950s, with the four-firm concentration ratio varying between 71 and 89 per cent. It was least concentrated in the early 1960s, before becoming more so in the early 1970s. Some further discussion of the factors behind these changes can be found in the examination of the development of rock and roll in chapter 3. Moreover, as Bishop (2005) shows, the relationship between the major players in the music industry has itself been subject to a series of takeovers and mergers. This process is shown in figure 1.2.

The parent companies of two of the producers, which dominate the pop music industry, are also active in other sectors of the economy. They are conglomerates with a wide range of interests which focus in the media field. In an influential examination of the structure of contemporary media industries, Murdock and Golding (1977) suggest two reasons for this historical process of diversification, or horizontal integration, across different spheres on the part of the conglomerates, which produce a range of different products. They argue, first, that such strategies facilitate the maintenance of overall profits even when individual sectors suffer from a lack of potential for expansion as a result of falling demand; and, second, that the process provides the opportunity for one sector to 'cushion' another where profitability has declined because of other factors. However, it is clear that at some points this diversification can produce an unstable compromise, which can then lead to the parent company divesting itself of a specific area of operation. Thus, in the case of music, EMI was re-created as a music company in 1996, moving away from Thorn EMI, and 'Time Warner sold Warner Music to an investment group led by Edgar Bronfman Jr. in 2003' (Burkart 2005: 493–4). A current example of a horizontally integrated company is Bertelsmann (Bishop 2005: 447). As box 1.1 suggests, this remains a fluid situation.

An alternative, but sometimes related historical strategy is that of 'vertical integration', where 'oligopolistic concentration of the record industry was maintained by control of the total production flow from raw materials to wholesale sales' (Peterson and Berger 1990: 143). For example, an artist may record in a studio owned by a company which manufactures a disc from the recording at one of its plants, and which is then reviewed in a magazine owned by that company (which may also include

Table 1.1 *Number of firms and market shares in the weekly Top 10 of the popular music single record market, by year*

Year	Labels	Firms	Firms with only one hit	Concentration ratio	
				4-FIRM	8-FIRM
1948	11	11	5	81	95
1949	9	8	3	89	100
1950	11	10	3	76	97
1951	10	8	2	82	100
1952	12	11	5	77	95
1953	12	11	3	71	94
1954	13	12	4	73	93
1955	16	14	7	74	91
1956	22	20	10	66	76
1957	28	23	8	40	65
1958	35	31	19	36	60
1959	46	42	29	34	58
1960	45	39	20	28	52
1961	48	39	16	27	48
1962	52	41	21	25	46
1963	52	36	15	26	55
1964	53	37	17	34	51
1965	50	35	16	37	61
1966	49	31	13	38	61
1967	51	35	15	40	60
1968	46	30	17	42	61
1969	48	31	14	42	64
1970	41	23	5	51	71
1971	46	21	7	45	67
1972	49	20	5	48	68
1973	42	19	4	57	81

Source: Peterson and Berger 1990: 142

a review of the film made by the artist for a film company owned by the same conglomerate) and sold to the public in a shop also owned by the company. Aspects of Bertelsmann are also vertically integrated in this way (Bishop 2005: 448).

Indie labels and music 2.0

Within this overall picture of a market dominated by a small number of very large companies, attention has often been drawn to the innovative role of small 'independent' record companies. Thus, Peterson and Berger (1990) argue that a period of concentration in the music industry is followed by a burst of creativity when the previously unmet demand on the part of the public for different sounds is unleashed and fed by smaller innovative companies. They suggest that this happened during 1955–9

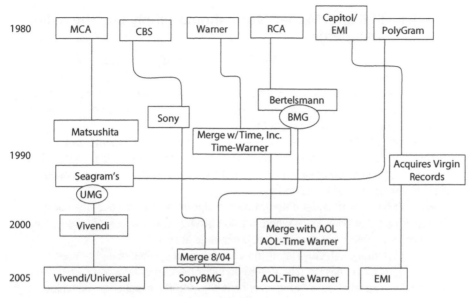

Figure 1.2 Industry consolidation, 1980–2005
Source: Bishop 2005: 448

after the advent of rock 'n' roll in 1955. A similar case can be made for the effects of punk in Britain during 1977 and subsequently, as well as for dance music in the late 1980s, though it is important to recognize that demand itself may be influenced by shifts in consumer preferences, which are related to wider changes in consumer culture.

This perceived situation has led some journalistic and academic writing to focus on the creative stance and effects of small, 'independent' record companies such as Atlantic (Gillett 1988), Stax (Guralnick 1991), Chess (Cohodas 2000), SST (Azzerad 2001), Postcard (Reynolds 2005) and Factory (Middles 2009), as well as UK independents such as Rough Trade, Beggars Banquet, 4AD and Cherry Red Records (Ogg 2009), all of which are perceived to have produced particularly distinctive music. It is suggested that the smallness and intimacy of such companies facilitated the production of particularly innovative sounds, which broke free from the standardized products of the dominant record companies. Furthermore, it is argued that such companies were better able to represent the aspirations and feelings of their artists and audiences than the large corporations.

Negus offers a critique of such approaches. He maintains that a dichotomous distinction between the large, conservative conglomerates and the small, innovative independents is misleading, as the recording industry is actually 'a web of major and minor companies' (1992: 17). Thus, larger companies will, for example, fund smaller ones to develop particular artists, set up 'independent looking' companies of their own, and adopt small group working practices which resemble those in smaller companies. More recent academic writing has similarly pointed to the complexities of the relationship between the 'independents' and the majors (for example, Lee 1995; Hesmondhalgh 1997, 1998; and, in general for the cultural industries, Hesmondhalgh 2002, 2012).

Box 1.1   EMI and Warner Music should simply bite the bullet and merge

The saga must rank as one of the longest-running, most inconclusive, takeovers in corporate history.

It has emerged that EMI-owner Terra Firma met with Edgar Bronfman, Warner's chief executive, several times last year, but talks on a deal ran aground yet again over price and the two have not met since.

'There are £1.6bn in value terms of synergies out of any such merger but neither side could agree who should get the benefit of those synergies so that deal fell apart,' said one source of what is at least the fifth time the pair have looked likely to link up only to fail to do so.

While EMI has been under different ownerships in the past decade, the curse of running a music company – where passion often gets in the way of sense – has surely played a role in some of the failed marriage attempts.

The Terra Firma chief, Guy Hands, may be a shrewd businessman, but even the private equity player has been unable to dodge some of problems associated with owning a record label. As a music lover he is enjoying the experience. Watching him dancing and singing at a recent Lily Allen gig alongside colleagues and family provided some insight.

Mr Hands' EMI may have taken writedowns and amassed a large debt pile but Terra Firma is still the proud owner of the company behind Coldplay's *Viva la Vida*, last year's best-seller. You would be unlikely to see such passion in other less glamorous sectors, such as mining or chemicals.

Mr Hands believes that Terra Firma's EMI under marketer Elio Leoni-Sceti has had clever ideas. In many ways, Terra Firma is right to have some faith. EMI did report a threefold increase in earnings to £163m in the year to March, boosted by the Coldplay album. And Mr Leoni-Sceti is undoubtedly having the right ideas – from deals with video-games makers and music websites Spotify and Muzu.tv, to selling the rights from lyrics of classic songs, including *Radio Ga Ga* and *Somewhere Over the Rainbow*, to Sainsbury's for a range of baby clothes.

However, there is only so much he can do. EMI – and Warner – would benefit greatly from increased scale. According to the latest Informa figures, EMI held the smallest recorded music market share of the major companies, with its slice of sales falling from 9.9pc in 2007 to 9.6pc in 2008. Universal increased its revenue market share to 28.7pc from 28.1pc in 2007, Sony BMG followed with 21.1pc and Warner Music's share was 14.9pc.

EMI Music Publishing also lost the top spot in music publishing, been beaten into second place by Universal with a share of 18.3pc.

Scale matters in the music industry. No more is it just a question of keeping up with Universal and Sony BMG, size is necessary to prove that, in the world of MySpace and YouTube, the record label model still works.

Scale would also give EMI and Warner Music greater strength in negotiations – particularly after Warner Music's recent scuffle with YouTube, where the label demanded that thousands of its videos from artists be taken down.

The financial pressures on EMI are clear. It emerged last week that a further

£28m has been injected into Maltby Capital, EMI's holding company, to keep it within the terms of its debt agreement. Terra Firma acquired EMI in 2007 with £2.6bn of finance provided by Citigroup. The large debt load is no doubt one barrier to a tie-up. In March, Terra Firma's accounts showed it had taken a €1.3bn (£1.2bn) writedown on EMI – half of what it paid for the company.

Debt at Warner has also become less of an issue. It is raising $1.1bn (£670m) through a bond sale, which it plans to use along with cash reserves to pay off its bank debt. Some industry analysts believe that Mr Bronfman knows a deal makes sense and has been judiciously managing his label's balance sheet to move on EMI in anticipation of it eventually collapsing under its debt.

The financial complexities of any deal between the pair are clear – not to mention the challenges that would arise from the characters involved in negotiating on both sides. It is, after all, not clear who would buy who in a merger, or who would run the joint entity.

Nevertheless, EMI and Warner Music should try to find a way round their differences. It is no secret the music industry has changed. Regulation is unlikely to prove problematic this time around and the growing force of the internet means the record labels must band together to combat it. While the music industry does work together to some extent, another large player would create a much-needed force at a time when many are questioning the viability of labels.

Source: Amanda Andrews, *Daily Telegraph*, 2 June 2009

It is illuminating in this respect to consider the example of 2 Tone Records. As the detailed discussion reproduced in box 1.2 explains, the first title on 2 Tone, *Gangsters* by the Specials, was recorded 'independently' and then manufactured and distributed by Rough Trade, an 'independent' record company. Radio airplay and live appearances by The Specials led to record industry attention and an interesting deal with Chrysalis Records.

Negus draws attention to the webs and networks that operate in the music industry:

> These organisational webs, of units within a company and connections to smaller companies, enable entertainment corporations to gain access to material and artists, and to operate a coordinating, monitoring and surveillance operation rather than just centralised control. The corporation can still shape the nature of these webs through the use and distribution of investment. But it is a tight–loose approach, rather than a rigidly hierarchical form of organisation; tight enough to ensure a degree of predictability and stability in dealing with collaborators, but loose enough to manoeuvre, redirect or even reverse company activity. (1992: 19)

Additionally, Negus has considered the place of specific genres within large record companies. A good example of some of the complexities involved is that of rap and hip-hop (see also chapters 2 and 4). Negus points out that this is more often considered 'as an aesthetic form of African-American expression: a resistant, oppositional, counter-cultural style created via the appropriation of technology and existing musical signs and symbols (scratching, sampling, mixing), drawing on a long tradition of diasporic creativity' (1999: 82). Negus adds consideration of the music industry. Thus, the music industry develops and uses rap and in turn the music has been very

Box 1.2   The birth of 2 Tone Records

This further stamp of approval from John Peel only added to the circus of record company suits that turned up at every gig, along with the likes of new wave fave Elvis Costello, who was an early convert to the 2 Tone sound. A&M, Arista, Island, CBS, Virgin, Warner Bros., they were all sniffing around, offering larger and larger amounts of money to get the hottest property on the market at the time. Christ! Mick Jagger was turning up in person to represent Rolling Stone Records! The band couldn't believe it was all happening to them, but rather than get carried away with it all, they knew exactly what they wanted out of any deal. A distribution deal for their 2 Tone label, giving them the freedom to record what they wanted and to sign other groups of their choice.

At the end of the day, it was Chrysalis who finally got the Special A.K.A. to put pen to paper by agreeing to their demands. . . . The stumbling block with other labels had been 2 Tone. Everyone wanted the Specials, but nobody wanted the label. At Chrysalis too, there were some arguments over creating a separate label identity, but in the end it was agreed to do just that because the band were too good to lose.

The 2 Tone idea might have put the others off, but the extra money involved turned out to be peanuts. 2 Tone was allowed to record ten singles a year by any band and Chrysalis were obliged to release at least six of them.

The budget for each single was only £1,000, and so it was just like giving the Specials another ten grand advance with the added bonus of the chance to discover new talent and more chart success. For that, the Specials signed a five album deal, with options up to eight LPs. With most bands doing well if they are still in business after the 'difficult second album', Chrysalis were certainly taking no chances about losing their new signings half way along the road to Beatledom.

2 Tone was never a separate entity from Chrysalis, although those directly in control decided what was released on it. In effect it was just a trading name for Chrysalis. There were no fancy 2 Tone contracts and bands on 2 Tone were actually signed to Chrysalis. For this, Chrysalis paid 2 Tone a 2 per cent royalty on top of that offered to the bands.

2 Tone might have been a revolutionary challenge to what had gone before, but when all was said and done Chrysalis still held all of the aces.

Source: Marshall 1990: 17

successful commercially. Divisions have been set up within major companies to deal with genres such as rap (and country and salsa), and these divisions are themselves reorganized as musical genres are reconstituted. The major companies have also formulated relationships with smaller ones. However, the use in rap and hip-hop has generated a range of issues concerning copyright (see below), as 'rap is perceived to be less attractive in terms of the criteria through which long-term catalogue value is accorded' (ibid.: 94).

The interconnections between the small and the dominant companies in the music industry can be characterized in a fashion which reflects the influence of writers who maintain that Fordist methods of mass production (so called after the model of

Fordism	Post-Fordism
Mass consumption	Fragmented niche markets
Technology dedicated to the production of one product	General flexible machinery
Mass, assembly-line production	Short-run batch production
Semi-skilled workers	Multiskilled workers
Taylorist management strategy	'Human relations' management strategy
General or industrial unions	No unions or 'company unionism'/ no-strike deals
Centralized national bargaining	Decentralized local or plant-level bargaining
Geographically dispersed branch plants	Geographically concentrated/new industrial districts/flexible specialist communities

Figure 1.3 Ideal types of Fordism and post-Fordism
Source: Bagguley 1991: 155

Ford's development of the mass production of cars) are increasingly being replaced by post-Fordist (or flexible) ones in contemporary capitalist societies. The differences between these regimes are summarized in figure 1.3.

According to Bagguley, the 'central element of a Fordist economic structure is mass production articulated to mass consumption' (1991: 154). Thus, the characterization of the culture industry produced by Adorno, which was considered at length in the Introduction, could be said to depict a Fordist structure. Standardized goods would emerge from production lines, under the control of a hierarchical management, to be consumed by a public with very little choice over what was available to them. In a post-Fordist system, there would be far more flexibility in production: work groups would often be organized into teams with a variety of tasks – a move towards the production of a greater range of goods addressed to different markets with the aim of giving consumers a wider choice. For the post-Fordist industry, 'the emphasis is on breaking down rigid job classifications both horizontally between functions and vertically within the hierarchy of authority, implying "multiskilling" on the one hand, and participation on the other' (ibid.: 157).

Hence, it can be argued that working practices in a small company might not be that different from those in a small team in a much bigger one which has moved away from Fordism and bureaucracy. Negus (1992: 14–16) argues that this process has occurred in the music industry, resulting 'in a proliferation of project groups and team-based working practices' and contributing 'to a blurring of previous hierarchical distinctions' (ibid.: 15). This is reinforced by the fact that even very large companies are split into divisions, often based around different genres, with degrees of autonomy.

However, there are a number of criticisms that can be made of this idea of post-Fordism. Bagguley (1991) suggests that it concentrates mainly on the manufacturing industry to the neglect of services, and that it tends both to ignore divisions of race and gender and to overestimate the extent of the spread of post-Fordist practices, which may be confined to a relatively small number of industries in specific locations in the world. Such developments have also complicated the arguments about cycles of concentration and innovation in the music industry that were first articulated by Peterson and Berger (1990). In carrying out an analysis of the USA between 1948 and 1973, Peterson and Berger argued that they had shown 'a link between market structure and musical diversity and musical innovation' (Ross 2005: 477), which involves the following:

> Changes in market concentration lead to diversity in musical form, which in turn leads to musical innovation; this musical innovation leads to market competition, which results in further musical innovation as each record company attempts to find a new musical form to stimulate consumer demand; innovation slows down as record companies strive to gain the largest share of the market for the most popular new musical form (secondary concentration) and finally, this market concentration starts the cycle over again. (Ibid: 478)

Since Peterson and Berger's paper was first published in 1975, a number of researchers have extended the analysis. Most straightforwardly, this has meant updating the time span beyond 1975, but it has also led to significant refinement of how the processes identified by the two authors are measured. Thus, for example, Peterson and Berger examined musical diversity through the number and variation in singles reaching the *Billboard* weekly chart. While this captured diversity well in the 1960s, when singles charts were very significant and sales of singles were high, it is not such a useful indicator in the twenty-first century. Moreover, as pointed out above, big companies have diversified their output partly by introducing large numbers of different 'labels' (which may look to the casual consumer like 'independent' companies). Thus, while advocates of the approach suggest that the cycles approach has much to recommend it, as it captures in general terms some plausible relationships, it needs to recognize the new modes of delivery of music (for example, via downloading and streaming) and the way in which large companies have diversified their activities over time. Thus, even if these companies do control 85 per cent of recorded output, it might be thought to be less significant if that output is much more diverse than it was twenty or thirty years ago.

A connected development in the culture industries of the digital age has been a shift in authority from those people directly concerned with production to those who are essentially concerned with other aspects of the company. Marketing departments, for example, have been engaged in extending their traditional remit, consisting of sales, record promotion, PR and advertising, to marketing functions that respond to a fast-changing music industry landscape, thus including functions such as 'video promotion, corporate sponsorship, new media marketing, grassroots marketing and tour support' (Hull et al. 2011: 229). The different dimensions of what this actually means for the working practices in a record company and the promotion of artists is examined in more detail in chapter 2.

Writing in 2005, Kusek and Leonhard depicted large music companies as 'conservative' forces in resisting change wherever they can. In a context where they see demand for digital music-sharing on the part of consumers to be building up, they say that 'Just about every new transformative technology was fought, tooth and nail, until it could no longer be contained, discredited, or sued out of existence, and only *then* it was reluctantly embraced, its providers acquired and controlled, then put to work to bring in the bacon' (2005: 140). Knopper (2009) tracks the transition of the major record labels from trying to fight peer-to-peer services by employing technological (e.g. DRM) and legal means through to the momentous announcement by EMI in 2007 that they will make most of their catalogue available online, followed by the similar decisions by the rest of the majors.

At that time, in the mid-2000s, the music industry and wider society were at the cusp of mainstreaming and proliferation of what Young and Collins (2010) term Music 2.0. The phenomenon encapsulates relevant qualities and dimensions of Web 2.0 technologies, determined by the participatory culture where 'the producers are the audience, the act of making is the act of watching, and every link is both the point of departure and destination' (Kelly 2005, as quoted by Young and Collins 2010: 340). Young and Collins argue that the communication and distribution potential of the Internet is impacting on the music industry's 'top-down' relationships and leading to the establishment of a novel set of relationships within the new media environment, influenced by participatory cultures. They suggest that the introduction of new technologies has resulted in the two main 'seismic shifts': first, the increase in accessibility and on-demand consumption of digital music through either legal or illegal channels; second, and related, an ongoing process of 'disintermediation' where a more direct relationship is forged between artists and their audiences.

When writing about the music 'in the cloud' (a metaphor used for the Internet), Wikström identifies three basic features of the new music industry landscape: connectivity vs. control, service vs. product, and amateur vs. professional (2009: 5–9). For Wikström, 'the new music industry dynamic is characterized by high connectivity and little control' (ibid.: 6), where members of the audience are forging better informed and stronger connections that allow for an increased and more efficient flow of music, usually through various online channels. This is in contrast with the old music industry economy, marked by low connectivity between audience members, where music companies acted as important intermediaries between artists and their audiences. According to Wikström, music of a new music economy ought to be thought of as a 'service' rather than a product, meaning that a physical good is inseparable from the content – that is, from music itself. The key to the success of the service is its ability to provide a path through a vast quantity of information, guiding the consumers and helping them to navigate the content. Finally, the rise of the amateur or the non-professional who makes a creative impact 'in the cloud' is not to be underestimated. New technologies promote and facilitate new forms of creative output where members of the audience can 'create, remix and publish content online' (ibid.: 7) and artists can directly reach previously unreachable audiences. Nonetheless, where does this leave the traditional structure of the music industry, and what happens to the existing roles of the record labels? Having conducted a primary research into musicians' attitudes towards de-institutionalization and democratization of the production and distribution parts of the music industry, and upon situating their findings within discourses of the impact of Web 2.0 technologies, Young and Collins conclude:

> For established bands, Music 2.0 presents a range of opportunities in addition to existing marketing and distribution channels. It allows them to communicate more easily with fans and to forge relationships that are reinforced in 'real world'

engagements such as music sales and attendance at live performances. Less established bands undoubtedly have more opportunity for exposure than in the past. But
our research confirms our instinct that the mechanisms of Music 2.0 do not guarantee 'success'; building new relationships demands time and effort, and the new distribution mechanisms still require complex negotiation. Music 2.0 requires musicians
to act as marketers, managers, and lawyers – or to employ others to act in those roles
on their behalf. (Ibid.: 354)

Bogdanović's (2009) findings, based on research with amateur musicians, are in
line with the above. After some initial enthusiasm and excitement about the new
music platforms such as MySpace, the majority of the musicians recognized their
limitations as both promotional and distribution tools. While, on account of the
notion that 'If you're not on MySpace, you don't exist' (boyd 2007: 1), they continue to
maintain their presence on various social networking platforms, the majority pursue
more traditional forms of exposure such as frequenting live gigs, networking in offline
music spaces, employing a band manager and making a direct contact with record
companies and the press.

'Products' of the music industry

Through most of its history, 78-rpm shellac discs, 7-inch 45-rpm records, stereo LPs,
compact audio-cassettes and compact discs were the functional artefacts produced
by the music industry. Then, in the second half on the 1990s, our understanding of a
musical product rapidly began to evolve, with the emergence of MP3, P2P networks,
smart phones and fast, broadband Internet connections. We will address the impact
of digital music later in this section. First, we provide a historical outline and examine the effect of wider societal and technological changes on the value and sales of
traditional musical products.

Hung and Morencos have usefully shown the fluctuation in the history of sales
for the record industry worldwide. In discussing the period 1969–89, they examined
three phases. The first phase, from 1969 to 1978, involved expansion, with the value of
retail sales increasing from 'USD 2 billion in 1969 to USD 10.2 billion in 1978' (1990:
64). The second phase, a recession from 1979 to 1984, corresponds to the general
world recession and the increased effects of home taping made easier by the market
penetration of cassettes. The third phase, recovery, developed from 1985, when the
value of sales of sound recordings increased, as shown in figure 1.5.

Hung and Morencos expected that this expansion would continue. Thus, the value
of world music sales in 1992 was US$28,893 million, compared with US$26,361 million in 1991. CDs were increasingly important in these sales figures. For example, their
worldwide sales value went up from US$975 million in 1991 to US$1,163 million in 1992.
However, once the effects of the CD boom began to wear off, sales began to contract, and
the retail value of world sales fell, from US$39,716 in 2000 to US$33,614 in 2004. Over this
period, sales of CDs fell from 2,454 million units in 2000 to 2,111 units in 2004, while DVD
sales went from 12 million units to 180 million units over the same period (BPI 2005:
102). Although in 2011 the overall worldwide recorded music trade revenue was down
by 3 per cent, and physical format sales were down by 8.7 per cent, physical formats still
constituted 61 per cent of world sales (BPI Yearbook 2012: 88). Other aspects and trends
in sales are considered in chapter 7, from the point of view of the consumption of music.

		Market value (trade income US $m)	% Change from 2010	Share of global revenues (%)
1	USA	4,372.9	−0.1	26.3
2	Japan	4,087.7	−7.0	24.6
3	Germany	1,473.7	−0.2	8.9
4	UK	1,433.7	−3.1	8.6
5	France	1,002.2	−3.7	6.0
6	Australia	475.2	5.7	2.9
7	Canada	434.0	2.6	2.6
8	Brazil	262.6	8.6	1.6
9	Netherlands	240.2	−12.1	1.4
10	Italy	239.9	−6.4	1.4

Figure 1.4 Top 10 international markets 2011
Source: International Federation of the Phonographic Industry

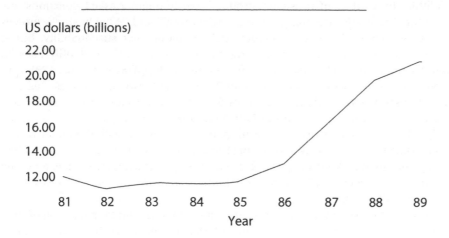

Figure 1.5 World sales of sound recordings, 1981–9
Source: International Federation of the Phonographic Industry 1990

Peer-to-peer (P2P) file-sharing services such as Napster played a significant part in the process of 'disintermediation' or democratization of distribution (Young and Collins 2010: 341) in the popular music industry. Napster existed as a free music file-sharing service until the legal action by the music industry in 1999. It was closed in 2000 and replaced in the UK by the new 'legal' Napster in 2004. Subsequent to the increase in popularity of P2P file-sharing, the introduction of digital audio/media players and the emergence of portable digital music devices (MP3 players), a number of digital music download services or 'stores' were established. The best known is iTunes, launched in 2003 and by 2010 accounting for about 70 per cent of the global music download sales. Digital music stores offer purchases or paid downloads of music files (and increasingly other products such as audio books, DVDs, podcast subscriptions, games, etc.), providing alternative formats to what is traditionally thought of as a music product. Music streaming, on the other hand, challenges the concept of ownership of a popular music product or an artefact, as well as disrupting a host of practices associated with the industry's income collection business models. Well-established services such as Last.fm and Spotify allow users to stream music files, store them in music libraries, share their libraries with other users, and listen to them on portable music devices such as smart phones without having to download or purchase the files. User profiles are created through 'scrobbling' – 'Scrobbling a song means that when you listen to it, the name of the song is sent to Last.fm and added to your music profile' (www.last.fm/help/faq?category=Scrobbling, accessed 3 December 2010) – leading to the recommendations based on the existing user taste as well as possibilities to branch into similar genres. In their infancy, streaming services were perceived as a good way to discover new music and revisit some of the old favourites, free of charge. However, with ever expanding music catalogues and the increased portability of the music libraries (e.g. availability of the Spotify app on mobile devices), streamed music listened to on a portable device is rapidly replacing paid-for music downloads.

Within the context of music as 'product', two frequently asked questions are: 'How can free music streaming services make profit?' and 'What business models do they employ?' There is an ongoing debate about their sustainability, but at present they are funded by advertising and user subscriptions. Spotify uses an advertisement-supported revenue or 'freemium' model (Wikström 2009: 179), with a free version featuring adverts of about 30 seconds between songs, as well as a Premium service available for a monthly fee, where users can have an advert-free listening experience. Spotify also offers song downloads in partnership with the 7 Digital online music store. As a result of the deals signed with the major record labels (Universal, EMI, Sony and Warner) and the deals with the large independent aggregators such as Merlin, Spotify's music catalogue is extensive. It has emerged that the majors receive 18 per cent of Spotify shares while Merlin receives 1 per cent (Lindvall 2009).

However, the issue of the artist royalties and compensation for streaming of their music is persistent. Following reports in 2009 that, despite more than a million plays of her hit single 'Poker Face' on Spotify, Lady Gaga received just $167, as well as the attack on the service by BASCA (British Academy of Songwriters, Composers and Authors) for its 'tiny' royalties, Paul Brown, Spotify's senior vice-president of Strategic Partnership, claimed that the figure was out of date and misleading, relating to a short period of time after the service was launched and covering only royalties due from STIM (the Swedish collecting society).

Additionally, our conversations with working musicians suggest that amateur musicians in particular are very reluctant to use streaming services on account of an established perception that other artists do not benefit financially. On the other hand, there are some emerging indications that younger listeners, those frequently labelled 'digital natives', are happy to embrace the no-cost model of streaming services.

As a response to ever increasing popularity of such music streaming services as Spotify, record labels and ISPs have been trying to devise and agree on an alternative revenue model where a label's offering would in some way be bundled with ISP services such as broadband, mobile and TV subscriptions. Virgin Media would be one such bundle. However, the labels have so far failed to agree on the proposal of unlimited downloads for a monthly fee, as well as what the cost of the subscription would be. In the meantime, Spotify signed a deal with Swedish ISP Telia in 2009, bundling Spotify Premium with its TV, broadband and mobile services and resulting in a good uptake of Spotify Premium in Sweden (Behind the music 2009).

The contribution of ad-supported or free streaming services to the UK music industry's revenue went from £2.4 million in 2008 to £11.4 million in 2011. Nonetheless, it contributes only 1.4 per cent to its overall revenue, while sales of physical formats still account for 64.6 per cent (BPI Yearbook 2012). According to the BPI, overall album sales dropped by 5.6 per cent in 2011, while digital album downloads rose by 26.6 per cent, cushioning the overall drop in album sales. 2011 was the eighth consecutive year of growth in the sales of singles, with an increase of 10 per cent on 2010. The percentage of digital album sales also increased, from 1.8 per cent in 2006 to 23.5 per cent in 2011. According to the BPI, 99.3 per cent of the UK's singles market in 2011 was digital.

The increase in sales of singles and the struggle of the album are reflecting a wider phenomenon of 'unbundling' or 'à la carte' consumption of popular music products enabled by the digital distribution. And yet, from time to time there are reports of resurgence of interest in traditional music industry products such as vinyl records and cassette tapes. In 2010 Amazon.co.uk reported stocking up more than 250,000 vinyl albums to meet the demand, while the Yahoo search engine has seen a 210 per cent rise in searches using the phrase 'blank cassette tapes'. There are a number of small independent record labels such as Captured Tracks in New York City and Night School Records based in London that release music on cassette tapes, particularly in CS (cassette single) format.

Despite the intermittent niche resurgence in interest in some of traditional or 'retro' formats, the digital music markets continue to grow and dominate consumption in the recording industry globally. According to the IFPI *Digital Music Report* (IFPI 2012), digital music revenues in 2011 constituted 32 per cent of record company revenues globally, a rise of 29 per cent on 2010, which could be attributed to diversification and growth of convenience in new subscription-based music consumption models such as Spotify, as well as with record companies making a number of subscription deals with ISPs and mobile operators. The report estimates that 3.6 billion downloads were purchased globally in 2011, with both singles and album sales growing. The subscription services have also recorded a growth, with a number of global paying subscribers rising from 8.2 million in 2010 to 13.4 million in 2011.

Digital piracy is defined as a continuing problem, with an estimated 28 per cent of global Internet users accessing unauthorized services each month. With the live performance market alone offering 'no guarantee of growing revenues', every other income stream continues to be explored. The following sections examine one such area, that of the rights in the music industry, and the ongoing changes brought about by the digital era.

Income from rights

Income derived from rights has always been very significant, and 'a considerable part of the turn-over of the music industry is now being derived from "the exchange of immaterial items" based on the rights to produce a musical work or its performance'

(Fabbri, 'Copyright: the dark side of the music business', *World Beat*, 1991, pp. 109–14, as quoted by Negus 1992: 12). As long ago as the mid-1980s, Frith saw that:

> For the music industry the age of manufacture is now over. Companies (and company profits) are no longer organised around making *things* but depend on the creation of *rights*. In the industry's own jargon, each piece of music represents 'a basket of rights'; the company task is to exploit as many of these rights as possible, not just those realised when it is sold in recorded form to the public, but also those realised when it is broadcast on radio or television, used on a film, commercial or video soundtrack, and so on. (1987: 57)

The ongoing digitization of the music industry processes and products resulted in the question of rights once again becoming exceptionally prominent and widely debated, with the entire industry being labelled 'a copyright industry' (Wikström 2009). Copyright in the context of the music industry centres on intellectual property right, which is 'the right given to the creators of original literary, dramatic, musical and artistic works, and [which] also extends to the creators of original sound recordings, films, broadcasts, cable programmes and the typographic arrangement of published editions' (*Cultural Trends* 1993: 56). In addition, 'The concept of copyright embodies the further principle that although the creator of the work may want to retain the copyright, he may allow others to use his material providing they pay him for it' (ibid.: 56). As is shown in figure 1.6, *three* types of rights can be identified, which are collected on different bases. Frith shows that these rights are subject to international variations. Thus, 'France and the USA, for example, have never acknowledged a performing right in records as such (and it was not until the 1976 Act that jukebox operators in the USA had to get a license from ASCAP/BMI for their use of songs as songs' (Frith 1987: 58; for more detail, see also Marshall 2005). A problem for the individual copyright owner is the collection of the income which should stem from the ownership of such rights, which is therefore undertaken by collecting societies.

The three types of rights identified in figure 1.6 are sometimes further grouped into performing and mechanical. PRS for Music was formed in 1997, bringing together two royalty collection societies – the Performing Right Society (PRS), founded in 1914, and the Mechanical Copyright Protection Society (MCPS), founded in 1924. The alliance is now the principal collecting agency for performing rights in Britain. It is a not-for-profit organization, and in 2011 it represented over 90,000 members from the ranks of songwriters, composers and music publishers. Through its licences

Right	Basis for collection
Performing	'for use of the musical material . . . collected on behalf of writers and publishers when music is performed or broadcast'
Public performance	'paid for the privilege of broadcasting or playing the actual recording (rather than the song) in public'
Mechanical	'paid to the copyright holder every time a particular song or piece of music is recorded'

Figure 1.6 Rights in the music industry
Source: Negus 1992: 13

it provides access to over 10 million songs. Royalties are collected through four main streams: broadcast and online, international, public performance sales and recorded media. PRS collections for 2011 were £630 million, with £557.2 million paid out to members. This represents an increase of 3.2 per cent on 2010.

Phonographic Performance Limited (PPL), which was founded in 1934, collects royalties for record companies and artists in the United Kingdom by licensing the use of recorded music (public performance, broadcast and new media use). In 2011 there were 8,500 record company members and 51,500 performer members of the society. The annual income from licence fees was £153.5 million, with distributable revenue of £130.8 million.

PPL operates a sister company, VPL (Video Performance Limited), which deals specifically with the licensing of music videos when they are played in public or broadcast on TV.

Box 1.3   PPL company history

PPL was formed in May 1934 by the record companies EMI and Decca Records, following a ground-breaking court case against a coffee shop in Bristol.

The coffee shop, Stephen Carwardine & Co, had been keeping its customers entertained by playing records. EMI, then called The Gramophone Company, argued it was against the law to play the record in public without first receiving the permission of the copyright owners. The judge agreed, establishing this as an important legal principle.

EMI and Decca formed Phonographic Performance Ltd (PPL) to carry out this licensing role and opened the first office in London.

There has been much technological, social and legal advancement since PPL was formed in the 1930s. The Copyright Act 1956 led to PPL's role expanding to cover the licensing of broadcasters that played recorded music. The popularity and growth of radio in the 1960s and 70s led to burgeoning PPL revenues. Further copyright law changes in 1988 strengthened PPL's licensing position.

In 1996, performers were given the rights to receive 'equitable remuneration' where recordings of their performances were played in public or broadcast – leading to PPL paying them royalties directly for the first time. Performer organisations PAMRA and AURA merged with PPL in 2006, leading to an annual meeting and dedicated board specifically for performers.

From collecting £1 million in our first decade of business to now collecting over £140 million a year, we are managing more rights for more members with a larger amount of money being paid out – enabling more licensees to play a greater variety of music. We have also branched out to collect royalties internationally for when our members' recordings have been played in other countries.

The digital age has brought ongoing challenges to the music industry and recorded music. We continue to fight to protect our members' rights and work with governments and leading industry bodies to ensure the creative industries are supported.

Source: www.ppluk.com/About-Us/Who-We-Are/Company-history/

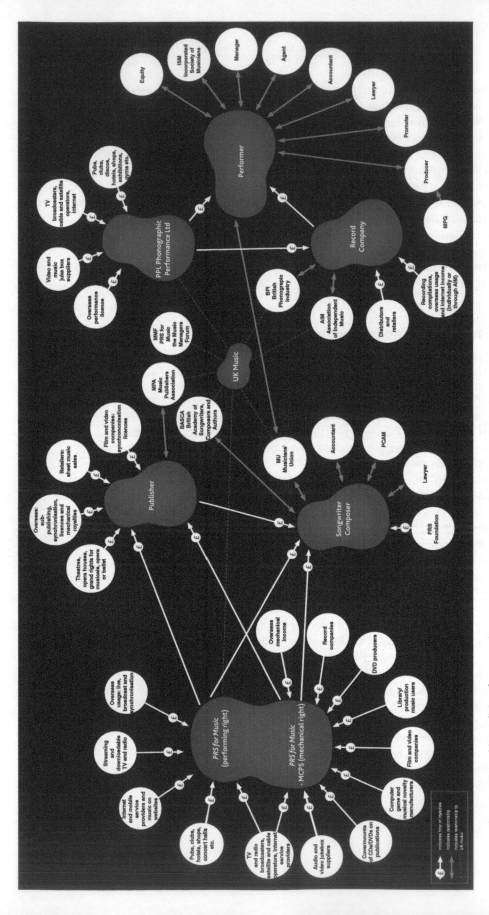

Figure 1.7 Making a living from music

Source: www.prsformusic.com

Licensing and digital piracy

In the contemporary music market, where physical sales are decreasing and income from mechanical rights is low, the revenue derived from licensing music is gathering significance (Wikström 2009: 93). Wikström outlines a number of reasons for the continually increasing importance of music licensing: a greater number of 'cloud'-based media outlets, which blur the traditional boundary between 'promotion outlets' such as television and radio and 'distribution outlets' such as records and CDs; the licensing of songs for commercial advertising as a promotional rather than a distribution strategy; the licensing of music soundtracks for use in computer games; and, finally, the licensing of music for mobile telephony (e.g. ringtones, callback tones). According to Wikström, since the start of the new millennium, music publishing has consistently challenged and encroached on what has traditionally been the domain of the record labels. One greatly quoted example of such infringement is the ownership of the master recording, which (together with the lyrics and the composition) in the new music economy is increasingly owned by the music publishers (ibid.: 99).

The ongoing development and mainstream use of the new digital technologies resulted in the need to find novel ways of protecting and regulating the music ownership rights. Digital Rights Management, or DRM, is widely used by rights owners to curb piracy. It works by relying on encryption that protects content, authentication systems, and decryption keys that allow only users with permission to access the content and so prevent illegal copying. Record labels adopted DRM to prevent copying of music files. However, one of the most popular music formats, MP3, is unencrypted and can be shared and played across a range of devices.

A suite of legislation known as the Digital Economy Act came into force in the UK in June 2010, impacting on the regulation of all creative industries, including popular music. A part that has received a lot of publicity relates to measures designed to discourage, prevent and punish illegal file-sharing. These include tracking down, suing and imposing 'technical measures' such as disconnecting or limiting Internet access of those persistently engaged in illegal activity. It is estimated that more than half of all traffic on the Internet in the UK is illegally shared content, resulting in substantial losses by the country's creative industries. The Act has provoked much debate, mostly around the issue of copyright infringement, and time will tell if the measures put in place will have any impact on the amount of illegal file-sharing or simply drive it underground. Similarly, in 2011 in the USA, the leading ISPs, such as AT&T, Cablevision, Comcast, Time Warner Cable, and Verizon, agreed with music and film industries to introduce a system of 'copyright alerts' under which up to six warnings will be sent to those suspected of copyright infringements/illegal downloading. Various measures, such as the reduction of Internet speed or a request to respond to an alert and discuss copyright issues, can be put in place. However, ISPs are not expected to disconnect a user from the Internet at any point. The approach thus is focused on change of behaviour rather than being solely punitive.

Box 1.4   Illegal downloading is suffocating the music industry

The BRIT Awards are the biggest night of the year for British music, and tonight the O2 will host the awards for the first time. This year's BRITs promise to be a true celebration of the very best contemporary British musical talent, with Mumford & Sons, Plan B, Take That, Tinie Tempah and The xx all vying for the Vivienne Westwood-styled trophy for album of the year, a new climax for the show.

The BRITs are the showcase for one of Britain's most important cultural exports. Watched by millions on the night, and by millions more around the world, the BRIT Awards send out a strong signal that the British music industry remains a significant creative powerhouse on the global stage.

This country can be incredibly proud of what British music has achieved in the last 50 years, from The Beatles and The Rolling Stones through Oasis, Spice Girls and Coldplay to Amy Winehouse and Florence + The Machine. This is testament to the talent and creativity of these artists and the cast of thousands that nurtures them and helps them succeed.

Music helps make Britain an exciting place to live and increases our reputation abroad. The UK is also one of only three countries that are net exporters of music, making it vital to future jobs and growth.

There has never been a better, more engaging time to be a music fan in Britain – especially online. There has been fast-paced innovation in digital platforms and there are now over 60 different legitimate services offering UK consumers access to vast music catalogues. I can say with total confidence that these services offer a better user experience than any pirate music site.

Music buyers using the new services are also getting better value than ever from this healthy competition. In 2002, a single cost £3.54 on average. In 2010, a single track download was just 82p. Very few consumer products outgun music when it comes to progressively attractive pricing.

The industry is listening hard to the needs of people who love music and this month we have launched an 'on air, on sale' policy, ensuring that songs are available to buy and stream from the day they are aired on radio.

But while the music business is transforming itself to face the challenges of the digital age, widespread illegal downloading continues to damage record labels both large and small. As revenues continue to fall, the considerable annual investment that music companies make in new artists remains under pressure.

The number of new British acts that broke through last year was the lowest on record. Britain is in no way suffering from a paucity of talent, but the entire music ecosystem remains distorted by illegal downloading. With only one in four songs downloaded over the internet acquired legitimately in Britain, there is still a huge way to go.

The biggest barrier to growth and innovation in the creative sector is the delay in implementing legislation to tackle the problem that was passed nearly 12 months ago. The industry is playing its part by encouraging new digital services, alongside campaigns appealing to the hearts and minds of music fans. But any weakening of our IP framework, now under major review, would represent a gigantic and unwelcome gamble on Britain's creative and cultural future.

Tonight's BRIT Awards celebrate Britain's outstanding talent and a world-class British industry. It is a poignant moment for us to reflect on how much music really means to us.

Source: David Joseph, *Daily Telegraph*, 15 February 2011

Branding

Frith has argued that, in an industry where 'failure is the norm' – referring to the failure in economic terms of covering the costs – one of the main strategies employed to maintain the profitability is 'star system'.

> Star-making, rather than record selling, is a record company's core activity; the latter is dependent on the former. This means that the music an act or artist makes has to fit a star image and personality; these days as much money is spent on image making as on music-making and no one gets signed to a record label without a discussion of how they will be marketed. (Frith 2001: 35)

At the level where an artist becomes a star – that is, when 'past sales successes are taken to guarantee their further sales successes' (Frith 2001: 35) and where marketing of a star becomes marketing of a star brand – a trademark to protect it can be applied. As Lury explains: 'A trademark provides a legal shield around the name, slogan, shape, or character image and, in conjunction with product licensing, makes it possible for the original proprietor to transfer this sign to second and third parties for a limited period of time in exchange for royalties' (1993: 85). It has been suggested that such developments are taking place across a number of different media. Indeed, it may be that they enable performers to move between different media more easily through the transfer of their image, and thus to break down the divisions which exist between media. What has been termed 'branding' – 'the forging of links of image and perception between a range of products' (ibid.: 87) – facilitates the development of images that are transferable between different media and into increasingly diverse spheres of consumption. For example, Kusek and Leonhard argue:

> Hip-hop culture has become a de-facto part of mainstream culture through the combined power of music, merchandise, and marketing. Brands such as Baby Phat, Roc-A-Wear, Sean Jean, Phat Farm, Shandy, and Snoop Dogg are among the leading brands of hip-hop inspired clothing and merchandising businesses and are making many of hip-hop's smartest artists very wealthy. According to Simmons Lathan Media Group, 45.3 million consumers worldwide spend $12.6 billion annually on hip-hop media and merchandise. The hip-hop success formula has a lot more to do with creating far-reaching musician business than just selling CDs. (2005: 118)

Such transferability of images means that the music industry is increasingly connected to other media industries. This process is clearly speeding up under the impact of the digitalization of cultural goods, where boundaries between CDs and DVDs are being eroded and television, radio, MP3 and telephones are being integrated. As is discussed elsewhere in this book (especially chapters 2 and 5), one of

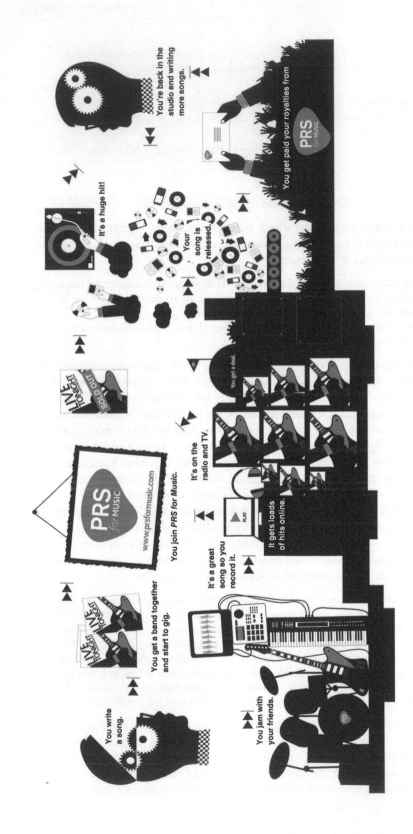

Figure 1.8 'The story of your song'

Source: www.prsformusic.com

the implications of these developments is the increasingly prominent view that the music industry should be examined not primarily in terms of *manufacturing* but in the context of the promotion of images and signs. Thus, it may equally be seen as a *service* industry, where the product is an experience. In important respects, advertising and promotional practices (Wernick 1991; Lury 1993) are central to contemporary culture. They are not simply added on to a previously produced product. Promotion of goods across different sectors is more and more important. Madonna is not simply a recording artist but an image that connects a number of different areas of culture. Of course, problems arise for the images and the companies whose profitability is connected to it when the personal life of the real person affects the image.

If the image definition of such products or brands is clear enough, they can be sold all over the world, without alterations for different cultures and markets – rather like Coca-Cola, for example. This sort of characterization leads to three important issues: the way in which media are converging, the effects of new technologies on the protection of rights, and the globalization of the music industry and its products.

Aside from representing the industry's response to a decrease in record sales, the 360-degree record deal model can be viewed as a recent example of utilizing brands, consisting of a number of associated experiences and the values attached to them, to generate profit. In a 'classic' record deal, a label receives a percentage of album sales, while the artist's main source of income is touring and merchandise. In the new music economy, a 360-degree deal means that the labels get about 10 per cent of all revenue streams that are associated with their marketing and branding of a band or an artist, which can include touring and merchandise, endorsements, sponsorship, book deals, and so on. In addition they still get about 90 to 95 per cent of record sales income. Perhaps because 360-degree deals emerged at the time of falling record sales, the arguments surrounding them tend to focus on record labels' exploitation of what has traditionally been the main income stream for the artists. The majority of artists, including some internationally recognized names, openly acknowledge that such deals are in no way beneficial for them. There is, however, a different strand of the debate where a move to 360-degree deals is perceived not purely in economic benefit terms but within a context of the shifting role the record companies play in the development of a band or an artist. Thus, it has been suggested that 360-degree deals or multiple rights deals are a natural progression of the music industry becoming a service industry, where labels are the brand marketers and the brand covers a number of brand-associated 'experiences' extending way beyond recorded music and live performances. Such contracts arguably work well for established brands such as JayZ, Shakira and Madonna (all of whom have signed deals with Live Nation) but are unlikely to benefit lesser-known artists. Taking all into consideration, it would be more beneficial for the latter to produce and distribute their own music while hiring an agency to deal with the promotional, business and marketing aspects.

Globalization and the transmission of music

It was explained earlier in this chapter that the main markets for pop music products are in the United States, Europe and Japan. The United States and Britain have in turn dominated the production of popular music for sale in the world market (Negus 1992; see also Burnett 1996). It seems likely that world markets will be increasingly opened

Culture 1 ⟨⟷⟩ Culture 2

Figure 1.9 Cultural exchange
Source: Wallis and Malm 1990: 173

up to the products of these music industries. Though often relatively small in terms of size, the markets in many of the countries outside the established main markets are among some of the fastest growing in the world. These include countries in Latin America (e.g. Bolivia and Chile), Eastern Europe (e.g. Poland and Hungary), Africa (e.g. Nigeria), the Middle East (e.g. Israel) and Asia (e.g. Taiwan). It seems obvious that the nature of domestic music production may be affected by the attempts of the big music companies to sell in these markets.

Such a process is but a specific example of the process that has been characterized as 'globalization'. There has been a major debate concerning this idea (and, in a wider sense, considerable political protest around it) since the late 1980s (Robertson and White 2005). It was argued that new modes of global connection had been developed on the basis of a range of economic and political processes such as state deregulation and economic restructuring. While at one point it seemed possible to suggest that this was likely to lead to the obliteration of 'local' cultural forms, writers on globalization realized that it was not happening in any straightforward sense. To take account of this process, the concept of 'glocalization' was coined by Robertson (1995) to capture the way that globalization was producing new modes of local attachment (for further discussion of these issues, see Savage et al. 2005).

In such a globalizing context, Wallis and Malm (1990: 173–8) have argued that patterns of cultural transmission can be classified into four types: 'cultural exchange', 'cultural dominance', 'cultural imperialism' and 'transculturation'. In cultural exchange (see figure 1.9): 'two or more cultures or subcultures interact and exchange features under fairly loose forms and more or less equal terms' (ibid.: 173). An example of this process would be the (illegal) copying of a CD which is exchanged on a reciprocal basis with a friend. In more global terms, it could entail the ways in which reggae adopted elements from American soul groups which have then been fed back to African forms in subsequent years (see, for example, the work of Cheikh Lô).

In cultural dominance (see figure 1.10), by contrast, one form of culture is imposed by a powerful group on a weaker one. For example, in school we may be forced to

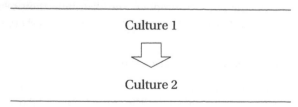

Culture 1

⬇

Culture 2

Figure 1.10 Cultural dominance
Source: Wallis and Malm 1990: 174

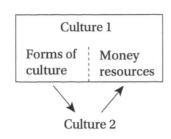

Figure 1.11 Cultural imperialism
Source: Wallis and Malm 1990: 175

listen to particular forms of music to the exclusion of others because the approved forms were perceived to be 'proper' music. Such a process occurred on a wider scale in Africa, where 'missionaries working in Kenya and Tanzania supported by a colonial administration exerted pressure on local culture. Schools were established at mission stations where native pupils were taught a mixture of European and Christian values and music' (Wallis and Malm 1990: 175).

In cultural imperialism (see figure 1.11), 'cultural dominance is augmented by the transfer of money and/or resources from dominated to dominating culture group' (Wallis and Malm 1990: 175). Wallis and Malm suggest that 'examples of the money transferred are profits made by subsidiaries of record companies belonging to the dominating culture, or copyright money. The resources can be gifted musicians, pieces of music, or unique traditional musical instruments which are removed to museums in a dominating culture area' (ibid.). It has been argued that the dominance of the United States in the transmission of music represents a form of cultural imperialism. This was a great concern in Britain in the 1950s, when commentators such as Richard Hoggart (1958) were appalled by the prospect of the Americanization of British popular culture by rock 'n' roll and other American cultural forms (Hebdige 1988).

Garofalo has pointed to three main problems with this thesis of cultural imperialism. He argues, first, that it tends to underestimate the amount of resistance to domination that can occur, even in subjugated cultures. Second, he maintains that it tends to 'conflate economic power and cultural effects' (Garofalo 1992a: 4). It is important to recognize in this argument that cultural dominance does not simply follow economic dominance. Third, Garofalo contends that the cultural imperialism thesis often rests on the premise that unspoilt cultures of the dominated are corrupted by the imposed cultures from the West. In criticism of this aspect of the cultural imperialism thesis, Collins argues that the forms of 'Western' music that are influential in South Africa are actually developments of forms which were earlier exported from Africa in the days of slavery. These forms are being reclaimed in interaction with music developed along a different route in Africa itself. Collins argues that:

> 20th century African popular performers have found three ways of circumventing the problem of 'cultural imperialism' and producing a viable contemporary art form in touch with the common person. These are through the progressive Africanisation or de-acculturation of genres which were initially modelled on foreign ones, by the

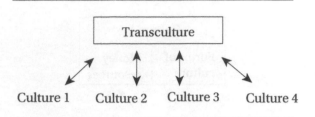

Figure 1.12 Transculture
Source: Wallis and Malm 1990: 177

> creative use of the black dance-music 'feedback' from the New world, and by contin-
> uing the old African tradition of protest music. (1992: 194)

Garofalo's view is that reality is more complicated than the thesis of cultural imperialism allows and that the complexities may be better understood through the concept
of transculturation.

'Transculturation' is the result of the worldwide establishment of the transnational
corporations in the field of culture, the corresponding spread of technology, and the
development of international marketing networks for what can be termed transna-
tionalized culture, or 'transculture' (Wallis and Malm, 1990: 176; see figure 1.12). The
emergence of 'world music' could be seen as an example of this process. Another
term which therefore could be used for this sort of culture is *global* culture. The music
of Madonna or Michael Jackson might be said to be transcultural, or a form of global
culture. As Garofalo argues: 'Can it be that the 25 million or so people outside the
United States who bought Michael Jackson's *Thriller* were all simply the unwitting
dupes of imperialist power? Or, is it conceivable that Jackson produced an album
which resonated with the cultural sensibilities of a broad international audience?'
(1992a: 6).

The effects of this process may be leading towards the creation of what Appadurai
has called 'mediascapes':

> 'Mediascapes', whether produced by private or state interests, tend to be image-
> centered, narrative-based accounts of strips of reality, and what they offer to those
> who experience and transform them is a series of elements (such as characters, plots
> and textual forms) out of which scripts can be formed of imagined lives, their own as
> well as those of others living in other places. (1990: 299)

Thus, it may be that globally we are witnessing the creation and expansion of
mediascapes made up of a variety of elements which are used in alternative ways
in different places by particular groups of people. Furthermore, such mediascapes
would not be the product of one group or controlling organization but involve complex negotiations and struggles around the placing together of different elements.
The mediascape is like a landscape, in that it can be seen in different ways from
alternative perspectives and is relatively open to different uses. The idea suggests
that configurations of media are very complex and that, while they are affected
by the operation of power, they are not simply subject to the whims of powerful
corporations or governments. A landscape may be affected by the decisions of the
powerful – a motorway may be built through it, for instance – but such decisions may

be fought, or parts of the landscape may come under the control of smaller owners, and so on.

In this sort of approach the attempt is made to move away from more simplistic accounts resting on notions of the overpowering strength of a few capitalist corporations who can do more or less as they want. It suggests that more attention should be paid to the production (and consumption) of music in specific local contexts as part of a consideration of the interaction of the global and the local. However, it is important to recognize the leading role of large corporations and to study their aims and the potential effects they can have in a detailed fashion.

Three summary points can be made. First, these processes are dynamic and contradictory. As can be argued, globalization does not mean that everything is becoming the same. As Tomlinson suggests: 'From the instrumental point of view of capitalism, then, connectivity works towards increasing a *functional* proximity. It doesn't make all places the same, but creates globalized spaces and connecting corridors which ease the flow of capital (including its commodities and its personnel) by matching the time–space compression of connectivity with a degree of cultural "compression"' (1999: 7). What is occurring is what Tomlinson, following Robertson, terms 'unicity' – 'a sense that the world is becoming, for the first time in history, a single social and cultural setting' (ibid.: 9). In one sense this defines the nature of the transculture discussed in this section so far.

Second, different aspects of globalization are connected. Thus, the consumption of a CD as part of a way of life of an individual (see chapter 9) will depend on the social interaction of those who made it (see chapter 2), who may be globally separated, the political processes that facilitate trade, and the economic patterns of production and organization that led to its being produced and marketed (see chapters 2 and 3).

Third, the practices of globalization are contested. This may be the overt struggle that has led to violent and explicit confrontations around specific meetings of the global elite, the organization of pop/rock concerts, and so on. However, the practices of hybridization involve modes of contestation as well as accommodation and the production of new forms through collaboration.

Thus, Appadurai's approach (see also Appadurai 1996) is very important, since it draws attention to how people reconstruct their patterns of local living as they confront a range of other people and processes, as well as how they imagine other places and processes to be (see further Savage et al. 2005). A number of studies of musical reconstitution in different parts of the world can be seen as offering evidence for the complex reconstitution of cultural forms rather than the obliteration of one by another (Taylor 1997; Bennett 2000).

Ho (2003) shows how the development of Cantopop in Hong Kong (music that is sung in Cantonese) emerged in the 1970s as a 'local' form in response to the desire for music in the local language rather than in English or Mandarin Chinese. This is termed a process of localization. However, as time passed, Cantopop was itself promoted by the large record companies and became influenced by musical innovation in other parts of the world. In this sense, Ho argues, it is multicultural. Indeed, as the need to increase market share has come further to the fore, Cantopop artists now sing in Mandarin as well and have explored a range of different genres, not just 'formulaic romantic ballads and brain-dead dance tunes' (ibid.: 151). Hong Kong pop has thus been influenced by music from the USA and Britain, as well as Japan, China, Taiwan

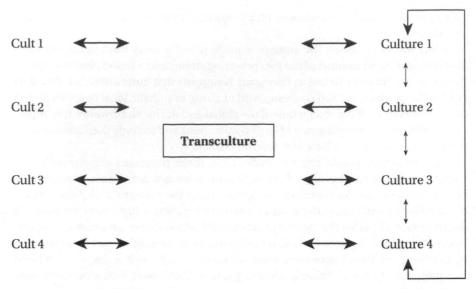

Figure 1.13 Glocalization

and Korea. In the production of 'new creative fusions', '[t]he story of Hong Kong pop in its global–local interaction is not only a case of cultural (western) imperialism and the Asianisation of Asia, but also involves a process of negotiated cultural identities as expressed in the language of Cantonese and other representational means' (ibid.: 154). Similar sorts of argument can be made about the effects of rock in China (de Kloet 2003).

As such ideas progress, it can be suggested that a new stage of development has been reached in addition to that discussed by Wallis and Malm. As well as producing a transculture and feeding back to it, local cultures are relating to other cultures and how they are imagined to be. Such a characterization can be represented diagrammatically, as in figure 1.13.

Some authors suggest that the notions of the local and global in popular music are extremely problematic. Fairley argues that the global and the local offer different perspectives on what is fundamentally one process:

> From one perspective the term globalization is used to describe the process in which local musicians may be seen to lose their local identities as they begin to employ musical elements from the global soundscape, from 'transnational' musical forms (like rock). From another it is used to describe the way in which local musicians adopt local sounds, and may appropriate local 'traditional' copyrights. In both cases arguments are about motives as well as effects. Many musical cases do not fit into either of these perspectives. (Fairley 2001: 273)

The complexity of interplay between the global and local musics has been shown by Kahn-Harris (2000). Through his analysis of the career of the Brazilian band Sepultura and 'the unique way in which they responded to globalization', he demonstrated that the global success of the band enabled their return to local sounds, exemplified by their album *Roots* (1996), which signalled the return to the band's roots not simply by its title and lyrics but also by the incorporation of Brazilian percussion instruments and the recording with the Xavanta tribe. As such it represented an attempt at construction of a particular form of musical locale and Brazilianness, which was then to be consumed on a global scale and attain an enormous commercial success.

The recent global success of a South Korean musician, PSY, with 'Gangnam Style' is a good example of how features of globalization, such as swift communication, rapid access to information and cultural exchange unbounded by geographical, material borders, can have impact on life and the consumption of a song. 'Gangnam Style' was released in July 2012 and, according to PSY, originally produced for local K-pop (Korean pop) fans. It went viral on YouTube in August 2012, reaching 1.2 billion views in January 2013, and the song had topped music charts in over thirty countries by the end of 2012. PSY became an international sensation, and his success led to increased interest and expansion of K-pop (a genre that, despite its huge popularity in Asia, has failed to establish itself in the Western world). Global demand for the song has led to radio stations discarding their traditional reluctance to play foreign-language songs.

If music is viewed as a process involving a number or relationships that inform its production and consumption, and not simply as a macro-economic analysis (see Laing 2008) of global power relationships and revenues, then a much more complex picture begins to emerge. Fairley thus calls for consideration of activities undertaken by complex local networks of musicians, entrepreneurs, record companies, festivals, media outlets, and so on, in order to understand music 'as a process within which meanings through experiences are generated' (2001: 287).

Furthermore, in an age marked by the participatory online culture, where globally expanding 'imagined communities' are formed around all music-related interests and practices, a useful approach may be to think about 'virtual diaspora' (Pinard and Jacobs: 2006), unbound by geographical borders and cut loose from the idea of nationhood.

Summary

This chapter has considered:

- the current patterns of ownership and control in the pop music industry, pointing to the concentration of the industry;
- the status of 'independent' record companies and the ideas of Fordism and post-Fordism;
- ongoing processes of digitization and disintermediation, music 'in the cloud', Music 2.0, and the new music industry 'landscapes';
- the nature of the markets for the products of the pop music industry;
- the importance of copyright, distinguishing different types of rights, the value of the income they generate, and the membership of the collecting societies in the United Kingdom;
- branding;
- some characterizations of processes of cultural exchange and transmission, including a discussion of the thesis of cultural imperialism and trends towards transculturation, globalization and glocalization.

2 The Social Production of Music

In chapter 1 we outlined some of the key features in the transformation of the music industry in the 2000s and explored a number of pertinent issues associated with the recent changes. We focused on what could be termed as 'the music publishing stream' (Hull et al. 2011) through an examination of the economic structure and organization of the pop music industry.

This chapter extends some of the key arguments from chapter 1 by considering different facets of music production. It begins with a reflection on the recent digital 'turn' in music, characterized by the introduction of digital music production technologies and the resultant changes in the distribution and consumption of music. An examination of pop music and technology sets the scene for the discussion of the meanings associated with music-making in the digital era, such as those of musicianship, authenticity and creativity. It goes on to summarize the key and evolving roles within 'the recording stream' through an overview of 'the pop process'.

Without musicians there would be no music – and consequently no music industry at all. With the aim of focusing on the more 'micro'-aspects of music-making, the chapter concludes with the discussion of some of the most important sociological studies of musicians. In addition to introducing the key issues raised by those studies, our aim is to pose the question about the extent of the impact of the ongoing transformation of popular music domains on the roles, practices and meanings associated with music-making.

Pop music and technology

In the mid-2000s a lively academic and industry debate was taking place about the 'disintermediation' of music as a result of new channels of music-sharing and distribution, such as peer-to-peer networks. This then broadened to include the potential of emergent social networking sites such as MySpace and Facebook, with their capacity to facilitate direct communication between artists and their audiences. The discussants tended to fall into two camps – those who glimpsed an enormous liberating and creative potential in the new technologies and those who were cautious about their impact and employment, waiting to see what responses the music industry, now very concerned about the economic implications of such changes, will come up with.

Some aspects of the debate are summed up very well in an exchange between Professor Marcus Breen, head of the School of Communications and Media, Bond University, Australia, and Eamonn Forde, a freelance music business and technology journalist. Breen puts forward an argument for the removal of 'the middleman' or 'disintermediation' of the relationship between an artist and their audience facilitated by the Internet, resulting in 'a Direct Access Relationship between producer and

consumer' (Breen and Forde 2004: 80). As part of a struggle over the control of distribution and circulation of popular music, he envisages the enormous changes in the
organization of the music industry. While acknowledging the shift, Forde points out
a number of responses already taking place at legislative, organizational and technological levels. He argues that 'online' is just another channel for distribution which
can coexist with physical formats and maintains that the record companies continue
to play vital roles:

> Take the record company away and what are you left with? A free-floating morass of
> MP3s online that is impossible to navigate. The music industry's failure rate is anec-
> dotally around ninety-two per cent (or ten in every twelve acts and this does not even
> consider the thousands of acts they turn away at the A & R gate . . . Record companies
> gatekeep but also invest in the development of an act. How are the 'new online-only
> bands' going to pay for studio time, for example? Where will people find out about
> these new acts? How will they be mediated to the consumer? (Ibid.: 85)

Forde's focus on the music industry's agenda is problematic for Breen, who in
turn wishes not only to question the impact brought about by the new technologies but also to examine the reasons for a wider music culture and creativity being
'overwhelmed' by marketing and sales. He suggests that the introduction of digital
technology ought to be used as a platform for a public debate 'about popular music
production and ownership', allowing the interests of different parties to be heard
(e.g. record companies, musicians, audiences) and improving the ways in which we
experience and connect with music.

Writing around the same time, Kusek and Leonhard (2005) offer a glimpse into
the future of music, envisioning it as ubiquitous and free flowing, and the current
music streaming services arguably come close to enabling such experiences for
their users. Kusek and Leonhard's prediction about the merging of the functions and
roles within music companies (e.g. music publishing, touring, merchandising, artist
management) are more or less reflected in the existing 360-degree business models,
discussed in chapter 1. Before examining the industry's response to advancements in media technologies in further detail, there are two important matters that
require attention and clarification: first, the definition of technology and, second,
the general nature of the interaction which is being suggested. We shall examine
those issues before returning to the industry's response to advancements in media
technologies.

In a classic discussion, MacKenzie and Wajcman (1985) suggest that there are
three definitions of technology. First, technology may be defined as 'sets of physical objects' – irons, buses, cars, iPods, smart phones, eReaders, and so on. Second,
technology may refer to human activities as well as simple physical objects. These
physical objects only become technology when they are used in human activity: 'a
computer without programs and programmers is simply a useless collection of bits of
metal, plastic and silicon' (ibid.: 3). Third, there is a definition of technology not only
as objects and activity but as knowledge as well. In this approach, technology is not
really technology without 'know-how'. When a student uses a laptop to present his or
her work through a series of Powerpoint slides, he or she has to know how to switch it
on, run the software application, enter and exit a full screen mode or play some audio
and video clips. These are relatively simple forms of knowledge and activity, and

many forms of technology require more detailed and expert knowledge and more complicated operations for them to function properly.

It is often assumed that technology is very important in affecting the nature and development of society. In its strongest versions, this thesis is called *technological determinism*. In an important discussion and critique of this thesis, the cultural theorist and critic Raymond Williams suggests that 'The basic assumption of technological determinism is that a new technology – a printing press or a communications satellite – "emerges" from technical study and experiment. It then changes the society or the sector in which it has "emerged". "We" adapt to it because it is the new modern way' (1983: 129). In a similar vein, MacKenzie and Wajcman propose that technological determinism 'is the theory that technology is indeed an independent factor, and that changes in technology cause social changes. In its strongest version, the theory claims that change in technology is the most important cause of change in society' (1985: 4). These writers argue that the thesis of technological determinism rests on two important premises: first, a prior separation of technology from society, where technology is at some point seen to be outside society; and, second, on the idea that 'technical change causes social change' in a direct and unmediated sort of way.

There are two major problems with simple technological determinism. First, 'the characteristics of a society play a major part in deciding which technologies are adopted' (MacKenzie and Wajcman 1985: 6). If this is accepted, it is hard to see technology as an independent factor. One point here is that technologies may be invented but then not be developed, or fail, for social reasons. Some technologies lose out for reasons that are not necessarily simply technological. Thus the cartridge (eight-track cartridge or tape that utilized the magnetic tape sound-recording technology) lost out in a battle with the cassette (utilizing the same magnetic tape sound-recording technology) and the Beta video system (analogue videocassette magnetic tape-recording format developed by Sony, released in 1975) lost out to VHS (developed by the Japanese corporation JVC). There is currently a well-publicized battle of uncertain outcome taking place between Blu-ray and HD DVD, both using optical storage technologies. Second, 'the same technology may have very different "effects" in different situations' (ibid.).

On the basis of the discussion so far, it is difficult to sustain the thesis of clear or simple technological determinism. However, as MacKenzie and Wajcman point out, this does not mean that technology is not important and they draw attention to three areas where technology can have decisive specific effects. First, technologies can be political, as they can be developed and designed to eliminate certain social developments and encourage others. Thus the 'New York builder Robert Moses designed road systems to facilitate the travel of certain types of people and hinder that of others' (MacKenzie and Wajcman 1985: 7; see Rose 1994 and chapter 4 for more on this and the development of hip-hop). Moreover, some technologies are more compatible with some social relations than others. Hence, it can be argued that 'basing energy supply around a nuclear technology that requires plutonium may enhance pressure for stronger state surveillance to prevent the theft of plutonium and help erode traditional civil liberties' (MacKenzie and Wajcman 1985: 7).

Second, technology can have long-term specific effects. Thus, for example, once a road is built or sited in a particular place, it is difficult to alter it. Critics argue that the decision to build the M25 around London has had long-term effects on the habits of car-drivers and that it began a process of expansion of the width of the road in a process which is supposed to ease congestion, but which actually turns out to be self-defeating as more traffic uses it at each stage of expansion. Third, technology can have very significant environmental and ecological effects, as the debates over pollution, acid rain and nuclear power demonstrate so clearly.

In this argument, technology is not independent and directly determining but one of a number of factors which interrelate to produce specific results. Other factors to which MacKenzie and Wajcman draw attention are economics, gender and the state. Thus, technologies are invested in for particular reasons, often in the search for market advantage or profit. They are frequently related to particular conceptions of gender and the arrangement of households and, finally, are sometimes financed by the state for military reasons, among others.

Williams (1983) argues that technological determinism can often mesh with, and influence, forms of cultural pessimism, where, along with other factors, the development of new forms of technology is held to lead to forms of cultural decline. Thus the increasing development of computer technologies and games is thought, by some commentators, to result in a deterioration in the ability of schoolchildren to concentrate on books, especially the sorts of book that are held to be of high standard. In the area of music it has been suggested that the introduction of new technologies leads to a decline in forms of previously established and valued standards of musicianship.

The discussion so far has raised a number of issues for consideration in the examination of technology and pop music. It is necessary, first, to define the sort of technology that is being discussed; second, to consider whether some accounts slip into a sort of simple technological determinism, where technology is seen to change social arrangements on its own; third, to look at the specific effects of technology; and, fourth, to examine the other factors which are affecting social and technological change. A complete study of the relations between different technologies and pop is a long way beyond the scope of this book, and useful detailed and historical accounts can be found in the work of Steve Jones (1992) and Théberge (1997).

Toynbee offers a useful conceptualization. In accord with his idea of the selection of possibles discussed earlier in this chapter, he argues that there is what he terms a 'technosphere' – an area of 'imaginary possibilities and constraints which lies between performance on one side and the more or less remote reception of sound on another' (Toynbee 2000: 69). Thus, the technosphere may be more or less immediate and simple – the performer plays an acoustic guitar and people sitting in front of him or her hear it immediately – or exceedingly complex – for example, where a track is made up of a number of different sections from a variety of sources recorded in different times and places, mixed in several locations and then distributed over a range of formats, such as computers, CDs, DVDs and mobile devices.

Toynbee identifies three main 'tendencies' in the technosphere and the type of music involved. These develop in broad historical succession. First, there is the 'documentary' mode, where the idea is 'to carry the truth of an original unmediated performance event across the air to listeners' (2000: 70). This idea was dominant from the 1920s to the 1950s. Second, there is another approach that existed through the twentieth century, which Toynbee labels 'ventriloquism'. Here, an instrument or the human voice becomes an extension of the body. The instrument and voice act as an intermediary between the body and the technosphere itself. Toynbee gives the following examples of this relationship: 'scat singing [as in jazz where the singer does not articulate words], the playing of the electric guitar, amplifier and effects, or scratching and editing tropes performed by the DJ' (ibid.). Third, there is the strategy that developed from the 1950s onwards, where the desire is 'to construct a sonic environment, a virtual dimensionality which never existed "originally"' (ibid.). This sort of approach has become more significant as advances in technology have opened up new possibilities.

There are pessimistic, optimistic and more balanced views of technologies and the ways they can be used. Pessimistic accounts suggest, sometimes in a technologically determinist fashion, that they will inevitably have negative effects, leading to the decline of musicianship, the end of true musical creativity and the development of a kind of 'programmed' music, perhaps along the lines suggested by the theories of Adorno which were examined in the Introduction. However, such accounts are difficult to sustain because of the general problems of technological determinism identified earlier: the technology is somehow seen as independent of society in the first place, and technologies can have different effects in alternative social situations.

A far more complex pessimistic account has been provided by Théberge (1989), who argues that the development of new technologies of musical production has led to increasing rationalization in the studio. This process is guided by the twin desires on the part of the producers for 'economic efficiency' and 'technical control'. Théberge maintains that this process involves the rationalization of music production along the Weberian lines outlined in chapter 1. The producer and the engineer take control of this overall rationalized process and 'enter directly into musical practice' (1989: 101). The producers do not engage in a dialogue with the musicians or carry out their wishes but are increasingly moving towards a situation where they are in control of the process, by which finished recordings are created from multi-tracks in the studio. As Goodwin argues:

> Théberge sees the process of multitracking, then, as deeply ideological, creating an illusion of community and interaction, where in fact there is only a simulation created by the manipulation of separate, rationalized elements. These elements are apparently fused, partly through stereo imaging and the application of electronic reverberation (which can be used to construct the illusion that the individual parts were recorded in the same acoustic space) in the final mix. (1992: 82)

This pessimistic account expects music to be increasingly rationalized, programmed and controlled. More optimistic accounts suggest otherwise, arguing that the development of new technologies can lead to more creativity as difficult operations become more easy to perform. Further, it has been argued that there is a form of democratization involved in the process whereby the wider availability of these technologies leads to the possibility that more people can be involved in musical creativity. In response to a more celebratory account, Goodwin calls for some caution, suggesting that

> There are clearly dangers in thinking about music as though it were a free-floating mystery, a social practice unconnected to actual conditions of production. As students of pop we need to know exactly how the means of musical production impact upon the sounds themselves. But in undertaking that task we have to recognize also that the definitions of music and musician can change. The new technologies of pop music have not created new music. But they have facilitated new possibilities. (Ibid.: 97)

Such an approach suggests the need for complex sociological investigation which locates the technology in context, and echoes the view of Steve Jones that there are new roles developing in the production of music. These involve a shift from the relationships and interaction between the musician, the producer and the recording engineer, which have characterized music production in recent years (and which will continue to exist in many areas), to those relationships which obtain between performers, programmers and performer-programmers (Jones 1992: 12). In this vein, Toynbee argues that 'technical and musical functions ... have been completely elided. MIDI musicians are always programmers and technicians too' (2000: 94). This shows how the technical and the musical are intertwined, rather than one determining the other.

An excellent example of the complexities of this situation can be found in the work of Schloss (2004), who reports on an ethnographic study of the practices of the producers of 'sample-based hip-hop' music. Schloss is interested in the way in which this hip-hop music is produced and the 'ethics' and practices around it rather than in the other dominant trends that have constituted the literature on hip-hop (see chapter 4). It is significant that this has much in common with the studies of local music-making considered earlier in this chapter:

> Most of the producers I spoke with worked long hours at mundane jobs, received the equipment as gifts from their parents, or were given used equipment by older siblings or peers who had lost interest in using it. In other words, the reality in most cases is precisely what hip-hop's critics would presumably like to hear; a story of hard-working, close knit families with a certain amount of disposable income and a willingness to invest that income in their children's artistic pursuits. (Schloss 2004: 30)

This music is based around 'beats' – 'musical collages composed of brief segments of recorded sound' (ibid.: 2). The producers sample music from pre-existing records. Their preferred way of doing this is to search out old vinyl records through their own endeavours. Schloss points to the significance for this musician subculture of 'digging in the crates' for vinyl that other producers do not have. In this respect, it has some commonalities with the record-collecting culture (ibid.: 58) and operates as a form of distinction (see chapter 6). Thus, while there are some producers who will use CDs to sample from, this is not the preferred medium. The producers have a clear sense of what sounds 'right' to them, and this guides their aesthetic creativity – 'sampling is not valued because it is convenient, but because it is beautiful' (ibid.: 65). Furthermore, the producers have clear views about what should and should not be sampled – for example, it should not be something that someone else has recently sampled. Moreover, the technologically informed creative process of hip-hop itself takes place in the sort of social contexts described in this and the previous chapter. A particular issue is the complexity of the clearance of copyright for sampled material. Schloss shows that 'a substantial number of people, including artists, lawyers, copyright holders, and their various representatives and assistants, must approve any given sample request – and any one of them can veto it by simply ignoring, forgetting or otherwise failing to respond to it' (ibid.: 179).

Thus this example brings together a number of themes from this chapter and the previous one in emphasizing the complex practices of a group of music creators.

This creation involves technological dexterity but is not defined and determined by the technology, as human beings are making deliberate choices about what sounds right to them.

The industry response

Using Napoli's (1998) model of the media institutions' reactions to new technologies, Furgason provides a succinct account of four distinct stages in the major labels' response to technological advances that revolutionized music distribution. These are complacency, resistance, differentiation and diversification. Furgason traces the problem of 'complacency' to the introduction of CD technology and the major labels' repackaging of 'old copyrighted material into new, high-priced configurations such as boxed sets of an artist's career' (Furgason 2008: 152), which, while increasing their profits, diverted their attention from the impact on their businesses of fast-moving digital technologies.

When the MP3 technology took off in the mid-1990s, in combination with increasingly faster Internet connections and thus shorter download times (in 1993 it took about four hours to download a three-minute song; Furgason 2008: 153), the industry began to realize that MP3s were beating their traditional distribution systems. After the initial delay they responded by providing a small quantity of downloads on their own websites. The content, however, was not equal to that available through peer-to-peer distribution channels and, combined with the prices corresponding to those of retail CDs, made the entire venture unattractive to users who were seeking greater choices and better-value (albeit often illegal) alternatives.

The industry then moved into a different stage, defined by Furgason as rhetorical, legal and economic forms of resistance. The rhetorical resistance took a form of 'persuasive communication efforts', such as PR campaigns about the financial harm to the industry from illegal music file-sharing, as well as the attempts to educate audiences about legal and copyright implications of sharing a song online. This was followed by the 'legal resistance' through a series of lawsuits against illegal download providers, with the closure of Napster in 2000 representing a pinnacle of such efforts. In the United States the 'economic resistance' included the formation of a large consortium of the major recording labels, telecommunication companies and electronic companies (Furgason 2008: 160) under the name the Secure Digital Music Initiative (SDMI), with the aim of 'protecting music online'. One of the technological intervention attempts was watermarking of CDs – adding tones that could be detected by electronic equipment when the music is played, however inaudible to the human ear. Watermarking was unsuccessful due to frequent faults in technology and for not being very user friendly.

The subsequent stage of the industry's response was 'differentiation', where the major labels began to introduce online subscription-based services for music downloads. Already lagging behind, and having to renegotiate numerous deals with artists and publishers for their new online distribution models, the labels were not able to offer a repertoire of music that was extensive and attractive enough to users. Additionally, in reflecting the price of retail CDs, the cost of subscription service was deemed too high.

In the next stage, that of 'diversification', labels began to rely on the third-party distributors such as iTunes (launched in 2003), which provided a better choice of music content through one platform and continued to increase the number of available and competitively priced tracks. As discussed in chapter 1, the introduction of streaming services such as Spotify, and the associated shift from the need to own music to the capacity simply to listen to it at any time (via mobile devices that support streaming services), is raising a new set of issues about available and profitable business models.

The above sections dealt primarily with the impact of new media technologies on the distribution of music. However, the profound effect has been felt in many roles associated with music production and consumption. Continuing with the technological theme, the sections that follow discuss the impact of the digital technologies on music-making and the meanings associated with musicianship, as well as various changes in the key roles in the recording stream.

Musicianship, creativity and authenticity in the 2000s

In *The Digital Musician* (2008), Hugill reflects on the relationships between the digital technologies which have marked much recent music-making and the meanings associated with the words 'musician' and 'musicianship'. Technological innovations have allowed musicians to access a range of audio production and manipulation tools which extend and possibly enhance existing music practices but also present musicians with challenges related to the degree and manner of engagement. Moreover, what was once the domain of 'engineers' and 'acousticians' is currently being offered at universities in the form of music technology courses. Hugill defines the digital musician as 'one who originates and performs, who creates and produces, and who harnesses the potential of technology in new and exciting ways' (2008: xiv).

In the digital era, the sound, like image and text before it, becomes data – a pool of information that can be manipulated and transformed almost endlessly (Hugill 2008: 5). Such possibilities raise important questions about both the nature of the practice (sound manipulation and production) and the meanings attached to being a musician. What traditionally distinguished and marked a musician as 'outstanding' was a high degree of 'musicianship' – frequently associated with instrumental music and implying a significant level of musical awareness, skill and artistry. Hugill argues that the following skills inform digital musicianship:

1 technological understanding and the ability to be creative with technology;
2 transliteracy, or the ability to '"read" across a range of software and tools, media and platforms and creative and performance situations' (ibid.: 122) rather than just music notation;
3 interactivity: human–computer interaction or human–human interaction mediated by digital technology;
4 reflective practice facilitated by the existing technology, which includes listening to, appraising and developing the material, or 'a dialogue between the musician and the musical material he or she creates' (ibid.: 127).

As part of her research on digital music-making, in 2011 Bogdanović spoke to a number of young musicians and aspiring producers who utilize digital audio recording tools on a regular basis. The view below of Steven sums up some of the themes and issues that have been raised in those conversations:

The nature of the digital medium in many ways would have us believe that the future is all about the 'hive mind' and the creative sum of our technological endeavours. In my view, this is not so. We have the opportunity to share our creative wares, but in my experience, most creatives prefer to undertake the project and complete it alone. This is fine in theory, but presents problems where the artists finds themselves creating in a vacuum. This usually leads to too much self analysis and self doubt. Not good when one is attempting to create one's masterpiece.

The isolation of performing all the production tasks by yourself, along with the necessity – and possibly vanity – of playing all the instruments yourself, leads in most cases to an inferior product. Not everyone is Prince and nor should they be. Community is at the heart of music and much of the best music has been made by groups rather than single individuals because music is about layers; it's a tapestry! Everyone wants to be a producer these days; a singular genius that has an identifiable sound. This may be because there's less cash to go around and everyone is scrambling for a niche or a way to distinguish themselves.

I find this hilarious as I have been involved in audio for 10 years and have never recorded to tape; neither have most others, but all the 'noobs' in internet forums are salivating over the latest analogue tape emulation and they have never so much as touched a tape machine.

Steven's remarks about working in a vacuum, and his feelings of isolation, uncertainty and self-doubt, and yet the vanity 'of playing all the instruments', are not new, unfamiliar or related just to digital audio recording processes. They can, however, be accentuated on account of the new working environments featuring compact digital audio workstations (DAWs) used for home recording. His comment about 'salivating over the latest analogue tape emulation' foregrounds a sense of nostalgia for the pre-digital era. Furthermore, digital musicians and their practices are often incorporated in the persistent and ongoing debate about music and authenticity. In the context of digital recording, authenticity is frequently associated with analogue sound and the race to replicate it in the digital recording through the employment of various plug-ins. More broadly, authenticity in popular music has been described as denoting uniqueness, originality, live performance, rock (as opposed to pop), art (as opposed to commerce), rawness, spontaneity, and so on, and has been studied on representational, cultural and personal levels (Barker and Taylor 2007). Minimalism, speed and lack of adornment in recordings are sometimes perceived as making a record sound more 'authentic': 'US indie act Hüsker Dü's early albums seem to have been recorded in little more than the time it took to play them' (Bannister 2006: 119).

Performing live, where an artist or a group engages in supposedly unmediated contact with their audiences, is often perceived as a marker of authenticity. In an interview with *Rolling Stone*, Neil Tennant of the Pet Shop Boys claimed that the band 'Can't cut it live . . . We're a pop group not a rock 'n' roll group' (Cook 1998: 11). Leach (2001: 147) describes such a statement as simply replacing one marker of authenticity (the ability to perform live) with another (honesty with their fans). For Auslander, live performance represents 'the secondary effect of mediating technologies' (2006: 86) because, at most large arena events such as concerts or sporting fixtures, the majority of the audience experience 'mediatized' performance relayed via big screens.

In the popular media much has been made of the perception that 'manufactured bands' (usually formed following an audition) or those entering the music business through talent shows such as *The X Factor*, are inauthentic, fabricated, commercial business 'products' that lack legitimacy. One example is the original 'manufactured' band, The Monkees, who were never inducted into the official Rock and Roll Hall of Fame, despite selling 65 million records and performing 200 concerts, including a tour with Jimi Hendrix. According to some critics, because they were formed following an audition and did not play their own instruments on the first two albums, combined with the fact that they used a number of highly regarded songwriters to build their repertoire (e.g. 'I'm a Believer' was written by Neil Diamond), they are considered an 'inauthentic', manufactured band. Matthew Stahl's article 'Authentic boy bands on TV? Performers and impresarios in *The Monkees* and *Making the Band*' (2002) takes up this theme by exploring the representation of boy bands in two television shows that were produced and broadcast in different eras (the 1960s and the 1990s–2000s). Similarly, Leach examines some of the most common 'authenticity markers' in relation to the Spice Girls, arguing that they present 'non-rock authenticity' by foregrounding their ordinariness (2001: 161). Additionally, their fans appreciate the polysemy in their presentation of authenticity, willingly engaging in the play and constructing different kinds of authenticity from the signifiers that are available to them.

The concept of authenticity is heavily imbued with the value most of us ascribe to artists and music we enjoy. According to Peterson, it is socially constructed, 'a claim that is made by or for someone, thing or performance and either accepted or rejected by relevant others'. As such, it can be attained through 'authenticity work' (2005: 1086) rather than found in objects and persons.

The pop process

Despite the continual transformation of the music industry outlined so far, many of the traditionally vital roles within record companies remain. The remit of many of these, however, is evolving and expanding, sometimes resulting in a shift of focus or an overlap of responsibility. This section examines these different places in the division of labour, how they interconnect, and the different contributions they make to the overall musical product. Negus (1992: 38) suggests that all record companies share a division of labour of the type shown in figure 2.1.

The Artist and Repertoire (A & R) division has primary responsibility for the signing and development of artists at the record company. However, in accord with the general points made by Abercrombie (1991), which were outlined in chapter 1, Negus suggests that other divisions and groups of staff, especially marketing divisions, have increased their influence over these dimensions in recent years (1992: 50; see also Negus 1999). Despite this, A & R remains very important and, according to Negus, has continued to work along principles set during the 1960s, when the 'rock tradition' developed. He suggests that six criteria are used in the assessment of potential artists:

1 the live, stage performance;
2 the originality and quality of the songs or material;
3 the recorded performance and voice;
4 their appearance and image;
5 their level of personal commitment, enthusiasm and motivation;
6 the achievements of the act so far. (1992: 53)

Box 2.1   The working practices of Martyn Ware

Martyn Ware was a founding member of both the Human League and Heaven 17 and is one of the UK's most successful and in-demand producers. His work includes Terence Trent d'Arby's *Hardline* album and hits for Tina Turner and Marc Almond. Martyn has also worked extensively writing music for film, theatre, television and radio. His most recent venture is the Illustrious Company, formed with long-term collaborator Vince Clarke (of Erasure, Yazoo and Depeche Mode), which makes original music soundscapes often in visual contexts. They recently staged a series of events called 'The Future of Sound'. See www.illustriouscompany.co.uk.

Please describe your creative use of technology, particularly digital technology.

I'm a Mac addict. I had one of the first Macs in the country in the 1980s. The Mac is central to just about everything we do, from composition through to soundscape assembly, through to 3-D surround-sound convolution. We use a proprietary system that has been built with our advice by Paul Gillieron Acoustic Design which enables us to move things around in three dimensions and actually see where things should be in a wireframe diagram. It can move up to sixteen different sound frames simultaneously at 25 frames per second. We also use Logic, an industry standard product, as a front-end. We also use Macs for all our business needs, designing websites, etc. And, although we are famous for using analogue synths, nowadays we use virtual instruments as well, so more or less everything we do is mediated through technology.

What music do you make?

It varies. My collaborator, Vince Clarke from Erasure, and myself compose together, creating soundscapes for exhibitions, events, etc., etc. We also do Hollywood-quality sound design in three dimensions. So, the work we do ranges from 3-D 'narratives' that have nothing to do with traditional music, through to traditional music pieces that are rendered in three dimensions.

The kind of music we create tends to be generally electronic and can be completely abstract or based on, say, folk history or recordings of the human voice. We are currently working on a project for the Royal Observatory at Greenwich which uses seven different sound fields based on sounds, from various observatories around the world, created by celestial events. That's pretty abstract for the listener, but it's all predicated on sounds that are relevant to the particular environment. We're also designing the reopening of the National Film Theatre, accompanied by giant projections from their newly digitised film library. So, we're doing a lot of stuff that involves reinterpreting in space existing historical or contextual content. From a commercial point of view, we work closely with commissioners to create a sense of immersion. So we did a piece for BP last year based on their six core values, from 'innovation' to 'green'. We extemporised around those ideas to create a sense of immersion in a sound environment.

Why do you make music?

Because it's the only means I have of making a living. And for pleasure. I tolerate no interference with the creative process. I never have done, throughout my career as a musician and writer, composer and producer. One of the conditions of me working is that I can't deal with working by committee, particularly when composing. For that reason, we don't do much work with the advertising world, for instance. The presumption in that kind of world is that if they pay you enough money they have the right to interfere. I'd rather earn less money and provide a clean path towards resolution of a creative idea. And it's my life, and has been before I got signed as a professional musician, since about 1972 when I bought my first synthesiser and started playing with imaginary bands, with my mates in Sheffield. It makes me laugh when people talk about retirement, because I'll be doing this until the day I die, if I can.

Is any of your sound-based work not 'music', as such?

I regard it all as music. Some people would say: 'That's not music'. It all has an artistic element. An example of the closest we would get to something that is not music is a piece we did for the Swansea National Waterfront Museum, with a friend called David Bickerstaff and a company called New Angle. One of the rooms was about how people used to shop in South Wales and the historical attitudes to money. This particular room had a long table with a responsive projection on it where you could touch items and they'd go into your shopping basket as you went along. They needed a sound element to make clear the information they wanted, and we had to do it in two different languages simultaneously. So we took this approach where we had multiple streams of information together with sound effects in three dimensions which if it was done in stereo would sound confusing, but when they are separated in space sound not confusing at all. It's like having several people in different corners of the room speaking several things in several languages, almost like a Samuel Beckett play, where some of it is abstraction but the majority is about getting information across in an interesting way. Without an artistic sensibility and experience of handling spatialised sound, this could be an absolute mess. So I regard the whole thing as being very creative at every level and very based on a knowledge of musical assembly, both in a compositional sense and in a production sense (my career is half-and-half composer/performer and producer).

Do you consider yourself a performer, a composer, a technologist, an engineer, some combination of these or, indeed, something else?

Good question. Nowadays, less of a performer, although during the 'Future of Sound' events I MC the whole thing, because I'm the most famous person involved and it's my baby anyway, so I can do what I want! I like public speaking now, whereas it used to horrify me. I've turned from a performer in the music sense to a performer in the didactic sense. Since I've had children (now aged eleven and nine), I've become much more interested in distributing the experience I've acquired over thirty years.

I think of myself more as a composer now, in the real sense of the word, than a writer. I'm a producer-composer. The skills I acquired as a producer were invaluable in terms of organising the material required to get a message across, especially in the complex world of 3-D sound and how that information is imparted to the observer. I don't like the word 'technologist', but I have become fascinated by technology. Our 3-D sound needs to be, or rather often is, accompanied by visual imagery. Interesting new forms come out of that collaboration. So I have become, of necessity, much more *au fait* with all the technologies that are out there to do with interaction, with digital manipulation of information, informatics and new forms of coding that enable you to do things that weren't previously possible in combining digital visual generative work and sound. So, I've expanded my skills base to incorporate a lot more things. I'm not an expert on all those things, but I know the *implications* of what a certain technology can bring. I don't need to know how an engine works to drive a car is the analogy, I suppose. But it's fascinating, and a prime reason for doing the Future of Sound, in which I encourage artists to collaborate with what we do, but also do works in progress. They're not always finished or polished, they're edgy. Sometimes they don't work properly or do totally unexpected things on the night. That interests me a lot more than creating something that's finished and polished. The most exciting thing for me has always been the early stages of creativity. The more things converged to the point of being finished, the less interested I became. For instance, mixing never excited me that much because I always knew exactly how I wanted a track to sound, and that was just a boring process of getting there. The creative process of collaboration and bouncing off other people was what excited me down the years, and that's why I've now created the seed conditions like when I started in the late 1970s/early 1980s.

What is the cultural context for your work? Are you influenced by music in other cultures? And other arts?

I'm definitely influenced by music from all around the world. I've always been very eclectic in my tastes, from way back, even before I was involved in making music. I don't think 'Ooh, I've just discovered music from Mali' or '. . . Tuvan open-throat singing.' Everything is music to me. I can't alter the context for my work. Everyone knows I'm an electronic musician. We've always tried to do electronics with soul, and that's what interests me, not just in musical terms but also in personal terms. I only work with people who approach what they do with soul, with a sense of humanity, of generosity and openness to new ideas. So the context for me is *innovation*, I think. I'm more interested in new forms than I am in perfecting existing forms.

What skills and attributes do you consider to be essential for you as a digital musician?

I can't think of anything that's particularly special about being a digital musician as opposed to any other kind of musician. You need a degree of talent, a good ear. I'm not a talented musician in the traditional sense: I struggle to play keyboards properly, I can only read music at a snail's pace, I never had any formal training.

The important thing is that I can conceptualise how I want something to sound, based on the timbres and melodic aspects – counterpoint, etc. I can hear a multitrack going on in my mind that I just have to get out. If I can't play some things I know people who can, or I can programme it. Open-mindedness is very important. People who buy a sequencer package have an interest in learning how to use it, but there is a big mistake that digital musicians nowadays often make. They have in their computer a tool of enormous power and diversity that enables them to create very quickly pieces that, on the surface, seem very complex and well rounded. The problem is that the ease with which it is created means that there is a lot of stuff out there that is, frankly, as shallow as a puddle. (I can't really criticise them because I would have done exactly the same thing in the early days, if I had had the tools.) What I would encourage digital musicians in particular to do is: take a step back, do a little thought and research about what you want to achieve before you start. We're in a situation now where you can switch your computer on and, within ten minutes, you can have something that 'does the job'. This is particularly prevalent in advertising, or when people put mp3s on a website. They say 'Isn't this brilliant?' The answer is: 'No, it's not brilliant, it's only OK.'

What digital musicians have to aim for is to escape the normal, pre-set paths that are offered to us at all times. All musicians, myself included, can go for the easy option, the lazy way, and it is always on offer today, particularly in computer composition. The most valuable advice I can offer people starting out on this path is: take a step back, look at what you are trying to achieve and do a bit of research. Make it hard for yourself. Limit your palette, even. Deliberately limiting yourself can enable more unique creations.

Do you have any other useful or relevant things to say about being a digital musician today?

The future is very exciting. We are in the early stages of virtual synth abilities. I do quite a bit of lecturing, and one warning flag I'd raise is that the standards in universities and colleges are not generally agreed. I personally think Logic is as good as anything, in terms of its breadth of capabilities and depth of possibilities. But I know a lot of colleges use Reason. I find a lot of these more 'user-friendly' platforms tend to lead you in facile directions. It is more constructive to start from scratch. I'll give you one interesting example. When I was working with Vince [Clarke] at a studio in America, he used to have, as people know, every synth on earth. He used to control them all using CB and Gate, and his programming controller was a BBC B computer (this was only four years ago) running a program called UI, of which he is the only remaining user. We'd discuss what we wanted to do for a while, then he'd say, 'Go away for half an hour'. When I came back, he'd got loads of different synths plugged up together, and programmed it . . . really amazing. If I suggested a change to more than one sound, within ten minutes he'd reprogrammed *everything*. To me this is a fantastic example of apparent complexity actually being much simpler than being pre-guided by software. We're all under more time and financial pressure than ever before, but I would still urge people to go off-piste from time to time, and even to start with a blank canvas, no pre-sets.

Source: Hugill 2008

directors

president or managing director

artist and repertoire   marketing   public relations
publicity and press radio   and television promotion
business affairs/finance and legal   manufacture and distribution
administration and secretarial

Figure 2.1 The division of labour in a record company
Source: Derived from Negus 1992: 38

The reference points for the predominantly male A & R staff, who may previously have worked as 'music writers, disc jockeys, musicians promoters and sales' (Negus 1992: 56), or who have come into the industry from the 'college rock tradition' (ibid.: 57), are the stars of the Anglo-American rock tradition. There is a certain antipathy to the video and more image-based pop bands which fall outside this tradition. This may be because an album band may have a longer life and can be expected to reap more consistent rewards for the company over a longer period of time. Moreover, in accord with this 'rock' tradition, importance is placed on the quality of live performance. This relates to the idea that rock is a public or 'street' form. Within rock and pop music, as in other areas of social life, the street has been seen as an area of male dominance and camaraderie. This is illustrated by a comment from a rare female worker in A & R, quoted by Negus: 'I'll tell you why I think there are not many women in it. Because, number one, it's a very chauvinistic industry, it really is. Number two, the A & R lifestyle does not suit the majority of women at all. The fact of going out every night to clubs, being up all night in sleazy, dodgy clubs or whatever' (ibid.: 59).

The extent to which the second outlined reason is still valid is debatable, as going out 'every night', seeking out and unearthing new talent, is not an activity that dominates the current A & R role. The introduction of the compact and modular digital audio technologies has meant that aspiring musicians can produce music quickly and cheaply, while various online social media platforms allow them to present their work to the target audience, including the A & R. Admittedly, while video footage of a live performance may fail to deliver all the nuances associated with the experience of a live gig, it can provide a relatively good indication of quality and presence in a live performance, allowing an A & R to make a decision if a particular band or an artist is indeed worth going to see live. Additionally, a new role, that of an 'independent A & R professional', has emerged and is becoming increasingly recognized and utilized. Independent A & R personnel work on a commission basis, aiming to generate income from as many sources as possible, across the boundaries of traditional music industry roles. In many ways, this role is a response to the changing environment of the music industry business, reliant on a full exploitation of all income streams while cutting down on talent development and nurturing artists. Instead, most major record companies prefer artists who already have 'momentum'. Moreover, in the current music industry climate, the division of labour between the roles of the record companies and the publishers is changing, with the publishers doing more and more A & R work. Some commentators have been pointing out the inevitability of the decline of the A & R role, brought about by the growing ability of artists to make and market their own music, using accessible recording technologies and the Internet. At a recent event on the future of music publishing, BMG Rights CEO Hartwig Masuch said: 'Currently, there is an A & R bottleneck which is stopping a lot of talent being recognised. There is a proliferation of systems that allow aspiring artists to make their own music and to monetise their works, for not very much money and this, along with the internet, will abolish that' (Masuch 2011).

Many aspiring musicians interviewed by Bogdanović (2009) dismissed this and equivalent perceptions, instead suggesting that the technologies that allow for their music to be heard do not necessarily guarantee an audience. Therefore, in order to succeed, most artists still have to rely on the marketing and promotion support from the record labels. Signing a record deal remains an important goal for many.

Once it has been decided that an act should be signed, it has to be developed and marketed from within the company. The interaction here between the A & R and marketing departments is central (Negus 1992: 63). The image of the group or artist is developed, with attention being paid to current trends. There may be an attempt to 'brand' the artist, in line with the general developments outlined in chapter 1. Thus, one executive interviewed by Negus 'spoke of attempting to "brand" artists. By this he meant that the unique quality of an act would become instantly recognisable and condensed into a specific image which could become a trademark. This director referred to the presentation of U2, who were not signed to the company he worked for, but whose marketing he spoke of with great admiration' (ibid.: 71).

It is important to understand that this process of 'branding' does not occur simply with the more recognizably 'pop' acts, such as Lady Gaga or Beyoncé, but is applicable to rock acts such as U2 or Bruce Springsteen, who are often thought to possess more 'authenticity'. These distinctions between pop and rock and their accrued meanings will be discussed more fully in chapter 3. The A & R and marketing departments both have their roles in the development of the product to be sold in the rock/ pop marketplace.

Negus examines the different aspects of these departments of the record company. For the most part, he emphasizes the collaborative nature of the interaction between these different activities (1992: 134). However, he also points to significant conflict in this domain. He maintains that A & R staff have become increasingly resentful of the intrusion of the promotional staff at earlier stages in the recruitment processes. The importance of marketing and promotion means that these activities are important in the shaping of a sound and image. Hence, in Negus's view, 'Many companies, responding to an increasing emphasis on marketing in the wider global economy, have attempted to make the informal dialogue between marketing and artist and repertoire more explicit by providing marketing with a formal veto on the artists who are signed' (ibid.: 148). The development of pop videos as promotional devices and their importance during the 1980s attests to the increasing importance of marketing and promotion and to their role within the creative process. Increasingly, promotional and marketing strategies are formulated at an earlier stage of the creation of a musical product, where a number of processes and tasks such as producing, engineering and mixing have been examined.

The producer tends to have overall control of the recording process, and he or she may be seen as filling the same sort of role as a director in film production. The A & R department will often try to match the artist with a producer who may have been successful previously with particular types of act and music. In the past, the producer may have been contracted to a particular company and have worked with a large number of that company's acts. However, by the early 1960s, producers were becoming akin to artists in their own right and some were known for their own sounds. A well-known case of this is Phil Spector, whose 'wall of sound' is still instantly recognizable and seen as his own invention, based on his orchestration of musicians and skills in the recording studio. A similar but less well-known example from the early 1960s in Britain can be found in the work of Joe Meek, whose sound, which can be found on recordings such as 'Telstar' and 'Robot' by The Tornados, still has devotees. Today, some producers such as The Neptunes (Pharrell Williams and Chad Hugo) and Dr Dre are as well known as the artists.

A similar movement towards greater importance can be traced for some record engineers. The distinction between the producer and engineer is put neatly by Negus, when he explains that, 'while the producer works as director of proceedings, the engineer is involved in technically finding the combination of settings to create the sounds required' (1992: 84). Some engineers have become quite well known, though they would normally be ranked below the record producer in importance. However, it should be recognized that the process by which some more established acts have become involved in the production of their own music facilitates the development of the role of the engineer, who would assist the group in putting into practice their own ideas – a role filled by some producers in the past. Furthermore, this points to some fluidity in the tasks performed by different people in the recording process over time.

- technology of recording
- recording aesthetic
- social organization of studio collaboration
- job responsibilities of the mixer
- occupational ideology of sound mixing

Figure 2.2 Dimensions of the modes of pop music production
Source: Derived from Kealy 1990

The process of development of occupation of the 'recording engineer' or 'sound mixer' has been traced by Kealy (1990), who suggests that there are three modes of collaboration in pop music production: 'craft-union', 'entrepreneurial' and 'art'. He characterizes these modes in terms of a number of different dimensions, as shown in figure 2.2. The content of these dimensions in the different modes is shown in figure 2.3. Kealy traces the development from the craft to the art modes of production. In the craft mode, which was dominant in the immediate post-war period, the recording engineer was expected to use mainly the acoustic properties of the studio to attempt to reproduce as far as possible a 'realistic' reproduction of a concert-hall sound. The occupation was organized around trade unions, and relationships in the studio were formal and demarcated, with little overlap between tasks. Kealy suggests that:

> The basic standard used to judge a sound mixer's work was whether the sound was 'in the grooves'. The good mixer-craftsman would make sure that unwanted sounds were not recorded or were at least minimized, that the desired sounds were recorded without distortion, and that the sounds were in balance. The recording technology

itself, and thus the sound mixer's work, was to be unobtrusive so as not to destroy the listener's illusion that he was sitting in Philharmonic Hall rather than in his living room. The art of recording was not to compete for the public's aesthetic attention to the art that was being recorded. (Ibid.: 211)

	Technology of recording	Recording aesthetic	Social organization	Job respon-sibilities	Occupational ideology
Craft	acoustic properties	realism	professional/ unionized	formal/ impersonal	'in the grooves'
Entrepren-eurial	tape	hit sound	fluid	open	selling
Art	multi-track	art	collaboration	rapport	expression

Figure 2.3 Craft, entrepreneurial and art modes of collaboration in popular music production
Source: Constructed from Kealy 1990

The entrepreneurial mode of sound recording developed during the 1950s. The introduction of tape for recording facilitated the introduction of new aesthetic and social relations. Smaller studios developed which wanted to create sounds that would result in hit records; they were not concerned with the reproduction of concert performance. The social organization of the studio loosened and the responsibilities of the mixer/engineer opened up, with the previous modes of craft unionism and professionalism breaking down. The studios became concerned to sell their sounds, both in terms of the labels that were often based in a small studio, such as Sun, in Memphis, which first recorded Elvis Presley in the mid-1950s, and Stax, also located in Memphis, which recorded a large number of soul singers and groups in the 1960s. There was a new entrepreneurial spirit, often built around the owner of the label, who was often directly involved in record production. Examples are Sam Phillips at Sun and Ahmet Ertegun at Atlantic.

The art mode of sound recording developed in the 1960s. Technology had further developed with the introduction of multi-track recording. The concern of many pop artists, and associated mixers and engineers, was how to produce an artistic statement which might be an experiment in sound. The engineer or mixer moved into a more collaborative relationship with the artist working in the studio, and there was a desire to establish a rapport between the engineer and the artist which would enable the collaborators to express themselves in the resulting music.

While these modes of organization can be seen as developing in a chronological fashion, it is important that they also be treated as ideal types. It can further be suggested that one does not necessarily replace the other. For example, it may be that bigger studios still operate in accordance with the craft mode, while smaller studios function predominantly in the entrepreneurial mode.

A related, but different, view to that of Kealy is expressed by Struthers, who distinguishes between 'three rival aesthetics of recorded music' (1987: 255): 'realism', 'perfectionism' and 'performance'. He suggests that realism was the earliest aesthetic, based in the idea that 'recordings should strive towards a faithful reproduction of the original performance' (ibid.: 242). Such realism became increasingly untenable, as 'using multi-track magnetic tape recording, the final recording is assembled and "reconstructed" from a number of fragments, and so there is no "original" of which that published recording can be a reproduction' (ibid.: 244). This leads to the perfectionism of which Struthers writes. The final aesthetic, performance, places emphasis on the performance of the musician, and his or her expressive qualities, which are captured in the recording.

The ways in which these different roles might be changing in relation to the introduction of new technology is considered in the next section. However, we want first to consider briefly some other dimensions to the pop production process. The places in the division of labour in a record company were summarized in figure 2.1 above. We have already examined the role of A & R and mentioned the importance of the marketing department and its close relationship with A & R. Negus (1992) points to the importance of a number of the other dimensions of the process, examining the intimate relationship between publicity and the music press, despite the critical reactions of media commentators, as illustrated in box 2.2 and box 2.3.

Like many other areas of society, pop and rock music can be seen as an aspect of a 'promotional culture' (Wernick 1991), where principles first formulated in the advertising of goods such as soap powder are increasingly applied to spheres such as politics and university life. Pop and rock are heavily promoted forms, and it can be argued that many of their meanings derive from their image in a marketplace. Music is promoted and analysed in the general press, the music press, music magazines and their online equivalents. Increasingly, it is endorsed and analysed through social media interaction, based on user-generated content; therefore the record companies may have 'the New Media Department' overseeing promotion and marketing opportunities on the Internet. Further, music has traditionally been promoted through the music video, or 'promo'. There is an extensive literature on video, which will be considered in chapter 5. Another important mode of advertising of musical wares is radio. A general examination of music and radio is beyond the scope of this book, being a topic in its own right. Such a general account can be found in the work of Barnard (2000). An extended consideration of the role of pirate radio in the 1960s is given by Chapman (1992) and an introductory account of radio in general can be found in Crisell (1994). More recent examinations have pointed to the fragmentation of contemporary radio into a number of different specialist stations (Barnes 1990). It seems likely that radio will remain important in generating record sales even if the stations become increasingly specialized, especially with the impact of digital radio stations. For further discussions of radio history, its structure, practices, context and prospects, see Barnard (2000), Hendy (2000) and Starkey (2004, 2011).

Music companies employ secretarial and administrative staff, often in familiar gendered roles of females supporting male staff. The products of the musical process also need to be manufactured and distributed, and many of the jobs in manufacture are performed by women, as illuminatingly discussed in the passage reproduced in box 2.4.

Hull and his colleagues (2011) identify some further structural divisions at the label level. These include the business affairs department, which deals with legal matters such as negotiating artist agreements, licensing and distribution deals. Depending on the size and the structure of the company, it may also deal with other business matters such as book-keeping, payroll and general finances. The accounting department performs a complex task of counting the sales and the payment of royalties, while

Box 2.2   Rock criticism in the music press

'The bulk of pop writing at any time is embroidered press office material; the majority of pop writers end up subbing advertorial for aftershave.' Rock musician Pat Kane takes rock critics to task.

Rock criticism? An oxymoron. The only truly critical acts in popular music are musical ones: I don't like the noises I hear around me, so I'm going to make or choose better/different ones. If rock 'n' roll is 'democracy in action – anyone can do it' (Lester Bangs), then why read others' opinions when you can make your own sounds, or choose your own soundscape? Your ears never tell you lies: rock critics *always* do.

And rock critics? For the most part, poxy morons. The bulk of pop writing at any time is embroidered press-office material; the majority of pop writers eventually settle for their own dusty little corner of a Condé Nast office, subbing advertorial for aftershave. The most interesting writers are the ones who endure, year after year, on magazines like *NME* or *Melody Maker*: forever foaming wildly at the next bunch of sallow-cheeked musical youth to come round the bend. They are particularly despicable. But at least they have their reasons.

Consider the basic lot of the long-term professional pop scrivener. It (I use the preposition wisely) is usually highly educated, yet utterly impoverished – a dangerous, distorting mixture. Despite years of training in the humanities, it finds itself reduced to a form of aesthete's beggary. The need to blag trips to Antwerp with Anthrax, or stuff down the crepes at some corporate mega-babe launch, reduces that precious critical distance to almost nil.

The reviews that result from this feudal employment are either slavishly reverential – which at least ensures that PR departments will keep the home-phone ringing. Or they're venomous and excessive – fuelled by self-loathing at continual compromise, and a kind of reckless bedsit nihilism.

I'll concede that these pressure-cooker conditions (young men and women writhing in the steam of their own insecurities and inadequacies) can make for some precocious writing. But it's a long trawl: and I usually just skim the pages looking for abusive references to a certain West-of-Scotland pop-soul duo by the name of . . .

Alright, I have an axe to grind: well, perhaps a machete to swing indiscriminately. My loathing of all rock critics – other than the self-evident pantheon (Marcus, Savage, Marsh, Bangs) – partly comes from having been at the end of some of their pathological attacks over the last eight years of my own career.

The golden rule that we broke at the start of our career and suffered for ever since was this: never give a more intelligent justification of your own music than the critic is able to. By doing so, you remove their whole raison d'être. Play the noble savage, hide your erudition under a comely fuzziness of mind, and the five-star ratings will be yours for as long as you want them. But push your own critical intellect too far and you will see the whites of their eyes.

A cursory flick through my cuttings renders up many such jewels of pundits-in-pique. 'May the bargain-bin save us from Sociological Pop Stars . . . Smart-Alec paranoid Scots, with gap sites where their shoulders should be . . . Tortuous lyrics, overripe melodies and everything framed in quotation marks. Don't they ever get tired of themselves?'

All this merely adjectival abuse – right down to the level of 'I've seen more soul in a billiard ball' and (I kid you not) 'Fuck off and die' – runs like water off a rocker's Gaultier. One can feel a certain empathy with the scattier rock critics; at least their writing displays a passionate, bilious commitment. Much more worrying is the advent of the Quality Music Establishment – represented pre-eminently by Q magazine but backed up by beanfeasts like the Mercury Music Awards (the 'Booker' of the pop world).

If the inky critic acts like a drunken gatekeeper between audience and artist – whose erratic behaviour at least allows the rocker all the random luck of schizophrenic reviewing – then the Quality Police are fully armed border guards. Only artists with corporate passports can get past them into the glare of public approval these days.

In an age of supposed relativism of taste and judgment, the presumption of Quality Rock-Crit is breathtaking: Q magazine proclaims its albums guide to be 'the best in the world', Professor Simon Frith, chair of the Mercury judging panel, has predicted that one day 'the endorsements of rock critics will have as much influence as the blurbs on book covers.'

What's behind this elevation of critical reasoning, of talk-about-pop music, is a major marketing crisis for the music business. Teenage singles buyers no longer lead musical taste, no longer create lasting stars: their rap and rave purchases have almost no connection to mainstream tastes in the album charts – the area that makes the corporations money. Over-25s mostly stick with established artists in their CD buying. So how do you get a 30-year-old married couple to risk their recession surplus on new releases?

Through elitist pop discourse, of course: the deliberate manipulation of status and credibility. If you're buying any new albums, intones the deep ideology of Q and the Mercury Awards, buy the ones that the experts say really matter. Rock academics and broadsheet scribblers, solicitors after the financial health of globe-straddling multinationals: same as it ever was. Only worse.

And the saddest thing about this current critical situation? That musicians and record companies are now looking for, or looking to be, 'Q-type' or 'Mercury's' artists: pointlessly chasing after criteria of excellence which these new, pumped-up commissars of rock can't even be consistent about themselves.

When pen-pushers start interfering with sound-makers – when the power of their response even shapes for a single second what musicians do musically – then the whole situation is completely upside down. They know the way, said Kenneth Tynan, but they can't drive the car. Music critics, get back under the Rock. And stay there.

Source: The Guardian, 6 September 1993

Box 2.3   Music critics love albums that the public hates

All right, it probably won't ever happen, but in the unlikely event that someone, one day, bets you a large amount of money that you won't be able to identify which person in a crowd of strangers is a music journalist – without asking them directly what they do for a living – here's how you win the bet. Go up to each person in turn and ask them to name their favourite Beatles track. The music journalist is the one who chooses 'Tomorrow Never Knows'.

You can be sure of two things. First, nobody who doesn't listen to music for a living will choose the final track on *Revolver*. An early pop gem such as 'I Wanna Hold Your Hand', perhaps, or a psychedelic masterpiece such as 'Strawberry Fields Forever', or a late-period sing-along such as 'Hey Jude', but not 'Tomorrow Never Knows'. Second, the music critic has to say 'Tomorrow Never Knows'. It's the law. If they choose 'Penny Lane' or 'Let It Be', they'll be drummed out of the union.

Like the rich, music journalists are different. Crucially, we hear music differently. Obviously, we shouldn't. In an ideal world, music critics would be a simple conduit between great music and the wider public. 'Here you go,' we should say, 'you'll love this' – and you would love it. The truth is a little different. While there is a large amount of music that is loved by critics and embraced by the record-buying/downloading public, and a similar amount that is shunned by both, there are albums that are adored by critics, but firmly resisted by almost everyone else, and albums that sell shedloads despite being ravaged by every critic in the land. The former group is epitomised by Captain Beefheart's *Trout Mask Replica*, the latter by *Bat out of Hell* – so let's call them Trouts and Bats.

There are different kinds of Trouts. Some are surely just about music critics showing off. Even if you admire the artistic intent behind *Metal Machine Music*, would you really want to listen to it? Then there are Trouts that are genuinely wonderful works, and critics shake their heads in sorrow that more people don't appreciate them, although we kind of understand why. Robert Wyatt typifies this group. Critics love him, but realise that his voice will strike most listeners as a bit odd on first hearing. In fact, 'Wyatting' has gained currency as a term describing the act of playing a song on a pub jukebox that you know will unsettle and annoy other customers. Fortunately, as well as being a brilliant songwriter and singer, Wyatt is also a thoroughly nice chap, with a great sense of humour, and professes himself 'honoured' by the association.

You might think that music critics would give up on these Trouts as lost causes, but no. We dig in our heels because we know we're right. Van Morrison's *Astral Weeks* is one of the best albums ever made; nobody much bought it, but critics never shut up about it. Eventually, 33 years later, it finally went gold. Okay, a lot of those sales will have been to music journalists replacing yet another worn-out copy, but still.

If Wyatt's voice or Morrison's masterpiece are far enough away from the musical mainstream to make their commercial limitations understandable, another batch of Trouts – wonderful pop music by Aimee Mann, Brendan Benson and one-non-hit-wonders Cardinal, masterful songwriting by John Hiatt or Randy Newman – seems to have all the necessary ingredients for commercial success, but never broke through beyond the 'critically acclaimed' level.

In part, this is explained by the importance of image in commercial success. Even in their younger days, Hiatt and Newman didn't carry themselves like pop stars, and while Mann gave it a go, she always looked uncomfortable in the role. Mainly, though, the discrepancy between Trouts and Bats is due to the fact that music critics are assessing music using different criteria than the rest of the world. Or, perhaps more accurately, we're using roughly the same criteria, but giving greater weight to some of them. Critics are particularly keen on authenticity, innovation, great lyrics and – most of all – a direct and identifiable connection between the emotions of the songwriter and the finished work. We're looking for the musical equivalent of a Jackson Pollock – it doesn't have to be pretty, but it must be genuine. If you take a look at the list of Bats, you'll note the almost complete absence of these qualities, in favour of attributes that critics often downweight – melody, entertainment value, immediacy, escapism, image.

Of course, these lists are merely the extremes. There is an awful lot of shared ground. If you think of some of the biggest hits of the past few years – the songs that were 'everywhere', such as 'Hey Ya', 'Crazy', 'Umbrella', 'Rehab' – they tick all the boxes. Critics adored them as much as the millions who bought them. We don't just like the 'difficult' stuff – although, saying that, you really ought to find room for a little Wyatt in your life.

CRITICS' FAVOURITES THAT THE PUBLIC HATES

1 Captain Beefheart, *Trout Mask Replica*
2 The Fall, *Hex Enduction Hour*
3 Nick Cave and the Bad Seeds, *Tender Prey*
4 The Flying Burrito Brothers, *The Gilded Palace of Sin*
5 Robert Wyatt, *Dondestan*
6 Ron Sexsmith, *Other Songs*
7 Lou Reed, *Metal Machine Music*
8 Dexy's Midnight Runners, *Don't Stand Me Down*
9 Palace Music, *Viva Last Blues*
10 Scott Walker, *Tilt*
11 Guided by Voices, *Bee Thousand*
12 Slint, *Spiderland*
13 Aimee Mann, *Whatever*
14 Randy Newman, *Sail Away*
15 Brendan Benson, *Alternative to Love*
16 Cardinal, *Cardinal*
17 Van Morrison, *Astral Weeks*
18 Love, *Forever Changes*
19 Big Star, *Radio City*
20 Vic Chesnutt, *Is the Actor Happy?*

PUBLIC FAVOURITES THAT THE CRITICS HATE

1 Meat Loaf, *Bat out of Hell*
2 Eagles, *Hotel California*
3 Norah Jones, *Come Away with Me*
4 James Blunt, *Back to Bedlam*
5 Céline Dion, *Falling into You*
6 Mariah Carey, *Music Box*
7 Shania Twain, *Come on Over*
8 Bon Jovi, *Slippery When Wet*
9 Billy Joel, *Greatest Hits*
10 Cher, *Believe*
11 Dido, *No Angel*
12 Lionel Richie, *Can't Slow Down*
13 Ricky Martin, *Ricky Martin*
14 Cranberries, *No Need to Argue*
15 Genesis, *We Can't Dance*
16 Pearl Jam, *Vs*
17 Supertramp, *Breakfast in America*
18 Simply Red, *Stars*
19 Robbie Williams, *Swing When You're Winning*
20 Jeff Wayne, *War of the Worlds*

Source: Mark Edwards, *Sunday Times*, 9 March 2008

Box 2.4   The other side of women in rock

This is the invisible, decidedly unglamorous side of the industry, the places where many of the 'women in rock' work. Most of the major labels – and, indirectly, the independents – probably employ as many women as men, perhaps even more: 'tea ladies', secretaries, receptionists, canteen staff, cleaners, and almost anyone servicing the needs of people within the industry will be female. Women also do all of the menial work that cannot yet be done more cheaply by machines: they assemble the basic parts of instruments, solder the wires and chips of electrical equipment and, in the pressing and packing plants, it is women who check the quality of discs, put them in their sleeves and pack shop orders into boxes ready for distribution. They are anonymous factory-workers at the bottom of the company hierarchy, and almost every record is handled by them at some point. Which gives them, if they choose to use it, an enormous amount of power. . . . EMI's plant at Middlesex is, in fact, reputed to be one of the better factories: it is unionized, working conditions are fair, and the company was happy to let me visit. The manager . . . is a large, middle-aged, genial man who calls his staff 'girls' (some of them are grandmothers), and thinks his secretary is wonderful. He forgot to mention her name: he calls her 'Darling'. He meant well.

Source: Steward and Garratt 1984: 63–4

manufacture and distribution are usually done via an outside entity or subsidiary (Hull et al. 2011: 182). Since its introduction in the late 1970s, the artist relations department (also known as artist development, product development or career development) has played an important role in co-ordinating the work of all other departments, aiming for an integrated, all-inclusive marketing and career development plan, therefore increasing chances for success and profitability. With the introduction of 360-degree deals, it is becoming an increasingly significant part of the overall 'service', sometimes coming under the 'artist services' division (ibid.:183–4). Within the structure of music group organization, such as Live Nation, artist services are horizontally aligned to music publishing and record label groups.

Having considered the relationship between popular music and technology as well as examined the nature of the production process and the evolving division of labour in the music industry, in the final section we introduce and discuss some of the most important sociological studies of musicians and music-making. We are undoubtedly living through an era of fast-changing music industry environments, and yet some elementary practices that inform and constitute music-making and performance seem to persist over time.

Musicians: culture, social origins, and performance

Jazz musicians

Reflecting on the academic research on popular music, Frith observes that there exists a modest body of empirical work on musicians and musical practices. However, the few existing studies are 'rather good'. Frith points out that those studies deal with 'journeymen and women of the popular music world' rather than with the most established and the most visible musicians – the stars (1996: 289). The relevance of ethnographic work lies in its examination and exposure of a wider set of meanings created and encountered by men and women who make and perform music. By looking beyond the most visible and most acclaimed participants, and by bringing into focus musical lives of 'ordinary' men and women, ethnographies seek to explore what music means to the participants and how it shapes their cultural identities.

In sociology, there is a strong tradition of bringing the 'ordinary' to the fore and understanding culture as 'a way of life', a subject of study equally worthy and significant as cultural artefacts produced by the great intellects and creative minds. Such a tradition has impacted on popular music studies, where over the past two decades there has been a noticeable development of focus, extending interest in music industries, textual analysis and audience studies to music scenes, local music-making, musical diasporas, and the impact of the latest technologies and role of music in everyday life (Bennett et al. 2006: 5).

One of the earliest and most important discussions of the culture of a group of musicians was written by the American sociologist Howard Becker (1963). Despite having worked as a jazz musician himself, Becker was interested in jazz musicians primarily as a 'deviant group', in connection with his revision of the sociology of deviance vis-à-vis the thesis of labelling, rather than with a detailed investigation of their occupational culture. Basing his account on the participant observation of jazz musicians in Chicago, Champaign-Urbana (Illinois) and Kansas City (Missouri), mainly in 1948–9, Becker focused on the following points:

> (1) the conceptions that musicians have of themselves and of the non-musicians for whom they work and the conflict they feel to be inherent in this relation; (2) the basic consensus underlying the reactions of both commercial and jazz musicians to this conflict; and (3) the feelings of isolation musicians have from the larger society and the way they segregate themselves from audience and community. (Ibid.: 83)

He argued that these musicians explicitly differentiated themselves from the rest of society, calling non-musicians 'squares'. The musician, as an artist, was expected to deviate from conventional ways of behaving. The 'square' was ignorant of the ways of musicians but was also feared as 'the ultimate source of commercial pressure' (ibid.: 90). Thus, the musician wished to follow his or her artistic sensibility and expression, but was in danger of being forced along the lines of commercialism by the dictates of the tastes of the 'square'. The musician reacted to the pressure generated by this situation in one of two main ways: either by remaining within the jazz community and attempting to stay true to his or her artistic beliefs or by compromising and going commercial. Both reactions were based on dislike of the 'square', which could lead, according to Becker, to the attempt on the part of the musicians to separate themselves physically from the audience.

Becker also discusses the nature of the career of these sorts of musician, extending his analysis to suggest that 'The antagonistic relationship between musicians and outsiders shapes the culture of the musician and likewise produces the major contingencies and crisis points in his career' (1963: 102). He shows how their career was based on an informal network of connections that helped the jazz musician to secure employment. However, those who controlled the most important cliques had adopted the commercial orientation. This further exacerbated the pressure of commercialism and the market on the individual, who sometimes responded by adopting 'the orientation of the craftsman' (ibid.: 112), where he or she was not interested in the music actually being played but focused on performing in a proficient or correct manner. In summary, with regard to the musician's career, Becker maintains that:

> [T]he emphasis of musicians on freedom from the interference inevitable in their work creates a new dimension of professional prestige which conflicts with the previously discussed job prestige in such a way that one cannot rank high in both. The greatest rewards are in the hands of those who have sacrificed their artistic independence, and who demand a similar sacrifice from those they recruit for these higher positions. This creates a dilemma for the individual musician, and his response determines the future course of his career. Refusing to submit means that all hope of achieving jobs of high prestige and income must be abandoned, while giving in to commercial pressures opens the way to success for them. (Ibid.: 113–14)

Becker argues that the family acts as a constraint or 'problem' for the male jazz musician, whose desire for freedom often clashes with the views of parents for the younger musician and of wives for older players. The jazz musicians therefore expressed, and attempted to live out, a particular type of masculinity, based around notions of freedom of artistic expression and liberation from family ties. The centrality of this to male musicians is brought home by the analysis by Bayton (1990, 1998), who shows that women musicians had to cope with the demands of children and family life in the way that male partners did not. Thus, babysitting arrangements would be the woman's responsibility, and children and babies would often have to be taken to band practices, something that was never the case for male musicians.

Becker's work is important because it identifies some key aspects of the culture of these musicians, including the difference between art and commerce and the dislike of the audiences who do not understand 'art'. However, it may not be possible to generalize from this group, which was studied at a particular time and place. It is important therefore to broaden the analysis by coming more up to date and by examining other forms of music.

White (1987) and Christian (1987) also examined the nature of jazz by themselves playing in jazz bands. White studied a professional band's engagement at a jazz club in Zurich and Christian researched various semi-professional bands in the English Midlands. White echoes many of Becker's points in his discussion, noting, for example, how some jazz musicians suggested that he should learn to read music, as 'you can do the shows and the cabaret thing – there's a lot of bread in all that game' (White 1987: 199). Furthermore, he argues that the lack of stability in the lives of the male jazz musicians interfered with the possibility of a stable family life (ibid.: 212).

The players studied by Christian had avoided the pressure towards commercialization by not becoming, or attempting to become, full-time jazz musicians. They earned small amounts of money, which were normally sufficient only to cover their costs and expenses (and in some cases not even these). The groups were subject to the market but mainly in the form of ensuring that they had a place to play. Christian explains that there is a

> precarious and fluctuating balance between, on the one hand, efforts to maintain musical integrity as expressed in the values and conventions held by most jazz musicians – that their music is not primarily a commercial commodity but a creative artistic activity – and, on the other hand, the need to operate within a market situation in order to find opportunities to play . . . compromises have to be made, sometimes in terms of what they play but more often in terms of the level of payment they can expect . . . most semi-pro jazzmen would rather not play at all than completely sell out to popular taste. (1987: 238–9)

The two main themes revealed first by Becker have been reinforced through this brief review of the culture of contemporary jazz musicians: first, the way in which musicians distinguish commerce from art; and, second, the desire for the musician to be perceived as an artist rather than being subservient to commercial goals (see also autobiographies and biographies of jazz stars that have much to say on these dilemmas: e.g. Carr 1999; Cole 2001; Davis and Troupe 1990). These themes also run through much contemporary rock and pop music, where they have been confronted in alternative ways by musicians in different social circumstances, as is shown in the next part of this section.

Art and pop

The most comprehensive tracing of the interconnections between art and pop music can be found in the work of Frith and Horne. Developing some aspects of the work of Becker, they are interested in 'how, in art schools, a particular tension between creativity and commerce is confronted and how pop music works as a solution' (1987: 3). They identify the structure and changing nature of the place of art schools in the English education system and show how attempts to make the art schools more vocational and responsive to the needs of industry ran up against the widely held conception of what it means to be an artist (ibid.: 30). The 'romantic' notion of the artist as a 'bohemian' entails ideas about individual creativity, freedom of artistic expression, the conflict between true art and the market, and so on.

From the late 1940s and early 1950s, when they connected to and bred a mode of appreciation of black American jazz, the art schools went on to attract and produce a significant number of the most important and influential rock musicians of subsequent decades. Frith and Horne identify three main waves of musicians: the rock bohemians, who 'simply picked up the bohemian attitude and carried it with them into progressive rock' (1987: 100), the pop art bands, 'who applied art theories to pop music making' (ibid.), and the pop situationists, who were central to the development of punk rock in the late 1970s. Some of the musicians and colleges involved are shown in figure 2.4. The art colleges provided both spaces for these bands and musicians to rehearse and practise and often their first audiences from other students at the college. The later musicians and bands, as well as some of their managers, wanted to put into practice some contemporary ideas about the relation between

Box 2.5   The art school career of Malcolm McLaren

In autumn 1963 [aged seventeen] Malcolm started evening classes in life drawing at St Martin's School of Art on Charing Cross Road but his mother objected to the nudes on display, so, still under the thumb of his family he transferred to 3-D design and graphics. To be accepted by the new system of art education, Malcolm needed two extra O levels, and enrolled in an Edgware school for a booster course. He passed, but was in the wrong educational area for St Martin's: instead, he was accepted by Harrow Art School to begin a Dip.AD in autumn 1964 . . . which, in his account of McLaren's early life, Fred Vermorel describes as 'the centre for miles around for Bohemian frenzy, mixing the local gay community with beatniks, drug pedlars, sexual delinquents and Mods'. . . . By degrees Malcolm began to see himself as an avant-gardist, searching for a key with which to unlock his deep anger and resentment. Between 1965 and 1968, he passed through a number of art schools and polytechnics (Reigate, Walthamstow, Chelsea, Chiswick) under a series of names falsified for the purpose of getting grants. Throughout this period he took up and discarded ideas from ideas then in currency. . . . Common to these was the idea of art being indivisible from everyday life, indivisible particularly from commerce and the environment. . . . Malcolm had entered Croydon [Art School] in the autumn of 1967: the course provided him with more freedom than hitherto and, as importantly, a community of peers . . . all were involved in a sit-in that developed in Croydon a week after the famous Hornsey Art School action. On 5 June [1968], the art students barricaded themselves in the annexe at South Norwood and issued a series of impossible demands. . . . After the Croydon sit-in, Malcolm Edwards entered Goldsmiths' in autumn 1968 to study film and photography.

Source: Savage 1991: 18, 23–4, 26, 28–9, 37

art and society and the political role of art through pop music. The art education of Malcolm McLaren, the future manager of the Sex Pistols, which is set out in box 2.5, is illustrative of some of the main themes outlined by Frith and Horne.

The earlier rock bohemians espoused notions of artistic freedom and individualism, which developed into their own attempts to produce pieces of rock art, often 'complex' in form. It was possible at that moment to sell lots of records (as albums) and still not to be seen to be 'selling out' to the marketplace, thus 'solving' the dilemma of the jazz musicians identified by Becker, by integrating art and commerce. The later situationists were more aware of the intertwining of pop, commerce and art. They were concerned not so much to remain authentic artists, and therefore to be above commerce, as to subvert both terms, suggesting that art and commerce were inextricably linked and that art could not be defined outside commercial relationships, which were not necessarily to be criticized. The art industry could be exploited from within; there was no need to attempt to create a 'pure' space outside it.

In his book *Lipstick Traces* (1993), Greil Marcus points to the interconnections between the Dadaist art movement of the Cabaret Voltaire in Zurich in 1916, the *Lettrists* in France in the 1940s and 1950s, the Situationists in Paris in the 1950s and 1960s, and punk rock in Britain in the 1970s. Such interconnections between art and pop music are also traced by Savage (1991) and for American punk by Heylin (1993). They came to the fore in the 1970s and have remained there ever since, reconstituting some of the dilemmas about being an artist and earning a living expressed by earlier generations of musicians. Commentators continue to show the role of arts education on popular music in the UK (see, for example, Harris 2003; Reynolds 2005).

The studies considered in this section so far have focused in the main on more professional musicians. However, music is also made, in the local context, by those who do not, in the immediate future anyway, expect to make a living from it. It is important therefore to consider the social processes at work in this realm and, furthermore, to remember that the musicians discussed by Becker and Frith and Horne will have started their careers by playing in local groups.

Local music-making

One of the most comprehensive and important studies of the nature of local music-making can be found in *On Becoming a Rock Musician* (1980), by H. Stith Bennett. While Bennett's study is based mainly on fieldwork done between 1970 and 1972 in the US state of Colorado, its general themes have applicability beyond that place and time. He divides his analysis into four main parts: 'group dynamics', 'rock ecology', 'mastering the technological component' and 'performance: aesthetics and the technological imperative'. Following the approach developed by Becker, Bennett traces the process through which a person becomes a local rock musician and plays to an audience. He identifies a number of stages in such a career, which are summarized in figure 2.5.

The budding rock musician has first to acquire an instrument. Most often, the first source of an instrument is the musician's parents. However, theft has also been used as a way of developing an individual's or a band's resources. There are well-documented cases of this in rock journalism. For example, Savage (1991) describes how Steve Jones of the Sex Pistols stole equipment in the early days of the band, and Rogan (1993) alludes to the illegal activities of Johnny Marr of the Smiths in the pur-

College	Musician
Liverpool	John Lennon, Deaf School, Orchestral Manoeuvres in the Dark
Newcastle	Eric Burdon
Sidcup	Phil May, Dick Taylor, Keith Richards
Ealing	Ron Wood, Pete Townsend, Thunderclap Newman, Freddy Mercury
Kingston	Eric Clapton, Keith Relf, Sandy Denny, John Renbourne, Tom McGuiness
Camberwell	Syd Barrett
Wimbledon	Jeff Beck
Hornsey	Ray Davies, Roger Glover, Adam Ant, Viv Albertine, Mike Barson, G. Lewis, Rob Gotobed, Lester Square, Steve Walsh
Croydon	Mike Vernon
Sutton	Jimmy Page
Harrow	Charlie Watts, Marco Pirroni
Hammersmith	Cat Stevens
Newcastle University	Bryan Ferry
Ipswich/Winchester	Brian Eno
Royal College	John Foxx and Ultravox
St Martin's	Glen Matlock, Lora Logic
Central	Lene Lovich, Les Chappell, Joe Strummer
Epsom	Richard Butler
Northampton	Kevin Haskins and Bauhaus
Coventry	Hazel O'Connor, Jerry Dammers, the Specials, Selecter, 2 Tone movement
Leeds	Marc Almond and Soft Cell, Green Gartside, the Mekons
Manchester	Linder, the Ludus
Edinburgh	Joe Callis, the Rezillos
Sheffield	Richard Kirk

Figure 2.4 Art schools and pop musicians in Britain
Source: Adapted from Frith and Horne 1987

Stage
1   acquiring an instrument
2   finding someone to play with and a place to play
3   increasing skills and forming groups
4   getting songs
5   working-up or 'getting-down'
6   structuring the set
7   finding a gig
8   getting to the gig
9   playing the room

Figure 2.5 Stages in the local rock career
Source: Adapted from Bennett 1980

suit of a new guitar and amplifier. According to Bennett, the problems involved in the acquisition of instruments and equipment represent economic barriers to becoming a rock musician.

After the instrument has been acquired, the beginner often attempts to learn to play on his or her own. This might involve trying to play along with some favourite records. However, most beginners realize that they can learn only so much in this way and begin to seek other musicians to play with. This can happen in different ways, but it often involves contacts with friends or friends of friends, who might form the nucleus of the beginner's first group. Groups form and re-form very quickly and can often be very loose in membership. Further, groups can often re-form out of pools of musicians who have been in a variety of groups. Bennett suggests that this is also often based on networks of friends and acquaintances. However, bulletin boards in colleges, for example, were also significant. In other contexts, advertisements in music papers have brought band members together. After people have come together to form a budding group, it is important for them to find somewhere to practise. Given the space needed and the noise produced by using electric instrumentation, this can often be quite difficult. Garages and basements were the sorts of places often used by the bands studied by Bennett. These factors constitute a social barrier for the budding rock musician.

Individual skills	Group skills		
	decrease	same	increase
decrease	3	4	5
same	9	2	6
increase	8	7	1

Situations 1, 2, and 3 are stable group configurations.
    1 = a 'good' group: the beginning of steady gigs
    2 = a transitional stage: the end of steady gigs
    3 = a disintegrative stage: 'natural death'

Situations 4, 5, and 6 are unstable group configurations which result in 'firing and hiring' – the individual is displayed by the group: an individual status degradation ceremony, or a group status enhancement ceremony.

Situations 7, 8, and 9 are unstable group configurations which result in 'quitting and looking' – the group is displaced by the individual: an individual status enhancement ceremony, or a group status degradation ceremony.

Figure 2.6 The levelling process of attributed musical skills in rock groups
Source: Reprinted from *On Becoming a Rock Musician*, by H. Stith Bennett (Amherst: University of Massachusetts Press, 1980: 31), copyright © 1980 by The University of Massachusetts Press.

As has already been noted, Bennett points to a rapid turnover in the membership of groups. He suggests that the relationship between the skills of the individual relative to the rest of the group is very important in this process (summarized in figure 2.6). Bennett gives as a graphic example a 'musical status degradation ceremony':

We had picked Mike up in Denver where he was sorta hanging out after his group in Texas broke up. For a while there everything was cool and we were playing steady, but we were progressing too . . . you know what I mean? . . . playing new songs and doing originals and getting our sets really together. Then you'd start hearing these mistakes in the bass, it was really ragged . . . just sorta falling apart. The thing is Mike was getting hung up on speed. First he was just popping and finally he was shooting up every morning. And he just looked like shit warmed over. Finally we just had to get rid of him, he was bringing the whole group down'. (Piano player, quoted in Bennett 1980: 33)

In the main, the sorts of group studied by Bennett were 'copy' groups who relied on non-original material. This meant that group practice and rehearsals mainly involved the 'getting' of songs from a record. The groups did not use sheet music or musical notation in this process but developed their material by a process of trial and error from the recorded form. There are important issues here concerning the way in which a recorded form, which might involve extensive multi-tracking and over-dubbing, is transformed into something that can be played live by a small group of four or five musicians. Bennett argues that the local musician listens to the recordings with a 'recording consciousness' (1980: 126), which enables him or her both to hear the different components of the recordings and the technical aspects of its construction and to translate these into practical ways of playing in the local group. Furthermore, he suggests: '[A]fter a song is gotten it must be transformed into a performable entity. After a song may be known in its individual parts it cannot be said that the group knows the song until the process of working-up (which is not so ironically also known as getting-down) has been concluded' (ibid.: 145).

This involves repetitive practice. The next stage in the process is the organization of the worked-up songs into a set or sets, which often entails thinking through the pacing of the performance and trying to produce an overall effect out of the discrete elements that have been learned as separate songs.

The groups have to find gigs and get to the gig. As this normally involves transporting themselves and the equipment, access to a van is very important, and a musician with a van might be accommodated within a group in preference to a more accomplished player without one. Bennett divides gigs into four main categories: social (including sponsored ones with free admission and break-even and fundraising types), which 'refers to situations which are concerned with pure sociation events, gatherings, which are primarily ends in themselves' (1980: 85); ceremonial (for example, weddings); bar; and concert. Concert gigs are relatively rare and are normally played by the local group as a support for the more well-known group. The bar gig is very important to the local group (which, given the male nature of most bars, will affect the potential for participation of women). As Bennett says in general about the bar:

The economic mainstay of local groups is the local bar. A bar gig is a more complex economic event for the group than either the social or ceremonial one-nighter – it could mean 'Friday and Saturday nights' or 'six nights a week' depending upon the clientele the bar services, but it always means a performance reality which is purchased as entertainment in the same way as mixed drinks and bar chatter. Bar owners and managers consider the group an economic investment which draws customers to the site; from their viewpoint they are paying the group for the number of bodies it pulls through the door. (Ibid.: 91)

The group has to adapt and set up its equipment to play the room, which can affect the nature of the performance and the musical event in different ways. The physical make-up and acoustics of rooms can have effects. There are also important differences between playing inside and outside.

Bennett's book is important in illustrating many different aspects of the local musician's life and career and, like Becker's work, for illuminating some of the dilemmas encountered: finding someone to play with, deciding what to play, agreeing on the time to practise, and so on. However, despite its continuing general pertinence, it is subject to some limitations: first, it is now rather dated; second, it discusses rock music of a particular type and period; third, it is located in the main in one place; and, fourth, the musicians considered are mainly men, and Bennett plays little attention to the issue of gender. It is important, therefore, to examine some other, more recent, accounts of local music-making to extend the scope of the approach pioneered by Bennett.

A later study of the making of rock music in a local context can be found in *Rock Culture in Liverpool* (1991), by Sara Cohen. Cohen spent a year between October 1985 and October 1986 carrying out unstructured interviews and participant observation on 'bands without record contracts that therefore functioned on the margins of the industry' (ibid.: 5). The sorts of band she studied tended to have been together for between two and three years and to consist of four or five white men aged between twenty and thirty. The pattern of instrumentation in the groups tended to be similar, being guitar- and drum-based. Cohen focuses on two of these bands in particular: the Jactars and Crikey it's the Cromptons!

Cohen makes a number of important points about the bands and different aspects of local music-making, some of which echo, in a rather different context, the themes developed by both Becker and Bennett. First, she shows how the groups are based in particular social settings and how important their participation in one studio was, as they tended to interact with other bands based at Vulcan Studios in Liverpool. Second, she examines the issues around the gaining of the instruments for the band, centred on the difficulties of securing the necessary finance.

Third, Cohen discusses the way in which the bands developed their own songs. The bands she studied were interested primarily in writing their own material. They would play the occasional cover version, but an important aspect of their self-perception as musicians was their originality. This contrasts with the copy groups examined by Bennett. Cohen points to 'four main themes implicit in the music-making of the Jactars': an 'emphasis upon natural talent', a 'simple and clean sound', 'originality', and 'musical incompetence as style', which were shared by Crikey it's the Cromptons! (1991: 169). There were differences between the bands in the ways in which they developed their material, but they had similar notions of creativity and originality. In part, this stemmed from a post-punk ethos of creativity, to be developed outside what the bands themselves saw as the established sounds of a mass culture.

Fourth, despite this anti-commercialism, the bands were interested in getting record deals. Cohen describes in some detail the reactions of record companies to the material sent to them by the bands, and the letter's attempts to get record companies to listen to their music. Thus, the bands were seeking success even if this was defined in terms that did not include doing anything to sell records. Likewise, more than 50 per cent of the wider sample of local bands studied by Cohen had some kind of management (1991: 59). However, despite this, legal and financial affairs remained difficult and were often implicated in the break-up of bands.

In addition to the points noted so far (and there are other aspects which make Cohen's book useful in the developing literature on local music-making), it is the fifth factor that is the most important: the bands' masculinity and attitudes towards women. Cohen notes how the relations between different bands tended to be like gang rivalry (1991: 35). Furthermore, the band was a social unit: being in a band was a 'way of life' (ibid.: 38) for the male members, and the only woman member of one of the bands was systematically marginalized. These practices and attitudes were reinforced by the performances. Women were seen in terms of visual image (ibid.: 81), not as musicians, and were hence involved as 'mostly backing singers and non-instrumentalists' (ibid.: 206). In Cohen's account, at gigs 'the community and solidarity the bands strove for was predominantly masculine. While women generally liked to dance, their male counterparts were reluctant to do so' (ibid.: 101). Women were viewed as a problem for the bands and were 'actively excluded'. This reinforces the theme identified by Becker, where wives and families were seen to be a 'problem' for the male jazz musician, and also the gendered nature of music-making identified by Bayton (1990, 1992, 1993, 1998).

These themes are comprehensively discussed by Bayton. In *Frock Rock* (1998), which examines female music-makers in the 1980s and mid-1990s, Bayton shows that women still make up only around 15 per cent of musical performers (ibid.: 23), and even those that do perform – apart from those who reach star status – tend to be written out of the histories of music. Bayton seeks to explain why there have been 'so few women playing instruments in bands' (ibid.: 25) and shows that there are a number of constraints on women engaging in music-making (some of which will affect men, though in different ways). She divides these constraining factors into two broad types: material and ideological. The material factors include the need to secure equipment and transport, the necessity for space and time to practise, and the way in which female leisure time is constrained by parents and partners. Male musicians often exclude female players, and the rock musical style is masculine, which is further explored by Bayton in terms of the construction and reproduction of ideologies of femininity, which are class differentiated in some respects.

Despite these significant material and ideological constraints, some women do become involved in music-making. Bayton offers an analysis of the 'routes into rock' by which this can be facilitated. She discusses the parts played by having a musical family, being classically trained, having an art education, being involved in drama, gender rebellion, having boyfriends or husbands who are musicians, attending higher education and having female role models. Bayton argues for the importance of punk (and what is now most often termed post-punk; see, for example, Reynolds 2005) in the late 1970s in opening space for more women to be involved in music-making at local levels (1998: 68). This was also significantly affected by feminist and lesbian politics of the time, which encouraged female creativity and provided places for practice and performance. These points are summarized in figure 2.7.

Bayton then analyses the nature of the processes that confront women once they have begun to get involved in music-making. Again, some of these are similar to those discussed by authors such as Bennett (1980) and Cohen (1991), but Bayton draws out some of the particular processes that affect women, such as the fact that

Constraints	Escapes
childhood femininity	gender rebellion
family	unusual/musical family
technophobia	unusual family/school
	women's music projects
teenage femininity	bohemian/artist
(via mass media and female peer groups)	rebel identity
material constraints	feminist collectives
equipment space, money, time	political collectives
	women's music projects
	unusual boyfriends and husbands
ideological constraints	feminism
(dual standard of morality etc.)	lesbianism
	Riot Grrrl
	Girl Power
exclusion by male music-making peer	women's music projects
groups and by male bands	women's bands
exclusion by promoters	DIY feminist venues
male-dominated gigs	
hostile male audiences	women-only gigs
sexploitative managers	DIY administration
	supportive husbands/managers
sexist PA crew	DIY feminist PA
	feminist courses in sound engineering
female compartments	punk, Riot Grrrl, and feminist
alternatives in the record promotion	DIY record production and distribution
industry (esp. light pop/vocals)	

Figure 2.7 Constraints and escapes for women musicians
Source: Bayton 1998: 190

they are more likely to join a band at an earlier stage of learning an instrument and are less likely to practise in the parental home. The all-women bands considered by Bayton tended to be more democratic in operation than those examined by Bennett and to be more involved in writing original material. There are further issues for women to confront once they are playing in public, such as sexual harassment on a number of levels, the image and style that is to be projected, and so on. Some of the dilemmas involved here are captured in box 2.6, which can also be read in the context of semiotics (see chapter 5). In addition, women have to confront the sexism of the music industry. While some practitioners and commentators perceive that there have been some improvements for women since the 1980s, Bayton argues that there is still a long way to go before 'there are as many women playing in rock bands as men' (1998: 209).

Building on the gender dimensions of Cohen's (1991) and Bayton's (1998) work, Bogdanović (2009) examined the associated processes of music and gender enculturation as well as the concepts of homosociality, hegemonic masculinity and

Box 2.6   Dilemmas of dress for female performers

SHAREEN (Ms45): I have to think too hard. I shouldn't have to. All female dress is drag. All female dress is some kind of signifier and the thing that pisses me off as a band is if we showed up in a little gold lamé dress and false eyelashes we would be heard differently than if we show up in jeans and t-shirts. And, goddamn it, there are some days that I want to wear a gold lamé dress and false eyelashes. Then there's the ridiculous cat fight mythology. If one of them is wearing a pretty little gold lamé dress and the other one's wearing jeans, they say, 'Oh, that's the pretty one and that's the dykey one.' And it's like, 'What? No, I really want to wear comfy shoes today. Give me a fucking break. . . . Since clothing is such a signifier, I'm trying to figure out ways that I can have a better sense of humour without putting myself into the Barbie category. That's taken some manipulation.

Source: Bayton 1998: 112

bandhood. Her findings demonstrate that the experiences, values and behaviour of men who make and perform music are wide-ranging and multiple, and that their gender identities/masculinities are non-monolithic. Instead, many amateur and semi-professional male musicians face an array of cultural and ideological constraints identified by Bayton as significant for female musicians.

A very comprehensive study of local music-making was undertaken in Milton Keynes by the anthropologist Ruth Finnegan between 1980 and 1984. In *The Hidden Musicians* (1989), Finnegan describes seven musical worlds which she found in this English new town: classical, brass band, folk, musical theatre, jazz, country and western, and rock and pop. She draws a series of contrasts between the worlds (which can often overlap, as members can belong to more than one) in terms of how the playing of music is learned, how it is performed and how it is written. She identifies a number of different social institutions which support music and the patterns of organization of the musical worlds and, in general, points to the importance of music to everyday life in Milton Keynes in providing pathways for urban living. In this respect, Finnegan's detailed empirical study suggests that music is a core activity in the structuring of contemporary social life – an argument that has been made in far more theoretical terms by writers such as John Shepherd (for example, 1991). It is also an important part of those works that consider the role of music consumption in everyday life (e.g. DeNora 2000; Laughey 2006; see chapter 10).

Finnegan shows the large number and variety of bands that were active in the pop and rock world at this time. She divides them into three main categories. First, there were 'the young, relatively inexperienced and recently formed bands' (1989: 110), often formed by people still at school. Second, there were the groups 'who had left school and were beginning to perform in local clubs or youth clubs for a small fee' (ibid.: 111). Third, there were those bands which 'had established a secure position in pub and club circuits, outside as well as within Milton Keynes, played in upwards of 50 or 100 performances a year, and, while still towards the amateur rather than the professional end of the scale, brought in substantial fees' (ibid.: 114). Despite the existence of these different types of band, some overall patterns were identified. First, the groups were made up predominantly of men; second, they aimed at giving live performances; and, third, they wanted to be paid, though remuneration varied greatly.

Finnegan uses her detailed research to confront some of the main themes arising from the literature on pop music. First, she argues that pop music cannot be seen simply as the music of youth, since the category of youth is cross-cut by many other social divisions and youth is actually a fairly wide category, encompassing people of a variety of ages: 'Youth predominated, for even mixed audiences also included young people, but family audiences were nothing unusual and it would be misleading to conclude – despite the widespread image – that rock bands played exclusively to either teenagers or young people under 25' (1989: 123–4). Second, she examines the view that pop music is produced by those who are uneducated or unemployed and again finds this assumption to be unwarranted. She suggests that the picture on education was mixed and that, 'of band members who gave details, nearly two-thirds were in jobs' (ibid.: 124). This figure in particular might not hold for other times and places, as at this point Milton Keynes could be said to be relatively prosperous. Third, Finnegan examines the idea that pop music expresses a form of rebellion. This is a theme which is treated at greater length in chapter 3, though Finnegan suggests that evidence from her study makes it difficult to generalize about this, and the idea of protest was not 'generally borne out by this study' (ibid.: 127).

Finnegan argues that there were a number of common themes running through the rock and pop music world. First, the musicians tended to possess less knowledge about other players compared with members of other musical worlds. However, certain individuals would be well known. Second, there were shared ideas about playing and learning. Echoing the account by Bennett (1980), the pop musicians were self-taught and joined bands in the early stages of learning an instrument. Moreover, there was a common pattern to the instrumentation in the bands, where 'the standard combination was guitars (rhythm and lead), bass guitar, and drums, together with vocals' (Finnegan 1989: 129). The most important common feature of the pop musician's world, according to Finnegan, was 'their interest in expressing their own views and personality through music-making' (ibid.). She argues that this is a 'stress on individuality and artistic creation which accords ill with the mass theorists' delineation of popular music (ibid.). However, for the mass theorists such as Adorno, this may be a 'false' individuality and creativity, and they would not necessarily accept the participants' own view of their creativity.

According to Finnegan, such creativity was often expressed in the musicians' desire to compose their own music, where 'playing in a band provided a medium where players could express their own personal aesthetic vision and through their music achieve a sense of controlling their own values, destiny and self-identity' (1989: 130). This brings the discussion back to the themes raised by Becker, as the notion of self-expression repeats the idea of the artist, above commerce, at the core of the jazz musicians' beliefs. However, it should be remembered that these ideas of artistic achievement and autonomy may be more wished for than actually achieved. Moreover, it may be easier for the local musician to remain relatively separated from the music industry, as he or she may not have to deal with it to any great extent. This becomes more difficult as the artist seeks to earn a living from his or her activities and raises issues of the extent to which the musician can remain authentic as an artist, in the way that many musicians express, rather than 'selling out'. This theme will be returned to in this book. However, before it can be considered, attention needs to be given to some of the processes at work in the institutions which these musicians confront and which some of them will become part of, and in many ways, as the discussion continues, it should become clearer that the opposition between creativity and industry is oversimplified.

In this context, Toynbee (2000) offers a useful framework for analysis of the dynamic of such creativity. Toynbee argues that those who make popular music can be defined as creators who operate in a field that places some limits on the nature and extent of their creativity. This may involve a range of roles, as Kusek and Leonhard suggest:

> What this means is that a musician does not have to be a recording artist or a performer to thrive in today's music industry. It means that you may be, at different times, a songwriter, lyricist, performer, band member, entertainer, promoter, entrepreneur, fashion designer, producer, teacher, or small business manager. Being 'creative' in the music business often means wearing several hats, doing several things at the same time, and picking up new skills on the fly. (2005: 21)

However, the 'freedom' in such a situation should not be overestimated. In Toynbee's words, 'the unit of creativity is a small one' (2000: 35). Musicians work in a context of 'possibles', where possibility of innovation is subject to some constraints. What can be analysed is the selection of possible modes of innovation or the likelihood of the selection of ways forward. Patterns of possibles, once established, can then be pursued over a long period of time. Toynbee suggests that the career of the Rolling Stones is a good example of this. Other artists shift ground more rapidly and explore a wider range of possibles. An example of this might be the work over time of an artist such as Elvis Costello, who has worked, for instance, in a new-wave/punk context, in country styles, with a string quartet and in producing ballads with Burt Bacharach. Costello's initial commercial success expanded the musical fields in which he could subsequently work, or expanded his range of possibles, while still being able to make a living. This contrasts with the constraints on Becker's jazz musicians. Moreover, as is shown in the study of three different young bands making music in contrasting localities in Sweden, such creativity and learning is a crucial aspect of the many dimensions of the pleasures and motivations of playing music (see Fornäs et al. 1995). For those interested in music ethnography, Drew (2001), Taylor (2003), Schloss (2004) and Fonarow (2006) provide further relevant examples.

Summary

This chapter has considered

- the interactions between technology and pop production in general and, more specifically, the digital 'turn' in production, distribution and consumption of music;
- the meanings and practices associated with being a musician in the digital era, focusing on the concepts of musicianship and authenticity;
- the nature of some of the most important parts of the pop production process, including the changing roles within the recording industry;

- some important studies of jazz musicians which point to issues of art and commerce in their lives;
- evidence of the interconnections between art and pop music-making;
- some important dimensions and accounts of music-making at the more specific and everyday level.

PART II

TEXT

Following the production–text–audience scheme of the book, Part II engages with music as text. Chapter 3 sets the scene by providing an overview of the historical development of different types of popular music, before engaging with the important issue of the politics of rock and an associated examination of the interconnection between gender, sexuality and power in popular music.

Chapter 4 utilizes a similar approach and applies it to 'black music' – its definitions, histories, development, place and status within wider socio-musical contexts. Informed by musicology and semiotics, chapter 5 explores the form/structure of music and the ways in which it conveys meaning. Chapter 6 extends the analysis to the performance of music and accompanying activities such as dancing, as well as the construction and 'performance' of identities through a range of extra-musical activities such as record collecting.

Together, the four chapters in this part of the book look at the nature and structure of musical texts, the complex ways in which they communicate meaning, and the wider social contexts and practices that inform and facilitate such communication.

3 History, Politics and Sexuality

This chapter, the first of four to focus on the texts of popular music, begins the move away from the direct consideration of the production dimension of the framework outlined in the Introduction. However, in accord with the sociological orientation of the book, these texts are set in context. The chapter aims, first, to provide an account of the recent development of pop and rock music which locates the wider meanings of these forms in different political and economic contexts, developing some of the analysis from earlier chapters by including descriptive material on the development of contemporary pop music; second, to take up some of these wider meanings through an analysis of the interconnections between pop and political action and meaning; and, third, further to consider some of these political and social meanings through a discussion of pop's relations to gender and sexuality.

The chapter also introduces some themes which continue to resonate in the discussion of pop music: considerations of the value of pop music and why it is that some forms are valued more highly than others and the extent to which forms of pop music are an authentic expression of individuals or social groups. These themes are further pursued in subsequent chapters.

The development of rock and roll

Richard Middleton has located the development of rock and roll since the mid-1950s in a wider historical context of musical and cultural change. He suggests that three 'moments' of important social change in music as a whole have occurred in the West, though at different points in time in different societies. The first of these, which Middleton calls a 'bourgeois revolution', occurred in Britain between the late eighteenth century and the middle of the nineteenth. During this period, a music industry developed which was dominated by the commercialism of the capitalist, or bourgeois, class and 'most musical production is in the hands of or is mediated by commercial music publishers, concert organizers and promoters, theatre and public house managers' (Middleton 1990: 13). By the mid-1850s, there was a 'congruence across a range of different musical practices, resulting in a not exactly homogeneous musical field but one clearly dominated by a bourgeois synthesis' (ibid.). As Middleton shows:

> With variants, this relative congruence of musical technique, repertoire and practice stretched across light opera, bourgeois domestic song, the brass band and mass choral movements and the now more rationally organized music hall; it even penetrated the broadside and orally transmitted song genres of the industrial areas. Street music was gradually banished, political song pushed tight proletarian enclaves, and the musical avant-garde characteristic of earlier in the century was either

marginalized or assimilated, as brass bands played Wagner and parlour singers juxtaposed Schubert and Schumann with more commercial products. (Ibid.)

The second period of change began by the 1890s, when new forms of mass culture, generated by the new monopoly capitalism, appeared. Large corporations became more important in international marketplaces, and American forms, such as ragtime and early jazz, became more popular, showing a tendency to overshadow national music forms. Middleton locates the third period of change after the Second World War, especially with the birth of rock 'n' roll, and argues that this was the 'moment' of 'pop culture'. At this point, there were the beginnings of increasing corporate domination, which coexisted with more local initiatives often found in particular sectors of the population. There were technological changes based around electronic systems, and young working-class people became significant movers in musical creation. This system became relatively stabilized by the late 1960s, when

> new social patterns, technologies and musical styles had been substantially assimilated into a reorganized music-industrial system: a transnational oligopoly of vast entertainment corporations, supplied to some extent by 'independent' producers; serviced by mass audience radio and TV channels (with some 'minority' shows and channels), by a symbiotically pliant music press and by related leisure-products businesses; and directing itself at a series of separate audiences whose distinctness is less subcultural than a creature of market researchers' consumer profiles. (Middleton 1990: 15)

This view suggests that, despite the significant changes that are happening around digitization, contemporary music is dominated by the large corporations discussed in chapter 1. Small or independent companies feed the larger ones. However, as was noted in chapter 1, some writers have argued that 'independent' companies based in specific locations were central to the development of rock and roll. To consider such approaches, it is necessary to examine the context in which rock developed. Gillett (1983) periodizes the development of rock in the way shown in figure 3.1. This periodization and terminology reflect a critical judgement of worth on Gillett's part which values the 'roughness' of rock 'n' roll over the later, blander, rock and roll. Rock 'n' roll is a hybrid which developed out of previous musical forms, most importantly black music, country music, folk music and previous pop forms (Frith 1983: 12–38). According to Gillett, it contained a number of different styles, which are listed in figure 3.2.

This diversity in rock 'n' roll reflected the internal diversity of some of its source materials. Thus, in discussing black music (a topic explored more fully in chapter 4), Gillett points to the number of different types of rhythm and blues music, which itself is an all-encompassing label used to categorize music produced for the black market. It replaced the earlier description of 'race music'. The different types of rhythm and

Up to 1958	rock 'n' roll
1958–1964	rock and roll
1964–	rock

Figure 3.1 Periodization of the development of rock
Source: Adapted from Gillett 1983

1 'northern band rock 'n' roll' (for example, Bill Haley)
2 'the New Orleans dance blues'
3 'Memphis country rock (also known as rockabilly)'
4 'Chicago rhythm and blues'
5 'vocal group rock 'n' roll'

All 'depended for their dance beat on contemporary Negro dance rhythms'

Figure 3.2 The five styles of rock 'n' roll
Source: Adapted from Gillett 1983: 23

blues music discussed by Gillett (1983) are the 'Dancehall Blues', the 'Club Blues', 'Bar Blues', Gospel and what he calls the 'Group Sounds'.

The pivotal figure in rock 'n' roll is Elvis Presley. Gillett (1983) interprets the relationship of Presley with other musicians and the producer Sam Phillips in the studio in a way that brings out the creative roles of the participants in the new rockabilly or Memphis country rock. Some extracts from Gillett's interpretation appear in box 3.1.

So far, this brief consideration of the development of rock 'n' roll has centred on the transformations within the music itself, how it related to earlier, source, material, and some of the processes which went on in the studio at its creative moment. However, it is important to consider its social context in more detail. In his discussion of the development of rock 'n' roll in Memphis, Gordon (1995) shows the cultural importance of a wrestler (Sputnick Monroe) and a film Western hero (Lash Larue). In addition, like other commentators on Memphis, such as Guralnick (1995), he points to the importance of Dewey Phillips's radio show, where Elvis Presley's first records were aired. A key piece of sociological analysis of the wider context of the development of rock 'n' roll has been written by Peterson (1990), which links this history to other factors.

Peterson asks the question 'why 1955?' – that is, why was there such a fundamental shift in the nature of American popular music between 1954 and 1956? He suggests that previous analyses have tended to point to three main reasons: first, the role of particular creative individuals, such as Elvis Presley; second, changes in the nature of the audience for popular music, in particular the influence of those individuals born after the Second World War; and, third, changes in the media industries themselves.

Peterson criticizes both the first and second of these explanations. He argues that the first accords too great a role to the creative genius of particular individuals (though he does not suggest that these individuals were without talent). Rather, he maintains that at particular points in time certain individuals come to the fore because of a specific set of social conditions, which operate as a kind of pattern of selecting mechanisms. Peterson argues, therefore, that there are always more talented artists in existence than those who achieve prominence at any one particular time. His argument against the second mode of explanation is more straightforward. He points out that, in 1954, 'the oldest of the baby-boomers were only nine years old and half had not been born yet' (1990: 98). This leaves him free to develop a case that stresses the place of contextual factors in the development of rock. In general, Peterson has been associated with the 'production-of-culture' perspective, which argues that there are six factors that 'shape' the development of culture: 'law, technology, industry

Box 3.1   The development of rockabilly in Memphis

Presley was the most commercially successful of a number of Memphis singers
who evolved what they themselves called 'country rock' and what others, record
collectors and people in the industry, have called 'rockabilly'. Country rock
was basically a Southern white version of 12-bar boogie blues, shouted with a
minimum of subtlety by ex-hillbilly singers over an accompaniment featuring
electric guitar, standup bass, and – from 1956 – drums, still taboo in Nashville.
The style evolved partly from the imaginative guidance of a Memphis radio station
engineer, Sam Phillips, who entered the recording business by supervising sessions
with local blues singers and leasing the masters to a number of independent
companies (Chess in Chicago, owned by the Chess brothers, or Modern/RPM in
Los Angeles, owned by the Bihari brothers). The success of some of these singers,
notably B. B. King and Howlin' Wolf, encouraged Phillips to form his own label,
Sun, and two of the singers he recorded for his own label, Little Junior Parker and
Rufus Thomas, had hit records in the Negro market.

The Memphis blues singers used small bands which featured piano, guitar, and
saxophone. No particular dominant style linked them all, but common to many of
their records was a kind of intimate atmosphere created by the simple and cheap,
but unorthodox, 'tape delay echo' recording technique of Phillips. The singers
invariably made their personal presence felt on the records, menacingly in Howlin'
Wolf's case, impatiently in Junior Parker's. These recordings, and other more
traditional blues, and rhythm and blues records issued by Sun, were known to a
substantial number of white youths through the South, and presented a source
of song material and stylistic inspiration that was in many ways more satisfactory
than the orthodox country and western culture.

Jimmie Rodgers sang the 'white blues' in the twenties but Elvis Presley was the
first to make it work as pop music. According to the legend of his recording debut,
his discovery by Sam Phillips was casual and lucky. Presley is said to have attracted
the attention of Phillips when he used Sun's studios to cut a record for his
mother's birthday present; Phillips encouraged him to make a record with proper
accompaniment, and the two men were rewarded with a local hit from one of the
sides, 'That's All Right'.

The story of Presley's discovery has the elements of romance, coincidence, and
fate that legends need, and in fact seems to be true, but it is likely that if Phillips
and Presley had not met, two other such people would soon have done what they
did – merge rhythm and blues with country and western styles and material, and
come up with a new style. In the panhandle of west Texas, in Arkansas, in north
Louisiana, and in Memphis there were other singers whose cultural and musical
experience were comparable to Presley's; indeed, some of them followed him into
the Sun studios, while others tried studios in Nashville and Clovis, New Mexico.

It is difficult to assess how great a part Sam Phillips played in influencing his
singers – among other things, by introducing them to blues records – and how
much they already knew. Presley told one interviewer:

> I'd play [guitar] along with the radio or phonograph, and taught myself the
> chord positions. We were a religious family, going round together to sing at

camp meetings and revivals, and I'd take my guitar with us when I could. I also dug the real low-down Mississippi singers, mostly Big Bill Broonzy and Big Boy Crudup, although they would scold me at home for listening to them.

'Sinful music', the townsfolk in Memphis said it was. Which never bothered me, I guess.

In the same interview, Presley stressed the importance of Phillips:

Mr Phillips said he'd coach me if I'd come over to the studio as often as I could. It must have been a year and a half before he gave me an actual session. At last he let me try a western song – and it sounded terrible. But the second idea he had was the one that jelled.

'You want to make some blues?' he suggested over the 'phone, knowing I'd always been a sucker for that kind of jive. He mentioned Big Boy Crudup's name and maybe others too. I don't remember.

All I know is, I hung up and ran 15 blocks to Mr Phillips' office before he'd gotten off the line – or so he tells me. We talked about the Crudup records I knew – 'Cool Disposition', 'Rock Me, Mama', 'Hey Mama', 'Everything's All Right', and others, but settled for 'That's All Right', one of my top favourites. . . .

What Presley achieved was certainly not 'the same thing' as the men he copied. On 'That's All Right' and 'Mystery Train' (written and first recorded by Junior Parker for Sun), he evolved a personal version of this style, singing high and clear, breathless and impatient, varying his rhythmic emphasis with a confidence and inventiveness that were exceptional for a white singer. The sound suggested a young white man celebrating freedom, ready to do anything, go anywhere, pausing long enough for apologies and even regrets and recriminations, but then hustling on towards the new. He was best on fast songs, when his impatient singing matched the urgent rhythm from bass (Bill Black) and guitar (Scotty Moore). Each of his five Sun singles backed a blues song with a country and western song, most of them already familiar to the respective audiences; each sold better than its predecessor, and increasing numbers of people discovered Presley either through radio broadcasts or through his stage appearances.

But Presley did not reach the mass popular music audience with his Sun records, which sold mainly to audiences in the South and to the minority country and western audience elsewhere. Only after Presley's contract was bought by RCA-Victor did his records make the national top ten, and the songs on these records were not in a country rock style. At Victor, under the supervision of Chet Atkins, Presley's records featured vocal groups, heavily electrified guitars, and drums, all of which were considered alien by both country and western audiences and by the audience for country rock music. Responding to these unfamiliar intrusions in his accompaniment, Presley's voice became much more theatrical and selfconscious as he sought to contrive excitement and emotion which he had seemed to achieve on his Sun records without any evident forethought.

> Presley's success for Sun, and later for RCA-Victor, encouraged Phillips to try other singers with comparable styles and material, and attracted to his studios young southerners with similar interests. Carl Perkins and Warren Smith from the Memphis area, Roy Orbison from west Texas, Johnny Cash, Conway Twitty, and Charlie Rich from Arkansas, and Jerry Lee Lewis from northern Louisiana brought songs, demonstration tapes, and their ambitions to Phillips, who switched almost completely from black singers to white singers once the latter became commercially successful.
>
> *Source:* Gillett 1983: 26–9

structure, organisation structure, occupational career and market' (ibid.). In the main body of his article, he explores how these factors influenced the events of 1955.

Peterson begins with law and technology, which are thought to have a significant role in defining the ways in which the other factors operate. With respect to law, he identifies three important aspects: copyright, patent law and Federal Communications Commission (FCC) regulation. He argues, for example, that the main copyright collecting agency for public performance, the American Society of Composers, Authors and Publishers (ASCAP), which controlled the reproduction of music by ensuring that only certain forms were allowed on the radio, was challenged by a rival organization, Broadcast Music Incorporated (BMI), which had been formed by the radio networks when they had failed to agree over licensing fees. Because of ASCAP's control over more traditional radio-type material, BMI utilized other types of music which had previously been excluded from radio airplay. Thus, a struggle over rights revenue (see further, chapter 1) is seen as one of the contributing factors to the development of rock. However, this conflict occurred in the early 1940s, so it does not on its own explain the outbreak of rock. In terms of patent law, Peterson examines the struggle between different companies over the ownership of different record formats which led, by the early 1950s, to the existence of the long-playing 33⅓-rpm and the 45-rpm record. The latter was particularly important, as it was aimed at the pop market and was far more robust than the fragile 78-rpm disc which it replaced. Thus, the 45-rpm record could be distributed much more easily by smaller record companies. Finally, in terms of FCC regulation, there was a great increase in the number of radio stations that were licensed to broadcast.

The introduction of the 45-rpm record was a form of technological innovation. Peterson draws attention to two other important technological innovations: the introduction of television and the development of the transistor radio. Television is significant, in the main, for its effects on radio. The big networks that had previously controlled radio moved into television, which they have continued to dominate in the USA, where local television stations are affiliated to NBC, CBS or ABC. Smaller, more specialized radio stations were set up. Much of the traditional radio programming (for example, soap operas) moved over to the new medium. Second, there was the introduction into America of cheap, portable radios from Japan.

In discussing industry structure, organization structure, occupational careers and the market, Peterson draws comparisons between the situation in 1948 and in 1958. He provides much detail in describing a movement over this ten-year period, from the control of the industry by a small number of companies which produced, distributed and manufactured musical products to relatively more diverse and 'entrepreneurial' situations (see also the discussion of these developments in the Introduction). As Peterson summarizes:

> In the early 1950s, the music industry was blind to the large and growing unsatiated demand for greater variety in music and deaf to the efforts of musicians that might have satisfied that demand. The music industry was financially as well as aesthetically committed to the big band-crooner style of popular music of the time, and, because of its oligopolistic control of the production, distribution and marketing of new music, was able to thwart the marketing of alternative styles.

Then with the transfer of network radio programming to television, radio turned to playing records as the cheapest effective form of programming. The arrival of cheap transistor radios and the development of the top 40 radio-as-jukebox format meant that a much larger number and far wider range of music was exposed to the audience. Using the new durable 45 rpm records, and taking advantage of the developing network of independent record distributors, numerous independent record companies experimented with a wide range of new sounds in an effort to tap the unsatiated market demand. In a matter of two dozen months between late 1954 and early 1957 rock was forged in this caldron of entrepreneurial creativity. (1990: 113–14)

Peterson provides a very important and illuminating sociological account of the social context of the development of rock in the United States. However, it is important to note two problems with his approach. First, it is not always clear at a particular moment whether he is contextualizing the development of rock or explaining its development. At the beginning of his article, he stresses the explanatory. However, as the piece develops, he becomes more involved in drawing comparisons across time which are not, in themselves, explanations, as it is not clear precisely what effects the factors are thought to have. Second, Peterson's focus is on the United States, and his account is not necessarily very helpful in explaining the development of rock in other societies, such as Britain.

The latter has been examined by Bradley (1992) in the context of the 'composite account of rock 'n' roll'. His clear summaries of what he sees as myths about the development of rock are reproduced in box 3.2.

Bradley identifies a number of problems with the 'composite account', which are also of general relevance to work on the history and meaning of rock:

1 Many accounts neglect 'the problem of understanding and explaining the phenomenon of white kids responding to black styles' (Bradley 1992: 14). This is an area which is explored in chapters 4 and 6.
2 There is a tendency to neglect the phenomenon of the development of the group. Bradley suggests that the idea of a small group of musicians playing together is a new departure for white music in the 1950s.
3 There is a gender blindness in many of the standard accounts which neglects or plays down the 'maleness' of rock 'n' roll.
4 The accounts do not pay enough attention to the nature of amateurism in rock music production and the development of local pop music-making in the 1950s.

Aspects of these sorts of criticism have been dealt with in some of the more recent work on rock and pop, which is summarized and examined at other points in this

Box 3.2   The composite account of rock 'n' roll

It is possible to construct a sort of standard composite account of the main events and developments known as 'rock 'n' roll' . . .. It consists of a list of factors on which they more or less all agree, and on which they confer major causal status in relation to the rise of rock 'n' roll and beat music. It also involves a starting definition or delimitation of the body of musical artists, and records, radio and TV shows, which make up the phenomenon of rock 'n' roll and beat music.

The USA

The following is a summary of what might be called the standard view, the agreed wisdom, or the prevalent *myth* about early American rock 'n' roll.

1 'Popular music' already exists in the early and mid-1950s as an industry, with its 'major' and 'independent' recording companies, publishing houses, radio stations, etc. 'Live' venues exist in most towns and cities, while for records a whole infrastructure of distribution and sales outlets, as well as large chains of juke boxes, are well established. Trade magazines, magazines for listeners, and the charts or hit parades all serve promotional functions. The popular music audience already includes almost the whole population. Profits are high and, consequently, plant and other investments are expanding; this is especially true of record production, which, having all but died during the Depression and the war years, is growing dramatically, on the basis of improved and still improving materials (vinyl replacing shellac) and technology (hi-fidelity and, later in the 1950s, transistorization of radios).

2 'Popular music' also exists already as a *tradition* familiar to virtually all American listeners and musicians. Certain styles are nationally established as 'popular', others are more locally based (country music), or are excluded, to some degree, from the national popular charts ('race' music, as gospel, blues and rhythm and blues were then called), though they are closely related to popular music, in being often catered for by the same companies, and in providing numerous popular artists. There are also several varieties of jazz, from 'traditional' to 'modern', each of which is less than fully familiar but by no means unknown to the 'mass' of the listening public. Both modern jazz and country music enjoy 'booms' in the late 1940s and early 1950s, but these are not on the scale of the rock 'n' roll developments which follow.

   The presence of a black, working-class population in every major city of the USA by 1950, a result of migrations mainly from the First World War onwards, means that local radio stations and record stores almost everywhere reflect, to a significant degree, the tastes of these communities. And since neither radio-dial-twiddling nor shopping-around can be censored, despite the industry's compulsive categorizing, young white people in ever-increasing numbers do listen to the music which is becoming known as 'rhythm 'n' blues' and 'rock and roll' (or rock 'n' roll) in these years. Those local DJs, juke-box operators and independent record store and record label owners who are close to this development take note, and begin to consciously promote this music for white listeners.

Most of the authors agree, to some extent, that the 'boring', 'bland', 'sentimental' state of the nationally popular (among whites) music of the early 1950s, as a whole, contributes to the defection of these young white listeners, but they all argue this in a very generalized, sweeping way, and all argue for different exceptions. Their problems with regard to verbalizing musical meaning are clearly displayed in this difficulty or weakness which they all share.

3 A 'post-war boom' in the USA is the economic background to a new scale of working-class and middle-class 'affluence' in the 1950s. Both pocket money and widely available part-time work swell the disposable income of 'teenagers' at high school, while wages are often relatively high in the first years of work, in comparison with the 1930s and 1940s. The overall effect is to create a large group, throughout the country, of independent young or 'teenage' consumers, of relatively high spending power, even despite the rise in numbers staying on longer at school.

Most of the rock histories use the term 'teenagers' uncritically, ignoring the fact that it was a neologism of the late 1940s or early 1950s, replete with many new connotations. The connotations which are clearly retained in the rock historians' appropriation of the term are (a) a style of *leisure*, and of *consumption*, found among 'kids' from the ages of 13–14 to the early 1920s, (b) a certain exuberance or rowdiness, which can become a threatening wildness, and which includes (c) a foregrounding of sexual practices (dating, going steady, courtship in general, and the 'threat' of 'sex before marriage'). Behind these implications of the term, we can also see clearly that the standard notion of 'the teenager' is usually of a boy, not a girl, and that the 'threat' of sex is a threat *of* boys *against* girls, as seen *by* parents, teachers, etc. These things, sadly, remain unsaid in the rock histories.

4 The search for 'novelty', derived from the competitive economic character of the pop industry, and in particular from attempts by 'independent' record companies to outflank 'majors', leads to 'cover versions' of dance blues and vocal group successes from the 'race' market, being offered on the mainly white pop market as a whole. In a sense, this is merely the equivalent of the raids on jazz and on country music of the same years, but partly it is also the result of an 'authentic' pressure from existing teenage audiences, as spotted by adventurous DJs and independent studio producers. These 'cover versions' are normally produced by 'acceptable' white artists, and involve some changes in musical style, and some cleaning up of lyrics on occasions, but none the less they have the side-effect, when successful, of arousing some interest in the originals, and the longer-term effect of familiarizing the white pop audiences with some of the conventions of the black styles. Some groups of white musicians actually begin to specialize in a 'half-way' style, notably Bill Haley and the Comets, whose 'Shake Rattle and Roll' is a cover version of a rhythm 'n' blues hit, while 'Rock around the Clock' is an original number modelled on the work of black artists to some extent.

5 A cluster of media events combines to shoot the Haley style, and that of some others, into national prominence, notably the use of the music in the sound track of *Blackboard Jungle*, a successful film about 'wild' adolescents, and subsequently

the appearances of Elvis Presley on the Nashville TV show 'Grand Old Opry', and later on the nationally screened 'Ed Sullivan Show'. Later come other films, such as *Rock around the Clock* and *The Girl Can't Help It*.

6 At this point, the competitive logic of the industry once again influences developments, producing a race to imitate the initial successes and to promote the music with all the resources available. In particular, again, the 'independents' see their chance to compete on more equal terms with the 'majors', since both are relatively new to the style, and neither is very sure at first of how to predict who and what will be successful. Literally dozens of young artists are signed up, especially by independent companies, to produce rock 'n' roll; others are converted overnight, from aspiring crooners or country singers into imitation Elvises.

The very over-production and financial chaos which result help to ensure that this situation cannot last, and by about 1958–9 in the USA, the initial 'explosion' of production of, and enthusiasm for, rock 'n' roll is over. However, the consequences of this period of upheaval are that one or two independent companies do indeed establish themselves as small majors, that a new generation of producers, artists and song writers becomes established in the industry, and also that some black rhythm 'n' blues artists share in the explosion, singing their own music more or less as they would be doing anyway, but reaching young white audiences. Fats Domino, Little Richard, Chuck Berry, Jackie Wilson, Lloyd Price, Larry Williams and the Coasters are among those who owe their wider success to this upheaval.

Britain

Each of the rock histories devotes a section to Britain (though not normally to any other country), tracing the story of the impact of rock 'n' roll (and of the home-produced 'skiffle') and placing these events, usually, as 'background' to the Beatles and the 'beat-boom' years of 1963–6. I would argue very strongly that the view which sees the period 1955–63 in Britain as a mere 'background' to later beat, and other later styles, is heavily distorted by an almost fetishistic attention to the charts (i.e. the successes of the Beatles, etc.), and that, sales of records notwithstanding, the development of a 'youth culture' in Britain, and of a music *of* that youth culture, can only be understood by reversing that emphasis. In a very real sense, there is an element of *myth* in the way rock histories skip from one commercial peak to another, or from one 'great artist' to another, ignoring almost totally the social roots of both the music-making and the listening, which ought to be among their objects of study. Nonetheless, the main points of a composite account can again be enumerated, this time relying, however, on a slightly different list of books.

1 The pop industry is already international. American music already features strongly in British record stores, and on Radio Luxembourg, while the BBC allows a little of it into the major popular radio shows. British artists 'cover' most big US hits themselves. Equally, and very importantly, American films are readily available at British cinemas. Any BBC resistance to 'American trash' is

out-flanked by the rise of records and by films; and when ITV comes along, it exhibits no scruples in adding to this trend with its pop shows. In any event, pop music coverage on radio and TV is on a very small scale in these years, by 1990s standards, and young listeners rely heavily on record buying and jukeboxes.

2 The Teddy boys already exist, chiefly in London, before rock 'n' roll arrives in Britain. They probably originate (according to Hebdige) in the traditional working-class areas of South and East London in the early 1950s. Their style of dress is, in part, an imitation of the Edwardian man about town, but in other respects, they imitate American models. The interest in unusual clothes itself is odd (and new?) among male, working-class Londoners, as is the responsiveness to rapid change in fashions of music which follows in the mid-1950s. Hebdige calls this style 'a focus for an illicit delinquent identity' and points out its connection to a fantasy of America. The phenomenon apparently needs only publicity to spread: only later does commercial exploitation of the style move in.

3 The absence of a large black community with its own musical life (though this was beginning to take shape in the major cities), and also the resistance to pop and rock in general, and American pop and rock in particular, which is maintained by the BBC, combine to give the films which feature rock 'n' roll a greater importance in Britain than in the USA. The film *Rock around the Clock*, and its title song, are adopted by Teds in particular and teenagers in general all over Britain in 1955–6: various 'riots', and the occasional destruction of cinema seats to make room for dancing, gain the music and the audiences much notoriety, orchestrated by the newspapers into a full-scale 'moral panic'. This reaction tends to make rock 'n' roll a sort of badge of defiant identity, rather than just another fad of taste, for the kids involved.

4 Skiffle, a musical style taken initially from traditional jazz bands, coincides with this early rock 'n' roll enthusiasm and, being slightly more respectable in origins, is accepted as a quaint offshoot of jazz or folk music, even by the BBC, who launch '6/5 Special' as a TV pop show specializing in skiffle. One of the important things about this style is that its great simplicity, and the cheapness of using home-made instruments, lead to a wave of amateur and semi-professional imitations by the kids themselves. (What almost every account omits to mention, but is nonetheless true, is that it is *boys*, specifically and almost exclusively, who take up playing skiffle.) This craze lasts from 1956 to 1958 or so, after which amateurism continues, but now mainly in imitation of American rock and post-rock musics.

5 At the same time as amateurism becomes firmly established among teenagers, by about 1957 or 1958, the 'real' rock 'n' roll records from the USA dry up, and post-rock 'balladeers' and British artists exhibiting little or no rock influence come to dominate record sales and radio and TV shows, Tommy Steele, Marty Wilde and Cliff Richard perhaps being the most rock-influenced of these. Some of the new 'rock-pop' records lack the prominent beat of rock 'n' roll, and most are also highly 'arranged' products; on both counts they are not seen as good models by the teenage amateurs, who aim chiefly for a lively dance music. The result is that young audiences seeking live dance music turn away from the charts, just as

some American teenagers did in the early 1950s. A live dance music style which becomes known as 'the big beat', and later as 'beat', develops, as does a standard group format of lead and bass guitars, sometimes a third ('rhythm') guitar, drums and vocalist(s), sometimes with a piano or organ, or a harmonica. This beat music thrives most strongly in the provincial British cities where the hit-making, and indeed, record-making, machinery is virtually non-existent (Liverpool, Birmingham, Glasgow, Manchester, Newcastle).

6 A somewhat more self-conscious movement of rejection of the charts leads to the British 'rhythm and blues' movement, chiefly in their milieux. Though this has much in common with the earlier and later jazz booms, in being mainly middle class and often idealistically anti-commercial, it also resembles beat and rock 'n' roll in many ways: it is performed by small groups (four or five members, with guitars and drums the chief instruments), it uses electrical amplification, and it includes a lot of dance music with a strong beat. The Rolling Stones, the Animals and the Zombies are among many representatives of this movement who become pop successes, while other more 'uncompromising' groups have less success in the early and mid-1960s but strongly influence the later 'British blues', 'underground' and 'heavy' rock developments (John Mayall, Alexis Korner's Blues Incorporated, etc.)

Source: Bradley 1992: 9–14

book. However, the discussion so far illuminates two significant factors that will continue to be developed through the rest of this chapter. First, there is the value placed upon particular textual forms of popular music by critics and commentators (see also chapter 5). As we have seen, Gillett conveys approval of a particular form through his use of the term 'rock 'n' roll' and his denigration of the more 'sanitized' 'rock and roll'. In this account, 'rock 'n' roll' somehow stands for freedom and expression and 'rock and roll' for constraint and manipulation. We shall see how rock came to have a particular meaning in the 1960s with connotations of opposition and resistance, especially when compared to pop music. Thus, definitions of textual types or genres are not just of academic interest but also convey meaning to a much wider audience. This is often connected with politics in the broadest sense.

Second, there are the interconnected issues of gender and sexuality. Bradley (1992) comments on the maleness of many of the accounts of the development of rock. Related to this is the way in which pop music has often been seen as 'immature' or superficial because of its implied audience among young women. The femininity of pop is something implicitly problematic for male writers. Such themes can be explored as we take the story of the development of pop more up to date (see also, Chambers 1985; Reynolds and Press 1995).

Rock and pop in the 1960s and 1970s

The conventional account of the development of rock and pop sees a bland period between the late 1950s and 1963. This is the period where, according to Gillett, the excitement of rock 'n' roll is replaced by standardized music industry 'products' such as Fabian in the United States and Cliff Richard in Britain. A perceived shift occurs with the rise to fame of The Beatles in 1963 in Britain and 1964 in the United States. While in many respects The Beatles were partly located within more 'conventional' forms and packaged in a show-business sort of way, their reappropriation of black music styles opened the way for a series of developments during the 1960s. Partly, they are important for the way in which they brought together different styles, integrating forms of black soul with rock and roll. They acted as a bridge between the rock 'n' roll of, for example, Chuck Berry and more pop-oriented material. It is possible to say that they integrated pop and rock and led the field in producing a kind of unified audience which was to exist for a good part of the 1960s. The suggestion here, then, is that there is normally recognized to be a difference between rock and pop which runs through the development of the forms since the 1950s. However, at certain points these forms are intertwined. Indeed, some writers, such as Grossberg (1983), have argued that, in detail, it is actually very difficult to separate them. In part, this has to do with the role of more detailed analysis of the actual nature of the sounds themselves. This is an issue taken up in chapter 5.

The Beatles opened the space for the development of rock music in the 1960s. There were many different strands of this. In Britain there were a number of groups that utilized blues-based themes and structures and a continuing appropriation of black American forms. Sometimes black American musicians developed the styles themselves, Jimi Hendrix being the most notable example. He played in r 'n' b groups in America in the early 1960s before moving to Britain in 1966 to team up with two white musicians to form the Jimi Hendrix Experience.

Rock music sold in large quantities and was often seen by its producers and audience to involve the communication of authentic artistic consciousness and to have important things to say about contemporary events. At this time, there developed an audience for rock which seemed open to a number of different styles. Of course, this is not to say that there were not different tastes within the audience and different types of rock. There clearly were. However, by comparison with the polarization between different forms in the early 1960s and the increased separation of forms in subsequent years, these differences were not so clear-cut. There were perhaps more divisions in the United States, though it is possible to argue that forms of fragmentation of the rock pop audience really begin to appear around 1968, between West and East coasts and forms such as 'Folk-Rock (1965–6), largely a phenomenon of New York and Los Angeles, and its wandering son, the San Francisco Sound (1966–7)' (Heylin 1993: 3) and the embryonic East Coast scene centred around the Velvet Underground.

Throughout the 1960s in Britain there had been differences between the influence of more contemporary black sounds in the form of soul and earlier forms, such as blues, which fed the more guitar-oriented rock bands. In the early to mid-1960s these could be integrated, as the extract from the journalist Cliff White's diary in box 3.3 shows. However, by the end of the 1960s and the early 1970s, a greater degree of fragmentation had set in.

Looking back from the twenty-first century, it is possible to see the beginnings of forms which were to separate more and more as time went on. It has become increasingly common to date the beginnings of the genre of heavy metal to the work of Black Sabbath, Deep Purple and Led Zeppelin in the late 1960s and early 1970s (Weinstein

Box 3.3   Cliff White's 1964 diary

Fri	Oct 30	Jimmy Reed, Sugar Pie De Santo, The Dixie Cups on Ready, Steady, Go.
Sat	Oct 31	Saw Jimmy Reed at Club Noreik. Had to miss John Lee Hooker at Flamingo.
Mon	Nov 2	Saw Carl Perkins, Tommy Tucker, The Animals at Gaumont State. Had to miss Jimmy Reed at Flamingo.
Wed	Nov 4	Martha & Vandellas on Top Of The Pops.
Fri	Nov 6	Martha & Vandellas, Kim Weston on RSG.
Mon	Nov 9	My birthday. Still alive.
Tues	Nov 10	Martha & Vandellas on Pop Inn.
Fri	Nov 13	Saw The Isley Brothers at East Ham Granada. Had to miss The Soul Sisters at Flamingo.
Sat	Nov 14	Perkins, Tucker etc. at Finsbury Park Astoria.
Mon	Nov 16	Down to The Scene with the mob as usual.
Wed	Nov 18	Saw Jimmy Reed at Flamingo. Chatted with him for about an hour backstage. Great bloke.
Thurs	Nov 19	Took some records up to Jimmy's hotel and had breakfast with him. Geezer called Al Smith from Vee Jay was there. Nice enough bloke but seemed more keen to talk about Betty Everett than Jimmy.
Fri	Nov 20	Jerry Lee, Marvin Gaye, The Stones on RSG.
Sat	Nov 21	Saw Jerry Lee at Club Noreik.
Sun	Nov 22	Load of us went down to Brighton to see Jerry Lee again.
Mon	Nov 23	Saw Jimmy Reed at British Legion Hall, South Harrow. Had to miss Jerry Lee at Eltham Baths.
Thurs	Nov 26	Saw Howlin' Wolf and Hubert Sumlin at Marquee.

Source: C. White, sleeve notes for Jimmy Reed: *Upside Your Head*
Courtesy of Charly Records CRB 1003, 1980

1991; Walser 1993). Also, the 'pomp' or 'classical' rock of groups such as ELP, Yes and Genesis can be clearly identified, as can the influence and popularity of some forms of British folk rock, such as Fairport Convention. While the followers of all these forms may now see them as separate types, they might not have been seen thus in the early 1970s, when it was perfectly possible to be a fan of all three.

What did open up in a clear way in the late 1960s and early 1970s was a new divide between what was perceived to be the more serious – and, somehow, more 'authentic' – rock music and 'commercial' pop music. Devotees of rock could be scathing in their attacks on pop and commercialism, and criticism of groups seen to be 'selling out' became exceptionally shrill. This accusation, which continues to this day, despite the way in which Britpop musicians legitimated commercial success (Harris 2003), was regularly hurled at musicians such as Marc Bolan, who stopped being a hero of the so-called underground when his singles began to sell on the mass market. It had of course been made against Bob Dylan when he moved from acoustic to electric instruments in the mid-1960s. Pop meant singles and chart success; rock meant albums and was serious. It is important to recognize that the distinction was not necessarily built around the size of the audience. The rock groups sold lots of albums, but their 'serious' intent and content seemed to protect them from the criticism of 'selling out'. The criteria of values did not depend on sales. There are political issues here which are considered in more detail later in this chapter.

There were forms that bridged this increasing divide between rock and pop in the early 1970s, in particular the association of different artists under the heading of glam rock. Some of these bands were clearly seen to be pop groups oriented to top-20 success, examples including The Sweet and Gary Glitter; however, others straddled, and in lots of ways reconstructed, the divide between rock and pop, most notably David Bowie and Roxy Music. Both of these showed the influence of the later forms of connection between art and pop influence considered by Frith and Horne (1987), as discussed in chapter 2. This crossing and breaking down of the barrier which had been erected between pop and rock was to be influential on developments in both Britain and the United States in the mid- to late 1970s, where art, pop and rock intertwined to produce punk rock.

There has been a certain amount of rather nationalistic debate on the origins of punk. This was certainly an issue at the time when various factions wanted to claim punk as their own. However, it is more useful to see American and British punk as interlinked and interacting forms and to leave aside rather pointless debates about originality and ownership. The beginnings of American punk can be traced through from the forms of East Coast rock art collaboration, of which the Velvet Underground is the clearest example (Heylin 1993). Such collaborations, together with the influence of glam rock and the pub rock movement of the mid-1970s, combined to produce the punk and new waves of 1976 and 1977 (Laing 1985; Savage 1991). These often explicitly attacked the rock values, which were seen to have been corrupted through the 1970s as rock stars became richer and more detached from their audiences. However, most important for the present chronicle was the way in which punk attempted to draw on black forms, most notably Jamaican reggae, in the production of something that was neither pop nor rock and which made no attempt to integrate the two. Thus, initially, punk went against the album ethic of the rock bands and the kind of top-20 promotion strategies of the pop groups. Singles became important again, but they were to be produced in an 'independent' and amateur manner, even though, as was discussed in chapter 2, there are clear difficulties with the notion of independence used here. This integrative moment did not last very long before a new – and qualitatively different (on some accounts) – form of fragmentation occurred in the 1980s and 1990s.

Rock and pop in the 1980s and 1990s

Some see the punk period as a watershed. It represents an attempt, first, in its desire for independence and the short three-minute song, to regain the spirit of the early days of rock 'n' roll; and, second, to reintegrate the pop and rock forms which had increasingly split during the 1970s. It also marks an important point in the fragmentation that was to develop further during the 1980s and 1990s. Thus, in Britain, the early 1980s saw both the integration of punk and reggae in the 2 Tone movement (see chapter 1), which updated 1960s Jamaican ska with a punk framework, and the development of new pop, as represented initially by the groups labelled as the 'New

Romantics'. Slightly later came the new 'rock' bands such as Big Country and, more enduringly and popularly, U2. During the later stages of the punk period, heavy metal reasserted itself in Britain and, subsequently, in the 1980s in the United States, where it has been argued that heavy metal moved to the centre of the popular music field (Walser 1993).

The 1980s saw a launch of MTV, the first television channel devoted entirely to music, and with it the rise in popularity of the music video. Music genre crossovers became increasingly acceptable and popular. A much quoted example is the British band New Order, who combined their trademark impassive vocals with synth pop melodies and the New York club scene sound. In 1982 they released 'Blue Monday', the bestselling British 12-inch single of all times. According to Haslam, 'Blue Monday' 'borrowed' from several different musical traditions: "'Blue Monday was really influenced by four songs", he [Bernard Sumner] once told me. "The arrangement came from Dirty talk by Klein & MBO, the beat came from a track off a Donna Summer LP, there was a sample from Radioactivity by Kraftwerk, and the general influence on the style of the song was Sylvester's (You make me feel) Mighty Real." (2000: 299)

As the 1980s progressed, other forms, such as hip-hop from America, increased in importance and influenced white music in different ways. There has been the continued existence of what has been known as the independent or indie sector, though, as has been noted at several points so far, it is not always easy to specify what this is independent of or from. All this has led to fluidity between the different types of music, where it has become, argue many commentators, more and more difficult to sustain the sorts of definition of rock and pop which seemed to have some analytic purchase in the 1960s and 1970s. There has been a breakdown of barriers, it is suggested, so that it was, for example, possible for Michael Jackson to employ heavy metal forms as associated with Eddie Van Halen on his *Thriller* album of 1983. Furthermore, it has been argued that fragmentation into many different forms of music and the interactions between such forms represented postmodernism and the effects of this process in popular music.

Towards the end of the 1980s influences of Detroit and Chicago club culture began to be felt in the clubs in the UK. 1988 is commonly known as 'second summer of love', epitomized by the Madchester scene, the bands such as Happy Mondays and the Stone Roses, as well as the famous Haçienda club with its acid house scene.

The early 1990s were marked by the emergence and popularity of grunge sound, with Nirvana and Pearl Jam releasing influential albums in 1991 (*Nevermind* and *Ten*) which went on to make a significant impact in the musical mainstream. Sometimes referred to as 'Seattle sound', grunge was influenced by indie or alternative rock, hardcore punk and heavy metal sound. A parallel development in the UK, and for some commentators a direct response to grunge, was a rise of Britpop, exemplified by the bands such as Blur, Suede, Pulp and Oasis. Those bands were drawing on musical influences from the British musical past of glam rock, punk rock and arty punk, and regularly topping the charts.

The decade continued to bring many genre crossovers (pop punk; nu metal – combining grunge, metal and hip-hop; rapcore – rap and rock; industrial metal; electronica – influenced by dance sound but aimed at home listening on account of its down tempo) characteristic of postmodern pastiche, where bringing together and combining elements of different styles becomes a norm.

Music in the 2000s

As discussed in chapters 1 and 2, the start of the new millennium was marked by the 'new' digital era in music, which has transformed the way in which music is produced, distributed and consumed. While new recording technologies in many ways liberated the ways in which music can be recorded and produced, thus acting as a democratizing feature and allowing so-called bedroom producers to flower, almost conversely live music became relevant once again, mostly because of the recognition that live performance is an important income stream for the record companies and the artists. At one end of the popular music spectrum, the talent shows such as *The X Factor* on both sides of the Atlantic attract thousands of wannabees and millions of viewers, and yet remain associated with lack of authenticity, commercialism, manufactured acts and the notion of selling out. At the other end, the emergence and an extraordinary rise in popularity of social networking sites such as MySpace, Last.fm, SoundCloud and Bandcamp provided a platform for all music, giving a space for 'alternative', unsigned artists to be heard. Genre crossovers continue to occur, with labels such as 'synthpop', 'Nu-disco' and 'electro hop' being attached to various types of sound. 'Post' became a prefix used to describe a range of revivals, such as 'post-grunge'. In the early 2000s, garage rock and post-punk were resurrected by bands such as The Strokes, the White Stripes and Franz Ferdinand. Emo sound (with origins in hardcore punk's subgenre known as emotional core or emocore) and aesthetic (fashion, hairstyle) entered the mainstream with the success of Jimmy Eat World's *Bleed American* (2001) platinum-selling album. Eminem, who was named as the Best Artist of the Decade by *Billboard* magazine, is often thought to have brought hip-hop to the mainstream.

The important point to consider is the extent to which the democratization of popular music spaces, combined with fragmentation of the boundary between 'rock' and 'pop' and generic crossovers which are becoming a norm, is an example of postmodernism. This point is developed in the final section of this chapter, through the discussion of Madonna.

Pop and politics

Pop music has been seen as an important social force in many different ways. In this section, attention is drawn to the connections between pop and politics along three different dimensions. First, there is the way in which pop or rock is seen as in some way oppositional to established values in the broadest sense. Second, there are the interconnections between rock and politics, as understood in a more conventional way, as concerning political parties, the government, the state, and so on. This leads, third, to a consideration of definitions of censorship – how such processes should be understood and how they occur in different ways in specific contexts.

As has been discussed above, the development of rock 'n' roll in the 1950s is often presented as a kind of liberation from the dullness of American and British life of the period. It is seen to have opened up new possibilities for self-expression and to have broken down the conventions and stuffiness of everyday life. Rock was vibrant and something that authority did not like. In this account there is something inherently oppositional about rock. In the 1960s, ideas about this oppositional status were entailed in rock's characterization as the music of protest, the 'movement' or the underground. A clear version of this argument has been expressed by Bradley, who argues that rock music is a 'collective, collectivizing, communal phenomenon' (1992: 118). Rock is both produced in a communal fashion, in groups and bands, for example, and consumed communally at concerts, in clubs, and so on. For Bradley, it was primarily the music of youth:

> Youth culture involves a resistance to atomization and massification, and to the boredom, the loneliness, the fear and the experiential vicariousness they produce. The unique position of post-war teenagers, physically adult yet excluded from adult roles and responsibilities, with considerable disposable cash, and familiar from early childhood with the products of the modern mass media, healthy, well-fed and energetic, yet involved in less hard physical work than many of their ancestors – this privileged, new position seemed merely to throw into sharp relief for them the limitations, frustrations and oppressiveness of their existence in other respects, and to give them the opportunity to respond in new ways to these conditions. Music-use became one of the main chosen instruments of their response. (Ibid.: 96)

In Bradley's account, rock music, therefore, is resistant. In its connections to youth culture, it resists and relates to feelings, about the family, school and the media. Further, it is connected to issues of boredom and the attempt to overcome the mundane nature of society. Rock also resists the atomization or individuation of contemporary life in its construction of communities, which are often to exclude the adult world. All in all, in Bradley's phrase, rock involves a 'resistant communality' (ibid.: 131). Other aspects of the relation between rock and youth groups will be discussed in chapters 7, 8 and 9.

This sort of stance concerning the oppositional character of rock developed rapidly during the 1960s. However, the decline of some of the ideals of that period and the activities of some rock stars which led them to be perceived as a part of a capitalist commercial venture threw the idea into crisis. In lots of ways, punk was built on that crisis and attempted to renew the idea that rock was an active political force. This occurred specifically through the activities of organizations such as Rock Against Racism in the late 1970s (Widgery 1986; Frith and Street 1992) and Red Wedge in the 1980s and, in a broad sense, through the antagonism of some of the new groups to the established record industry by the ethic of do-it-yourself which punk spawned (see, more generally, McKay 1996). These raised expectations about the inherent oppositional nature of rock which have often, somewhat paradoxically, given rise to some of its strongest criticisms. Authors who believed strongly in this stance become disillusioned and then point to the role of the rock industry in the corruption of the original ideal. Thus, much writing on rock has characterized a cycle of supposed innovation and opposition being literally bought off by the activities of the big record companies and their agents. The writing on punk was no different. A number of these views are captured by Burchill and Parsons:

> In 1978 every record company is waking up to find a somewhat superfluous punk combo on its doorstep. Supply and demand? But you can't supply something that there's no demand for.
>
> Never mind, kid, there'll soon be another washing-machine/spot cream/rock-band on the market to solve all your problems and keep you quiet/off the street/distracted from the real enemy/content till the next pay-day. Anyhow, God Save Rock and Roll . . . it made you a Consumer, a potential Moron . . .
>
> IT'S ONLY ROCK AND ROLL AND IT'S PLASTIC, PLASTIC, YES IT IS!!!!!! (1978: 96)

The problem with this sort of approach, of seeing the music as 'corrupted' by the industry and consumerism, is that it is difficult now – and indeed it may always have been difficult – to suggest that rock or pop was ever outside the structures of the record industry and capitalism. If the arguments of Negus (1992) that the record industry is a web of connections between the small and the large, which were examined in chapter 1, are taken seriously, it is hard to see where the pure spaces for creation outside the context of commercial relations exist. Further, the postmodernist argument that the boundaries between art and commerce are increasingly breaking down also suggests that commercial relationships are unavoidable, but this does not necessarily make musical products corrupt, inauthentic or valueless.

There is another version of rock and the record industry which suggests that it was always a capitalist con-trick or part of an industrialized society anyway. Some of these general accounts were also considered in the Introduction, where some of the problems associated with them were identified. It is important to point out again that the examination of the politics of rock needs to take place in a more specific context where the assertions are of a less general nature.

Grossberg has carried out an investigation of this kind. Building on a framework developed by Raymond Williams (1973), he argues that rock can produce three types of boundary between its followers and dominant culture: oppositional, alternative and independent. He defines these boundaries in the following way: 'Oppositional rock and roll presents itself as a direct challenge or threat to the dominant culture', whereas alternative rock 'mounts only an implicit attack on the dominant culture.' 'Independent rock and roll does not present itself as a challenge, either explicitly or implicitly, to the dominant culture although it may function as such' (1983: 110). Grossberg shows that there are crucial differences between different forms of rock with regard to their critical potential. He also identifies the way in which rock can be co-opted, which he examines at greater length in his book *We Gotta Get Out of This Place* (1992b). An example of this could be the celebration of the Queen's Golden Jubilee in 2002, which included a large rock concert in London with established 'mainstream' stars. Moreover, there have been forms of rock that have expressed right-wing political views (see, for example, Barber-Kersovan 2003) and controversies over the politics of lyrics in forms such as death metal (Kahn-Harris 2003). This leads into the second part of this discussion of pop and politics.

The direct connection of rock with politics in the case of Rock Against Racism in the late 1970s and Red Wedge in the 1980s has already been mentioned. In the 1960s, rock was often seen as the music of protest continuing those 'folk' forms which had been connected with the working class, often by middle-class intellectual members of revolutionary political parties (Harker 1980). There have been various other direct connections between pop music and political activism (McKay 2005) – for example, the free festival movement in the 1970s (Clarke 1982), which continued in the struggles around the festivals and activities of so-called new-age travellers in the 1990s. Groups on the right have also connected their politics to rock music. In the late 1970s the fascist right in Britain founded a group known as Rock Against Communism, and the Oi Skinhead Rock of the early 1980s is often related to fascist activity in various countries (Barber-Kersovan 2003). Rock and pop have been connected in rather different ways to politics since the 1980s through a number of charitable concerts such as Live Aid in 1985 and Live8 in 2005, and in more direct ways around the Nelson Mandela concerts in London.

Garofalo (1992c: 26–35) discusses four potential functions that such events may have: fundraising, consciousness-raising, artist activism and agitation. According to Garofalo, Live Aid in 1985 raised $67 million. Such events might raise the consciousness of the public about issues such as poverty and debt and political figures such as Nelson Mandela. Furthermore, they could deepen artist involvement in politics and contribute, perhaps indirectly, to political change.

In discussing such events, it is important to consider the issues and outcomes in a specific way. This has been done in other accounts of rock and politics, and some of the most interesting connections have been drawn in the context of events in Eastern Europe in the late 1980s. Influential work by Wicke opens up the issues in a clear manner (see also on this topic, and the politics of rock more generally, Street 2012). Wicke (1992a, though see also, for example, Wicke 1992b and Wicke and Shepherd 1993) suggests that rock music played a significant role in the disintegration of East Germany in 1989. During September of that year musicians in that country issued a statement which argued, from a leftist position, for greater democracy. This had been prompted by the exodus of young people to the West via Hungary, which had been going on throughout 1989, and which the East German authorities had tried to conceal, though the information was freely available in the Western media. The musicians' statement was read out at numerous state-sponsored performances held to celebrate the fortieth anniversary of the foundation of the German Democratic Republic on 7 October 1989. The attempts to prevent this by the state security forces led to conflict with audiences which continued after 7 October.

The fact that rock music could have such effects was based on three preconditions. First, East Germany's rock musicians had been organized by the state under the Committee for Entertainment Arts. This represented an attempt 'to render the musicians susceptible to forms of state-imposed discipline' (Wicke 1992a: 201). Second, the performances of the musicians provided a clear space for debates on political ideas, not least because other media were closed to such discussion. Third, the authorities interpreted lyrics in political terms, 'finding nearly every lyric to be politically disruptive' (ibid.). Audiences interpreted songs in this way as well, finding their own politically disruptive messages in them. Through these processes, rock music had become politicized by the state, the performers and the audiences.

Wicke argues that the state had been worried about the potential for opposition expressed by rock music since the middle of the 1960s, at first trying to argue that it had no place in a socialist society. This strategy was altered in the early 1970s to one that tried to incorporate rock music under the umbrella of state organization. However, this proved very difficult to sustain, and by the mid-1970s the state was forced into a number of public struggles with rock musicians. By the late 1980s, in a strategy of 'divide and rule', it was attempting to split the musicians between the younger and older elements. Thus, the state's own attempts to incorporate rock, to neutralize the threat that it was perceived to pose, had actually led to the further politicization of the music and, indeed, provided mechanisms for the expression of opposition from within state umbrella organizations themselves. Furthermore, once the state had fallen, the way was open to the influx of Western bands which eliminated the indigenous rock music scene, showing the linkages between this form of rock and the state itself. In Wicke's words:

But just as East German rock music was born and lived as an oppositional cultural and political force during Honecker's years in power, it is now in the process of dying with him. With the fall of the Berlin Wall has come a radical change in the music scene in the former communist territory. Having achieved their revolutionary cultural and political goals, German musicians from the East have for the most part been quickly (and sadly) forgotten in the flood of commercial popular culture that has swept in from the West. (1992a: 206)

Pekacz (1994) has argued that accounts such as Wicke's have overestimated the role of rock music in political change in Eastern Europe and the extent to which it opposed the established regimes. She maintains that, in fact, the government in such societies was much less monolithic and doctrinaire than is suggested by Wicke and that rock music entered into a number of everyday accommodations with it. Below the level of state rhetoric, rock musicians and state functionaries often shared common frames of reference. In sum, Wicke, in this view, romanticizes the oppositional role of rock partly by overemphasizing the unity of the structures it confronted. This is rather similar to those 1960s accounts of the oppositional status of rock which saw it as fighting an all-pervasive 'system'.

However, the recent example of the arrest and imprisonment of the Russian 'anti-Putin' female punk group Pussy Riot signals the operation of an extremely vigilant state censorship regime. Following their February 2012 performance of a song titled 'Virgin Mary, Redeem Us of Putin', in Christ the Saviour Cathedral in Moscow, three members of the band were arrested and faced up to seven years' imprisonment for 'hooliganism'. The news of their situation spread rapidly across various social media platforms, and, in the weeks and months following, many established punk bloggers (e.g. John Robb on http://louderthanwar.com/) and 'sympathisers' tried to raise the profile of the case, calling for the release of the women. By the summer of 2012 the news of Pussy Riot's actions and arrest had reached the mainstream media, as well as caught the eye of high-profile artists such as Yoko Ono, Anthony Kiedis (Red Hot Chili Peppers) and Madonna, who publicly expressed their support. Following Madonna's remarks about freedom of expression and her call to release the band members during her Moscow concert, Russian Deputy Prime Minister Dmitry Rogozin took to his official Twitter account, posting: 'Every former w. . . seeks to lecture everyone on morality as she gets older. Especially during tours and gigs abroad.' In August 2012 the International Association for the Study of Popular Music put out a statement condemning the detention of Pussy Riot members and seeking their immediate release. The statement foregrounds the historic link between popular music and protest: 'Historically, popular music has often been used as a peaceful and effective means of conveying political protest. While such expressions may appear provocative and challenging to some, such protests should never be mistaken for criminality' (www. iaspm.net/).

On 17 August 2012, Nadezhda Tolokonnikova, aged twenty-three, Maria Alekhina, twenty-four, and Yekaterina Samutsevich, thirty, were convicted of 'hooliganism on the grounds of religious hatred'. In October, Nadezhda Tolokonnikova and Maria Alekhina were sentenced to two years' in prison by a Moscow court, while Yekaterina Samutsevich was given a suspended sentence and released. Following the verdict and sentencing, protests were held in support of the band members in a number of cities across the world – including Belgrade, Kiev, Berlin, Sofia, London, Dublin and

Box 3.4   Dissenting voices

Growing protest

2009 Political art group Voina, headed by Pyotr Verzilov, splits into two factions.
March 2011 Female members of Voina, including Verzilov's wife Nadezhda Tolokonnikova, study feminist punk movement "riot grrrl" and form Pussy Riot.
14 December 2011 Pussy Riot hold a concert on the roof of the detention centre where anti-Putin blogger Alexei Navalny is being held.
20 January 2012 They perform a short song, Putin Pissed Himself, on a platform in front of St Basil's Cathedral in Moscow's Red Square, opposite the Kremlin. Eight members are detained but later released.
21 February Now infamous protest, staged in Christ the Saviour cathedral in Moscow. The performance lasts less than five minutes and the song Virgin Mary, Redeem Us of Putin divides opinion within Russian Orthodox church.
3 March Six band members are detained, but only Maria Alekhina and Nadezhda Tolokonnikova are arrested for hooliganism after 'punk prayer'.
16 March A third member, Yekaterina Samutsevich, is arrested. If convicted, the trio face up to seven years in prison.
27 June Artist Alexander Ivanov, poet Lev Rubinstein and satirist Viktor Shenderovich, along with nearly 25,000 other supporters, sign an open letter published on the website of liberal radio station Ekho Moskvy calling for the trio's release after a court extends their detention without setting a trial date.
20 July A judge extends their jail time by six months.
23 July The request for President Putin to appear at the trial (due to start 30 July) is rejected.
27 July International support is triggered by the US rockers Faith No More inviting Pussy Riot to join them on stage in Moscow.

Source: Olivia Mace, The Observer, 29 July 2012

Barcelona. Nadezhda Tolokonnikova and Maria Alyokhina were released from prison in December 2013, on the eve of the Sochi Winter Olympic Games and following the passing of an amnesty law. They have dismissed their release as a publicity stunt. The story continues to cause much debate about state censorship, the freedom of speech and the role of popular culture in facilitating dissenting voices, across a variety of alternative and mainstream media.

Other studies have explored the complexities of the 'censorship' process in societies such as South Africa during the time of apartheid (Drewett 2003) and communist China (de Kloet 2003). In both these cases it is shown how artists and record companies sought to subvert the rules of censorship in a number of ways. One of these is by changing the lyrics of songs that were being sent to the censor for checking, so that the real meaning was covered up. This could be done by simple substitution of words, as Drewett (2003: 158) explains with respect to the sending of work to the South African Broadcasting Corporation (SABC): 'Many musicians tried to sneak controversial ideas onto radio using innovative methods. Keith Berelowitz of Carte Blanche revealed that they submitted counterfeit lyric sheets with albums sent to the SABC, replacing controversial words with ones that had a similar sound. In one instance they changed "policeman" to "please man'" (personal interview with Berelowitz, 15 April 1998). In 1985 Shifty Records released a compilation album of rebel rhythms called *A Naartjie in Our Sosatie* ('A tangerine in our kebab'), a play on 'Anarchy in our society'. In another case, the group Bright Blue 'used symbolic lyrics to sing about a man living in fear within a heavily repressive society' (ibid.: 159). Similar processes take place in China.

To evaluate the political significance of rock, it is important to consider the way in which the different forms of music operate within specific constellations of political forces and how the impact of rock and pop musicians in mega-events concerning issues such as world poverty continue to provoke debate about political effects. The third strand of this discussion, then, is that it is difficult to have, or to develop, a general account or theory of the political nature of rock music, especially given the complexities of the situations. This sort of approach has been usefully developed over time by John Street (e.g. 2012), who suggestively points out that the politics of pop music are formed in the relationship between commerce and ideals. He uses the example of the 1970 Isle of Wight Festival to argue that

> The entrepreneurs, like the musicians, were caught between political idealism and commercial reality, between belief and the bottom line. Arguably, it is this tension which actually generates pop's finest moments and its truest politics. Utopian fantasies tend to issue in bland sounds, and self-righteous polemics in dull tunes. The politics of popular music are best animated by the attempt to combine commercial logic with romantic ideals. (Street 2001: 244)

For Street, popular music has both 'the power to represent and the power to effect' (ibid.: 245) – that is, music can capture feelings and wishes and have influence. However, these are capacities rather than guarantees, and the precise extent of representation and effect will depend on the specific context and the case.

This line of argument has been usefully explored by Cloonan vis-à-vis the significant issue of the definition of censorship. This is done in the wider context of policing, which is used 'to convey the variety of ways in which popular music can be regulated, restricted, and repressed' (Cloonan and Garofalo 2003: 3). Cloonan argues that it is important to explain what is meant by censorship. This is not straightforward: 'The essence of the problem lies in drawing up a definition which is narrow enough to exclude apparently frivolous examples but broad enough to include incidents other than overt attempts by governments and other agencies to prevent musical expression' (ibid.: 15). This leads him to the following definition: 'censorship is the process by which an agent (or agents) attempts to, and/or succeeds in, significantly altering, and/or curtailing, the freedom of expression of another agent with a view to limiting the likely audience for that expression' (ibid.). This allows a variety of activities to be considered under this heading, from the 'market-based decisions within the music industry to the actions of official or state censorship agencies' (ibid.), and it leads Cloonan to a useful categorization of the way that censorship can operate on a number of levels. He discusses three main levels: 'prior restraint, restriction, and suppression' (ibid.: 17–18).

Prior restraint involves a process such as preventing a band from recording. Cloonan suggests that practices of the music industry (see chapters 1 and 2) can be seen as prior restraint: 'By not signing artists, record companies can effectively act as censors in the sense that, for whatever reason, they are acting to restrict an artist's audience. This is not to say that all decisions not to sign artists are acts of censorship, but rather that they can have censorial implications for the artists concerned' (Cloonan and Garofalo 2003: 17). Restriction can be more visible and direct, as it involves 'the imposing of certain conditions upon the placement or ownership of products' (ibid.). Thus, 'In western Europe and North America, the most frequently cited examples of popular music censorship – banning of records from the radio – are examples of restriction' (ibid.). Finally, suppression involves 'attempts by a government or legal system to enforce a moral and/or political code' (ibid.: 18).

This sort of approach means that Cloonan is able to consider a range of processes of the policing for popular music without necessarily suggesting that they involve the more overt forms of censorship. This indicates that a range of social, economic and political processes can be discussed in terms of how they affect the communication of a text to an audience (see the range of factors in case of the development of rock and roll above). Thus, while this involves the general definition of the processes involved, it also draws attention to the need to consider the specifics of those processes. It is not possible to see policing and regulation in China and the USA (Fischer 2003) in precisely the same ways, but having an overall framework enables these comparisons to be drawn in finer detail. This reinforces the critical comments on general accounts of rock discussed in the Introduction. Such accounts are further complicated when the relations between rock, gender and sexuality are considered.

Rock, gender and sexuality

It was suggested earlier that the more conventional accounts of the development of rock point to its initial power and resistance (in rock 'n' roll) which was transformed as the music industry moved in (producing rock and roll). Further, there was a clear barrier built between rock and pop at a later date. It has been argued that these accounts reflect hierarchies of gender in popular music and society. The classic case for this interpretation has been made by Simon Frith and Angela McRobbie (1990). Frith and McRobbie's initial suggestion is that rock music cannot be analysed either as simply a product of the culture industry, and hence as a commodity which acts ideologically to incorporate its consumers, or in its subcultural consumption by different audience groups. They argue that rock's meanings, especially in the construction and representation of sexuality, are rather more complex than these rather general accounts allow.

Frith and McRobbie contend that male domination of the music industry leads to representations of masculinity in contemporary pop music. They identify two main types of pop music, which they label 'cock rock' and 'teenybop'. Cock rock is 'music making in which performance is an explicit, crude and often aggressive expression of male sexuality', its 'performers are aggressive, dominating, and boastful, and they constantly seek to remind the audience of their prowess, their control' – the 'image is the rampant male traveller, smashing hotels and groupies alike. Musically, such rock takes off from the sexual frankness of rhythm and blues but adds a cruder male physicality (hardness, control, virtuosity)' (Frith and McRobbie 1990: 374). Teenybop, according to Frith and McRobbie, is consumed mainly by girls, whose teenybop idol's 'image is based on self-pity, vulnerability, and need'. This finds a different form of musical expression from cock rock: 'In teenybop, male sexuality is transformed into a spiritual yearning carrying only hints of sexual interaction. What is needed is not so much someone to screw as a sensitive and sympathetic soulmate, someone to support and nourish the incompetent male adolescent as he grows up' (ibid.: 375).

There are artists who seem to fit fairly clearly into these categories (many heavy metal groups have been seen as examples of cock rock and singers and groups such as Justin Bieber, Take That and One Direction as teenyboppers), though Frith and McRobbie point out that there can be important crossovers between the two. They argue that these textual and performance types connect to different audiences. Boys, as the consumers of cock rock, are active. They attempt to follow guitar-playing idols into the music industry, and attendance at the cock rock concert is active. Furthermore, suggest Frith and McRobbie, this attendance is collective. Boys are in and form groups. The female fans of the teenybopper are, by contrast, relatively passive and individual. They consume as individuals. Their aim as performers is to be singers, or else to face the kind of exaggerated aggression associated with such musicians as Janis Joplin, with the attendant dangers of self-destruction. In addition, Frith and McRobbie suggest that teenybop idols can be used in different ways by the girl audiences as a form of collective appropriation and resistance to school norms. Aspects of this will be considered at later points in this book.

In Frith and McRobbie's view the conventional accounts of the decline of rock 'n' roll are actually accounts of its feminization (1990: 383). Furthermore, they begin a process of attempting to look beyond the lyrics of a song to investigate its gendered meaning in musical terms. The vehicle for this is a comparison of Tammy Wynette's 'Stand by Your Man' with Helen Reddy's 'I Am Woman', which values Wynette over Reddy:

> The lyrics of 'Stand by Your Man' celebrate women's duty to men, implore women to enjoy subordinating themselves to men's needs – lyrically the song is a ballad of sexual submissiveness. But the female authority of Tammy Wynette's voice involves a knowledge of the world that is in clear contrast to the gooey idealism of Helen Reddy's sound. 'Sometimes it's hard to be a woman', Tammy Wynette begins, and you can hear that Tammy Wynette knows why her voice is a collective one. 'I am woman', sings Helen Reddy, and what you hear is the voice of an idealized consumer, even if the commodity for consumption in this instance is a package version of women's liberation. (Ibid.: 385)

In their article, Frith and McRobbie address a number of important themes:

- the idea that it is important to go beyond a focus on the rock industry or the consumption of rock;
- a characterization of the music industry as male-dominated;
- the characterization of the different forms of masculinity entailed in 'cock rock' and 'teenybop';
- the interconnections between these textual and performance forms and audiences;
- the attempt to move beyond lyrics in the characterization of the worth of songs;
- the argument regarding the feminization of rock 'n' roll.

In a subsequent critique of this piece, Frith suggests that, in 'a jumble of good and bad arguments', there was a confusion of 'issues of sex and issues of gender'. Sex was somehow seen as an essence, rather than something that, like gender, was subject to forms of construction. This argument rejects the idea that there is a core to sex which was simply expressed in music. Music plays a significant part in the construction of gender and sexuality. However, Frith says that 'the most misleading of our original arguments was the distinction between male activity and female passivity when, in fact, consumption is as important to the sexual significance of pop as production' (1990: 422). The original article tended to emphasize the ways in which music was produced at the expense of its consumption. This is an important theme. The Introduction to this book has suggested that it is as important to examine audience appropriations of texts as it is to look at their production, and this is discussed at length in chapters 7, 8 and 9.

Another problem with Frith and McRobbie's argument is that it was originally written in the 1970s, long before the many developments in pop music that have taken place since. In the final section of this chapter, we want to examine some of these through a brief discussion of the most discussed pop figure of the period: Madonna.

Madonna: pop, politics, gender and sexuality

The ongoing Madonna phenomenon raises issues in the three areas that have been discussed in this chapter: the distinction between rock and pop; the politics of pop music and its connections with power; and gender and sexuality. These three areas will be considered in turn. (For an extended examination of Madonna, see, for example, Schwichtenberg 1993, which contains a number of important contributions to the discussion here; also Guilbert 2002; Fouz-Hernández and Jarman-Ivens 2004.)

First, there is the relationship between rock and pop. Early interpretations and accounts of Madonna tended to focus on her implication in the pop industry. She was seen as an inauthentic product of the culture industry who was involved in the exploitation of others for the gain of that industry. Madonna was sometimes contrasted with another popular woman singer of the early and mid-1980s, namely Cyndi Lauper, whose work was seen to be more thoughtful and authentic. However, as time has passed, these debates have been reconstituted. Partly in connection with the increased salience in popular culture of the debates around postmodernism, there was a heightened recognition of the problems of the definition of authenticity and what this can mean in an increasingly commercialized, commodified and media-saturated society. Hence, while Madonna seemed to have come from what would normally be seen as pop beginnings, her work, in some accounts, has been at the forefront of the breaking down of this particular barrier. Further, this could be seen as crossing the divisions between art and commerce in a way consistent with the development of postmodernism. However, Madonna has sometimes asserted her own rights and authenticity as an individual artist. An example of this occurs in the documentary film *In Bed with Madonna* (1991, aka *Truth or Dare*), in which she argues against the censorship of her show on the grounds of artistic freedom, using a notion of individual authenticity close to that expressed by rock artists (and expressed by the jazz musicians studied by Becker – see chapter 2), which itself derives from earlier conceptions of the nature of the artist. However, an alternative interpretation would stress that this is in itself a kind of pose for particular purposes, which has little to do with what Madonna really is, even if there is any point in exploring such an issue. It is significant that this produces ongoing tensions in Madonna's career. Thus, with the release in 2005 of her CD *Confessions on a Dance Floor*, critics suggested that Madonna had returned to disco and dance music in an attempt to secure a larger (pop) audience in the wake of her more artistic attempts to convey 'authentic' personal and social messages in releases such as *Ray of Light* (1998), *Music* (2000) and *American Life* (2003), though it is important to note that these in themselves depended on collaborations with other popular artists and producers of the time.

Second, there is the issue of politics. If Madonna can be seen by some as transcending debates about authenticity, she also connects to new ideas about a form of politics based in ideas of play, the 'freeing' and reconstitution of identity, again in ways connected to the advocates of postmodernism. In an introductory discussion of the idea of identity, Hall (1992) distinguishes three concepts of identity: 'Enlightenment', 'sociological' and 'postmodern'. The Enlightenment concept rested on notions of there being an essential core to identity which was born with the individual and unfolded through his or her life. The sociological concept argued that a coherent identity is formed in relations with others and thus develops and changes over time. The postmodern subject is thought to have no fixed or essential identity. In postmodern societies, identities have become 'dislocated'.

It can be suggested that earlier constructions of politics could be related to the search for new forms of identity as the oppressed or dominated threw off those forms which colluded with oppression and implicated them in the operation of power. These forms of identity could be seen to be relatively stable and to enable the new identity to be expressed in a way that opposed the dominant order. Thus, the standardized identity of the pop consumer as characterized by Adorno might be replaced with the more sophisticated identity of the follower of serious music who would recognize the way in which the culture industry used pop music to reproduce inequalities. This sort of politics can be seen to rest on a sociological concept of identity, where the subject can be changed, or switched over, as social conditions change.

Some more recent forms of politics, however, suggest that the stability of such identities is problematic in that they freeze the fluidity of contemporary identities and, indeed, often involve the privileging of one construction of identity over another. Thus, talking of a working-class identity might neglect the different identities of black and white workers and, for example, subsume the black identity in the white one. Similar arguments have been made against forms of feminism that do not take account of the different identities of black and white women. In some recent politics, there is a celebration of the idea that there is not a true or real identity but a multiplicity of identities which operate in different circumstances. In these respects, Madonna has, it is argued, caught the notion that there is no real identity, no authentic way of being, and has become involved in the play of masks and surfaces rather than in a search for the truth and the underlying reality. Thus the shifts in Madonna's representation of self – and indeed physical appearance – can be seen in this light. As she gets older, yet more layers have been added to this play, such as the roles of wife and mother and the relationship between the USA and the UK. This allows further dimensions of activity to be brought to bear and in turn fuels debates on what Madonna is doing. This has one function of keeping her in the public eye and reconstituting the nature of her stardom and the nature of her celebrity.

Due to her constant reinvention, transformation and appropriation of cultural signifiers, some commentators accuse Madonna of 'cultural tourism', particularly in relation to her playful visual engagement with queer sexuality and ethnicity. Within the discourse of postmodernism, such flirtation with a range of cultural or identity signifiers is seen not as negative but rather as necessary. Patricia Waugh writes:

> The concept of a 'woman's identity' functions in terms both of affirmation and nega-
> tion, even within feminism itself. There can be no simple legitimation for feminists
> in throwing off 'false consciousness' and revealing a true but 'deeply' buried female
> self. Indeed, to embrace the essentialism of this notion of 'difference' is to come
> dangerously close to reproducing that very patriarchal construction of gender which
> feminists have set out to contest . . .' (Waugh 1992:189)

This argument can be developed further by referring to the notion of 'womanliness as a masquerade', introduced in 1929 by Joan Riviere and later developed by Judith Butler. Riviere argued that women adopt a mask of womanliness in order to 'stave off male jealousy and reprisal . . . for any incursions into the power appropriated by men' (Cranny-Francis 1995: 27). In her work, Butler (see further chapter 6) uses the notion of 'masquerade' further to examine and reassess the ways in which gender, sex and sexualities are constituted.

Musically, too, Madonna is accused of 'borrowing' and 'latching onto' trends, with many reviewers of her 2008 album *Hard Candy* commenting on her attempt (albeit belated in this case) to jump on the hip-hop wagon by working with Timbaland and The Neptunes (producers) as well as collaborating with Pharrell Williams (of The Neptunes) and Justin Timberlake.

If Madonna the performer symbolizes the dislocated, decentred and fragmented postmodern identity, maintained through self-invention, transformation (in both style and sound), pastiche and performativity, then arguably she resists various cultural appropriations, thus perpetuating and maintaining a multiplicity of discourses about herself. One such discourse based on the postmodern play of visual signs is the recent 'Alejandro' video by Lady Gaga – a form of pastiche of Madonna's work where numerous references are made to different Madonna 'periods', including black and white images resembling her Vogue phase, the mourning present in her Evita period, imagery associated with bondage that punctuates much of her work, and the religious signifiers of 'Like a Prayer'.

In relation to the third area, gender and sexuality, Madonna is held to have exhibited a form of play with gender roles which overcomes the privileging of one form of gender as that to be emulated and which represents a form of freedom from straitjackets. Furthermore, the sense that she is in control of her own destiny and image has projected the idea of her being a strong woman who is generally in control, rather than someone who is manipulated by the men who dominate the pop music industry. In terms of sexuality, Madonna has connected to forms of culture and politics which value the transgression of established sexual norms concerning violence and pornography. It is argued that her videos and books, such as *Sex*, bring forms of sexual representation which had been hidden into the mainstream. This process makes visible forms of sexuality that had been obscured or denigrated by the mainstream culture and may lead to greater tolerance of those who engage in what have been described as 'perverted' practices. Moreover, the representations associated with *Confessions on a Dance Floor* stimulated debates in the popular press about the appropriate forms of behaviour for a woman born in 1958 with children.

Madonna continues to have an interesting relationship with feminism. In *On Stage and on the Record* (2003) she declared herself as a humanist rather than a feminist. She is seen as a positive female role model by some, mainly due to the perceptions that she destabilizes and threatens the norms of the heavily masculine music industry. On the other hand, her flirtation with the femme fatale image and incorporation of what some feminists would argue is pornographic material in her videos means her presence is perceived as confirming and reinforcing gender stereotypes.

Furthermore, there has been consideration of the way in which Madonna serves as a hero to younger generations of women ('wannabees') who are tired of the older forms of politics and of the sterility of their everyday lives. This might also now apply to older women. However, there are others who reject the idea of Madonna as an icon. Schulze and her colleagues (1993) point to four critical accounts of Madonna among those who hate her. She is seen as the lowest form of culture, as 'the lowest form of irresponsible culture, a social disease', as 'the lowest form of the feminine' and 'as the antithesis of feminism'. They also suggest that these critics feel that they are going against the dominant ideas of Madonna as a 'good thing'; they are, in the phrase of Schulze et al., 'resistive readers'.

This debate about the worth of Madonna and her connections to cultural politics has carried through into other dimensions of academic and popular debate where, for example, the merits of boundary-breaking, transgression and play have been much discussed, often in relation to gender and race. This debate throws into sharp relief many of the issues examined in this chapter. First, the distinction between rock and pop has often entailed judgements of value and assumptions about gender. For example, the evaluation of rock has often involved the privileging of masculinity. Second, general arguments about the relation between pop and politics require revision if the ideas associated with postmodernism, fragmentation and cultural difference are taken seriously, as more needs to be made of the specific contexts in which political practices occur. Arguments about politics need to be considered with respect to particular cases, as the extended discussion of the East German situation in the 1980s showed. Third, it is important to recognize that, while the approach pioneered by Frith and McRobbie is still illuminating in certain respects, contemporary gender relations and feminine identities are far more complex. Issues of gender and sexuality should be discussed in a way that recognizes such complexity.

While the theme of new ways of thinking about sex, gender and sexuality is taken up in detail in chapter 6, it can be argued that recent popular musicology (see also chapter 5) has explored a number of different dimensions of how the study of female performers allows reconsideration of key issues raised in this chapter. For example, Whiteley (2000b: 136–51) examines the textual strategies of Madonna's work in the context of the feminist theory of Luce Irigaray concerning 'plurality, play and difference' (ibid.: 150). This is a specific example of how Whiteley combines analysis of the overall social context and feminist and cultural theory with the discussion of music, lyrics and visual representation to produce new insights into the way in which a range of female performers (for example, Janis Joplin, Joni Mitchell, Patti Smith, k.d. lang, Tracey Chapman and the Spice Girls) express and construct identities and different spaces for women to speak in a manner that explores new political directions.

The release of Madonna's 2012 album *MDNA* and the PR campaign accompanying it continue to produce a lively debate about gender, sexuality and, this time round more prominently, age. Suzanne Moore and Liz Jones reflect some of the issues that have dominated the debate.

Box 3.5 I have always compared myself to Madonna

God, I am exhausted and I haven't even started. At my age, your knees creak, you feel constantly tired, your features start sliding down your face, you are forever in some souped-up cardy or improbable shrug because of the 'arms crisis', and, as if that were not enough, you have to compare yourself to bloomin' Madonna in her bra and knickers. I have always compared myself to her, not because I am an all-singing/dancing army of one, but because she is always there: the prism through which women and ageing are refracted. Her relentless quest for hipness, her groin thrusted into my face, her humourless attempts at self-deprecating ordinariness, her trying-on of personae – the hunting, shooting, fishing/lady author who likes a pint one was particularly bad. All of this drives me mad. But then, like any old flame, she reminds me suddenly of the original fire by doing what she does best. I love that she annoys so many with her collection of children/boyfriends/dancers, that she will insist on making another record, and that she does not know the meaning of 'age appropriate'.

A woman doing as she damn well pleases pleases me, but the debate is tired. Should she be more 'dignified'? Like, say, Mick Jagger? Should she even wear fishnet tights?

This, of course, has upset Liz Jones in the Daily Mail. I confess I don't look like Liz or Madge, but I didn't know fishnets over the age of 50 were actually illegal. Jones seems to think only a shroud will do. I presume Prada does a nice one. 'After 50 you have no erogenous zones. Accept it. Move on. Cover up,' says Jones.

Actually, this 'Please put it away, Madonna' schtick has been going on for 30 years through the cut-off belly tops, conical bras and leotards to the new short shorts. My daughters also find her now generally 'old and disgusting'. As for bringing in Nicki Minaj, my 21-year-old sternly told me: 'That is bad, Mum. She is basically selling sex to young girls.' Well I should coco? Isn't that what music is for? Selling sex. To girls. And boys. And gays. MDNA returns Madonna precisely to this arena where the alchemy of female desire and pure ambition sync joyously. The dancefloor is the place where barriers melt away: at its best this music represents a transcendence and liberation that no other genre achieves. It is about the physicality of sex and sweat and chemicals, which Madonna appropriates, calling it MDNA while refusing drugs. In come the superstar DJs, MIA and Minaj – all part of the bricolage as Madonna hedges her bets. This is the divorce album, apparently. She possibly wants to shoot Guy Ritchie in the head (who doesn't, frankly?) and boasts that she can do 10 things at once (again, who can't?). It is only when she is back with producer William Orbit that it really works, but then Orbit could make the national anthem sound like a trippy globule of loss and lust.

That the music is secondary to the spectacle does not mean it does not sell, though I know no one who buys her or ever thought she was cool. If you want dance music, go straight to the sources that she pilfers from.

What I do rate, though, is her drive. When she turned herself from a sexual subject into a sex object for her book Sex, I attended an academic conference about her overcompensating for her 'lack'. They were Lacanians. Lack meant lack of a phallus. How I laughed. But I remember wondering how she would do sex and motherhood. She may not know the theories, but like any autodidact her instincts are impeccable. She simply wore a shirt that said 'Mutha' on the front and 'Fucker' on the back.

Oddly, though, her lyrics remain mostly inane but sometimes sadly truthful. 'I traded fame for love' was the first line of Ray of Light. On MDNA she is older and has done the marriage thing. 'I tried to be your wife/diminished myself, and I swallowed my light.' But the best thing remains. 'Only when I'm dancing can I feel this free . . .'

Dancing – somehow that is what it all comes back to. Her life is a dance of control and the freedom comes from keeping moving. Her body is not so much a temple as a corporate HQ that is her business. Why should she not parade it? Her face may be full of filler, another terrible film may be in the bag, but here she is looking amazing being ravished by ripped Latinos and crying black tears. What's not to like?

The late, great Steven Wells once called her oeuvre the 'carry on shagging school of feminism' but in the end it is not just about sex. What upsets people about Madonna is not her sex drive but her insatiable need to be taken seriously. She won't stop. Her work ethic is the polar opposite of what the music aspires to: losing yourself. This is why Madonna's age means nothing, not just because she looks good but because she knows the one erogenous zone that women never need to cover up is our minds. Hers is restless, insatiable and refuses to play by the rules. That is a kind of freedom most women never attain. Long may she continue to divide and rule.

Source: Suzanne Moore, *The Guardian*, 28 March 2012

Box 3.6 Oh, Madge! The bottom line is no woman over 50 should really be wearing fishnets

When Madonna wore fishnet stockings the first time around, it was 1990. Back then, she teamed them with a polka-dot jacket, black shorts, a bowler hat and a gamine crop. There was a huge dollop of attitude, too, and rather ballsy humour.

I remember she grabbed her crotch onstage in those little shorts. She looked incredible.

The outfit was not her idea, of course: she was mixing Marlene Dietrich with Liza Minnelli in Cabaret. She knew fishnets infer sadomasochism. They are slutty, especially if riddled with holes, and so segued nicely into her irreverent schtick.

She had a dancer's buttocks and thighs but, most importantly, she was only 32 years old. I remember my 32-year-old buttocks rather fondly: I enveloped them in tiny olive green Calvin Klein shorts and fishnet tights, topped off with a gold Katharine Hamnett waistcoat, and took them to a disco in Marbella.

Fast forward 21 years, and my 53-year-old bottom now has the consistency of unrisen dough. I keep expecting Delia Smith to turn up at my house with a rolling pin, and dust me with flour. I'd no more wear my olive shorts these days than a snow-washed denim blouson.

But here Madonna is again in fishnet tights. And even briefer satin shorts. She seems these days to be channelling Bette Davis, or some sad relic from the Eighties, what with the arm warmers and Karl Lagerfeld for Chanel fingerless gloves. The awful quiff reminds me of the redoubtable fashion critic Suzy Menkes.

Now, I know these comments might be rather harsh, but so is growing old. It's ghastly. I reckon I've had as much plastic surgery as Madonna appears to have had, an equally large vat of filler squished into my cheeks because the pads of fat that used to lurk there have migrated to my knees.

But while our faces might still look freakishly young, it's our bodies that betray us, no matter how many hours we've spent flat on our backs in a Pilates studio.

I might be the same dress size I was aged 32, but that's about all that has remained the same. My ankles are now riddled with blue veins. My earlobes are heading rather worryingly towards my shoulders.

Note how Madge always wears those fingerless gloves: I'd wager she's developing liver spots, or at least the skin on the back of her hands is now so thin she could read her reviews through it.

I'm not saying women over 50 should stick to embroidered salmon twin sets and the M&S classics range, hiding behind great big bauble necklaces and shoulder pads.

I still wear outfits I've owned since 1990: hipster trousers with mannish tailored jackets, baggy combat trousers, microscopic Prada T-shirts. Toe rings worn with Havaiana flip flops. My Gucci embellished boot-cut jeans.

But there is an increasingly large pile of clothes destined for Oxfam, not the Oscars. Even though we children of the Fifties are so much better preserved than our mothers (and my mum didn't have one single natural tooth in her head aged 49), there are still some garments that have a definite sell-by date.

Ultra skinny jeans: just too gynaecologically explicit and thrombosis threatening. Anything pink, or with a bow. Sleeveless vests. I'm also thinking of giving up wearing platforms, as I've become increasingly worried about breaking my ankle and ending up on a mixed-sex geriatric ward.

Shorts are a distant memory, along with 20–20 eyesight and getting out of a chair without a groan. In fact, I can no longer wear anything above the knee, as I now have Demi Moore-like knee wrinkles.

Revealing my decolletage is tricky, too, as the jutting bones reveal me as not old, but long dead. And I'm one of the lucky ones. It's far easier to grow old gracefully if your style has always been quite pared down, minimal and mannish, as mine has been: I always think the likes of Jo Wood, with her uniform of biker jackets and lots of black, can glide smoothly into senility pretty much unfettered.

But if you have always favoured ra-ra skirts, prom dresses and Jean Paul Gaultier conical bras, you might want to plan a great big bonfire.

Of course you can look fabulous over 50, but there is a crucial difference between being well groomed, a la Anne Robinson, and looking like a superannuated Barbie, a la Carol Vorderman, whose body-conscious Roland Mouret dress worn for a lunch with girlfriends was so tight we could see her kidneys, while a red-carpet gown worn at the National TV awards showed off way too much cleavage.

It doesn't matter if you are as toned and honed as Madonna: it's simply not dignified to pull on an Herve Leger bandage mini dress just because you can.

Julianne Moore might be a goddess, but I don't want to see her upper arms or stomach (I found the sex scene in The Kids Are Alright gut churning, given I saw it with a boyfriend. I had never let him see my fifty-something rump in broad daylight, and here he was getting it writ large, across a 100ft screen).

Past 50, it is all about choosing classic shapes that fit well, and exposing as little flesh as possible. Too much anything – fake eyelashes, fake tan, sequins, satin and flesh – only accentuates your slide into antiquity.

I never felt so silly or envious as when I saw Jenny Agutter, who turns 60 this year, being interviewed on The One Show on BBC1. How serene, how unadulterated is she? Putting eyelash extensions on Jenny Agutter would be like giving the Queen a gold tooth. Wrong. And unnecessary.

I think being a fashion victim over 50, caring too much about trends and colours and hem-lines and whether men notice you or not, reveals something way more horrifying than crepey skin or a stomach with the consistency of cold porridge.

It shows that there is a yawning cavern in your soul where something more meaningful should be, such as, ooh, I don't know, a family, or love, or even gardening.

I find it a bit sad when I go to the shows in Paris, as I did earlier this month, and see women in their 60s shedding tears over a peplum skirt. An older woman in head-to-toe crazy, clashing printed pyjamas just looks as though she has escaped from her carer.

For a 53-year-old woman to play the fashionable sex kitten is a bit sad, to be honest.

I'm embarrassed for Madonna – she is letting the side down. Memo to the postmenopausal: forget the fashion mantra of only exposing one erogenous zone at a time. After 50 you have no erogenous zones. Accept it. Move on. Cover up.

Source: Liz Jones, *Daily Mail*, 27 March 2012

Summary

This chapter has considered:

- the development and meaning of various types of popular music, pointing to the location of the beginnings of rock and roll in a complex social context;
- discussions of the distinction between rock and pop and some of implications of this;

- the politics of rock music in general and specific senses, raising issues of the extent to which pop music opposes a dominant culture and the connections of rock with the state;
- the interconnections between gender, sexuality and pop music, using classic work by Frith and McRobbie to provide a springboard for debate;
- the Madonna phenomenon in terms of the issues raised by the chapter.

4 'Black Music': Genres and Social Constructions

This chapter develops some of the themes introduced in chapter 3, as ascriptions of value and claims about authenticity have run through debates about the implications and wider resonances of 'black music'. The chapter opens with a discussion of the important issue of how 'black music' is actually defined. This is important in itself as it introduces debates and raises concerns about the extent to which an 'essence' of black music can be defined in musical or sociological terms. Furthermore, it introduces issues concerning the political implications of black music and the ascription of the label 'black'. This is followed by an examination of the development of blues and soul, which is used to point to some important sociological dimensions of the evolution of these forms. A look at the reggae tradition elaborates on these themes and connects the discussion to specific debates about realism, modernism and post-modernism. The implication of this section of the chapter is that the development of specific forms of reggae can be understood through the utilization of ideal types of textual forms, which are themselves to be understood in social context. This theme is followed through into a consideration of rap and hip-hop culture that reviews some of the debates about this form, which have centred on ideas of resistance, space and place, expression and gender. The chapter is used to raise more general issues of how forms of music influence each other and how they can be related to ascribed characteristics.

Defining black music

The concept of 'black music' has in the past and in everyday criticism often been used in an unreflective way, where it is assumed that it is the music performed by black people. However, several questions have been posed to such a view. First, would a black musician performing a song by Lennon and McCartney or a black opera singer performing a piece from the European classical tradition count as black music (Oliver 1990)? Second, how is a black person actually defined and recognized? In some accounts of black music there was a danger of reproducing stereotypes of natural racial difference. From such a racist angle, black people are held to have natural abilities in music-making or dancing, and so on. However, as Oliver explains:

> To follow this argument through one has to confront the problem of genetic admixture through intermarriage and cross-fertility between races. The outcome of miscegenation between people of different racial stocks over generations inevitably leads to the diminution of some genetic traits and the dominance of others. They're expressed most visibly and physically in, for instance, lightening of skin hue, or differences in hair section and, hence, changes in hair growth. If abilities are genetically related, the diminution or dominance of some would also seem to be the inevitable result of such

racial cross-breeding, but the vast literature on race does not bear this out. Nor does common experience: in the jazz field, for instance, dark-skinned Louis Armstrong, Bessie Smith or Charlie Parker are not rated as being the musical superiors (or inferiors, for that matter) of light-hued Jelly-Roll Morton, Billie Holiday or Lester Young; at least, not on account of the presumed 'blackness' of their genes. (Ibid.: 6)

Furthermore, as Hatch and Millward have argued, blackness varied according to legal definition between different states in the United States:

Legally speaking, the definition as to what constituted a black person varied from state to state under the 'Jim Crow' laws. In Alabama, Arkansas, and Mississippi, anyone with a 'visible' and/or 'appreciable' degree of 'Negro blood' was subject to segregational laws as a black person, whereas in Indiana and Louisiana the colour line was drawn at one-eighth and one-sixteenth Negro blood respectively. Clearly, then, it was possible to change one's status – and therefore legal rights – by moving from one state to another. (1987: 117)

On the basis of the argument advanced by Oliver and Hatch and Millward, it is difficult to maintain that there is a genetic or biological base to 'black music' which marks it off from other forms. A similar point has been made by Tagg, who also suggests that it is difficult to find common features in what has commonly been classed as black music. He argues that four musical characteristics are often used to define 'blackness' of what is sometimes called 'Afro-American' music: 'blue notes', 'call-and-response techniques', 'syncopation' and 'improvisation' (Tagg 1989: 288). Tagg maintains that none of these characteristics can be used to identify a discrete category of black music and argues that the term black music should not be used. He concludes by noting:

Scepticism towards the supposed pair of opposites 'black' or 'Afro-American music' versus 'European music' has two main grounds: (1) musicological because no satisfactory definitions of any terms are provided and (2) ideological. The latter is particularly important because not only does the implied dichotomy pre-ordain certain sets of feeling and behaviour for one race and deny them to the other, it also turns the overriding question of class into a matter of race or ethnicity. (Ibid.: 295)

Tagg argues for a position which can be seen as 'anti-essentialist' (Gilroy 1993), in that he rejects the idea that there is an essence to black music. Despite such criticisms, some writers have continued to argue that the concept of black music has some importance. In Hatch and Millward's account, the music made by black people is related to their oppression in the United States, and they point out that these oppressions and inequalities are often cut across by class, locality, and so on. They argue for a pluralistic account of pop music, which rejects the idea that some forms are more authentic than others. This allows for the study of the complexity of the relations between different textual forms of music and the inputs into them without prior suggestions that one is more 'true' or authentic than another. Thus, on Hatch and Millward's (1987: 120) account, 'pop music has always depended upon the interaction between white and black traditions', and they back up their argument with the example of the development of forms such as the blues. They do not take this position in order to reduce the importance of black musicians vis-à-vis pop music – a position that they are keen to emphasize. However, they suggest that there is no need to oversimplify and consider just one form of music to be authentically black.

Oliver also uses a pluralistic notion to form the basis for the investigations that make up his edited collection of articles on black music in Britain. He argues: "'[B]lack music" is that which is recognized and accepted as such by its creators, performers and hearers . . . encompassing the music of those who see themselves as black, and whose musics have unifying characteristics which justify their recognition as specific genres: peculiar patterns of "sonic order" in John Blacking's phrase' (1990: 8). In this view, black music is that which is socially defined as such. This is a form of sociological approach that emphasizes the actor's own point of view rather than adopting some 'objective' standard of judgement. However, there are problems with such an account, as there may be different or competing definitions of what black music is. The music of Michael Jackson, for example, might be seen as black by some but not by others. But it may also be argued that, in sociological terms, such disagreements over 'blackness' are relatively fruitless, as they will run into the sorts of difficulty already outlined above. More important, it may be suggested, is an examination of complex roots of Jackson's music (and indeed his identity) and how it is produced and consumed in particular ways. This is not to say that the attribution of blackness has no effect. However, this is most important in the consideration of how particular forms of music articulate and connect to political issues.

It can be argued, therefore, that context and political meaning are important in the discussion of 'black music', and that some of the more relativistic arguments might tend to neglect this. Consider, for example, Maya Angelou's account of attending *Porgy and Bess*, reproduced in box 4.1. Here, a clear expression of the pleasure in a 'black' performance can be seen, in a way that conveys how Angelou's eyes are opened, and how, as a result, a commitment to black culture and expression might develop.

The discussion so far has the following implications. It has been suggested, first, that it is difficult to sustain the idea that black music is based in biological factors. Second, that, in the development of many forms of popular music, the interaction between black and white has been crucial. Third, that this does not necessarily denigrate or undervalue the contribution of black people to popular music. As Hatch and Millward argue, 'those designated as black have made the major contribution to the development of pop music from its earliest origins' (1987: 116). Fourth, that some, more relativist, writers have concluded that the term 'black music' should not be used, as it tends to imply the existence of a black musical or racial essence. Fifth, that sociological investigation into the development of those forms that have been designated as black needs to take into account the complex social contexts and locations which have led to the development of such forms. Sixth, that such investigation will often lead to consideration of the political meaning and roles of such forms, in both the general and the specific variants identified in chapter 3. In a seeming paradox, this may lead to the reassertion of the importance of the ascription of the label 'black music'.

One of the strongest arguments along these lines has been made by Paul Gilroy (1987, 1993), who suggests that many discussions of black music downplay its political importance: 'There are three core themes around which the anti-capitalist aspects of black expressive culture have been articulated' (1987: 199). These are detailed in figure 4.1. Gilroy's approach, called 'anti-anti-essentialism' (1993: 102), recognizes that a biological or natural core to black culture and black music cannot be found and argues against attempts to suggest that, because of this, there can be no such category as black culture. His notion of black culture is based in social practices and social

Box 4.1   Maya Angelou at *Porgy and Bess*

If *New Faces of 1953* excited the pulses of San Franciscans, *Porgy and Bess* set their hearts afire. Reviewers and columnists raved about Leontyne Price and William Warfield in the title roles and praised the entire company. The troupe had already successfully toured other parts of the United States, Europe and South America . . .

I went to the theater ready to be entertained, but not expecting a riot of emotion. Price and Warfield sang; they threaded their voices with music and spellbound the audience with their wizardry. Even the chorus performed with such verve that a viewer could easily believe each singer was competing for a leading part.

By intermission I had been totally consumed. I had laughed and cried, exulted and mourned, and expected the second act to produce no new emotions. I returned to my seat prepared for a repetition of great music.

The curtain rose on a picnic in progress. The revelers were church members led by a pious old woman who forbade dancing, drinking and even laughing. Cab Calloway as Sportin' Life pranced out in cream-colored suit and tried to paganize the Christians.

He sang 'It Ain't Necessarily So,' strutting as if he was speaking *ex cathedra*.

The audience applauded loudly, interrupting the stage action. Then a young woman broke away from a group of singers near the wings. She raced to the center of the stage and began to dance.

The sopranos sang a contrapuntal high-toned encouragement and baritones urged the young woman on. The old lady tried to catch her, to stop the idolatrous dance, but the dancer moved out of her reach, flinging her legs high, carrying the music in her body as if it were a private thing, given into her care and protection. I nearly screamed with delight and envy. I wanted to be with her on the stage letting the music fly through my body. Her torso seemed to lose solidity and float, defying gravity. I wanted to be with her. No, I wanted to *be* her.

In the second act, Warfield, as the crippled Porgy, dragged the audience into despair. Even kneeling, he was a large man, broad and thick-chested. His physical size made his affliction and his loss of Bess even sadder. The resonant voice straddled the music and rode it, controlling it.

I remained in my seat after the curtain fell and allowed people to climb over my knees to reach the aisle. I was stunned. *Porgy and Bess* had shown me the greatest array of Negro talent I had ever seen.

Source: Angelou 1985:126–7

Copyright © Maya Angelou 1976. Published by Virago Press 1985

definitions, though the process of call and response is seen as central to the structure of black music (ibid.: 78). It can be argued, then, that the identification of categories of black culture and black music is intimately connected to a range of social and political issues.

In order to examine these issues more closely – as well as those concerning the ascription of cultural value and authenticity – this chapter traces the development

- A critique of productivism: work, the labour process and the division of labour under capitalism.
- A critique of the state revolving around a plea for the disassociation of law from domination, which denounces state brutality, militarism and exterminism.
- A passionate belief in the importance of history and the historical process. This is presented as an antidote to the suppression of historical and temporal perception under late capitalism.

Figure 4.1 Core anti-capitalist themes in black expressive culture
Source: Gilroy 1987: 199

and meanings of blues and soul in the United States, the rise of ska and reggae in Jamaica, and the implications of rap and hip-hop culture. This will involve elaborating on the history and discussion of modernism and postmodernism. The focus here will be on 'African-American' and 'African-Caribbean' music. It is important to note that there are many other forms of 'black' music which have been relatively neglected in the sociological study of pop music or which have implicitly not been recognized as 'black'. An important exception to this trend is Oliver's edited collection (1990), where the contemporary development of styles such as Bhangra is considered (Banerji and Baumann 1990). However, this does not overcome the fact that writing on black music, often by white people, has implicitly constructed a black tradition which tends to exclude 'Asian' styles (Sharma et al. 1996). This has been highlighted by the success of performers such as Cornershop, Talvin Singh and Apache Indian, whose work foregrounds interconnections between different ethnic groups. Some have argued that rap and hip-hop music facilitates such developments, as will be examined later in the chapter. It also raises general issues of the ascription of ethnic identities and how people live them. This discussion should also be read in the context of the examination of globalization in chapter 1.

Blues and soul

In chapter 3 it was noted how rock 'n' roll developed in part from rhythm and blues (r 'n' b). Following Gillett (1983), five forms of r 'n' b can be identified in the post-Second World War period:

1 'dancehall blues'
2 'club blues'
3 'bar blues'
4 gospel
5 'group sounds'.

These distinctions illuminate the diversity of r 'n' b, which encompassed a variety of different types of music, and the connections between these forms and particular social contexts. Gillett suggests that there are a number of musical characteristics of the blues or r 'n' b. First, all the forms had a dance rhythm, which distinguished r 'n' b from post-war jazz, 'which was rarely recorded as dance music and which could therefore dispense with the convention of maintaining a particular beat throughout a song' (1983: 122–3). Second, Gillett suggests that:

> In rhythm and blues, the soloists were generally more 'selfish', concerned to express their own feelings, depending on the rest of the band to keep the beat going and the volume up while they blew their hearts out and their heads off. In jazz, there was usually more interplay between musicians, more exploration into melody and harmony, less reliance on the emotional force of the musician's tone. (Ibid.: 123)

Third, in Gillett's view, the blues entailed the communication of character on the part of the performers.

Having thus established the common features of r 'n' b, Gillett examines the nature of the five categories in some detail. He identifies three subtypes of the dancehall blues: 'big band blues; shout, scream and cry blues; and combo blues' (1983: 124). The dancehall blues, as the name suggests, were performed for large audiences as a backdrop to dancing. The large dance bands often contained a main singer and a saxophonist, whose roles became more important with the passage of time. The 'jump combos' were particularly important in the development of rock 'n' roll, leading to the popularity of performers such as Bill Haley, Chuck Berry and Fats Domino. In Gillett's account, the jump or combo blues was an exuberant music, which 'served to express whatever confidence people felt on the [US] West Coast during and after the war, the quieter club blues expressed the more dominant mood there, one tinged with despondency' (ibid.: 142). One of the first to play in this style was Nat 'King' Cole.

The bar blues developed in US cities as rural blacks migrated. In particular, much of what is familiar as the electrified blues which fed into rock 'n' roll in the 1950s, influencing rock music in the 1960s, was associated with the movement of black performers from the Mississippi Delta in the South to cities such as Memphis in Tennessee and especially to Chicago. As Guralnick explains, 'the blues came out of Mississippi, sniffed around in Memphis and then settled in Chicago where it is most likely it will peacefully live out the rest of its days' (1992: 46). This Delta style was distinctive, as Palmer suggests:

> The Mississippi Delta's blues musicians sang with unmatched intensity in a gritty, melodically circumscribed, highly ornamented style that was closer to field hollers than it was to other blues. Guitar and piano accompaniments were percussive and hypnotic, and many Delta guitarists mastered the art of fretting the instrument with a slider or bottleneck; they made the instrument 'talk' in strikingly speechlike inflections. (1981: 44)

The originators of the style tended to play and record for local audiences throughout the South, often living in a hand-to-mouth manner. They recorded their music for the local black market, though they were also recorded in a more anthropological way by 'field researchers' as representatives of a kind of 'folk music', which placed a particular connotation of 'authenticity' on music that was often commercial in its aims and context. The musicians entertained, and developed their skills, at parties and social gatherings on large southern plantations.

The style originated with Charley Patton and was developed by such figures as Son House, Robert Johnson and, perhaps most famously, Muddy Waters. Waters was born in 1915 in the Mississippi Delta, grew up in Clarksdale and played at fish fries for local audiences. Having moved north to Chicago in 1943, in the late 1940s he recorded for a label called Aristocrat, which had been formed by the Chess brothers, who were immigrants from Poland. The label was subsequently renamed Chess, and in 1950 Muddy Waters had his first 'hit':

> [This] meant you sold probably 60,000 copies in the race market and almost exclu-
> sively around Chicago, Gary, St Louis, Memphis and the South. There was no distri-
> bution on the coast, there was no radio air play, and the money that was involved
> would certainly seem small by today's inflated standards. Even so it was enough to
> make Muddy Waters a star. (Guralnick 1992: 69)

Waters continued to have hits through the 1950s, though his star waned as the decade
progressed. His work continued to influence white musicians and he was subsequently
'rediscovered' at many points. His career is important, as it illustrates a number of social
processes: first, the origination of a style in a particular local setting, though the style
may have been developed out of commercially available recordings; second, the way in
which the music was performed in social contexts for the local market; third, the movement of the music to a different, more urban, social setting; fourth, the recording of that
music for the local market; and fifth, the wider taking up of the music at various points
by different international markets. These are common processes in the development of
black music, and they will be further considered in the discussion of reggae below.

Gillett's characterization of the nature of the blues as a musical form was introduced above. Other writers have suggested that it is less easy to define its essence
than might be thought. Thus Guralnick argues:

> What is blues then? Well, it's a lot easier to keep on saying what blues is not. It isn't
> necessarily sad music. It doesn't tell a story. It neither makes nor alludes to minor
> chords. It is for the most part self-accompanied. It follows certain basis progressions
> (I–IV–V–IV–I or tonic, subdominant, dominant chord patterns). It is not a music
> of particular technical accomplishment. In the end you come back to the famil-
> iar conundrum; if you have to ask, well then you're just not going to understand.
> Because blues is little more than a feeling. And what could be more durable or more
> fleeting and ephemeral than just that? (1992: 41)

These difficulties are also brought out by the more detailed discussion of the musical
structure of the blues in the extract from Hatch and Millward (1987) reproduced in
box 4.2.

The fourth and fifth forms of r 'n' b discussed by Gillett (gospel and group sounds)
fed into the development of soul music during the 1960s. As Guralnick (1991: 21) suggests, 'the story of soul music can be seen largely as the story of the introduction of
the gospel strain into the secular world of rhythm and blues'. Soul was, in Guralnick's
account, 'Southern by definition if not by actual geography' (ibid.: 6) and centred in
three main cities: Memphis in Tennessee, Macon in Georgia, and Muscle Shoals in
Alabama (ibid.: 8). A similar story can be told for soul as for the blues, with a movement from the local to the wider international market over a very short space of
time, so that figures such as Otis Redding, James Brown and Aretha Franklin became
international stars whose work remains enduringly popular.

As with other forms, there is a variety of different soul styles, though some commentators such as Guralnick have pointed to common features. He suggests that
'soul music is a music that keeps hinting at a conclusion, keeps straining at the
boundaries – of melody and convention – that it has imposed upon itself' (1991: 7).
However, of importance from Guralnick's account is the following:

> The one other irreducible component of Southern soul music was its racial mix, and
> here, too, opinion remains divided about its precise significance. To some it is just

Box 4.2   Blues as a musical type

As a musical type the blues is not easy to describe. Traditionally, writers on the subject take the other, emotional, meaning of the term too seriously in attempts to delineate the genre. Yet for its fans the music is immediately recognizable, but via its structure rather than through its supposedly 'sorrowful' qualities. In fact, as a music the blues is no more sorrowful than, for instance, popular, art-music, hillbilly, or many 'folk' musics. Hillbilly music in particular, and especially the modern 'country and western' variety, has a far stronger tradition of overt expression of sad and sorrowful themes, in the manner of the 'tear-jerker'. Like most songs, blues reflects human life in general, though concentrating on the experiences relevant to the singer/composer and immediate audience. Blues songs are thus, not surprisingly, concerned with such topics as sexual relations, travelling, drinking, being broke, work and the lack of it, etc., etc. If there is one central emotional attitude typical of the music it is that of *irony*. And whether this represents a cathartic method for overcoming the 'blues', as many writers . . . claim, is mere psychological speculation. For the number of psychological states involved in blues singing may well be as many as there are performers. Some undoubtedly did it for the money, a normal motivation for professional entertainers. Still others quite obviously saw themselves as 'artists' with something important to give to the world (among these we would count at least Skip James, Robert Johnson and Muddy Waters).

The ironic qualities of the music have always been enhanced by the prevailing musical structure of the blues: though this has very often been described as being, wholly or partly, in a 'minor key', that is, really not an adequate representation of the music's structural properties. The melodic patterns of blues very often look like minor tunes, particularly when transcribed. Yet the aural effect, which is far more important, is one closer to harshness than to the traditional minor effect of 'sad' sounds. Thus many European and Anglo-American 'folk' songs which contain minor intervals in their melodies often look, on paper, similar to blues songs, yet when heard they sound very different. In fact many of the musics, including country and western, which do specialize in sorrowful sounds, use certain major key melodic patterns to achieve the required 'sad sound'.

The 'harsh' tonality in blues is particularly apparent in what Robert Palmer, following Muddy Waters, calls the 'deep blues', i.e. those with their roots in the Delta. These have a structure based on the 'blues pentatonic'. This mode is composed of the first, fourth and fifth tones of the scale plus 'altered' (or 'accidental') thirds and sevenths. The altered thirds and sevenths constitute what have come to be known as the 'bluenotes'. Though the 'bluenote' phenomenon is difficult to describe within the terminology of western musical theory, it constitutes a tone in between minor and major tones. That is, the major tone is 'leant on', flattening it somewhat, or the minor is sharpened in the same manner. On the guitar this can be done by bending the strings with the left hand; and on the piano an equivalent effect can be obtained by means of 'crushing' the notes (that is by playing adjacent notes at the *same time*, so blending them). The techniques required for the vocal expression of the mode are more difficult to master than many people seem to realize, and little more than a handful of those who have been recorded can be considered virtuosos. Prominent among those are Bessie Smith, Robert Johnson, Muddy Waters, Elvis Presley, Ray Charles and Aretha Franklin.

As these and a few other artists have illustrated, blues singing requires vocal range, intensity and the most delicate control. But it also requires the ability to provide subtle melodic and rhythmic improvisation. Bessie Smith's 'Gulf Coast Blues' (1923) is a wonderful demonstration of these qualities, as is Robert Johnson's 'Come On In My Kitchen' (1936), in which he shows to perfection the technique of using the guitar as a 'second voice' by matching the tones and textures of voice and guitar. And Muddy Waters's recording of 'Long Distance Call' (1951) exhibits beautifully the subtlety of vocal mannerisms involved in all the most accomplished blues singing. This is especially apparent in the first line of the final verse, as he sings

> Hear my phone ringing, sounds like a long distance call,

sliding effortlessly between the major and the 'blue' tones, with just the right mixture of hope and bitterness in his voice.

Elvis Presley may seem a surprising, even a perverse, choice to anyone who has yet to listen closely to his best work in the blues field, though few would deny the awesome qualities of his voice. Despite Presley's well-established brilliance on his *Sun* recordings, perhaps his most convincing performance as a blues vocalist is on his version of the Lowell Fulson number 'Reconsider Baby' (1960), cut during the sessions immediately following his army release.

Ray Charles and Aretha Franklin are better known as soul singers. Yet unlike many of the gospel-trained vocalists who stuck closely to the major scale in their secular performances, as in the case of Sam Cooke, Charles and Franklin have often recorded songs with melody lines based upon the blues pentatonic. Charles's 'What'd I Say' (1959) and Franklin's 'I Never Loved A Man' (1967) are perfect examples of this aspect of their work.

The melodic structure is the basic *musical* component of the country blues song. Of the three fundamental song components, *lyrics*, *melody*, and *harmony*, it is the last named that is of least importance to the genre. For country blues are typically constructed so as to maximize the compatibility of their lyrical and melodic components. Thus the central 'logic' of the music is that of 'horizontal' (i.e. melodic) rather than that of 'vertical' (i.e. harmonic) coherence. It is a particular feature of Delta blues, for instance, that vocal and guitar parts are sung and played in unison, especially in the case of recordings where the vocal part is accompanied by 'bottleneck' style guitar, wherein the voice and guitar 'echo' each other. Harmony in country blues is an embellishment, secondary to the melodic line, which has become more important as blues have increasingly been played in bands.

An all too common method of describing the 'fundamental' musical structure of blues, particularly by writers with a jazz or popular music background, is that proposing a 'typical' chord sequence. It is ubiquitously given as:

```
1st line        ---/---/---/---/
chord symbols    I     I     I     I
2nd line        ---/---/---/---/
chord symbols   IV    IV     I     I
3rd line        ---/---/---/---/
chord symbols    V    IV     I     I
```

Thus the 'typical, twelve-bar' blues is commonly described, in shorthand, as being of an AAB, I–IV–V–IV–I, form (wherein the AAB shows that the first, lyrical, line of the stanza is repeated).

However, the descriptive outline given above seriously distorts the structure of country blues. For not only does it imply that a particular harmonic progression is a crucial part of the music's structure; it also ignores the phenomenon of 'bluenotes' in the music. The more enlightened commentators at least include in such outlines symbols such as I^{7dim} and IV^{7dim} to denote the use of diminished chords. Without the addition of diminished chords the outline resembles a boogie progression rather than that of a blues. And even as an outline of boogie progressions it is little more than a very basic, practical, guide, providing a simplified 'musical map' for those who wish to strum out a boogie pattern, for instance.

Given the fundamental *melodic* nature of blues structures, the outline does not even give an adequate guide to (chordal) guitar accompaniment. Country blues often begin on the dominant (i.e. Vth) tone of the scale. Furthermore, the actual chord position used to 'cover' the vocal line can be one of several, including that of the Vth chord, confined in the outline to the third stanza. Many Delta and Chicago 'downhome' blues commence with a diminished seventh (^{7dim}) tone. These include the Muddy Waters recording of 'Long Distance Call', in respect of the stanza quoted above. A chord progression which conforms to the verbal part, as appearing on the record, could be:

```
chording:   I7dim  7ma   IV   IV7dim  IV  V
vocal:      Hear my   phone ring——ing——
chording:   V    V  IV IV   IV7dim  I
vocal:      Sounds like a long dis——tance call
```

Beginning the verse on the diminished seventh, as Muddy Waters does here, is a common feature of Delta, and Delta-derived blues. Moreover, the melodic structure of the whole line is typical of that blues strain. Thus the tune of the first two lines of the verse is noticeably similar to those of, for instance, B. B. King's 'Rock Me Mama' (1961) and Robert Johnson's 'Rambling On My Mind' (1936). The line is composed of two musical phrases the progressive structure of which conform to typical phrases of Delta blues. And the construction of blues songs by means of stringing together a number of lyrical and musical phrases has always been the basis of both continuity and change in that music.

Source: Hatch and Millward 1987: 59–63

one more variation on the old racist story: black workers, white owners. I have spoken earlier of my own confusion and my ultimate conviction that here was a partnership. But it was a partnership with a difference: the principals brought to it such divergent outlooks and experiences that even if they had grown up in the same little town, they were as widely separated as if there had been an ocean between them. And when they came together, it may well have been their strangeness to each other, as well as their familiarity, that caused the cultural explosion. (Ibid.: 10)

This returns the discussion to the theme considered at the beginning of this chapter, concerning the difficulties of clearly defining and separating black and white musics. In this section, several points have been demonstrated. First, that forms of black music have tended to develop in particular local and commercial contexts (for example, dances and bars), where a number of influences were brought together, in performances for black audiences. Second, that such forms have then been transmitted to wider audiences where they are then developed in other ways. Third, that it is possible, though often relatively difficult, to convey the precise musical texture of these forms of music. These are themes to be taken up in the next section, on ska and reggae.

Ska and reggae

Reggae developed in the 1960s in Jamaica from two previous related forms – ska and rock steady – which had themselves grown out of music popular in Jamaica earlier in the 1950s and 1960s. These were the calypso-like mento form, the drum music particularly associated with country-based Rastafarian religious groups, and the American r 'n' b sounds that were available in Jamaica from radio stations based in the southern states of the USA (Clarke 1980: 57–8; Hebdige 1987: 23–70; Jones 1988: 18–23).

Ska and rock steady, like reggae, addressed themes of importance to the everyday life of those in a less well-off position in Jamaican society. For example, in the 1960s there was a cycle of songs whose lyrics debated the rights and wrongs of the rude boy phenomenon. Musical argument about the rude boys of the West Kingston ghetto considered their morals and ethics as well as the extent to which their law-breaking could be seen as an expression of political and social protest, or whether they should be seen as murderers and thieves who were simply hurting their own people. Lyrics of the current songs took different positions on these issues.

Reggae as a specific form developed from rock steady. As Clarke explains:

> In its formation, Rock Steady began to express the specifically Jamaican experience as diversely as possible. Political protest was on the increase, but songs speaking of other themes were also part and parcel of the music scene. By 1968 Rock Steady was evidently being overtaken by another type of rhythmic invention, Reggae, which was faster and a synthesis of both Rock Steady and Ska. (1980: 96)

By the late 1960s reggae existed as a distinct musical form. At this point it began to address, in a direct fashion, themes articulated in Rastafari. There were many precursors to the development of Rasta, but perhaps the most important, and the most celebrated in the 1960s and 1970s, was the work of Marcus Garvey, a black Jamaican who formed the Universal Negro Improvement Association (UNIA) in both Jamaica

1   The belief in the divinity of Haile Selassie I. The Rasta term for God is Jah, which
    some commentators see as derived from Yahweh.
2   The characterization of white-dominated society as *Babylon*. There are obvious
    biblical reference points. Babylon can stand for different conceptions of white
    society, ranging from the society as a whole to its manifestations in particular
    oppressive agencies such as the police.
3   The centrality of Africa, though there has been debate about whether repatriation to
    Ethiopia or Africa in general actually means physical repatriation or whether it can
    be seen on a more spiritual plane, connected to other movements of Pan-Africanism.
4   The use of marijuana (ganga) as an aid to discussion and 'reasoning'. Marijuana is a
    sacred or religious plant, and is used as part of the cleansing of the body.
5   Dressing in particular ways including the growth of dreadlocks for males, the wearing
    of headscarves by women. Also important is the display of the red, gold and green
    colours of Ethiopia.
6   The following of a specific diet. A taboo on pork is as important as the attempt to
    follow what, in other cultures, might be termed an 'organic' diet.
7   A particular system of language, including the use of I-words. Thus, 'I and I' used to
    mean we, with a notion of the individual consciousness within the collectivity being
    stressed. There are a large number of I-words. Other examples include stressing the 'I'
    at the end of Rastafari.
8   A division of gender roles. The 'elevation' of the woman as the 'Queen'.

Figure 4.2 Some key features of Rastafari

and the USA in the early part of the twentieth century. Garvey and his organization
stressed black pride and ideas of repatriation or return to Africa. He formed a company called the Black Star Line, which was to purchase ships to take those who had
been forcibly removed by whites back to their African homelands.

Marcus Garvey is significant for his iteration of many themes that were to become
part of Rastafari, such as black pride and the idea of Africa as a homeland. However, his
direct significance is on a different level. As Clarke states: 'Garvey's main contribution
to the birth of Rastafari, however, was his prophecy to "Look to Africa, when a black
king shall be crowned, for the day of deliverance is near"' (1980: 38). The coronation of
Ras Tafari (Head Prince) as Haile Selassie I of Ethiopia in 1930 was seen as the answer
to Marcus Garvey's suggestion, though, as Clarke notes, Garvey might have known
rather more about the political and social situation in Ethiopia and Africa and the likely
imminence of this event than some of those who subsequently followed his words.

Some of the key themes and features of Rastafari are listed in figure 4.2 (see also
Owens 1979; Gilroy 1987). Rasta themes were increasingly articulated in reggae in the
late 1960s and the 1970s. However, it is important to recognize that there were different styles of reggae. Three different forms can be distinguished: the vocal group, the
DJ/talkover and the dub. The vocal group style is perhaps the most familiar form of
reggae; perhaps its most well-known exponents were the Wailers and the subsequent
work of Bob Marley. The vocals are foregrounded, either those of the main vocalist
or the harmony of the small group. The DJ/talkover style, where the DJ talks over the
basic rhythm track, originated in the sound systems of Jamaica, where the record

producer who controlled the sound system, providing the music at dances, produced a particular rhythm which the DJs talked over at the dance, supplying words addressing individual and social concerns. These were then subsequently recorded and issued as records in their own right. This form alerts us to the central importance of the sound system and the live experience in this form of Jamaican music, in a similar way to which the blues functioned in black communities in the southern states of the USA. In the dub form, the basic rhythm track is doctored by the producer, so that electronic tricks can be played with it. Again, this points to the importance of the record producer in Jamaican music.

Rasta themes were brought to wide prominence by the work of Bob Marley, though the mass circulation of reggae has been interpreted as another form of white exploitation of an indigenous black form. Thus Clarke quotes from an interview he conducted with a black record producer:

> Now, all this heavy Reggae music sells a lot in Afrika, but who gets the money? Virgin, Lightning. . . . There are millions of pounds that come out of Afrika, but whose pockets does it go into? The same white man that these Reggae artists sing about, that they are gonna cut his head off, down with colonialism, and up with Rastafari. Those white companies enjoy that, man, because they are using those same words to sell you and me (i.e. black people)! (1980: 168)

Reggae and ska had been popular with young white people in the late 1960s in Britain (see further, chapter 7), and the more developed, politicized and Rasta-influenced reggae was popular in the late 1970s with the followers of punk. Early ska records were reinterpreted by the 2 Tone bands in the late 1970s and early 1980s, leading to the blurring of the edges between punk and reggae. Thus, a form produced originally in a black local context achieved wide circulation. The implications of this require further consideration through specific analytic categories.

Realism, modernism, postmodernism, folk culture and reggae

Realism can be defined as consisting of three elements (Abercrombie et al. 1992). First, realist cultural forms offer a window on some kind of other world. This does not have to be 'our' world and, indeed, very often it is not, but it is a world that has plausibility for us and is coherent in everyday ways. Characters have familiar motivations. Often the constructed world is related in some way to our world. However, popular fictions construct their own world, which relates to ours, and within that world there is both coherence and plausibility. Second, realism mobilizes a particular kind of narrative which is constructed through cause and effect and which often consists of a beginning, a middle and an end. Third, realism conceals the process of its own production and the fact that it is a fiction. The audience is often encouraged to think that they have dropped in on a world that exists independently of them and the producers of it. We 'suspend disbelief', to employ the common phrase.

There are many different realisms which have developed on the basis of this essential structure. For example, in a discussion of the US television soap opera *Dallas*, Ang identifies an emotional realism which she contrasts with 'empiricist' and 'classical' realism (1986: 45). However, the basic structure of realism can be contrasted with modernism and postmodernism.

Modernism exposes a different world. Rather than acting as a window, it focuses or refracts to show different elements of a world in a new light. The familiar world is made strange; a deeper reality of a different kind is alluded to, or explored. As Featherstone (1988) explains, narrative is fractured and the familiar patterns of cause and effect are shattered or self-consciously set in juxtaposition to other forms. Modernism is authored in an important sense. The author is central as the manipulator of the language of the representation and may be central as a site for the exploration of consciousness. Language and the play of language are central. Modernism in its classical development was a creature of high culture and the late nineteenth century, related to the city and particular forms of new 'border crossing' experience (Williams 1989).

Modernism differs from postmodernism. Postmodernism does not offer a window on a separate world or encourage the search for a different reality; rather, it suggests that our own world consists of images and discourses that cannot be known in an independent fashion. Further, postmodernism suggests that the world has lost meaning, or is simply the site of a clashing of incommensurate discourses that can only be juxtaposed and not ranked in order of importance. There is no truth or reality to be found in this scenario. Narrative may be fragmented, construct a 'knowing self', or refer to a number of other texts or narratives. Different elements from different discourses or genres are placed together in one work of art. Jim Collins discusses the novel *The Name of the Rose* by Umberto Eco as a postmodernist text in this manner, explaining that:

> The Sherlock Holmes story is only one of a wide range of discourses invoked by the text. Eco intersperses A. Conan Doyle with Roger Bacon, William of Occam, and a host of diverse medieval works, along with frequent 'flash forwards' to contemporary figures (e.g. the monastery's chief librarian Jorge of Burgos, or, Jorge Borges). But the single most important intertext is 'fictional' and ironically serves as the justification of the interpenetration of detective and philosophical discourses. The key to the mystery within *The Name of the Rose*, responsible for so much murder and mayhem, is Aristotle's legendary 'lost' study of comedy, and it is this fictive text which serves to accentuate the power of discourse in and of itself. (1989: 62)

Postmodernism also plays with ideas of production and authorship. An example of this is David Byrne's film *True Stories*, a fictional documentary about a Texan town. Byrne (who led the group Talking Heads) appears as narrator of the documentary, implying control over the narrative on his part. However, he often undercuts this by foregrounding his own lack of understanding of events or by forgetting information that he wanted to convey to the audience. At points the film appears realist, but it is revealed to have been produced by the use of devices such as having Byrne step through a scenic backdrop. Authorship and production are revealed in a jokey manner.

At any one time, these forms (or ideal types) of culture may be in conflict with each other and may represent yet another form of culture which it is important to consider. This is the concept of folk culture, which has been used in diverse ways in the study of music (Middleton 1990: 127–54). In the current discussion, folk culture refers to forms of culture that are tightly linked to particular social groups and which are not subject to mass distribution, even if they are electronically reproduced. In many respects they are not realist, as they do not open a window on a different world, do not use conventional narratives of cause and effect, and do not conceal the production process. The

	Folk	Realism	Modernism	Postmodernism
World	'bounded' or local	clear window	strange	discursively
	supernatural or	secular	opaque	structured
	religious			
Narrative	episodic	cause and effect	fragmented	cause and effect
		beginning–		with incorporation
		middle–end		of other texts
Production	immediate –	concealed	foregrounded	playful +
	performance based			problematic

Figure 4.3 Ideal types of folk culture, realism, modernism and postmodernism
Source: Abercrombie et al. 1992

reggae tradition can be examined through these categories, which are summarized in figure 4.3.

The pre-ska forms identified above were essentially folk forms. This does not mean that they were unchanging, 'traditional' or 'authentic', but that they were rooted in particular social groups and specific localities. Ska was important, as it began increasingly to address social and political issues in Jamaican society. The music itself was distinctive, with a new 'jerky' sound. In this form can be found the beginnings of social realism in music in Jamaica – for example, concerning rude boys and criminality – which was to be so important during the 1960s. This direct, documentary and declamatory realism was to carry on running through Jamaican music. Themes of love and romance were played down by contrast with the earlier American r 'n' b-influenced forms (Clarke 1980: 72). This social realism was to become more and more pronounced in the mid-1960s, when the audiences for these forms were predominantly local or in the black Jamaican communities overseas, in particular in Britain. At this point, ska and Jamaican forms did begin to have a certain wider impact. For example, Chris Blackwell set up Island Records and Millie Small had a number one hit in Britain. However, despite this success, the main audience was not ultimately made up of whites but of blacks – in particular, working-class blacks. The music addressed some of the struggles of these groups directly: against the police, the upper-class forces in Jamaica and gang leaders who preyed on the community.

The music was not 'owned' by the sorts of people who played it or were its main audience, as it was controlled by entrepreneurs who produced the records and employed the musicians in an exploitative manner. Within this context, the role of the male record producer as entrepreneur and businessman was paramount. The musician was an employee. The musicians themselves may have recognized their own skills and looked to the great figures of black American jazz for their inspiration, but their own social position resembled that of an underclass of employees with little hope of considering themselves as 'artists' in the 'romantic' or 'classical' sense. Their own struggles were with their employers, to whom they had to sell their labour power. One of the essential problems for the musician, that of earning a living, was solved through a clear set of industrialized social relationships.

As has already been suggested, sound systems were also important. The latest sound was prized (as it still is) as a means of establishing a distinctive or novel feel and reputation. Through the concealment of the source of the sound, there was often an attempt to prevent quick mass distribution, though, of course, record sales were important and could be stimulated once a following for a particular track had been developed at dances. At this point, while there had been some success in Britain, the music was still a folk form in the way defined above, though the transition to realism was well under way.

The realist tradition in reggae developed during the 1960s. Importantly, the sort of social realism already discussed continued to develop as ska turned into rock steady and then into reggae. The reggae that was popular in Britain in the late 1960s was essentially a familiar sort of form. The lyrics tended to address themes of love and loss; the instrumentals were rather simple, albeit danceable, tracks that held few surprises. Themes deriving from Rastafari also increased in importance. In the early 1970s these different aspects of the form were combined in the work of the Wailers and, most importantly, in the figure of Bob Marley (Davis 1984; White 1984).

Marley and the Wailers brought together many of the different aspects so far discussed. In developing what can be called an 'international' style of reggae, the Wailers drew on Rastafarian themes and imagery and addressed social issues such as the illegality of marijuana, police harassment and the conditions of slum-dwellers, as well as the themes of love and romance. They represent the high-water mark of reggae realism.

The Wailers' music opened a window on a particular, coherent world centred in black Jamaican life, rested on narratives about oppression, exploitation and love, and increasingly concealed the manner of its own production through more sophisticated recording techniques. This last was aided by the process of international success. The smoothing off of the rough edges of the Wailers' music after they were taken up by Chris Blackwell and Island Records is well documented and is sometimes seen as a typical dilution of the music's power for commercial purposes. However, it can also be described as an essential part of the perfection of the realist reggae form. Furthermore, the music was packaged in a way that made it more acceptable to those who were used to the form and content of Anglo-American rock, which had itself moved through a realist phase in the 1960s (Goodwin 1991: 178).

A further important aspect of this process should be noted. Increasingly, Bob Marley was marketed as an international star, which no doubt precipitated the split of the original Wailers, as the other two founder members (Peter Tosh and Bunny Wailer) were left behind. This process rested on the promotion of Marley as an artist in a way that had been relatively unfamiliar in the reggae tradition up to that point, but which paralleled the usage of such ideas employed in Western art traditions. Marley was seen as the creative genius behind the originality of the Wailers' music. During the 1970s various other artists were promoted in this way, which can be seen as central to the strategies of the international music industry as described in chapters 1 and 2, though many seemed rather uncomfortable in the role (for further discussion of the construction of pop music stars through video, see chapter 5).

By the mid- to late 1970s, reggae had taken off as a recognized international style that would be 'marketed internationally as reggae' (Gilroy 1993: 95), and it was particularly successful. It had moved into the album market and was integrated into the white mainstream. Its own concerns and focus were developed to the highest realist point. The texts sought to open a window on a particular world, utilized narrative lines that were structured by conventional understandings of cause and effect and which reached conclusions or closure, and which seemed to be produced in a seamless manner, concealing the complexity of production.

Such developments leave those who wish to innovate with two main options: either to carry forward the realist strategy that had been so successful for Marley or to do something rather different. Some acts were promoted in ways that approached the former strategy, but innovators tended to move in the latter direction, extending developments which had been happening parallel to the consolidation of realism in reggae.

During the 1970s and into the 1980s, various reggae artists developed modernist forms. These were often based in some aspects of the forms that predated the realist phase. From the centrality of the sound system developed the two forms that encapsulate the modernist movement in reggae: dub and the DJ talkover.

In the dub style, there is play with sound itself. Rather than being smooth and developing in a familiar fashion, the music became disjointed and 'difficult' in ways that paralleled similar developments in art forms such as the novel and 'classical' music. Attention is directed to the form itself. The familiarity of the reggae sound is made strange, and attention is drawn to the role of the producer in the production of such strangeness. It is the artist as expert with sound that is important rather than as the commentator on romantic or social issues. Artistic experiment with the form is valued for its own sake; as with modernist art, it is the form that is the focus.

The second style did similar things, though the focus was on the voice rather than the sound. The toaster would follow his or her inclinations in voicing over the often familiar rhythm track. These words possessed a degree of narrative, but key phrases were often repeated and drawn attention to. Language itself became important rather than being a means to represent something else of political or emotional importance.

Neither of these styles constructs or represents clearly any particular world, and the previous worlds constituted by reggae were dismantled and made strange in important ways. Narrative was broken and cause and effect of the rational kind are downplayed. Production and the role of the sound or language artist moved to the forefront.

Modernism in reggae does not simply follow on from realism in a straightforward sense, as variants evolved simultaneously. However, it is important to recognize the role of social and cultural struggle in these processes. The reggae artist, like all cultural producers, needs money to continue in operation and, above all, requires an audience to sustain a flow of finance. There are different strategies available to gain money and an audience. One way is to try to do something different from that which is already being done. However, in some respect innovation has to be based on what already exists. In the case of modernist reggae, this involves the resources of the tradition itself, the growing dominance of realist reggae and technical resource, such as the increasingly sophisticated recording technology. The modernist forms set themselves against the dominant realist tradition by using assets from the (folk) past, including key vocal phrases, biblical imagery and mythical themes filtered through the new technical developments. At this point, an avant-garde developed which took forward the claims of reggae as experimental. It could then be claimed, as a form of legitimation, that this was a more real form of reggae than the increasingly mass-accepted international style popularized by Marley and the Wailers. In this way the notion of the real might be used to ground a form that was moving away from the currently popular realist conventions.

Since the 1980s, as with other forms of popular music, there has been a mixing of reggae styles with soul (Hebdige 1987: 153–6), with rock and with dance music, not in a way that integrates them harmoniously but in a manner that allows the different discourses they entail to intertwine. It would be possible to analyse records such as Smiley Culture's 'Cockney Translation' (ibid.: 149–53; Gilroy 1987: 194–7), which plays with the relationship between white cockney speech and black patois, in a manner similar to Collins's consideration of *The Name of the Rose* mentioned above. Increasingly, discourses clash and 'mix' without one being the master or claiming dominance in a straightforward fashion (Collins 1989). The world has taken on a new complexity and an external view is not constructed; the music is within discourses that do not reflect the determination of cause and effect, but which are multiplied and multi-accented. Different ideas are juxtaposed. Production is not directly revealed or consciously elaborated, but neither is it concealed in the manner of realism. Rather, there is a play with production which is almost taken for granted. As the audience has become more aware of the process by which texts are put together, there is more fun to be had by playing on that knowledge. The consideration of this mixing of discourses can be developed through the examination of the development of hip-hop music since the 1980s.

Hip-hop and rap

The example of hip-hop allows further consideration of a number of issues that have run through this chapter so far. Since the rise to prominence of hip-hop from the late 1970s, an extensive literature has developed on the form. This has been summarized in seven broad areas: the history of hip-hop; authenticity; space and place; gender; politics and resistance; technology; and the culture industries (see Forman and Neal 2012). In this section I follow this logic and address these themes. It should also be remembered that some of these themes have already been considered elsewhere (see chapter 1 for hip-hop in the music industry and chapter 2 for discussion of the technologically informed nature of the making of hip-hop).

A particularly clear and influential discussion of the key issues around rap music has been written by Rose, whose contribution continues to be of ongoing importance. Rose's analysis is multilayered and examines a number of key issues already discussed above, but it emphasizes three key themes. These concern, first, the social and geographical context of the emergence of rap and hip-hop in New York City; second, the way in which rap is a development of 'traditions' in black culture; and, third, how new technology has facilitated the particular inflections that appear in rap. However, rap is not a radical departure from earlier forms of black expressive culture. Its key features, such as the way that it breaks the flow of the music and vocal yet rebuilds it through the layers of its construction, are based on such practices in other fields of cultural creation. Rose discusses how these processes of 'flow, layering and ruptures in line' (1994: 38) have been affected by the development of the sorts of new technology and processes discussed in chapter 2, leading to a number of stylistic innovations.

Rose also points to the work of a number of female rappers and discusses the importance of the way that rap and hip-hop consist of dialogue between different points of view. At times, this can take the form of boasting, which in itself can have extremely violent consequences for participants in the process, as the history of murder around hip-hop culture demonstrates. These processes around the dialogic nature of black popular music and culture have been extensively surveyed by such as Neal (1999).

Hip-hop and rap music came to wider prominence in 1979, though their roots can be found in other black musics (Toop 1984). Rap and hip-hop musics were a part of a wider hip-hop culture in New York, which included particular modes of dress, language, and so on. The music developed from DJs merging different records and sounds together in a way which seemed startling at the time but which now has become a part of everyday pop music, especially as it has been facilitated by the sorts of technology described in chapter 2. Experiments in sound and voice in rap were in part influenced by the Jamaican developments (Cross 1993: 15). However, one of the things that is distinctive about rap is the eclectic mix of elements. Toop quotes one of the pioneers of the style, Afrika Bambaataa, on his mixing strategy in the illuminating passage reproduced in box 4.3.

Rap had been developing through the 1970s before the first commercial records were released in 1979. These were a surprise to those at the core of the hip-hop scene, who were themselves quickly taken up by record companies and had their own records released. One of the key titles which exemplified the hip-hop cut-up style was 'The Adventures of Grandmaster Flash on the Wheels of Steel', by Grandmaster Flash (1981). As Toop explains, this is 'a devastating collage of Queen, Chic, The Sugarhill Gang's "8th Wonder", The Furious Five's "Birthday Party", Sequence and Spoonie Gee's "Monster Jam" and Blondie's "Rapture". It also overlaid a Disney-sounding story, the source of which Flash is keeping a firm secret' (1984: 106).

The sources of much of the material used in these recordings could be surprising. However, Toop suggests that the strategies involved elaborated black traditions:

> An underground movement indirectly inspired by a Cliff Richard percussion break might give the impression of a lemming-like abandonment of black traditions, but in a perverse way these cut-ups of unlikely records, whether by The Monkees or Yellow Magic Orchestra, were a recreation of the forthright emotion that at times looked like becoming a rarity in the mainstream of black music. They were a way of tearing the associations and the pre-packaging from the finished musical product and reconstructing it, ignoring its carefully considered intentions and restitching it into new music. As the process of recording music became increasingly fragmented in the 70s – a drum track laid down in Muscle Shoals, a back-up vocal in California, a lead voice in New York – so the implication began to exist that consumers might eventually be able to rejig a track according to their own preferences. (1984: 115)

At the same time as these experiments in sound and voice were taking place, there was a direct address to political issues in rap. As the name suggests, these were often raps about issues such as the denigration of black history and the current exploitation of black people (Gilroy 1987: 182–7). This had been a significant presence in American black culture from the late 1960s onwards. The soul tradition had taken such issues to wide prominence – for example, in the work of James Brown – and those artists politicized during the 1960s, such as the Last Poets and Gil Scott-Heron, directly confronted what were in their view the realities of black life. Thus, Scott-Heron's debut album, *Small Talk and 125th and Lennox* from 1970, contains some

Box 4.3   Afrika Bambaataa's mixing strategy

When I came on the scene after him I built in other types of records and I started getting a name for master of records. I started playing all forms of music. Myself, I used to play the weirdest stuff at a party. Everybody just thought I was crazy. When everybody was going crazy I would throw a commercial on to cool them out – I'd throw on *The Pink Panther* theme for everybody who thought they was cool like the Pink Panther, and then I would play 'Honky Tonk Woman' by the Rolling Stones and just keep that beat going. I'd play something from metal rock records like Grand Funk Railroad. 'Inside Looking Out' is just the bass and drumming . . . rrrrrmmmmmmmm . . . and everybody starts freaking out.

I used to like to catch the people who'd say, 'I don't like rock. I don't like Latin.' I'd throw on Mick Jagger – you'd see the blacks and the Spanish just *throwing* down, dancing crazy. I'd say, 'I thought you said you didn't like rock.' They'd say, 'Get out of here.' I'd say, 'Well, you just danced to the Rolling Stones.' 'You're kidding!'

I'd throw on 'Sergeant Pepper's Lonely Hearts club Band' – just that drum part. One, two, three, BAM – and they'd be screaming and partying. I'd throw on the Monkees, 'Mary Mary' – just the beat part where they'd go 'Mary, Mary, where are you going?' – and they'd start going crazy. I'd say, 'You just danced to the Monkees'. They'd say, 'You liar. I didn't dance to no Monkees'. I'd like to catch people who categorize records . . .

In the who-dares-wins delirium of the house parties, Bambaataa mixed up calypso, European and Japanese electronic music, Beethoven's Fifth Symphony and rock groups like Mountain; Kool DJ Herc spun the Doobie Brothers back-to-back with the Isley Brothers; Grandmaster Flash overlaid speech records and sound effects with the Last Poets; Symphonic B Boys Mixx cut up classical music on five turntables, and a multitude of unknowns unleashed turntable wizardry with their feet, heads, noses, teeth and tongues. In a crazy new sport of disc jockey acrobatics, musical experiment and virtuosity were being combined with showmanship. Earlier in black music history the same potent spirit had compelled Lionel Hampton to leap onto his drums, Big Jay McNeely to play screaming saxophone lying on the stage and the guitar aces – T Bone Walker, Earl Hooker, Johnny Guitar Watson and Jimi Hendrix – to pick the strings with their teeth or behind their heads.

Source: Toop 1984: 65–6, 105

of the themes that continued to run through his later output in tracks such as 'The Revolution Will Not be Televised' and 'Whitey on the Moon'. Scott-Heron's work was partly born from forms of oral poetry and his early music was minimalist. However, as it developed it worked in soul and jazz genres rather than connecting to hip-hop.

The work of Public Enemy, especially the albums *It takes a Nation of Millions to Hold Us Back* (1988) and *Fear of a Black Planet* (1990) and the track 'Fight the Power' (1989), directly confronted exploitation and oppression. For Dery: '[This work is] haunted by the ghosts of slaves flogged to death, Southern blacks lynched on trumped-up charges of raping white women, civil rights activists killed by Klansmen, Michael Stewart beaten to death by New York City Transit Police, Michael Griffith chased into the headlights of an oncoming car in Howard Beach and Yusef Hawkins shot in Besonhurst' (2004: 408). Moreover, as Rodman discusses at some length, this is also an attack on white music icons:

> 'Fight the Power' is nothing less than a call to arms – made by the most outspoken and militant rap group in contemporary popular music – against the ideas, institutions, and practices that maintain the political, social and cultural inequalities between whites and blacks in the US today. The song served as the musical centrepiece of *Do the Right Thing* (1989), Spike Lee's critically acclaimed film depicting twenty-four hours of racial tension in a predominantly black Brooklyn neighbourhood, and it subsequently appeared on Public Enemy's best-selling album, *Fear of a Black Planet*. 'Fight the Power' is probably the most widely known and recognized of all Public Enemy's songs, and its most frequently quoted lyrics are undoubtedly those concerning Elvis:

> Elvis was a hero to most
> But he never meant shit to me
> He's straight up racist
> That sucker was simple and plain
> Motherfuck him *and* John Wayne. (Rodman 1996: 44)

Perhaps the paradox here is that, despite such sentiments (or perhaps because of them), this music has been very successful with young white people (see below).

As hip-hop developed, music from the West Coast of the USA, and in particular Los Angeles, became more prominent (Cross 1993). The success of Niggaz with Attitude (NWA) was a key moment in the development of hip-hop. Their album *Straight Outta Compton* (1989) was widely commercially successful and also led to many of the questions that have been posed about 'gangsta rap', in particular about the way in which social and political concerns of African Americans were being examined in the form, the misogyny of the raps and the violence that was seemingly advocated by the participants.

These directions have continued as the form developed from the 1980s onwards, when it has been the lyrics of rap that have led to a range of controversies, especially over the way in which rap records have been held to promote violent solutions to black problems, to exhibit a kind of gang world-view and to denigrate women. This led to widespread news coverage of the music and the type of story reproduced in box 4.4, which have set many of the terms of mainstream debate about this type of music and culture. It is significant that this sort of 'concern' continues to play out. Thus, for example, in the context of urban riots in England in August 2011, comments on the late-night news analysis BBC TV programme *Newsnight* on 12 August 2011 by David Starkey caused controversy, as he commented that 'black' and gangster culture had become fashionable.

Beyond the level of drawing associations between violence and the music genre, by the media as well as by specific music culture participants, the real violence that was perpetrated by those involved has been a source of much controversy. As Kitwana argues:

> Probably no other event in rap's history has received as much coverage in the mainstream media as the so-called East Coast/West Coast beef–imagined and real

Box 4.4   Jay-Z at Hackney Weekend: but does hip-hop degrade or enhance?

'Success never smelled so sweet, I stink of success.' The lines by rapper and music mogul Jay-Z, who topped the bill at the BBC's Hackney Weekend festival on Saturday, are no vainglorious boast. From dealing crack on a Brooklyn housing project to an estimated personal worth of $450m (£288m), the rapper embodies the modern rags-to-riches tale. His stratospheric success reflects the evolution of a genre born on the impoverished streets of New York which now dominates the global music charts and cultural consciousness – a multiplatinum-plated success story at risk, critics argue, of drowning in its own excess.

Even as the 50,000-strong crowd recovers from seeing a lineup that throbbed with talent from both sides of the Atlantic, behind the scenes a heavyweight group of hip-hop artists, intellectuals and critics is asking: does rap enhance or degrade society?

Billed as the 'first ever global debate on hip-hop', speakers from rapper KRS-One to Victorian literature expert and hip-hop fan John Sutherland, David Cameron's youth adviser Shaun Bailey and hip-hop convert Jesse Jackson will gather at the Barbican on Tuesday for a debate organised by Intelligence Squared in partnership with Google+, bringing in voices from around the world via the company's 'hangout' technology. They will ask whether hip-hop is 'the authentic voice of the oppressed that turns anger into poetry and political action', or a 'glorification of all that holds back oppressed minorities and hinders them from mainstream assimilation'.

The Hackney Weekend's lineup proved that hip-hop artists have little difficulty finding their mainstream flow. On Saturday night, Nicki Minaj spat her brand of hip-hop pop before Jay-Z took to the stage, while on Sunday Britain's Plan B – back in the arms of his first love, hip-hop, having left the crooning and smart suits of his Strickland Banks era behind him –, Professor Green and Tinie Tempah will warm the stage by the Olympic Park for headliner Rihanna. 'This is hip-hop's moment,' said 1Xtra DJ and hip-hop artist Charlie Sloth. 'For the BBC to acknowledge that hip-hip is the dominant force in modern culture is huge.'

Last week, Ben Cooper, head of Radio 1, said of the Hackney Weekend: 'We're going into an area that I don't think any commercial operator would have gone into after the unrest of last year. That is the job of the BBC.'

Sloth added that local boys Labrinth – born and raised with nine siblings in Hackney – and Tottenham rapper Wretch 32 playing alongside stars like Jay-Z would send a positive message to the crowd, many of them residents of one of London's poorest boroughs, who were given priority in the ballot for free tickets. 'Seeing these artists up there, coming from the same place as they come from – it gives them hope, it shows what they can achieve.'

But for youth worker turned government youth adviser Shaun Bailey, the gangster lifestyle vaunted by some rappers creates a lack of respect for the black community. 'You've got a few people who do live a fug-life, a gangster life, and everybody else with their faces pressed up against the glass. They get to see it all, they get to hear it all but they don't have to suffer any of the consequences, any of the danger,' he said, in a video trailing the debate. 'It says to our young people, someone messes with you – blow their head off, literally. And you need to ask yourself: are we building massive hip-hop revenues on the backs of our young dead people?'

It is an argument echoed by Jason Whitlock, columnist for Fox Sports, who has declared categorically ahead of the event that 'hip-hop culture is dead'. Hijacked by 'prison culture' it now exists only to celebrate 'drug dealing, killing, disrespect, disrespect of women, sexism', he argues.

While blatant examples of misogyny abound in hip-hop – a recent line from Jay-Z and Kayne West's That's My Bitch boasts 'I paid for them titties, get your own' – there is space within the genre to challenge the sexism, according to dream hampton, co-author of Jay-Z's bestselling book Decoded. 'Is mainstream hip-hop sexist? Absolutely,' she said, in a phone interview from the US.

'But that is not the whole story – there are as many bitches and hos in the Bible as in hip-hop, but you can't have that conversation with a pastor. In hip-hop patriarchy can be discussed, confronted and laid bare, where others hide behind civil discourse and censure.' Others are likely to point out that hip-hop (the only genre to put such a 'terrific premium on linguistic inventiveness', according to Sutherland) now covers such a vast cultural and geographical space it is impossible to come down on either side of the argument. Speaking from Egypt, where he is at the vanguard of a small army of artists hoping to use rap's energy to document the Arab spring, rapper Deeb said hip-hop remained the genre of the underprivileged and oppressed and the act of posting a hip-hop track on YouTube was still 'a social and political' act. 'If there is a soundtrack to the Arab spring, I think hip-hop will have a few tracks on the CD,' he said.

But it's the turbo-charged bling of hip-hop – its obsession with private jets, designer labels and excess so at odds with the reality experienced by the majority of its fans – which leaves artists like 50 Cent and Jay-Z mere 'salesmen of commodity capitalism', according to Tricia Rose, professor of Africana studies at Brown University and author of The Hip Hop Wars. 'It's promoting a fiction, a fallacy of success that buys into a racist and corrupt system, where freedom and justice rarely feature,' she said.

Yet there was a danger of the debate becoming polarised, and useful debate being lost in the noise, she added. 'You're either a player or a hater,' she said. 'Blind attacks on hip-hop are used to justify a broad set of attacks on poor minority communities, but on the other hand few people in that world want to be critical of the negative influence of commercial hip-hop. The conversation is muted by that player/hater dialectic.'

Hackney-born Radio 1 DJ Trevor Nelson, when asked if he thought hip-hop enriched or degraded society, said: 'If we're going to be honest it does both – the beauty of hip-hop is that if you want to party, you can. If you want to preach, you can. There's no hip-hop committee. It's a free voice that goes straight to the point.' Despite the brashness and the bombast, the boasting and the bling, hip-hop remains a medium of expression for those with no voice in society, insisted 1 Xtra's Sloth. While Saturday's audience screamed to Jay-Z lyrics such as 'What's 50 grand to a muthafucka like me?', on Sunday they will hear Plan B's searing critique of post-riots Britain, Ill Manors: 'There's no such thing as broken Britain/We're just bloody broke in Britain/What needs fixing is the system/not shop windows down in Brixton.'

Whatever the debate concludes, for Sloth hip-hop is still the 'soundtrack to the struggle' and one we should get used to hearing. 'People thought the popularity of hip-hop was a phase,' he said. 'But it's more than that: it's a lifestyle – and it's here to stay.'

Source: Alexandra Topping, *The Guardian*, 24 June 2012

> antagonism between rappers and fans on the East Coast (mostly New York City) and the West Coast (mostly rappers and fans in Los Angeles). The conflict, which in print often centered on rap labels Death Row and Bad Boy, climaxed with the gangland-style murders of Tupac Shakur in 1996 and Biggie Smalls in 1997. In the wake of their deaths, many rappers participated in efforts to end the seemingly out-of-control antagonisms. From a rapper summit called by Louis Farrakhan's Nation of Islam to rap lyrics denouncing the East–West feud, rappers like Nas, Jay-Z, Common, Snoop, and others succeeded in reducing East–West antagonism. (2012: 458)

A theme that this sort of dispute and representation captures well is that of place and space. As has been considered, many of the discussions of the early days of rap and hip-hop place it very clearly in New York City. For Rose (1994), for example, hip-hop emerges in the context of the deindustrialization of the inner city area of the South Bronx, which had also been significantly affected by the construction of new roads to facilitate commuting from the suburbs into the business and commercial areas of the city. This has been a continuing theme. As Forman suggests, 'a particular image of hip-hop has been circulated, one that binds locale, resistance, innovation, affirmation, and cultural identity within a complex web of spatialized meanings and practices' (2012: 225; and see more generally Forman 2002). Moreover:

> The tales of originary sites of significance that describe local places and place-based activities emerge as crucial indicators for the shaping of attitudes and identities among hip-hop's entrepreneurs, including Def Jam founder Russell Simmons, James Smith of Rap-A-Lot Records, or Bad Boy Entertainment creator Sean 'Diddy' Combs, as well as among artists such as Eminem whose dysfunctional upbringing on Detroit's 8 Mile Road is now legendary. We might ask, can Jay Z be realistically disconnected from Brooklyn or Nas from Queens? Can Snoop Dogg be comprehended without acknowledging his Long Beach, California, roots, and can OutKast, the Goodie Mob or T.I. be isolated from Atlanta? Where these individuals are from is an essential element of who they are and what they project, whether in a broader regional sense of space or in the more finely nuanced and closely delineated scale of place. (Forman 2012: 225–6)

Space in general and specific places in particular are important as 'real' and as 'cultural' or imagined in hip-hop. Many of these meanings have been condensed in the idea of the 'hood' or 'neighbourhood'. This signals real places and forms of community and linkage as well as conflicts within local spaces. However, it can be asked how significant these specific meanings are as hip-hop has become globally successful. For example, while the meanings of OutKast may be linked to their origins in

Atlanta, an album such as *Speakerboxxx/The Love Below* (2003) was a top-ten hit in both the USA and UK in 2003–4, as was the single 'Hey Ya!' that was on it. The album was reviewed in the UK as a significant double album, often related to Prince's *Sign o' the Times* (1987) as well as efforts such as Bob Dylan's *Blonde on Blonde* (1966), The Beatles' *White Album* (1968) and the Rolling Stones' *Exile on Main Street* (1972). Thus, this work is located in a much broader context of other black music (see below) and the canon of 'rock'.

This also raises issues of authenticity and connections between social groups and modes of expression. Stephens (1992) has argued that, rather than advocating a kind of black separatism, rap actually creates a form of interracial dialogue. In his view, as whites and Latinos have become involved in rap-like forms, there has been the creation of new languages and a form of multiculturalism (see also Cross 1993; Bennett 2000). In advancing an argument that music cannot be seen as racially 'owned', Stephens notes the way in which black rap has borrowed from white sources and the pride in 'multicultural identity' advanced by Latino rappers. He offers an optimistic account of the development of the rap form, which he sees as a kind of 'transnational' or 'transcultural' form. His conclusion captures the essence of this argument:

> 'Black' music acts like a 'wave' at sporting events: once the wave starts rolling, you can't ask people not to stand up. When the call-and-response starts cooking, you can't pick and choose who's going to answer. It seems to me that instead of trying to draw colour lines around our music, we ought to be proud that black grooves are writing the bass lines to a new multicultural song. (Stephens 1992: 79)

In hip-hop, white rappers such as Third Base and Tony D, biracial rappers such as Rebel MC and Neneh Cherry, Latino Rappers such as Kid Frost and Black rappers such as KROne all use black music and liberation theory as a base. But they use this tradition inclusively. The outcrop can no longer be defined along colour lines. With this mutually created language, participants can engage in 'negotiation strategies' through which they can 'transcend the trappings of their respective cultures'. This dialogic discourse provides a model of our movement towards the cultural crossroads where we can truly come to know what diversity means.

The success of white rappers such as Eminem, whose work was produced by Dr Dre, previously a member of NWA, can perhaps be seen in these terms. Other examples that can be thought to illustrate these processes are the work of the Sudanese rapper Emmanuel Jal and the London based MIA. In this sense, a form of music that was originally located in place and sought to address issues of that place has become a global resource for the articulation of other themes and connected to other musical traditions. The success of artists such as 50 Cent, with connections to Dr Dre and Eminem, reinforces the point that, while this music retains themes that would have been at home in earlier stages of hip-hop, it can sell in very large quantities to a differentiated audience (see also Miller 2012; Perry 2012; Perullo 2012; Veran 2012).

In a more critical discussion, Irving has argued that 'much black music, which works to construct a space for the self-dependent black male subject, has excluded spaces for the construction of alternative femininities. This is especially true of rap music' (1993: 107). Irving argues that rap's exclusivity, which does not completely exclude white men, works against women. She contrasts this American situation with that found in contemporary British black music, which she suggests is far more open to a 'multi-subjectivity'. For Irving, the sexist and misogynistic terminology used in rap enables white male critics to identify with the black male position: 'Over and over, rapping is described in violent and phallic terms and, amongst both critics and performers, the sexism is a deliberate ploy to keep women off the turf' (ibid.: 114). She argues that this sort of male exclusionary practice can and has been overcome through some female rap records, such as those by M. C. Lyte and Roxanne Shante, which construct different positions for women. Irving's article is one of the most developed analyses of gender address and politics in this form of music.

In a rather more positive assessment of rap, Swendenberg (1992) argues that the form has been particularly successful in articulating a political message within the context of a mass-circulated form. Thus, rap constructs and reconstructs a black community which reinterprets the pre-existing forms of culture, in a far more radical way than punk, in a widely circulating form of music. However, Swendenberg neglects the sorts of argument that have been made about gender identified above, as well as the homophobia which he finds in much rap music, which he sees as 'shortcomings'.

Such debates have continued as rap and hip-hop music have become globally popular, being taken up and sometimes reconstituted in a wide range of places and spaces (see, for example Bennett 2000: 133–65). Hip-hop has therefore moved far beyond its origins in New York City and its subsequent development in Los Angeles. It has become a resource for a range of different artists and approaches. Thus, in addition to the female rappers considered by Rose and Irving, artists such as Missy Elliott have been successful. In working with the producer Timbaland, Elliott has addressed a range of concerns in the context of music that has often been very innovative. Moreover, the work of a range of artists, such as Mary J. Blige, who in many respects develop the soul tradition also incorporate aspects from rap and hip-hop (see Forman 2012).

While these moves have opened the way for various forms of rap and hip-hop, there has also been debate about the way in which these musics have been appropriated by the culture industries. This is a common theme in the discussion of popular music, as has been considered in this book. On one level, as Neal suggests: 'For some rappers, hip-hop's engagement with the mainstream has forced them to renegotiate between long-standing narratives within the black community that have equated mainstream acceptance with "selling out" and basic desires to craft a lifestyle out of their skills as visibility as rap artists' (2012: 632). However, with the increasing development of popular music artists as 'brands' (see chapter 1), they have further branched out into commercial activities (see e.g. Blair 2004; Hess 2012; Holmes Smith 2012). There has been discussion of hip-hop groups as corporate entities in this context. As Negus points out:

> Many rap musicians have recognized such connections and formed their own successful companies. Notable here is Wu-Wear, the clothing and accessory company established by the Wu-Tang Clan. This company have stores throughout the United States where you can purchase T-shirts, socks, baggy jeans, coffee mugs and key-chains, all featuring the distinctive Wu-Bat brand logo. (1999: 100)

The position of the texts of rap and hip-hop has therefore moved in a number of different directions. There has been a clear sense in which hip-hop has become part of 'mainstream' musical and commercial culture. As Kusek and Leonhard suggest: 'Hip-hop artists Simmins, L. L. Cool J., Missy Elliott, Eminem, Ludacris, Nelly, Sean Combs, and Jay-Z have shown corporate America that hip-hop can generate substantial dollars outside the recorded music industry' (2005: 118).

Conclusion

The discussion in this chapter suggests that ideal types of different cultural forms can be used in the analysis of black music. In particular, this was shown through the example of reggae music. However, a similar narrative could be developed for jazz. Thus, for example, Heble notes that 'jazz, developing from the early diatonic (and, if I can put it this way, realist) styles of ragtime, New Orleans, and Dixieland, has moved through the chromaticism of bebop and the modernism of atonality and free collective improvisation into what might be seen as more recent (postmodern) attempts at rehistoricization' (2000: 13). In addition, Peterson (1972), in a classic article, located the development of jazz in the relationships between folk, pop and fine art music (see also chapter 6).

The specific black forms were connected to social locations and social movements (see also, for example, DeVeaux 1997). In these locations, distinctive themes were often articulated which express, according to Gilroy (1987), some core aspects of black culture (see also, for example, Heble 2000; and Neal 1999). Such themes can sometimes facilitate dialogue between different ethnic groups, leading to the generation of new musical forms, such as Asian rap. These forms tend to have value ascribed to them because of their authenticity. However, this does raise problematic issues concerning the extent to which any artist can speak for a community. The discussion has been predicated on social definitions of black rather than essentialist forms, and has taken account of the wider social and political meanings of blackness. There remain problems with such descriptions. It may be that often used categorizations of black slide over and eradicate important social and political differences between different racial and gendered identities. The examination of rap brings some of these matters to the foreground, prompting consideration, for example, of the relation between 'black' and 'chicano' and male and female identities. In this respect, consideration of rap and the current fluidity of the relations between different musical forms further illuminates the discussion of politics and identity introduced in chapter 3 and exemplified through the discussion of Madonna. The valuation of the 'black' identities constructed for men by 'gangsta' rap or pornographic videos may be problematic for women (of all races), illuminating the complexity of contemporary cultural politics.

It is important to recognize that the discussion of 'black' music in this chapter has shown the importance of the consideration of different genres, but also how these genres have influenced each other. Thus, in his discussion of the group God's Property in a post-industrial soul context, Neal argues: "The group's mission was blatantly apparent on their first single release, a remix of the song "Stomp" which featured a bass line appropriated from Funkadelic's "One Nation Under a Groove" and liberal use of urban slang, Christian doctrine, and the stimulated gunshots, which had become popular in many Dancehall reggae recordings' (1999: 171).

This sort of context has increasingly informed the discussion of pivotal figures such as Miles Davis. Substantial considerations of Davis's electric music from the late

1960s onwards (e.g. Tingen 2001; Freeman 2005; Mandel 2008) discuss it in relation to the work of Jimi Hendrix and Sly Stone, for example, and show that it moved well beyond the boundaries of jazz. In addition, there were attempts at collaborations between Davis and Prince: Davis's last album showed the influence of hip-hop, and so on. However, much of Davis's work was also carried out in collaboration with the white arranger Gil Evans and producer Teo Macero and has been remixed by dance producers. It is significant that this music can increasingly be examined in such a wide context. In a number of ways this shows the progression of the study of popular music away from stereotypes to a situation where the specifics of contexts can be recognized.

Summary

This chapter has considered:

- the nature of 'black music' and some of the issues raised by the use of this concept;
- the textual development of blues and soul in the USA and the social contexts for these forms;
- the textual development of reggae in social context, utilizing distinctions between folk, realism, modernism and postmodernism, elaborating the arguments of chapter 2;
- the development of rap in its social context and some of the issues raised by this.

5 Text and Meaning

Chapter 5 is concerned with the ways in which pop music creates and conveys meaning. It involves examining, first, what conveys meaning; second, how meaning is conveyed; and, third, who conveys meaning. These threads run through the chapter, which begins with a consideration of how the established discipline of musicology has treated pop music. This is followed by a discussion of the way in which concepts deriving from structuralism and semiotics have been used in the study of the texts of popular music, which in turn leads into an examination of the relationship between words and music in the conveyance of musical meaning. Debates relating to musical meaning and the visual have been extended by the appearance in the 1980s of music video. Video is examined in some length in this chapter by contrasting the accounts of Kaplan (1987) and Goodwin (1993), before being revisited in the context of Web 2.0, marked by the participatory culture of co-creation as well as shifting motivations of the participants. This discussion therefore has more general provenance in the consideration of the relationship between music and visuals both in the creation of meaning and in the dual status of the music video as a cultural form (text) and a 'tool' for social interaction.

Musicology and pop music

Several writers have pointed to the way in which musicology, because of its origins in the study of Western classical music, neglects pop music. Middleton (1990), in an analysis that remains of significant importance (Griffiths 1999), suggests three areas where musicology has problems with the study of pop music. First is the terminology used in the musicological approach. According to Middleton, musicology uses value-laden terms such as harmony and tonality to the neglect of ideas such as rhythm and timbre. Furthermore, these terms are not used in a neutral fashion. In Middleton's view, a term such as melody suggests something to be valued, whereas tune suggests an everyday banal form:

> These connotations are ideological because they always involve selective, and often unconsciously formulated, conceptions of what music is. If this terminology is applied to other forms of music . . . [for instance, non-Western or pop forms] . . . clearly the results will be problematical. In many kinds of popular music, for example, harmony may not be the most important parameter; rhythm, pitch gradation, timbre and the whole ensemble of performance articulation techniques are often more important. (1990: 104)

Second, Middleton argues that there are problems with methodology, particularly in the use of notation in musicology. This leads to an emphasis on those parts of music that can be written down using conventional notation. However, many non-classical musics have features that cannot be expressed through the forms generated for the notation of European classical music. Furthermore, the focus on notation leads to the valuation of the score as representing what the music actually is. Again, this is not applicable in a direct way to other forms of music, where a score may not exist or where, as is the case with some pop music, it is created after the music has been recorded and marketed. Indeed, Middleton suggests that, 'Even in notated popular music – Tin Pan Alley ballad, music hall, vaudeville and minstrel songs, ragtime and nineteenth-century dances – the published sheet music, almost always for piano and voice and piano, sometimes 'simplified', acted to some extent as a prognostic device or a beside-the-fact spin-off' (ibid.: 106). The analyst who simply focused on the text of a pop song as written down with notes on a score would miss a number of the different ways in which such music creates meaning, including, for example, the nature of the performance given of the song. A number of these different dimensions to the creation of meaning are explored as this chapter progresses.

The third problem with musicology identified by Middleton concerns ideology. Musicology developed in nineteenth-century Europe to examine European classical music. While it has expanded its horizons somewhat, this is still its touchstone. Therefore, the claims of a particular kind of music are valued above others in a way that reproduces the tastes and practices of a particular powerful social group and marginalizes those of weaker social groups. The means by which other forms of music are judged against the classical European tradition leads the latter to be valued in ways that prop up established ways of thinking of music. This is a similar sort of point to that made by Middleton against Adorno, which was examined in the Introduction. In a further discussion, Middleton has summarized the key problems with 'the old-style musicological pop text' (2000: 4) in terms of the five points listed in box 5.1.

Given that '[t]he discipline of musicology traditionally is dedicated to the painstaking reconstruction, preservation, and transmission of a canon of great European masterworks' (McClary and Walser 1990: 280), the prospects for developing a musicological study of pop music would not seem promising. However, in recent years a number of writers have attempted to elaborate approaches which recognize that an analysis of the music can make a contribution. For example, Middleton (1990: 117) suggests that the critique of musicology which he so clearly sets out should not be taken too far, because this would block the proper understanding of how pop music works as music. Moreover, it would specifically obscure the connections that exist between the European classical tradition and popular music. Thus, Walser (1993) has shown how heavy metal makes use of the Baroque tradition from classical music. In general, Middleton argues that:

> The 'critique of musicology', then, should take aim not at 'art music' or musicology themselves – separating popular music off from them – but at a particular construction of musicology, based on a particular subject, conceived in a particular, ideologically organized way. Once the musical field as a whole is freed from the distorting grip of that ideology, the ground is cleared for a useful musicology to emerge. The metaphor should be not one of opposed spheres, or of decisive historical breaks, but of a geological formation, long-lived but fissured and liable to upheaval: the task is to remap the terrain. (1990: 122)

Box 5.1   Problems of the old-style musicological pop text

What exactly is wrong with the old-style musicological pop text? There have been many critiques. Usually the problems are seen as lying in the following areas:

(i)   There is a tendency to use inappropriate or loaded terminology. Terms like 'pandiatonic clusters' applied to pop songs really do tend to position them alongside Stravinsky, even though it is not at all clear that anything comparable is going on there, while, similarly, a phrase such as 'the primitively repetitive tune', for example, is weighed down with evaluative baggage.

(ii) There is a skewed focus. Traditionally, musicology is good with pitch structures and harmony, much less good with rhythm, poor with timbre, and this hierarchy is arguably not congruent with that obtaining in most pop music.

(iii) 'Notational centricity' (as Philip Tagg calls it) tends to equate the music with a score. This leads to an overemphasis on features that can be notated easily (such as fixed pitches) at the expense of others which cannot (complex rhythmic detail, pitch nuance, sound qualities).

(iv) The most common aesthetic is one of abstractionism. Musical meaning is equated with an idealized image of the 'work', contextualized process turned into abstract product. This procedure is at its most extreme in formalist modes of analysis, which tend to reduce meaning to effects of structure, ignoring emotional and corporeal aspects.

(v)   Listening is monologic. What the analyst hears is assumed to correlate with 'the music', and the possibility of variable aural readings is ignored.

Source: Middleton 2000: 4

McClary and Walser also want to reconfigure the musicological study of popular music, suggesting that it is important to study those aspects which 'trigger adulation in fans' (1990: 287), as these are central in the creation of meaning. Walser has expanded upon these points in his study of heavy metal music, where he argues that 'The danger of musical analysis is always that social meanings and power struggles become the forest that is lost for the trees of notes and chords. The necessity of musical analysis is that those notes and chords represent the differences that make some songs seem highly meaningful and powerful and others boring, inept, or irrelevant' (1993: 30). If this sort of argument is to be followed, it is necessary to consider the ways in which it has been suggested that music conveys meaning and can be analysed as a textual form. These ideas are developed in the next section.

Aspects of musical meaning

Much writing about the way in which music creates meaning has been influenced by structuralism and semiotics (or semiology). One important source of structuralism came from the linguistic theories of Ferdinand de Saussure (1857–1913), which were developed in the 1960s by influential writers such as Althusser, Barthes, Chomsky, Foucault, Lacan and Lévi-Strauss. Keat and Urry (1975: 124–6) identify the following main features of structuralism:

1 systems must be studied as a set of interrelated elements; individual elements should not be seen in isolation – for example, in a set of traffic lights, green means go only because red means stop;

2 an attempt to discover the structure which lies behind or beneath what is directly knowable;

3 the suggestion that the structure behind the directly visible is a product of the structural properties of the mind;

4 the methods of linguistics can be applied to other social and human sciences;

5 culture can be analysed in terms of binary oppositions – for example, between good and bad;

6 the adoption of a distinction between synchronic (static) and diachronic (changing) analyses;

7 the attempt to identify similar structures in different aspects of social life – for example, the standardized structure of pop music may be the same as the standardized structure of society.

Semiotics – or semiology – is the systematic study of signs. To introduce some of the concepts and ideas associated with these approaches, we can consider figure 5.1. Certain features of this photograph can be introduced immediately. It shows two women, one black and one white, sitting next to each other, arms linked, in a row of people. The black woman has short hair and is wearing a long white dress and

Figure 5.1 Rihanna and Katy Perry at the VMA MTV Awards, September 2012 (© Rex Features)

is holding a cup in her right hand. The white woman has long hair and is wearing a short, patterned black and white dress. The white woman is kissing the black woman's shoulder and, unlike other people in the photograph, is not looking out of the photograph's frame; instead her eyes are cast downwards. The photograph seems to be taken at some kind of public function. In the language of semiotics, this is what the photograph denotes. We can understand, or decode, such meanings in a fairly straightforward manner, as they are relatively objective.

However, the possession of other knowledge may facilitate a more detailed decoding of the photograph. Thus, the contemporary pop fan may recognize these women as singers Katy Perry and Rihanna. They may also know that the two artists are reported in the press to be the best of friends and that they have been consistently photographed together at various public outings. Further layers of meaning, or connotations, of the picture are built on the basis of this knowledge. These women are pop stars, and the photograph conveys ideas or discourses about the celebrity and friendship.

Still further layers of meaning can be added when the photograph is considered in the context of the two artists' careers and personal lives. The audiences familiar with Katy Perry's oeuvre would make an immediate connection between her action and her 2008 bestselling single 'I Kissed a Girl', which sold 8 million copies worldwide, topping the Billboard 100 chart for seven consecutive weeks and causing much controversy and criticism due both to its alleged appropriation of the gay lifestyle, with the purpose of gathering attention (and selling records), and its promotion of 'homosexualism'. They would no doubt further be aware of Perry's public claims of heterosexuality and her relationships with men (such as Russell Brand and John Mayer), as well as her assertions that the song is about fantasy and curiosity and the celebration of feminine beauty. Viewed in this way, the kiss on Rihanna's shoulder could be read as a playful remark on their 'womance'. Furthermore, such public displays of affection confirm the friendship between the two women amid speculations about Perry's alleged disapproval of Rihanna's continuous involvement with the singer Chris Brown (who in 2009 pled guilty to felony assault of his then girlfriend, and was sentenced to five years' probation and six months' community service).

The discussion of this photograph has introduced several important points:

1 that any image or text can be said to contain different layers or levels of meaning – in particular, there is a distinction between denotative and connotative levels;
2 that the nature of such meanings will depend on the context in which they are contained, or the surrounding circumstances – meaning is relational;
3 that some of the levels of meaning or codes are relatively neutral, or objective, whereas others will be saturated with social meanings or discourses;
4 that the recognition and elucidation of these different meanings involve analysis or decoding, which often depends on the nature of the knowledge and experience brought to the analysis.

Using the language of semiotics, the photograph can be said to be acting as a sign. The sign consists of two elements: the signifier and the signified. The signifier is a sound, printed word or image and the signified is a mental concept. This structure is represented in figure 5.2.

$$sign = signifier + signified$$

Figure 5.2 The structure of the sign

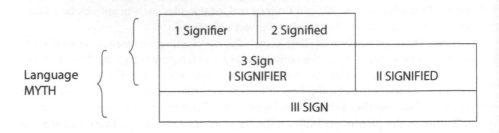

Figure 5.3 Language and myth
Source: Barthes 1976

The semiotic approach, which was developed from the study of language by de Saussure, has been applied widely. Thus, the French theorist Roland Barthes (1915–80) argues: '[T]ake a black pebble: I can make it signify in several ways, it is a mere signifier; but if I weigh it with a definite signified (a death sentence, for instance, in an anonymous vote), it will become a sign' (1976: 113). Barthes shows how different levels of meaning are associated (shown in figure 5.3). This demonstrates the relationship between the denotative or connotative levels of meaning. Barthes also writes here about the distinction between language and myth. For him, myths shore up existing structures of power, which favour the bourgeois class. Myths make what is historical or changeable appear to be natural and static.

Signs are organized into systems which convey meaning; in structuralist and semiotic approaches these systems are often called codes (Fiske and Hartley 1978: 59). Middleton (1990) suggests that a number of different levels of code structure popular music (shown in figure 5.4). Thus, if a track such as 'Born in the USA' by

langue: a general Western music code, governing the territory, roughly speaking, of functional tonality (starting, that is, about the sixteenth century and still largely current today);

norms: e.g. the mainstream conventions *c.* 1750–*c.* 1900, or those governing the post-1900 period; within these

sub-norms: Victorian, jazz age, 1960s, etc.; and

dialects: e.g. European, Euro-American, Afro-American; within these

styles: music hall, Tin Pan Alley, country, rock, punk, etc.; and

genres: ballad, dance-song, single, album, etc.; within many of these

sub-codes: e.g. within rock, rock 'n' roll, beat, rhythm and blues, progressive, etc.; and

idiolects: associated with particular composers and performers; within these
    work and performances.

Figure 5.4 Musical codes
Source: Middleton 1990: 174

Bruce Springsteen were to be analysed in these terms, we would see that the vocal, for example, contains characteristic figures of speech (or idiolects). We might argue that it was a rock song rather than a ballad. It might be Euro-American and be seen as a typical product of the 1980s, when rock took a particular direction – and so on, working up through the levels of code.

This sort of categorization can be used to inform discussions around the idea of competence. Middleton shows how Stefani distinguishes between 'high' and 'popular competence' and ability in the understanding or decoding of the code. High competence 'treats music as highly autonomous', suggesting that there is a set of distinctive skills which are needed to understand it properly. In contrast, 'popular competence appropriates music in a more global, heteronomous manner' (Middleton 1990: 175), perhaps connecting it more directly with everyday life. Furthermore: 'Popular competence can attach itself to any kind of music – though musics themselves coded in an analogous way are the most likely. Similarly, popular music can be listened to according to high competence principles (as is sometimes the case with professional performers). But a preponderance of popular music listening does seem to be of a popular competence type' (ibid.). This suggests, for example, that a piece of classical music could be decoded for its melody, but this would neglect other features that would be identified through the use of high competence.

The idea of musical code has been used in other ways by writers on popular music. For example, Bradley (1992) draws a broad distinction between the 'tonal-European code' and the 'Afro-American code', which he suggests are merged in the development of rock 'n' roll (see further chapter 3). In identifying these codes, Bradley draws upon the work of Chester (1990), who distinguishes between the extensional nature of classical music and the intensional structure of rock and other non-European musics. Chester argues that, in extensional classical music:

> Theme and variations, counterpoint, tonality (as used in classical composition) are all devices that build diachronically and synchronically outward from basic musical atoms. The complex is created by combination of the simple, which remains discrete and unchanged in the complex unity. Thus, a basic premise of classical music is rigorous adherence to standard timbres, not only for the various orchestral instruments, but even for the most flexible of all instruments, the human voice. (1990: 315)

By contrast, in intensional music, '[T]he basic musical units (played/sung notes) are not combined through space and time as simple elements into complex structures. The simple entity is that constituted by the parameters of melody, harmony and beat, while the complex is built up by modulation of the basic notes, and by inflection of the basic beat' (ibid.).

Another use of the idea of code can be found in the work of Sheila Whiteley (1992, 2000a), who mobilizes the idea of 'psychedelic coding' to study 1960s progressive rock. According to Whiteley, such coding, which included 'the manipulation of timbres (blurred, bright, overlapping), upward movement (and its comparison with psychedelic flight), harmonies (lurching, oscillating), rhythms (regular, irregular), [and] relationships (foreground, background)' (1992: 4), conveyed 'the hallucinogenic experience' in music.

The concept of style has been deployed in musicological discussion of rock by Moore (1993), who argues that it is possible to distinguish a general rock style, which

1   General cognitive processes. Here, methods relating to the schemes of sensorimotor-affective organization and symbolic-behavioural logic would be appropriate (for example, principles of same/different, strong/weak, up/down, and of proportion, grouping, contour and gesture).

2   Culturally determined applications of (1), specific to *musical* materials (for example, note-frames, time-frames, patterns of tonal and harmonic relationship). Generative theories come in here.

3   Style-specific syntaxes constructed from (2) (for example, available scales, intervals, rhythms, parameter relationships; preferred formulae, modes of combination). Distributionist, commutational and paradigmatic approaches are appropriate at this level.

4   Intra-opus patterns: the individual piece in all its uniqueness.

Figure 5.5 Levels of generative structure
Source: Middleton 1990: 214

includes a number of common features in areas such as rhythm and the voice, and a variety of different and specific styles within this general category.

The discussion so far has examined the ideas of sign and code as they have been used in semiotics. Middleton (1990: 214–20) suggests four dimensions along which music can be considered in structural terms, which develops the structuralist approach. He sees each of these as a continuum:

1   generative
2   syntagmatic
3   paradigmatic
4   processual.

Generative structure refers to the continuum between the deepest levels of the structure and those at the surface. This is similar to the idea of there being a hierarchy of codes, as considered above. Middleton's classification of generative levels is given in figure 5.5.

Syntagmatic analysis refers to the ways in which different musical units are combined to produce sequences of sounds. Thus, a pop song may be made up of a series of instrumental passages, verses, choruses, bridges, and so on. Likewise, to take another example, a meal may be thought of as a syntagmatic chain. In Britain, this might consist of a first course or starter, a main course and a pudding. Discussion of the precise contents of the different courses means moving the analysis on to the (third) paradigmatic level, as this refers to the alternatives that can be substituted into the different components of the syntagmatic chain. Thus, for example, a choice might be made between fish or meat for a main course.

Finally, Middleton considers the 'processual continuum'. He suggests that 'all musical events relate forward (through expectation and implication) and back (through memory), and their function and meaning change as the processual dynamic unfolds' (1990: 219). For Middleton, a full structural analysis has to consider the interconnections between these different dimensions.

An issue that has come under close scrutiny in much consideration of the creation

Table 5.1 *The subject matter of the lyrics of five punk groups*

	Punk	Top 50
Romantic and sexual relationships	21% (13)	60% (31)
Sexuality	15% (9)	–
First person feelings	25% (16)	3% (2)
Social and political comment	25% (16)	4% (2)
Music and dancing	7% (4)	18% (10)
Second and third person	7% (4)	3% (2)
Novelty	–	8% (4)
Instrumental	–	4% (2)

Figures in parentheses denote the actual number of songs in that category
Source: Laing 1985: 27; source for Top 50: Star File 1977

of musical meaning is the relationship between words and music. At this point, there-fore, we move away from the examination of themes deriving from structuralism and semiotics to focus on the issues raised in the examination of this relationship.

Words and music

Much analysis of pop music has focused on the meaning of the words or lyrics. Early attempts to study pop music (see Griffiths 1999) often considered the lyrics as a form of poetry, suggesting that certain pop writers could be seen as poets, and a lot of analysis of the works of Bob Dylan was carried out along these lines. Lyrics have also been studied in other ways. In some cases, the focus has been on the content of the lyrics. Thus, in his book-length study of punk rock, Laing (1985) shows the difference in subject matter between punk and Top 50 pop songs through content analysis, as shown in table 5.1. Punk songs were less concerned than pop songs with romantic and sexual relations and focused more on the nature of sexuality. Social and political comment was far more commonplace in the punk song than in the pop song. According to Ball and Smith, content analysis involves six steps:

> (1) selecting a topic and determining a research problem; (2) selecting a documen-tary source; (3) devising a set of analytic categories; (4) formulating an explicit set of instructions for using the categories to code the material; (5) establishing a prin-cipled basis for sampling the documents; and (6) counting the frequency of a given category or theme in the documents sampled. (1992: 21–2)

As with all forms of content analysis it is important to see how the different categories of content are defined, to consider the basis on which the sample has been arrived at, and so on. Further details on these matters can be found in Laing's book. However, as Laing recognizes, content analysis is a rather crude form of analysis. It tends to abstract the specific content from its context and does not pay much attention to the detail of the modes of expression in the lyrics.

In an attempt to overcome some of the problems of content analysis, more recent analysis of the lyrics of songs has studied different modes of expression and the ways in which the listener is addressed by them. One of the most consistent writers in this vein is Barbara Bradby (e.g. 1990, 1992; Bradby and Torode 2000), whose work is a form of discourse analysis. She suggests that lyrics and music construct and refer discourses in songs which have much wider significance. In the discussion of Madonna's 'Material Girl', which is reproduced in figure 5.6, Bradby lists the lyrics of the song as well as the discourses they refer to and construct – maternal, romance, everyday, money, school and teaching discourses. Further, she examines the pronouns (I, we, you, etc.) which address the other participants in the song's world and audience.

Machin too deals with discourses, identities, values and courses of action inherent in and communicated by lyrics with a view of providing a systematic way for conducting an analysis. In his application of critical discourse analysis, and with the aim or arriving at the meaning communicated by lyrics, the first step, he suggests, is to look for 'activity' or 'discourse schema' – that is, what happens in the song on a very basic level (Machin 2010: 78). Understanding this core level leads to an understanding of the values expressed by the song (e.g. sexual freedom, devotion, control, helplessness – frequently present in love songs). The second step, according to Machin, is to recognize the linguistic choices in terms of the key participants by noting who is included and who is excluded, and also whether the main participants in the lyrics are represented in generic, collective terms or as individuals. The next stage is to look at action and agency – that is, to recognize if the key participants are represented as active (e.g. travelling, working) or passive (self-reflective) (ibid.: 88). The presence of settings and circumstances of a 'story' should also be noted, such as 'streets' often referred to in rap music, 'roads' in rock, and 'hills' and 'streams' in folk (ibid.: 92), although those may not always be present in lyrical content. At the same time, Machin recognizes and points out that there are many lyrics without an activity schema – for example, the lyrics of 'Some Might Say' by Oasis:

> Some might say
> That sunshine follows thunder
> Go and tell it to the man who cannot shine
> Some might say
> That we should never ponder on our thoughts today 'cause they hold sway
> Over time. (Quoted in ibid.: 95)

Drawing on critical discourse analysis (CDA), Machin suggests that, beyond simply telling stories, lyrics communicate discourses of artists' identities, as well as reflecting and revealing cultural (contextual) discourses that surround them. While 'telling a story', an artist is making a series of semiotic choices in terms of the basic activity schema of the song, its setting, the identities represented, the status and activity of the participants, and so forth (Machin 2010: 77–8). At the level of the 'basic activity or discourse schema', Lana Del Rey's song 'Video Games' uses a female narrator to provide a description of two lovers spending time together ('playing video games', 'singing in the old bars', 'kissing in the blue dark'; see box 5.2). There is only one reference to other people – 'Watching all our friends fall in and out of Old Paul's' – with the narrative dominated by the pronouns 'I' and 'you', repeated throughout, and signalling an enclosed, intimate setting. Additionally, the successive repetition of 'you' in

> It's you, it's you, it's all for you
> Everything I do I tell you all the time
> Heaven is a place on earth with you
> Tell me all the things you want to do

[The figure] transcribes the lyrics of 'Material Girl', as actually performed on the record, which differs considerably from the neat verses reproduced on the inner sleeve of the album *Like a Virgin*. In addition, I have indicated the parts sung by the different voices in the performance, as follows:

Madonna as solo singer	= ordinary typeface
Madonna as girl-group, or female chorus, i.e.,	
using her own voice as backing vocal	= *italics*
MADONNA + MALE CHORUS OF THREE BACKING VOCALISTS	= CAPITALS
Madonna's voice as interrupting response	= {lyrics}
prominent electronic echo effects	= lyrics

Madonna, 'Material Girl', discourse analysis

Lyrics	Discourses	Pronouns
Intro.	(4 lines rhythm alone, then 4 lines with prominent melody in the bass)		
Verse 1	Some boys *kiss* me, some boys hug me	maternal/romance	– me
	I think they're OK	everyday	I – they
	If they don't give me proper credit	money/school	they – me
	I JUST WALK AWAY	everyday	I
Verse 2	They can beg and they can plead, but	romance	they
	They can't see the light, {That's right},	religious/everyday	they
	Cos the boy with the cold hard cash is	money/romance	
	ALWAYS MISTER RIGHT		
Chorus 1	Cos we're *living in a material world*	material	we
	And I am a material girl	material	I
	You know that we are *living in a material world*	material	you, we
	And I am a material girl	material	I
Verse 3	Some boys romance, some boys slow dance	romance	
	That's all right with me	everyday	me
	If they can't raise my interest then I	money	they, I –
	HAVE TO LET THEM BE	everyday	– them
Verse 4	Some boys try and some boys lie but	teaching maternal	I – them
	I don't let them play, {No way},	maternal	
	Only boys that save their pennies	maternal/money	
	MAKE MY RAINY DAY	everyday	
Chorus 2	Cos we're *living in a material world*	material	we
	And I am a material girl	material	I
	You know that we are *living in a material world*	material	you, we
	And I am a material girl	material	I
Chorus 3	Cos we're *living in a material world*	material	we
	And I am a material girl	material	I
	You know that we are *living in a material world*	material	you, we
	And I am a material girl	material	I

Figure 5.6 Discourse analysis of Madonna's 'Material Girl'
Source: Bradby 1992: 80–1

	Lyrics	Discourses	Pronouns
Instrumental Break 1			
	(4 lines of bass theme from intro. + voice 'ah's ending in 'ouch')		
Chorus 4	LI – VING IN A MA-TE-RI-AL WORLD	material	
	ma-te-ri-		
	LI – VING IN A MA-TE-RI-AL WORLD	material	
	-al		
	LI – VING IN A MA-TE-RI-AL WORLD	material	
	ma-te-ri-		
	LI – VING IN A MA-TE-RI-AL WORLD	material	
	-a-al		
Verse 5	Boys may come and boys may go and	everyday/romance	
	That's all right you see	everyday	you
	Experience has made me rich and	money/everyday	me
	NOW THEY'RE AFTER ME	everyday/romance	they – me
Chorus 5	Cos everybody's *living in a material world*	material	
	And I am a material girl	material	I
	You know that we are *living in a material world*	material	you, we
	And I am a material girl	material	I
Chorus 6	Cos we're *living in a material world*	material	we
	And I am a material girl	material	I
	You know that we are *living in a material world*	material	you, we I
	And I am a material girl	material	
Instrumental Break 2			
	(2 lines of bass theme from intro. + voice 'ah's, leading straight into)		
Voice	a material, a material,		
	a material, a material,		
Chorus 7	LI – VING IN A MA-TE-RI-AL WORLD	material	
	world ma-te-ri-		
	LI – VING IN A MA-TE-RI-AL WORLD	material	
	-al		
	LI – VING IN A MA-TE-RI-AL WORLD	material	
	ma-te-ri-		
	LI – VING IN A MA-TE-RI-AL WORLD	material	
	-a-al		
Chorus 8	LI – VING IN A MA-TE-RI-AL WORLD	material	
	ma-te-ri-		
	LI – VING IN A MA-TE-RI-AL WORLD	material	
	-al		
[fade]	LI – VING IN A MA-TE-RI-AL WORLD	material	
	ma-te-ri-		
	LI – VING IN A MA-TE-RI-AL WORLD	material	
	-a-al		

Figure 5.6 *(continued)*

Box 5.2   Lana Del Rey, 'Video Games'

Swinging in the backyard
Pull up in your fast car whistling my name
Open up a beer and you take it over here
And play a video game

I'm in his favorite sun dress
Watching me get undressed, take that body downtown
I say you the bestest, lean in for a big kiss
Put his favorite perfume on, go play a video game

It's you, it's you, it's all for you
Everything I do, I tell you all the time
Heaven is a place on earth with you
Tell me all the things you want to do

I heard that you like the bad girls
Honey, is that true? It's better than I ever even knew
They say that the world was built for two
Only worth living if somebody is loving you
Baby, now you do

Singing in the old bars
Swinging with the old stars, living for the fame
Kissing in the blue dark
Playing pool and wild darts, video games

He holds me in his big arms
Drunk and I am seeing stars this is all I think of
Watching all our friends fall in and out of Old Paul's
This is my idea of fun playing video games

It's you, it's you, it's all for you
Everything I do I tell you all the time
Heaven is a place on earth with you
Tell me all the things you want to do

I heard that you like the bad girls
Honey, is that true? It's better than I ever even knew
They say that the world was built for two
Only worth living if somebody is loving you
Baby, now you do
(Now you do)

It's you, it's you, it's all for you
Everything I do I tell you all the time
Heaven is a place on earth with you
Tell me all the things you want to do

> I heard that you like the bad girls
> Honey, is that true? It's better than I ever even knew
> They say that the world was built for two
> Only worth living if somebody is loving you
> Baby, now you do

foregrounds the narrator's focus on the other ('you', her man, her lover), leading to a gendering of status and an unequal 'distribution' of power due to the lack of lyrical response and thus a supposed lack of reciprocity.

'Video Games' is populated by action verbs such as 'swinging', 'pull up', 'whistling', 'open up', 'play', 'lean in'. They contribute to the construction of a dichotomy between masculinity and femininity: the male protagonist's associations with fast cars, the whistling of a woman's name, drinking beer and playing video games, and the depiction of the female through what she is wearing ('his favorite sun dress'), the way she is feeling ('drunk and I am seeing stars this is all I think of') and her position in relation to the man, summed up by the line 'it's all for you' (the dress, the perfume, the body on display, even finding pleasure in what in a different context could be read as tedious video-game playing).

On one level the lyrics reflect certain cultural norms associated with stereotypes of masculinity and femininity, such as:

- an active male and a passive female;
- feminine 'giving' and masculine 'taking';
- an infantilized (through use of infantile language in 'I say you are *bestest* lean in for a big kiss') and a submissive woman ('It's you, it's you, it's all for you everything I do');
- a powerful male ('He holds me in his big arms').

On another level, the lyrics reflect both the quiet enjoyment and excitement that may be found in the everyday (leisureliness and the intimacy of 'playing video games') as long as the backdrop for such an activity is the existence of love – 'Only worth living if somebody is loving you, Baby, now you do (Now you do)' – thus revealing further layers of meaning and the significance of sharing of a mundane experience.

This type of analysis goes well beyond the simplicities of content analysis. However, it does not overcome some of the issues raised by Frith (1988b) about the relations between words and music. Frith notes the centrality of content analysis to early discussions of popular music but argues that not only are such accounts overly simplistic, they also tend to relate the content of songs to general social attitudes or beliefs in a very straightforward fashion. He suggests that this neglects the sort of work that the song actually does through its lyrics and music. In his view, accounts which suggest that pop songs reflect the banality of mass culture are also prey to the same fault. Such a theory also occurred in rock music in the 1960s. Frith says: 'At its simplest, the theory of lyrical realism means asserting a direct relationship between a lyric and the social or emotional condition it describes and represents' (ibid.: 112). This theory of realism is different from that utilized in chapter 4. Frith uses the idea of lyrical realism to characterize those accounts that suggest a correspondence between the lyrics of a song and reality. The discussion of realism earlier referred to textual structure.

In lyrical realism, some songs are taken to be an authentic expression of social conditions or values, while others are inauthentic, but, in Frith's view, it is very difficult to establish the criteria on which such a judgement can be made. Furthermore, it is not always clear what reality the lyrics in the song are meant to be expressing. Frith's point is that simple links between the content of the words of a song and some reality which they are held to express are very difficult to establish. Because of this, he suggests, some writers have concluded that there is no need to pay attention to lyrics at all, also taking into account the evidence that, anyway, the audience is very often not aware what the lyrics are meant to signify, or else produce rather different interpretations of them. However, Frith argues that words are important. He suggests that they should be examined not as an expression of social conditions, social movements or the intentions of the great artist behind the song but as a 'sign of a voice', as: 'A song is always a performance and song words are always spoken out, heard in someone's accent. Songs are more like plays than poems; song words work as speech and speech acts, bearing meaning not just semantically, but also as structures of sound that are direct signs of emotion and marks of character' (1988b: 120).

Frith argues that analysis of songs should proceed in three directions. First, attention should be paid to the ways in which singers sing the song, as it is not just what is sung that is important. The pop or rock song is a performance (see further chapter 6). Second, analysis should locate the song in a genre. According to Frith, different genres, by which he means forms such as disco, punk, and so on, are understood in different ways by audiences and have different rules. Thus, 'The immediate critical task for the sociology of popular music is systematic genre analysis – how do words and voices work differently for different types of pop and audience?' (1988b: 121). Third, detailed consideration should be given to how songs work. For example, this could involve analysis of words as a form of rhythm and sound.

Frith's conclusions are that audiences often feel words and music and develop them in their imaginations. Thus, in his view, 'Pop love songs do not "reflect" emotions, then, but give people the romantic terms in which to articulate and so experience their emotions' (1988b: 123). It could be said, therefore, that, if this approach is adopted, those of us who listen to a lot of pop music have had our experiences and feelings couched in ways that derive from pop songs, and that our experiences are formed and interpreted in ways that are structured by those songs. Thus, for example, it may be difficult to divorce the experience of driving through America from prior knowledge of all those songs that concern the American road. This would suggest an intimate relation between music and social experience, such that music structures our social life (Shepherd 1991; DeNora 2000).

Frith's suggestive analysis is based in the pioneering work on the voice carried out by Roland Barthes, which we considered earlier in this chapter. Barthes (1990) argues that it is possible to analyse the 'grain' of the voice, distinguishing the pheno-song from the geno-song. The extract in box 5.3 encapsulates his approach.

In Barthes's view, some singers go beyond the expressive level to produce the pleasures of 'jouissance' in the audience. This is a very difficult term to translate from French, but it is often explained by contrasting it to *plaisir*. *Plaisir* refers to structured pleasures and feeling, while *jouissance* refers to something like the pleasure of orgasm. Some singers take us into particular forms of pleasure not through what they express in language and words, but through the physical effect they have on us.

Box 5.3   Pheno-song and geno-song

The *pheno-song* covers all the phenomena, all the features which belong to the structure of the language being sung, the rules of the genre, the coded form of the melisma, the composer's idiolect, the style of the interpretation: in short, everything in the performance which is in the service of communication, representation, expression, everything which it is customary to talk about, which forms the tissue of cultural values (the matter of acknowledged tastes, of fashions, of critical commentaries), which takes its bearing directly on the ideological alibis of a period ('subjectivity', 'expressivity', 'dramaticism', 'personality' of the artist). The *geno-song* is the volume of the singing and speaking voice, the space where significations germinate 'from within language and in its very materiality'; it forms a signifying play having nothing to do with communication, representation (of feelings), expression; it is that apex (or that depth) of production where the melody really works at the language – not at what it says, but the voluptuousness of its sounds-signifiers, of its letters – where melody explores how the language works and identifies with that work. It is, in a very simple word but which must be taken seriously, the *diction* of the language.

Source: Barthes 1990: 295
An essay published in *Image–Music–Text* by HarperCollins Publishers Ltd.

For one of us, Otis Redding's voice, especially on 'I've been loving you too long', has a physical effect, which might have something to do with the content of the lyric but has rather more to do with the effects of the 'grain of the voice'. More recently, the work of the 2005 Mercury prizewinner, Antony Hegarty (see the album *I am a Bird Now* by Antony and the Johnsons and subsequent work) can also be viewed in this light.

Middleton (1993), too, has argued that music can be related to bodily experience. For example, it is possible to see the connections between dance and music. Thus, one of the most recent directions for musical analysis has been to consider in far more detail how music is used and how much of its meaning and pleasure is connected to physical activity (see further chapter 6).

Much contemporary analysis of the pop music text has developed the insights summarized in this chapter so far. Middleton (2000) suggests that three main directions have been followed, all of which in different ways relate music and music analysis more thoroughly to context. First, there has been more location of music in ethnographic-type studies (see, for examples, chapter 2 above). Second, building on the sort of approach discussed above with respect to Bradby and Frith, there has been a focus on discourse rather than on the structures and semiotics of texts. The implications of this sort of development are further considered via the work of Judith Butler in chapter 6. In addition, as Middleton recognizes, work by such as Walser (1993) and Brackett (1995) has advanced these sorts of perspectives helpfully. For example, Brackett combines discussions of the structure and meaning of the work of such artists as Bing Crosby, Billie Holliday, Hank Williams, James Brown and Elvis Costello with useful connections to contexts. Third, there have been approaches that emphasize the concept of mediation. These explore the complex mesh of relations (or mediations) that connect music and define it in relation to many other mutually connecting influences and contexts: 'The musical worlds that we inhabit, then, are not clear sets, filled with autonomous entities which are foreign to each other and connected only via neutral "links": rather they are half-way worlds, without clear boundaries, filled with transient knots of variable meaning, practice and status' (Middleton 2000: 10). Negus (1996: 66) identifies three main senses of mediation: (1) the 'idea of coming in between', (2) 'a means of transmission' and (3) 'the idea that all objects, particularly works of art, are mediated by social relationships'. He argues that these ideas can be applied to the media in ways that illustrate some important institutional and textual processes.

In a text that collects together a number of articles which can be seen as representing the progress of popular musicology, Middleton's edited volume (2000) has chapters on the 'analysis of music' which look at the work of such artists as Randy Newman (Winkler 2000), Prince (Hawkins 2000) and Chuck Berry (Cubitt 2000). In addition, there is overview of the distinctive and influential approach of Tagg (2000). Another section examines the relationships between words and music. Here artists such as Peter Gabriel (Taylor 2000) and Bruce Springsteen (Griffiths 2000) are examined. Analysis is further broadened in a third section that brings in wider social contexts (for example, Whiteley 2000a; Moore 2000) and visuals (Björnberg 2000). Thus, this collection can be said to represent the state of an art that can be followed further in the pages of such journals as *Popular Music*.

This part of this chapter has explored a number of different dimensions of musical meaning. However, one dimension has been conspicuous by its relative absence in the discussion of the meaning of music so far: the visual.

From MTV to YouTube: sounds, words and images

This section gives an overview of some of the key arguments about the function and significance of the music video, most of which emerged in the 1980s following the establishment and rapid rise in popularity of MTV (Music Television channel). After the relatively stagnant period for academic engagement with the music video throughout the 1990s and early 2000s, the appearance of Web 2.0 and the subsequent rise in popularity of social networking, coupled with proliferation of the participatory digital cultures, brought the music video back to the fore. In contrast to the 'first wave' of academic interest, dominated by structuralist and poststructuralist approaches and frequently borrowing from traditions associated with reading and interpretation of cinematic content, the majority of the contemporary readings of the music video focus on its social, connective and participatory dimensions (e.g. Gauntlett 2011), in addition to recognizing it as a visual text and cultural artefact. This section will address the role played by the social networking sites such as YouTube in redefining the importance of the music video and the purpose it serves, within the broader attempts to understand music as multilayered text. Finally, it will give an example of analysis to demonstrate how sound, words and image work together multimodaly to create and communicate meaning.

As a number of writers have suggested, musical meaning has long been tied up with the visual. For example, Mundy (1999) explores the relationship of music to the visual in cinema, television and video. This view suggests that, in both production and consumption, music and the visual are entwined. Thus, from the beginnings of the cultural industries as a modern phenomenon, the production of music and, for example, film have been connected, in the sense that the companies involved would often have interests in both, or would be looking to combine the appeal to the two senses. This is even the case with the so-called silent cinema (ibid.). Moreover, the way in which audiences understand and access music is often connected to mass-distributed media forms. Bands will/used to be seen first on television – and so on. It is therefore possible to consider how music and visual meaning have been connected in the history of the cinema (for example, through musical films), television (*Popular Music* 2002; in programmes such as *Top of the Pops* or *Pop Idol*), or in specific promotional forms such as music videos that appear on broadcast and specialist TV channels.

Since the early 1980s a large literature on music videos has developed. A significant part of this focused on video as a visual text. One of the most important and comprehensive books which takes this approach is by Kaplan, who makes two important points about music videos in general. She argues, first, that they abandon the 'traditional narrational devices of most popular culture hitherto' (Kaplan 1987: 33); and, second, that 'they are routinely, and increasingly, self-reflexive' (ibid.: 34).

By the first point, Kaplan means that most music videos break with the relations between cause and effect, continuity, and time and space, which define the sort of realism described in chapter 4. Videos are edited in ways that differ from the classic conventions of the Hollywood film and thus disrupt our expectations of how a film should look. Furthermore, videos 'play off' earlier genres of film, such as the spy film, the Western or the horror film, as well as earlier familiar and popular movies. One of the most well-analysed and debated examples of this is the video for Madonna's *Material Girl*, which is a pastiche of the 1950s musical *Gentlemen Prefer Blondes*, starring Marilyn Monroe and Jane Russell.

With regard to the second general point, Kaplan argues that music videos often turn in on themselves: '[We] may see the video we are watching being played on a TV monitor within the frame; or the video shows us the production room in which a rock video is being made, which turns out to be the one we are watching' (1987: 34). An example of this is the video for the Human League's *Don't You Want Me?*. Videos, then, often expose the process of their making, something that most film and television in the realist mode seeks to prevent. Other videos comment on the nature of the music business, such as the video for David Bowie's *Jazzin' for Blue Jean*.

Through arguments of this nature, writers such as Kaplan maintained that music videos disrupt the realist illusion that we are watching a familiar world, structured by a set of realist narrative conventions of cause and effect, where the production process is concealed. In these respects, music video texts are often seen as postmodern. Another way in which they were thought to be postmodern was through their location on MTV itself, which, by going against the established conventions of broadcast television, such as a variety in programming to cater for different tastes, in its early days tended to break familiar patterns. It had been suggested that, because the music videos on MTV run into each other, they produce effects which blur the boundaries between different cultural experiences in classic postmodernist style.

Within this context, Kaplan identifies five main types of video, which are distinguished in figure 5.7. The first type is the romantic. In many respects this looks back to the 'soft rock' of the 1960s. Initially, it tended to be the province of female stars

		Modes (all use avant-garde strategies, especially self-reflexivity, play with the image, etc.)				
		Romantic	*Socially conscious*	*Nihilist*	*Classical*	*Post-modernist*
	Style	Narrative	Elements varied	Performance Anti-narrative	Narrative	Pastiche No linear images
Predominant MTV themes	Love/Sex	Loss and reunion (Pre-Oedipal)	Struggle for autonomy Love as problematic	Sadism/masochism Homoeroticism Androgyny (phallic)	The male gaze (voyeuristic fetishistic)	Play with Oedipal positions
	Authority	Parent figures (positive)	Parent and public figures Cultural critique	Nihilism Anarchy Violence	Male as subject Female as object	Nether for nor against authority (ambiguity)

Figure 5.7 Five main types of video on MTV
Source: Kaplan 1987: 55

and was less prevalent than some of the other forms. However, since 1983–4 it has increased in importance and has been associated with more male groups and singers. As the title of the category suggests, the videos are often about romance, addressing themes of love and loss. They may feature a narrative, but this is relatively weak and the focus is on emotions. In some ways this parallels the discussion of 'emotional realism' in television soap opera by such writers such as Ang (1986). The music in this sort of video tends to be tuneful and melodious rather than loud and overpowering.

Kaplan argues that the socially conscious type of video retains elements of the critical rock stance that was supposedly at the centre of 1960s and 1970s rock music. She suggests that this type of video is modernist in that it uses art to criticize established forms of authority and their associated forms of art and maintains that in the early 1980s three themes dominated this sort of video. First, there were anti-authority, anti-parental videos, which took a variety of different forms. Second, there were videos which concerned American foreign policy or 'specific social injustices, such as poverty' (1987: 75). These sorts of video were shown far less frequently than some of the other types. Examples are Bruce Springsteen's video for *Born in the USA* as a critique of post-Vietnam America and the Sun City video by Artists Against Apartheid. The third theme in the socially conscious category addresses 'women's oppression and the possibilities for female solidarity' (ibid.: 87). Thus, Kaplan argues that some videos address the problems faced by women in society and attempt to represent and construct forms of female solidarity.

This theme has been developed by Lewis (1993), who identifies forms of gender address to women in video. She writes that such videos use two distinct types of sign in particular ways. Thus: 'Access signs are those in which the privileged experience of boys and men is visually appropriated. The female video musicians textually enact an entrance into a male domain of activity and signification' (ibid.: 136). Discovery signs, by contrast, 'reference and celebrate distinctly female modes of cultural expression and experience. Discovery signs attempt to compensate in mediated form for female cultural marginalization by drawing pictures of activities in which females tend to engage apart from males' (ibid.: 137). Lewis finds evidence of these modes of address in work by Cyndi Lauper, Madonna, Pat Benatar and Tina Turner. However, she maintains that these sorts of video are relatively few and far between.

Kaplan relates the nihilist type of video to the 'originally anarchic positions of recent punk, new wave and heavy metal bands' (1987: 60). On MTV this was mainly the province of heavy metal bands. These videos often featured live concerts or re-creations of them. They rely on musical and visual shock. Sadistic and masochistic themes are often present, as are concerns with hate and destruction.

The classical video often relies on a more conventional, realist, narrative structure. However, they are also classical in 'retaining the voyeuristic/fetishistic gaze towards woman as objects of desire that feminist film theorists have spent so much time analyzing in relation to the classical Hollywood film' (Kaplan 1987: 61). Women are located in these videos to be looked at by men, both within the video itself and by the male spectator. A second type of classical video takes on and uses classical Hollywood film genre, which moves it more towards postmodernism.

The postmodern form of video (Kaplan's fifth type) involves a large element of play with images. When we watch these we often feel that we have lost a clear position from which to view. They do not put forward a clear 'line' or point of view; positions are advanced at one point in the video and are then undercut at a later point. While elements of this are present in all videos, they are exhibited to a far greater extent in this form.

Kaplan's account is one of the most detailed examinations of music video. However, there are some problems with it, the most important of which revolve around three issues: first, the nature of music video as promotion; second, the place of music in music video; and, third, the nature of the audience.

The first point concerns the nature of the video as a promotional device. While Kaplan opens her book by examining the commercial base of MTV and locates it in an institutional context, as her analysis develops it centres increasingly on the nature of the music video text as if it were a separate art form. In some respects this is perfectly legitimate, as it is possible to study texts using, for example, structural and semiotic methods, but it is important to remember that videos are embedded in a commercial context. Videos are produced in a very different context from classical or even contemporary Hollywood films and cannot simply be studied using concepts and categories derived from film and television analysis, without consideration of the specific applicability of such ideas to different media.

Second, the musical dimension often takes a secondary position in many discussions of music video. Kaplan's work develops out of her previous background as an analyst and theorist of film. Distinctions in the visuals are central, and musical differences tend to be discussed relative to these prior distinctions. In some writing, this aspect of music video has been almost ignored. Thus Frith criticizes the work of Browne and Fiske (1987), who, he says, compare Madonna's song-and-dance routine in the 'Material Girl' video with Marilyn Monroe's 'Diamonds are a Girl's Best Friend' in *Gentlemen Prefer Blondes*. 'The two songs', they assert, citing the lyrics in each case, 'are basically similar'. The differences are 'differences of tone'. 'Anyone who can hear a 1980s disco hit as "basically similar" to a 1950s theatre song is obviously deaf. Alas, it has been the deaf who have dominated pop video theory' (Frith 1988a: 221). Hence, our attention should be focused in videos as much on music as on visuals and the spoken word, suggesting that it is the relationships between these aspects that are important.

Third, Kaplan implies that the audience for the music video is of a particular type. However, this is based on an analysis of the text rather than on an investigation of the audience itself (for more general discussion of this issue, see chapter 6). Kaplan argues that, in the past, rock music addressed different cultural groupings, but that MTV utilizes a mass address: 'I will be arguing that MTV reproduces a kind of decenteredness, often called "postmodernist", that increasingly reflects young people's condition in the advanced stage of highly developed, technological capitalism evident in America' (1987: 5). And, later, she states:

> MTV simply takes over the history of rock and roll, flattening out all the distinct types into one continuous present. The teenage audience is now no longer seen as divided into distinct groups addressed by different kinds of rock music, but is constituted by the station as one decentered mass that absorbs all the types indiscriminately – without noting or knowing their historical origins. (Ibid.: 29)

However, it is not clear how this sort of approach can be reconciled with Kaplan's later comment, that 'Different groups of teenagers no doubt use MTV in different ways according to class, race and gender' (ibid.: 159).

Goodwin (1993) attempts to develop an analysis of video and MTV which takes into account these sorts of problem together with the illuminating approach taken by Kaplan. He stresses the promotional and industry context of music video and MTV, emphasizing the way in which the different products of media or cultural industries interlock in relations of multi-textuality (see also Wernick 1991).

> [This process] was exemplified, for instance, in the selling of the 1989 Warner Bros. film *Batman*, which involved tie-ins with the music industry (Prince's *Batman the Movie* LP, and the sound track from the film itself), publishing (including the Batman comic books, published by Warner Communications subsidiary D.C. Comics), television (through home video sales and rentals, and – eventually – cable and broadcast television rights), and merchandising (Batman bubble gum, breakfast cereal, and so on). (Goodwin 1993: 27)

Goodwin uses the ideas both of the interlocking nature of the media industries and of promotion and rights which were examined in chapter 1 to contextualize the development of music video. Video came about as a 'routine' way of promoting pop in the early 1980s at the same time as the development of the post-punk New Pop, which concentrated on issues of image and used new technologies in music-making. Television itself was expanding, and music videos were a cheap way of filling up airtime. Furthermore, 'music television very precisely addressed two trends in the 1980s: the aging of the rock audience and the growth (at least in the United States) of a youth culture that was not centred on music' (Goodwin 1993: 39). What Goodwin terms the 'music video cycle' is reproduced in figure 5.8. One important point to note about this cycle is the relatively insignificant role of

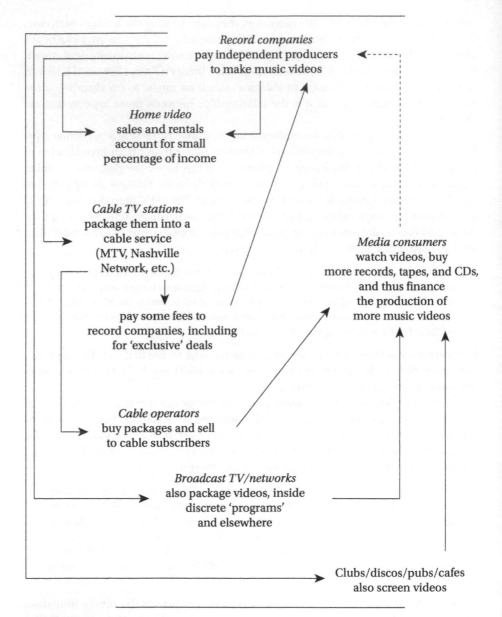

Figure 5.8 The music video cycle
Source: Goodwin 1993: 43

the sale of music videos as commodities themselves, as their main use is in the promotion of other goods. This still remained the case in 2011, when music video sales accounted for around 2 per cent of overall income in the music industry (BPI Yearbook 2012: 48).

Goodwin shows how MTV changed between 1981 and 1993, dividing its development into three stages: 1981–3, 1983–5 and 1986–93. The first phase was studied by some, such as Kaplan, who focused on the visual and postmodern nature of MTV.

At this point, MTV broadcast screen videos in a flow, and these videos themselves tended to break with narrative convention in the way identified by Kaplan (Goodwin 1993: 134). However, Goodwin maintains that developments during the second phase led away from this format. Most importantly, MTV was increasingly divided up into programme slots and the nature of the videos shown moved closer towards the performance type, with heavy metal music becoming ever more important. In August 1985 the ownership of MTV changed hands, from the founders Warner-Amex to Viacom International, and from 1986 onwards the trends that had appeared during the second period were consolidated. There were more programme slots and different sorts of musical material appeared. A typical MTV day, in March 1991, can be seen in figure 5.11.

Goodwin contextualizes music video and MTV far more than writers of other accounts have done. He also pays attention to the second problem that arises in accounts such as Kaplan's, identified above: the relative neglect of music. Goodwin argues that it is important to recognize how musical and visual dimensions to video are intertwined. Furthermore, he suggests that this is nothing new (see also Mundy 1999). Music has always made sense in relation to the visual associations that we in the audience give to it; hence certain forms of music suggest colours and images. Moreover, music has been connected with the visual through the media of film (early rock stars were promoted in film, especially Elvis Presley) and photographs. Goodwin's argument is that the 'visuals support the sound track' (1993: 70). Thus, for Goodwin, music videos are not films, and there is a clear danger of 'misreading the generic conventions of the form by applying rules carried over from another (inappropriate) genre or medium' (ibid.: 77).

Goodwin maintains that music in pop videos tends to close off meaning in ways that other writers on the form have neglected: 'we can find three kinds of closure or coherence that introduce a high degree of stability via the sound track: repetition, structural closure, and harmonic closure' (1993: 79). Pop songs, he asserts, are repetitive within themselves in alternating verse and chorus, for example. Furthermore, they resemble other pop songs (see the arguments of Adorno discussed in the Introduction) and are repeated across 'media sites', where the same song can be heard on the radio, TV, etc.

While such repetition might be held to suggest that pop songs do not resolve issues in the manner of the narrative realist text, Goodwin maintains that structural resolution does this in 'the way a song ends with the repetition of a chorus or refrain that "ties up" the song, perhaps as it fades out' (1993: 80). Such structural resolution is reinforced by 'harmonic resolution', which describes:

> the organization of the music itself around conventions of tonality and musical arrangement that both ground the music in a system of tonal relations that may be seen as the aural equivalent of the realist systems of 'looks' in cinema and often enable it to end with a musical 'resolution' which may be seen as the aural equivalent of a realist narrative reaching its conclusion. (Ibid.: 83)

However, despite his strong arguments for the centrality of music in the meaning structure of the music video, Goodwin recognizes 'that music video is relatively autonomous from the music, to a limited degree, in a number of ways' (ibid.: 85). He identifies and discusses four such ways:

ANATOMY OF A MUSIC VIDEO

Shooting a music video with American pop-star Selena Gomez and an international crew in Budapest, Hungary is an exercise in multi-cultural logistics to create
a product that appeals to a global audience. It begins with the studio recording,
and ends after a mad dash to the finish by scores of technicians, artists and——

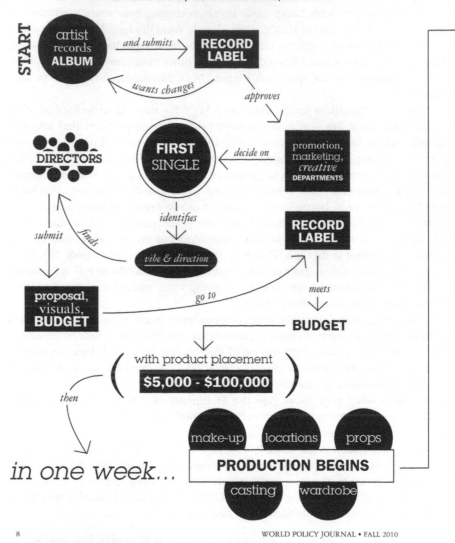

Figure 5.9 Anatomy of a Music Video
Source: World Policy Journal (2010), 27(3): 8

1 the visualization of the song may go beyond its meaning;
2 the clips seek to provide pleasure (sometimes, but by no means exclusively, of a
   narrative nature) in order to keep the viewer watching and to encourage repeated
   viewings;

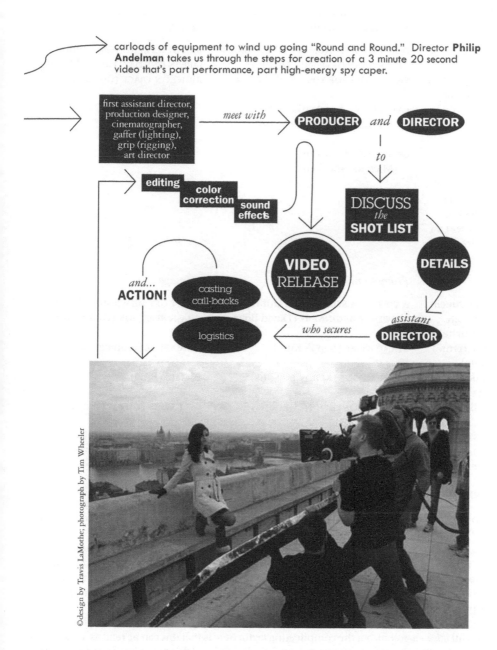

carloads of equipment to wind up going "Round and Round." Director **Philip Andelman** takes us through the steps for creation of a 3 minute 20 second video that's part performance, part high-energy spy caper.

first assistant director, production designer, cinematographer, gaffer (lighting), grip (rigging), art director

meet with → **PRODUCER** *and* **DIRECTOR**

to

DISCUSS *the* **SHOT LIST**

editing

color correction

sound effects

VIDEO RELEASE

DETAILS

and... **ACTION!**

casting call-backs

logistics

who secures

assistant **DIRECTOR**

©design by Travis LaMothe; photograph by Tim Wheeler

3   the clips might promote other commodities (such as films);
4   the clips might narrativize/display images of stardom that exceed any given individual song.

Like Kaplan, Goodwin points to the variety of different videos that are shown on MTV and categorizes them as shown in figure 5.10. It is possible to see some overlap between these categories and the types identified by Kaplan. For example, Goodwin's

Social criticism	Self-reflexive parody	Parody
SUN CITY (AAA)	DON'T LOSE MY NUMBER (Phil Collins)	BAD NEWS BEAT (Neil Young)
WAR (Springsteen)	JUST A GIGOLO (David Lee Roth)	LIFE IN ONE DAY (Howard Jones)
LIVES IN THE BALANCE (Jackson Browne)	THIS NOTE'S FOR YOU (Neil Young)	RIGHT ON TRACK (Breakfast Club)
TWO TRIBES (FGTH)	EAT IT ('Weird Al' Yankovic)	
RADIO CLASH (the Clash)	POP SINGER (John Mellencamp)	
JAMMIN' ME (Tom Petty)	ON THE GREENER SIDE (Michelle Shocked)	
SISTERS ARE DOIN' IT FOR THEMSELVES (Eurythmics)		
CULT OF PERSONALITY (Living Colour)		
ONE (Metallica)		

Pastiche	Promotion	Homage
RADIO GA GA (Queen)	A VIEW TO A KILL (Duran Duran)	DON'T GET ME WRONG (Pretenders)
THE ULTIMATE SIN (Ozzy Osbourne)	ABSOLUTE BEGINNERS (David Bowie)	CHAIN REACTION (Diana Ross)
MONEY FOR NOTHING (Dire Straits)	STAND BY ME (Ben E. King)	DR MABUSE (Propaganda)
MATERIAL GIRL (Madonna)	DANGER ZONE (Kenny Loggins)[a]	$E = MC^2$ (BAD)
THRILLER (Michael Jackson)	LAND OF CONFUSION (Genesis)[b]	TELL HER ABOUT IT (Billy Joel)
WHERE THE STREETS HAVE NO NAME (U2)	BATDANCE (Prince)	R.O.C.K. IN THE USA (John Cougar Mellencamp)
BIG TIME (Peter Gabriel)[c]	HEARTBEAT (Don Johnson)	
MEDIATE (INXS)		ROCKIT (Def Leppard)

[a] DANGER ZONE is especially interesting because it both promotes the film *Top Gun* and references (as pastiche?) the opening scene of Francis Ford Coppola's *Apocalypse Now*.

[b] LAND OF CONFUSION is not a movie trailer, as the other examples here are, but it does indirectly promote the British TV series *Spitting Image*, through its use of puppets. It also contains pastiche, in its joking reference to the montage sequence in Stanley Kubrick's *2001: A Space Odyssey*, in which the chimp's bone becomes a spaceship (here it is transformed into a telephone receiver held by the Phil Collins puppet).

[c] BIG TIME uses a pastichelike reference to the television series *Pee-Wee's Playhouse* (through its distorted, playful *mise-en-scène*), but the complicating factor here is that this can be read as an auteurist discourse, since the clip's director, Stephen Johnson, has also directed that television program. Read in that light, the clip should more accurately be classified as (self-?) promotion or homage.

AAA	Artists Against Apartheid
FGTH	Frankie goes to Hollywood
BAD	Big Audio Dynamite

Figure 5.10 Visual incorporation in music video
Source: Goodwin 1993: 161

social criticism category is not unlike Kaplan's socially conscious type of video, and Goodwin's category of self-reflexive parody is quite like Kaplan's postmodernist type. However, Goodwin points to the way that video is used as a promotional device for other texts and suggests a number of different ways in which music and visuals interact. He also considers different visualization of videos by audiences. On the basis of a small-scale audience study, he concludes, first, 'that the vast majority of students in this sample were able to note down visual images associated with the musical extract'; second, that there was 'a high degree of consensus on the kinds of iconography associated with each extract'; and, third, 'while a variety of mass-mediated imagery is invoked in these accounts, a significant amount of this imagery does not derive from music video (at least not in any clear, literal sense), and a good deal of it is clearly triggered by personal memory' (1993: 55). Goodwin also suggests that the kind of intertextuality in videos such as Madonna's *Material Girl* will not necessarily be recognized by the audience.

Goodwin's account is important, first, in developing a critique of the more unsubstantiated claims of those writers who have seen MTV and music video as postmodern in simple and clear senses; and, second, in providing a clear and historicized account of the promotional and industrial context of video. He alerts us to the interconnections of music and image in the way in which pop creates meaning. In more general respects, Goodwin's account explores a number of relationships that are not simply restricted to music videos. Thus, although his analysis is marked by the influence of specific cultural theories (postmodernism) and particular ways of characterizing the social context (for example, as postmodernity), the institutional, textual and consumption relationships that emerge continue to have ongoing force. As Mundy suggests: 'It is quite possible to see what might be termed a "music video aesthetic" at work across a range of contemporary cultural forms, including television, cinema and advertising; even if much of the original enthusiasm for music video as distinct cultural form has itself lessened' (Mundy 1999: 224). Thus, the link between the production of music and visual texts continues to work on a number of levels. For example, in terms of their pace and style, many contemporary movies have the characteristics of videos, and much contemporary TV is conducted to a beat. Moreover, these processes have impacted upon MTV, which has significantly changed its format: 'MTV has been forced to bend to advertising concerns and has changed its entire format, dropping music videos from a majority of its programming slots, and developing new show formats like *The Osbornes* to maintain or increase audience share' (Kusek and Leonhard 2005: 63). When it celebrated its thirtieth birthday on 1 August 2011, MTV was a global franchise, where music videos were taking up a relatively small space in its daily scheduling, and those mostly on its sister channels such as MTV music, MTV Base, MTV Rocks, MTV Classic and VH1. The primary MTV channel nowadays features shows such as *Geordie Shore, I Used To Be Fat, My Super Sweet 16* and *Teen Mom*. The enormous shift in programming on MTV can be illustrated by comparing a typical MTV schedule in 1991, when music videos or programmes about music featured prominently, with that in 2012, dominated by youth reality TV shows.

Guided by the popularity of sites such as YouTube and streaming services such as Spotify, and in an attempt to keep abreast of the fast-changing mobile technologies market, in 2012 MTV launched an iPhone and Android app called Under the Thumb. As well as allowing users to stream shows, the app has social co-viewing features. It is

7:00 a.m.	*Awake on the Wild Side*	00:00	Jersey Shore
9:00 a.m.	Music videos (Daisy Fuentes)	01:00	South Park
12:00 p.m.	Music videos (Andrew Daddo)	01:30	South Park
3:00 p.m.	*Spring Bread '91*	02:00	Real World San Diego
4.00 p.m.	*Yo! MTV Raps*	02:50	Best Of Cribs
4:30 p.m.	*Totally Pauly*	03:00	Teleshopping
6:00 p.m.	*Dial MTV*	06:00	Best Of Cribs
7:00 p.m.	*MTV's Half Hour Comedy Hour*	06:10	Teen Cribs
7:30 p.m.	*Hot Seat*	06:30	Teen Cribs
8:00 p.m.	*Prime with Martha Quinn*	06:55	Teen Cribs
10:00 p.m.	*House of Style*	07:15	Super Sweet 16
11:30 p.m.	*Bootleg MTV*	08:00	My Super Sweet 16
12:00 p.m.	*120 Minutes*	08:30	Friendzone
		09:00	Extreme Cribs
		09:30	Extreme Cribs
		10:05	16 and Pregnant: Adoption Special
		11:00	Teen Mom
		12:00	Plain Jane
		13:00	16 and Pregnant: Adoption Special
		14:00	Teen Mom
		14:55	Extreme Cribs
		15:25	Extreme Cribs
		15:50	Best of Cribs
		16:00	16 and Pregnant: Adoption Special
		17:00	Daria
		17:30	Daria
		18:00	The Fresh Prince of Bel Air
		18:30	The Fresh Prince of Bel Air
		19:00	The Fresh Prince of Bel Air
		19:30	The Fresh Prince of Bel Air
		20:00	Teen Mom
		21:30	New Pretty Little Liars
		22:30	Top 10 Most Outrageous Sex Myths
		23:00	New Geordie Shore

Figure 5.11 A typical MTV day in March 1991 (*Source:* Goodwin 1993: 143) and current scheduling

aimed at the generation of 'millennials' or 'digital natives' – 'basically kids or people who live at the pace of digital. They need to have content wherever they are, at any point, on any device' (Jones, quoted in Dredge 2012). The idea is that the users flick between viewing content and chatting about it, as well as being able to send invites to friends to co-view a particular programme at a specific time. MTV also wants users to link the app with Facebook to share their favourite shows.

At the heart of this development is an understanding of viewing as a social, shared activity, in very much the same way as viewing of television programmes was perceived as such at the time when one television per household was a norm. The difference, of course, is in portability and virtuality, rather than the physical presence required for active participation.

Railton and Watson (2011) revisit the music video and treat it not only as a promotional device serving the commercial agenda, which is to promote and sell the music and the artist, but also as a 'ubiquitous cultural product'. They suggest that, in an age of 'on demand' viewing through a multiplicity of platforms, the music video has the potential to lose its secondary status (to music or an artist) and to become a product in its own right. While their investigation focuses mainly on the politics of representation of ethnicity and gender, they make some useful typological summaries, building on Kaplan's and Goodwin's classifications. They point to a persistent tendency among some commentators to conflate music genre and video genre, while in reality there is frequently no evidence that they correspond. They are also critical of conflating the context of the music video distribution (e.g. MTV or YouTube) with the structure and meanings of video itself:

> Simply put, the music video becomes conflated, and confused, with the context of its distribution. This critical slippage not only tends to mask differences between individual music videos and the different generic structures of video, but also diverts critical attention away from the form and content of music videos themselves and shifts it towards the formal analysis of MTV as a putatively distinctive postmodern televisual phenomenon. (Railton and Watson 2011: 44)

Their own generic classification places music video in one of the following four categories.

1   Pseudo-documentary music video offers an illusion of 'privileged access' to the viewer by employing the documentary film stylistic devices, so that the artists *appear* to be in their 'natural' settings and conducting 'natural' practices associated with their profession, 'doing the job of being musicians, performers, stars' (ibid. 2011: 49). One of the examples given is the Metallica's 1992 video *Nothing Else Matters*, which shows how the song has been recorded in the studio.
2   Art music video abandons the attempt to capture the 'real life' of an artist or the band, instead 'appealing to notions of art and aesthetics' (ibid.: 51). It may borrow representational language from the tradition of animation, a particular art movement (e.g. surrealism) or experimental cinema. By making an association between the artist and an established, recognized and 'serious' artistic tradition, it acts as a legitimizing and authenticating device.
3   Narrative music video provides 'visual narration' for the content of the video but can also feature a narrative that is disconnected from the lyrical content.
4   Staged performance video is 'a performance explicitly staged for the purpose of producing a music video' (ibid.: 61) and is defined by closely choreographed routines, looking directly in the camera, and lip-synching. The aim is to foreground and legitimate the performance, as opposed to day-to-day practices of the artist/band, the narrative of the song or an artistic tradition that gives credibility to the artist.

Masculinity and music video

In examining the music video as one of the cultural forms through which identities, including gender, are represented and communicated, it is usually the representation of the female body and femininity that bear the greater scrutiny. Railton and Watson (2011) address this apparent lack of balance by discussing both the relative absence of the discourse about the male body in various cultural forms more generally and 'the absent presence of the male body' in music video specifically. Understanding masculinity as 'discursive, contingent, constructed and performed' (Railton and Watson 2011: 123) and adopting Connell's (1987) notion of 'hegemonic masculinity' as plural, non-monolithic and dynamic, together with the later notion of 'multiple hegemonic masculinities' (Connell and Messerschmidt 2005), they provide a reading of a number of music videos which employ various strategies to remove the male body from the frame of discourse. The three main strategies are the deletion, displacement and disguise of the male body. According to Railton and Watson, deletion is achieved through the use of abstraction and semi-abstraction (e.g. avoiding the representation of the human/male form altogether and focusing on light, colour, shape, and so on), a complete absence of the male artist and his replacement by women and female bodies, and the use of animation and animated characters (2011: 130–2).

The displacement of the male body can be due to filming and editing techniques which fragment the body (focusing on a particular body part and foregrounding skill/ musicianship – for example, fingers strumming the guitar strings) or through portrayal of exaggerated emotions by using extreme close-up shots or isolated settings.

The male body is frequently disguised by instruments or by oversized clothes (e.g. in hip-hop and r 'n' b videos), which stand in stark contrast to undersized garments worn by women. Another strategy used to 'disguise' the male body is to expose it but to make fun of it. Railton and Watson suggest that the ridicule de-sexualizes by disguising the male body in comedy.

Music video and YouTube

Writing in 2002, Frith suggested that most of the literature focusing on the music video seemed 'curiously overblown', with scholars from fields other than popular music (e.g. film studies, cultural and media studies) using popular music for 'general arguments about postmodernism' (Frith 2002: 278). Recent years have been marked by the revival of interest in music video brought about by a momentous rise in the use and popularity of various social networking platforms that enable video uploads. The best known is YouTube, launched in 2005. In 2006, following its purchase by Google Inc. for $1.6 billion, the site was streaming 100 million videos per day. Lady Gaga's *Telephone* video featuring Beyoncé amassed over 20 million views within a week of its release, signalling that the days of music video are not over just because it has disappeared from TV screens.

Naturally, not all of the streamed videos were music videos; however, the sheer volume of video traffic cannot be overlooked. Taking into consideration both production and the experience of consumption of music videos, two key changes ought to be noted. First is music videos are no longer viewed on television, old VHS tapes or DVDs, and instead are freely and instantly available online or on mobile devices. Second is the emergence of what is known as 'user-generated content' and the subsequent proliferation of fan videos online, enabled by a combination of faster broadband connections and embedded software for social media. Video-making as a form of vernacular activity is not new, and vidding – 'an art in which clips from television shows and movies are set to music to make an argument or tell a story' (Coppa 2009) – has a long tradition among female fans in particular. Unlike the tradition of vidding where a song/music is used to interpret the visuals or to give them a new meaning, images in many YouTube music videos are used to extend the meaning of song (communicated through music and lyrics).

Sociologically informed work focusing on the motivations of users for taking part in YouTube activities (creating, uploading, viewing and commenting on videos) is starting to emerge, and the evidence so far suggest that the main driver of participation is the desire for social interaction (e.g. Haridakis and Hanson 2009). In an ethnographic study into young people's engagement with online video-sharing on YouTube, Lange (2007) found that the most common practice among her participants was to post videos for friends and family to see and respond to. Similarly, Boulaire, Hervet and Graf (2010), whose research focused on digital participatory culture and creativity through analysis of amateur YouTube videos for Daft Punk's *Harder, Better, Faster, Stronger*, found that Web 2.0 technologies 'give rise to chains that link and connect individual minds, imaginations, interests, enthusiasms, talents, abilities and skills' (ibid.: 111). The focus on the participants' motivations to create, post and comment on music (and other types of videos) extends the existing studies of the music video both as 'a promo', a device that plays a part in the marketing process, and, in a visual semiotic approach, as a text that lends itself to visual encoding and reading. With the increase of user-generated content such as that on YouTube, or more recently Twitter's mobile app Vine, which allows the users to create and post short video clips of up to six seconds which can be shared on a variety of social networking services, the convenience, the speed and particularly the social dimension of (music) video production and consumption become increasingly pertinent: 'Interviewees reported that intelligent commentary on a video could stimulate closer social connections, if the video maker continues to communicate with and interact with the poster of the commentary' (Lange 2007).

In an ethnographic study of popular music identities and practices, Bogdanović (2009) found that social networking sites that enable embedding and sharing of videos, such as MySpace, YouTube and Facebook, provided the participants with platforms for self-presentation where uploaded music videos served as a form of cultural capital, signalling taste and thus aligning the musicians to a particular music genre, an ideological standpoint and associated set of practices. Additionally, easy access to a vast range of music material on YouTube facilitated nostalgic journeys to one's musical beginnings and the key musical influences.

Creative collaboration, co-viewing, discovery and recommendation often lead to the convergence of production and consumption of the music video, or what Gauntlett (2011), writing about wider online communities and practices, illustrates with the phrase 'making is connecting'. For Gauntlett, making is connecting on three levels: the level of actually connecting things or ideas to make something, the level of social connectivity where making and creativity lead to connections with others, and the level of connection with wider 'social and political environments' (2011: 2).

There is a growing body of work dealing with the legal and legislative dimensions and implications of user-generated and shared content, guided by the philosophy of 'sample, remix, mash, rip, burn', that cannot be addressed here at length. However, a recent case of the music video *Newport (Ymerodraeth State of Mind)* illustrates some important issues. A parody of the Jay-Z and Alicia Keys song 'Empire State of Mind', it appeared on YouTube on 20 July 2010 and was subsequently removed due to a copyright claim by EMI Music Publishing. Alex Warren and Terema Wainwright, the performers of the parody, met with Universal Records with the aim of exploring the release of their version as a charity single; however, seven writers of the original song refused permission for the record to be released and the video was removed from YouTube on 10 August 2010. Newport-based group Goldie Lookin Chain then released their 'parody of a parody' video, and in 2011 Comic Relief showcased a new parody video featuring Welsh celebrities. The original spoof can still be found on YouTube, reposted by several people, and it will presumably be pulled once YouTube becomes aware of it. *Newport* raises the issue of copyright and the distinction between an 'official' and 'unofficial' music video on YouTube, demonstrating that an 'unofficial' version and the video of a song can become very successful and viewed by millions of users. With the proliferation of fan music videos came a response from record companies. As a premium music video service with 2 billion worldwide streams and over 60 million unique visitors in the USA and Canada, VEVO hosts music videos from artists signed by Universal Music Group, Sony Music Entertainment and EMI, and Warner Music Group uses MTV networks to host its videos. While it is official music videos that remain most viewed (Boulaire et al. 2010: 112), the proliferation of unofficial or amateur versions calls for an understanding and examination of the genre as an evolving phenomenon. In addition to Goodwin's (1993) call for an exploration of the relationship between various texts and their associated context (e.g. film, soundtrack and merchandising), in an era where making facilitates connecting and vice versa, questions ought to be asked about the personal and social contexts of the individuals – that is, their motivations for creating content. In acknowledging the epistemic need for 'interdisciplinarity' and 'interprofessionalism', Tagg (2011) suggests that many researchers from non-musical, non-musicological backgrounds still struggle to address the music of popular music studies. In a similar vein, he recognizes that, while audio-only products have long been replaced by audiovisual products and services, the scholarly analysis that would competently engage with both is scarce or non-existent.

Summary

This chapter has considered a number of different areas of study and issues raised through the investigation of musical meaning:

- a critique of traditional musicology and contemporary arguments for the transformation of musicology to make it useful in the study of a variety of different forms of music;
- ways of studying musical meaning which derive in the main from the approaches of structuralism and semiotics; important concepts discussed here are code, structures and denotation and connotation;
- the interconnections between lyrics, words and music;
- the interconnections between musical and visual meanings, using music video as a well-known example, where Kaplan's (1987) work, representing a more

text-centred approach, was contrasted with the more contextualized perspective of Goodwin (1993);

- the transformation of the music video from a promotional device or 'promo' into a 'ubiquitous cultural product' in the age of Web 2.0, representation of gender in the music video and further generic classification, as discussed by Railton and Watson (2011);
- a brief overview of recent studies examining the motivations, role and impact of participatory cultural and music fan practices.

6 Performance, Dance, Distinction and the Body

This chapter explores a number of different aspects of the performance of popular music. It is significant that, despite the importance of performance to music (as opposed to the writing and reading of novels, for instance), it is only relatively recently that it has come under sustained academic scrutiny. In part this has stemmed from a more general and contemporary interest in how meaning is created in the modes of interaction that make up the performance situation. More specifically, the idea of performance has assumed a significant theoretical importance in academic work on culture and media. In no small part this is due to the influence of the work of the American writer Judith Butler on performativity, gender and sex. To reflect this importance, this chapter begins with an overview of the most salient parts of her work. One of the areas in which Butler has been influential is in theories and studies of the body. It can be seen that this is of specific interest given the role that dance has in relation to music. In addition to being a text that exists in various forms with the sorts of potential for study that have been overviewed in chapters 3, 4 and 5, music is danced to or – perhaps better, for reasons that are explored in this chapter – danced with. Again, it is rather surprising to note the relative neglect of this topic in the study of popular music until comparatively recently. To rectify this, to some extent, this chapter will consider some recent work that has studied and outlined theories that connect performance and dance with theories of the body. Two specific areas will be the practice known as moshing or slamdancing, which connects dancing to the notions of doing and participation, rebellion, resistance and gendered space, and the phenomenon of rave or, as it is now best known, dance culture, which has developed since the late 1980s. The examination of dance culture through the lens of performance, dance and the body also introduces two other themes that run through this chapter: distinction and identity.

One of the most influential academic studies of dance culture is Sarah Thornton's *Club Cultures* (1995). This will form the basis for the examination of dance culture in this chapter, in combination with other works that have usefully considered various aspects of the subject. In addition, this discussion introduces the important work on culture of the French sociologist Pierre Bourdieu. Bourdieu emphasizes the role of culture in the production and reproduction of cultural boundaries and hierarchies; his work in this area has assumed as much importance as that of Butler in recent years. It is significant that it has taken a lengthy period for these developments to be reflected in the study of popular music, and this aspect will be noted in this chapter. Ideas of distinction or, to use a Weberian formulation (see the Introduction), status are also played out in the collection of popular music, and aspects of this issue are discussed here (other facets of the consumption of popular music are further examined in chapters 7, 8 and 9). The issue of how collecting may contribute to the formulation and reformulation of identities is a point of departure here.

A number of the themes in this chapter are brought together at its close in an examination of Frith's *Performing Rites* (1996), which focuses our attention on ideas of performance and taste in useful and thought-provoking ways.

Judith Butler: performance, performativity, gender and the body

Judith Butler is best known for her highly influential book *Gender Trouble* (1990; 10th anniversary edition, 1999), which radicalized discussions of sex and gender. Arguing against biological determinism in these areas, she considers the way in which notions of sex and gender are performed and how they are socially malleable. These arguments have been very important in promoting the ideas of performance and performativity, which have grown in significance in media and cultural studies in recent years. Butler (1993) also analyses the social and discursive construction of human bodies. In later work (1997), she has examined the politics of speech and public utterances, which have been seen to be the cause of various forms of social harm. The discussion in this chapter will focus in particular on Butler's ideas of performance, performativity, gender, sex and the body, which are of most relevance to the nature of popular music performance.

Key aspects of Butler's approach are superficially relatively clear. As Bell puts it: 'gender, to cut a long story short, is an effect performatively produced' and 'identity is the effect of performance and not vice versa' (1999b: 3). In this view, identities such as gender are produced by discursive practice (Butler 1999: 184) and the performance of them in social processes, rather than being something essential that is given expression in action and practice: 'If gender attributes, however, are not expressive but performative, then these attributes effectively constitute the identity they are said to express or reveal' (ibid.: 180).

As Salih argues, this sort of approach 'has confused many people' (2002: 63). Salih demonstrates this by quoting the following from *Gender Trouble*: 'There is no gender identity behind the expressions of gender; that identity is performatively constituted by the very expressions that are said to be its results' (Butler 1990: 25), and she continues: 'How can there be a performance without a performer, an act without an actor? Actually Butler is not claiming that gender is a performance, and she distinguishes between performance and performativity (although at times in *Gender Trouble* the two terms seem to slide into one another)' (Salih 2002: 63). This was recognized by Butler herself, and she has sought to address the issue in subsequent work, as she says in the Preface to the tenth anniversary edition of *Gender Trouble*:

> Much of my work in recent years has been devoted to clarifying and revising the theory of performativity that is outlined in *Gender Trouble*. It is difficult to say precisely what performativity is not only because my own views on what 'performativity' might mean have changed over time, most often in response to excellent criticisms, but because so many others have taken it up and given their own formulations. . . . In the first instance, then, the performativity of gender revolves around this metalepsis, the way in which the anticipation of a gendered essence produces that which it posits as outside itself. Secondly, performativity is not a singular act, but a repetition and a ritual, which achieves its effects through its

naturalization in the context of a body, understood, in part, as a culturally sustained temporal duration. (1999: xiv–xv)

In crude terms, performance can be said to involve intention and action on the part of a constituted and volitional subject, whereas performativity is the process that constitutes the subject (and the body of the subject: see Butler 1993). Butler argues that:

> gender identity is a sequence of acts (an idea that has existential underpinnings), but she also argues that there is no pre-existing performer who does those acts, no doer behind the deed. Here she draws a distinction between *performance* (which presupposes the existence of a subject) and *performativity* (which does not). This does not mean that there is no subject, but that the subject is not exactly where we would expect to find it – i.e. 'behind' or 'before' its deeds – so that reading *Gender Trouble* will call for new and radical ways of looking at (or perhaps looking *for*) gender identity. (Salih 2002: 45)

So, even if there remain clear difficulties concerning how to distinguish between performance and performativity, Butler has drawn attention to how identities such as those of gender are produced in the context of social interaction. This has been very influential in the study of gender, which then sees such identities as having some degree of fluidity and which can be subverted by forms of 'drag', for example, or through processes of queering (Brett et al. 1994). An even more controversial aspect of Butler's work has been her argument that the body (or sex) is also constituted through such performative processes. On the face of it, this seems a difficult argument to sustain. After all, is it not clear what sex we are from the body parts that we have? However, as Salih maintains:

> A girl is not born a girl, but she is 'girled', to use Butler's coinage, at or before birth on the basis of whether she possesses a penis or a vagina. This is an arbitrary distinction, and Butler will argue that sexed body parts are *invested* with significance, so it would follow that infants could just as well be differentiated from each other on the basis of other parts – the size of their ear lobes, the colour of their eyes, the flexibility of their tongues. Far from being neutral, the perception and description of the body ('It's a girl!' etc.) is an interpellative performative statement, and the language that seems merely to describe the body actually constitutes it. Again, Butler is not refuting the 'existence' of matter, but she insists that matter can have no status outside a discourse that is always constitutive, always interpellative, and always performative. (2002: 80)

According to this argument, the body exists, but it always exists within discourses that give it materiality. As with many other of Butler's formulations, this has caused significant debate. However, it should be recognized that, at the very least, it opens up space for the reconsideration of a range of interacting processes. Thus, the extent to which bodies are culturally and socially defined can be discussed, as can the extent and the ways in which gender is something performed (perhaps differently in different contexts) and debated. If this is the case, sex and gender are not essential, are not pre-given, which entails the adoption of a position rather like that reached in the examination of black music in chapter 4. A potential step on from an anti-essentialist position (such as Butler's) is to recognize the social, political and cultural construction and reconstruction of bodies and identities, without moving to complete relativism. This sort of approach is captured in a comment on Butler made by Gilroy (whose work we considered in chapter 4), when he suggests that 'what he would like to see is a way of complementing her enquiries into the histories of subjectivity with a kind of enquiry into the history of solidarity, and intersubjectivity' (Bell 1999a: 36). The idea is to study the social constitution of the body, subjectivity, identities and communities. It is useful that this sort of agenda has been taken forward in studies of dance and the body, to which it is now possible to turn.

The body and dance

In recent years there has been renewed consideration of the place of the body in social and cultural theory, one of the sources of which comes from Butler's work, as discussed in this chapter so far. However, there have also been a number of other influences on this process. While classical sociologists and anthropologists had interests in a number of aspects of the body, there has been a significant move in recent years to consider various dimensions of the social construction of the body. Such approaches to the human body 'identify a range of social and cultural influences that shape its appearance and activity'; although there exists a variety of social constructionist approaches, what they 'have in common is an opposition to simplified essentialist explanations, i.e. explanations of bodily appearance and activity that assign sole or major significance to biological factors' (Longhurst et al. 2008: 199). Many different aspects of body construction and reconstitution have been examined, including the ways in which the body is disciplined by power and modified through diet and exercise, the gendering of bodies, and the way in which the body interacts with technology to produce the cyborg (see ibid.: 198–235). Furthermore, the social constructionist 'body project' can bring the cultural theory of writers such as Butler into dialogue with that of social constructionist sociologists, such as Garfinkel and Goffman (Thomas 2003). Despite the success of these developments in opening up new theory, it has been argued that, because of the way in which the body is seen as socially constructed, the material nature of the body disappears. As Thomas suggests: 'Recent developments in social and cultural theory, along with changes in the register of late capitalism, have been influential in bringing 'the body' out of the shadows and into the light of academe. But there has been mounting criticism, from a number of quarters, of the dominance of representational or discursive models at the expense of the lived body' (2003: 62).

If Thomas's argument is accepted, then there is a research agenda that combines the idea that the body (and its movement) is not simply a natural phenomenon but is subject to modes of social and cultural constitution, with the idea that both the body and its movement have a degree of materiality. Thus, educating the dancer involves training the body not only according to certain ideas of how it should move (it is thus constituted through discourse) but also in recognition of the fact that the body itself as a physical thing has to be altered. In pursuing this idea, Thomas argues that this opens the way for detailed ethnographic research on modes of dance.

To explore such possibilities, Thomas examines two modes of dance that can be seen as being at opposite ends of the spectrum of the disciplines of bodily movement: ballet and contact improvisation. Although they share features in common, such as the fact that they 'are both products of the western cultural and artistic tradition' (Thomas 2003: 108), there are significant illustrative differences between these two modes of dance. However, both illuminate the ideas of discursive construction and physicality. Thus, 'the ballet body provides a striking example of this process of objectification through its celebration of the ideals of visualism and the pursuit of the mastery of the body over nature. It is an athletic, highly tuned instrument through which the dancer's inner expression is given an outward form' (ibid.: 108–9). Contact improvisation, the beginnings of which can be traced from 'the counter-cultures of the 1960s and in the emergent critiques of the star images, hierarchies and codified techniques of western theatre dance (ballet and modern dance)' (ibid.: 109) is different:

> The contact body directs attention inwards to the body of the self through touch and weight. The body is ideally the subject and the object of attention in contact, in contrast to ballet where the bodily focus is objectified and fashioned through its visual appearance and projections in space and time. While ballet conspires with the visualism of western culture, contact improvisation colludes with the 'truth of the body' ideology encapsulated in a range of alternative body re-education techniques, such as the Alexander technique, which gained some ground in the 1970s. (Ibid.)

In addition to her consideration of these modes of dance, Thomas shows, through a number of other examples, the value of a more ethnographically formulated approach to the study of dance. As she says: 'In dancing, as the case studies in this book hopefully show, individual embodied subjects/subjectivities enact and "comment" on a variety of taken-for-granted social and cultural bodily relativities' (2003: 215). However, despite the innovative nature of her work, Thomas tends to downplay the role of music relative to dance.

In his work *The Male Dancer: Bodies, Spectacle, Sexualities* (2007), Burt foregrounds a theory of spectatorship in dance with focus on the male body. Giving a historical overview of the status of the male body in dance and the perceptions and expectations of the male dancer, he notes the ways in which Romanticism provided a scope for greater expressivity for a male artist:

> The Romantic genius was allowed a wide range of self-expression that would have been considered unacceptable in men not considered to be gifted. The way in which the Romantic composer might pound his piano while performing his own work, or the emotionalism of the Romantic poet, or the way the brush strokes betray the painter's emotions: the implicit or explicit physicality of all these seems to have been acceptable for artists in the nineteenth century. (2007: 18–19)

The romantic notions of 'physicality' of expressivity form an important part of discourses of authenticity in popular music, where passion, emotion, degree of vulnerability and presence/charisma are highly valued, and the body is often the main vehicle by which such qualities can be communicated. The theme of corporeal expressivity is carried on in the next two sections, which explore some key issues associated with two distinct cultural practices: moshing/slamming and raving.

Moshing/slamdancing

Moshing or slamdancing emerged in the late 1970s and early 1980s and is thought to represent a modification of the earlier punk dancing known as pogoing. In its earlier forms it was seen mostly at hardcore and punk gigs, but audiences engage in moshing while listening to live metal bands or any other type of music that lends itself to its energetic and vigorous nature. It takes place at 'the moshpit', 'the slampit' or simply 'the pit', an unmarked area usually just in front of the stage where a band is playing live. Tsistsos explains the connotations of the word 'pit': 'Naming this area the "pit" designates it as the site of some type of battle. Being part of the scene is about being rebellious, and the term "pit" suggests that this is the main site of rebellion' (1999: 405). The pit is a useful 'space' for examination of the relationship between music, body, gender, identity and dance. It is frequently described as a white male, homosocial space, defined by physicality, violence and the bodily expressions of 'authentic' emotions. Simon (1997: 150) points out the experience of moshing or slamming could be addressed from numerous perspectives, including:

- the psychological or neuropsychological point of view in terms of its ritualistic qualities (repetition of the moves) and its impact on the nervous system;
- by aligning it to a 'flow activity' marked by total involvement in an activity where 'the doing is the main thing';
- as a form of social or political protest;
- as a form of dance that offers escape and catharsis.

In an attempt to define the meaning of moshing or slamdancing, Simon examines it through a series of oppositions that define the pit, such as 'order/chaos, absorption of self in mass/centrality of individual asserting self, and violence/physicality' (1997: 149). He draws a parallel between some of the characteristics of the moshpit, such as 'violence/physicality, chaos/order, anonymity/individuality, speed and flux' (ibid.:155) and the culture of modernity. Although at one time, for example, it was possible to take slamming lessons in New York, and despite the existence of descriptive narrative accounts of how to do it, the rules of participation are learned mainly through practice. One of Simon's female respondents explains:

> It is very controlled even though it looks, like, wild and violent. You don't kick. There is a set way to wave your arms. It is a matter of creating and having your own space. Especially when someone clears a pit. They are recognized. For a while, when I first started going, that used to be a goal. It was respected to clear your own space. But there were ways to go about it. Taking your elbows at your sides and pushing back against the crowd. Then waving your arms in a confined circle fashion. The way you step, it is sort of like a march, like a jog . . . You didn't do it by being completely crazy. At a punk show I found it as a lot more like anything goes. I've seen at punk shows, people don't pick people up, when they fall, as readily as at hardcore shows. (Ibid.: 163)

Drawing on Foucault, Simon describes the pit as 'an embodied expression of disciplining power in action' (1997: 173) which serves two functions: to normalize bodies so that the pit works (dancers follow a certain set of unwritten rules and perform similar moves), while simultaneously allowing the participants a sense of expression, freedom and individuality. Here he recounts his own experience: 'I remember how, the first time I entered a pit, about three years ago, my initial fear – when I did not know anybody and was neither a punk nor a skinhead – was transformed into a feeling of complete submergence of myself to this mass of people, while I was simultaneously expressing myself in a way which felt free' (ibid.: 160–1).

Tsitsos (1999) builds on a number of the codes of dancing in a moshpit outlined by Simon, including rules of participation and the description of some of the moves (arm swinging, running counter-clockwise and colliding, crowdsurfing, stagediving). He further distinguishes between moshing and slamming, describing the former as 'slower and more exaggerated' and the latter as 'more frenetic in its movement' (1999: 406).

So far we have seen that the moshpit can be understood through an examination of the motivations and practices of the participants and the focus on the dancing body. It is also a highly gendered space. In her discussion of the audience's 'zones of participation', Fonarow (2006) describes three areas with associated practices: zone one, nearest to the stage and populated by the most devoted participants, of high density and significant movement; zone two, consisting of mostly still audience members focusing on stage performance; and, finally, zone three at the back of the venue, populated by those involved in other activities such as ordering drinks and talking (this zone tends to include the industry professionals). She points out a relative absence of women from zone one, as well as a visible lack of female participation in activities such as moshing, stage diving and crowd surfing.

Gruzelier's (2007) ethnographically informed discussion attempts to relate moshpit culture to theories of homosociality. Through what is perceived as violent interaction, he explores the stereotypes of aggression and violence associated with heavy metal culture, understood as male and masculine. He sees the moshpit as a space where male homosocial interaction is made visible and masculine dominance is asserted. In his exploration of its dynamics, rules and strategies, as well as by bringing female experience of the moshpit to the fore, Gruzelier suggests that its diversification – that is, its 'broadening demographic' – may lead both to the perception of a 'dilution of subcultural meaning' of a moshpit and to an increase of solidarity and inclusiveness of a musical genre and its practices (2007: 74).

The theme of opening up of a perceived gendered space, populated by gendered bodies in performance, is taken up by Williams, who writes about hardcore musical styles and masculinity: 'Beyond the violent mosh pits and stage-diving crowd antics, hardcore also dealt with lyrical issues that did not find a ready audience in the 1980s in the midst of apparently superficial, "candy coated" pop – that is, depression, identity crisis, and other personal demons' (2007: 151). She suggests that, because of changing cultural attitudes to masculinity, such themes and emotional weakness found their way into lyrical and musical expression of Emo (emotionally oriented rock) of the late 1990s and early 2000s, where 'the musical signifiers of emotional weakness – that is, such "undesirable" qualities [as] vulnerability, femininity, weakness' are combined with 'musical signifiers of aggression that are the bedrock of the punk/hardcore musical style' (ibid.: 152).

This section explored learning to dance through doing and participation, and the way in which the moves in slamming are determined by particular ideologies or rebellion and resistance. It outlined the understanding of the moshpit as a masculine, homosocial space but also hinted at possibilities for its widening and opening to include more egalitarian practices in which both sexes engage more or less equally. The next section introduces one such space – the club.

Box 6.1   Excerpt from *False Prophet*

The sound is incredibly loud. A hundred faces smile, laugh, grimace with exertion. I play a fast descending line and land on a low A that vibrates the floor-boards and the crowd responds with a general downward motion. I blast a fat chord as Stephen drops his microphone and dives onto the upraised hands of the audience, where he is bounced around like a gypsy bride while the chord feeds back, swells, and begins to howl as Debra kicks the foot switch that boosts her amplifier for a solo and I switch pickups, reduce volume, and scream.

Dancers slam into each other, one loses balance and is caught and righted, another falls down and is yanked back to his feet. People clamber onto the stage and dive into the crowd, are caught by those below and either set down or passed overhead to the rear or forward to be deposited on the stage to dive again. One guy takes a running dive and the four people under him, by reflex, move out of the way. I see Debra mouth 'ouch' as he hits the floor and is helped to his feet. People hug the PA speaker stacks to keep them from toppling on the crowd, three hold my microphone stand so I can keep singing without getting my teeth knocked out as bodies slam into everything. Tonal memory, hand and body motion, telepathy with the other players, and sound are all connected to the flailing mass. Everyone is making music.

It's a feedback loop – energy surges up from the crowd, into our bodies, out through our hands and voices to the dancers and back through us again, accompanied by a tremendous feeling of elation. The violinist and I exchange glances. Bow and pick and hammer-ons are thrillingly in sync. Tom-tom hits are small explosions, the kick drum is a concussion grenade, the marvellous myriad of psychophysical events that is music making is felt and seen as well as heard. Music is a total sensorial fact.

Source: Taylor 2003: 1–2

Raving

In the aftermath of the development of rave culture in late 1980s Britain, there developed both a journalistic (e.g. Reynolds 1998) and an academic literature (see below). One of the most influential studies of rave came from Thornton (1995), which is also discussed in the context of post-subcultural studies in chapter 9 (on different aspects of rave, see also chapters 7 and 8). Thornton draws on the ideas of the French sociologist Pierre Bourdieu (1930–2002), who has been particularly influential in the English-speaking world through his writing on culture and distinction. In reflecting on her book, it is therefore possible to explore some important themes in dance culture as well as to consider the work of this important sociologist, which will inform the consideration of ideas of distinction in this chapter.

Thornton argues that one of the salient features of dance culture (or, as she terms them, club cultures) is the way in which what she terms 'subcultural capital' is deployed. Some of the participants in this culture seek to advance their claims to being at the leading edge by being as 'hip' as possible to the most recent developments. According to Thornton, these are 'means by which young people negotiate and accumulate status within their own social worlds' (1995: 163). By defining themselves against what they perceive to be the 'mainstream', clubbers struggle over the capital that provides distinction in this area.

The framework for this argument comes from Bourdieu's *Distinction: A Social Critique of the Judgement of Taste* (1984). However, this work needs to be contextualized by his overall social theory. Bourdieu has been much concerned with a perennial issue in sociology, namely the relative weight to be accorded to the way in which human social life is determined by structural factors, such as the place of an individual in the class structure as defined by their occupation, or the extent to which individuals through social interaction have the power to create their own situations. Bourdieu addresses this debate through his idea of practice, which is captured in the notion of 'agents' engagement with the objective structures of the modern world, crystallized into those patterns of relations, with their specific determining force, that we call "fields" (economic power, politics, cultural production, etc.' (Fowler 2000: 1). Human beings internalize structures living within and producing what Bourdieu terms the 'habitus'. The habitus involves the habits that we develop, our disposition to look and classify the world in a particular way. It defines the world that we inhabit, but is not just about the knowledge that we possess of that world; it can be as much about our bodily habits or the way in which we move our body. In Bourdieu's argument, class is very important to the habitus in which we live, but it can also be seen as conditioned by gender, ethnicity, region, and so on. In some respects there are clear parallels with Butler's idea of performativity as discussed earlier in this chapter (see Butler 1997: 127–63; Salih 2002: 113). The habitus has been a very influential idea for thinking through the ways in which our position in the world is structured and lived.

In addition, Bourdieu has been particularly important in expanding and developing the idea of capital and applying it in new ways. This has been a significant general movement in the social sciences, which has built upon the basic insights of Karl Marx. In Bourdieu's formulation, it is not only economic capital that derives from money, income, economic investments, etc., but also cultural, social and symbolic capital. In general, in this idea 'there is a class, capitalists that controls the means of production – the process of pedagogic action or the education institutions (in homes, in schools, and so on). In addition, there is more attention to the more micro-social processes of capital deployment' (Lin 2001: 16). Cultural capital consists of such phenomena as knowledge, ways of life, ways of understanding the world and prestige. There are three main forms of cultural capital: embodied in 'long-lasting dispositions of the mind and body', objectified 'in the form of cultural goods', and institutionalized, 'resulting in such things as educational qualifications' (Skeggs 2001: 296). Social capital is based in social networks, connections or relationships. Symbolic capital is 'the form the different types of capital take once they are perceived and recognised as legitimate. Legitimation is the key mechanism in the conversion to power' (ibid.). Capital can be converted from one form to another; different forms might act in opposition to one another or can be enclaved. Thus, for example, those with high economic capital (the wealthy) might purchase a high-status education for their children, thus providing them with forms of cultural capital in educational qualifications and an understanding of 'high' culture such as literature and art. Attending high-status (and costly) schools may also provide a network of contacts (such as the often cited 'old-boy network') that might continue at university and in future life. It can be seen

$$[(habitus)(capital)] + field = practice$$

Figure 6.1 Bourdieu's formula
Source: Bourdieu 1984: 101

how this sort of 'conversion' might work, too, in the production of popular music, which will require some level of economic investment and forms of knowledge and understanding of music itself, as well as a network of contacts.

The final idea developed by Bourdieu which has been of significance is that of the 'field'. A field is an area of social life that has its own set of rules and expectations. Some forms of capital may be very important in some fields but are less important in others. However, it is possible to move between fields using the conversion of capital. Thus, economic capital may be of prime importance in the economic field but can also be used to advantageous effect in the political field. For Bourdieu, then, these concepts are linked, as he shows in the equation reproduced in figure 6.1.

To return to dance culture, it can be seen that to be part of the dance 'world' is to be involved in a habitus, which may involve forms of knowledge (for example, about clubs, DJs and records), ways of thinking (such as the idea that spending a significant period of time in a club is a good way to use time), ways of dressing (what are the appropriate clothes to wear) and ways of moving (as in the 'correct' modes of dancing). This habitus may be very significant in the dance music field but less significant in others (the field of education, for example). Within the field of dance music, which involves a habitus that is likely to be shared by the participants, some may seek to be seen as leaders. They might deploy their 'hipness' as subcultural capital in the way that Thornton describes. Moreover, their social contacts may be significant as well, as the extract in box 6.2 shows.

Thornton's study was one of the first extended academic discussions of the dance culture, and its deployment of the approach derived from Bourdieu has been influential. However, it has been subject to some criticism, as has some of the earlier work on rave culture that is discussed in Part III of this book. As Thomas explains, some of these studies actually neglect the nature of the dancing, and therefore body movement, that is such a significant part of the culture. She suggests that, 'despite noting the importance of Thornton's study to this emergent field of research, Malbon (1999) argues that she fails to attend to the experience of clubbing itself' (Thomas 2003: 207). Furthermore, she argues that more recent literature (for example, Malbon 1999, Bennett 2000, and Pini 2001) has a number of common themes, such as an ethnographic focus on the social patterns of club culture at a local level, an emphasis on the positive (and perhaps liberatory) aspects of dance culture, and the way in which these processes can lead to the production of new identities for the participants (Thomas 2003: 208–11). Such themes are also significantly present in the work of Jackson (2004).

Jackson, too, offers an ethnographic account of the clubbing experience, examining in some detail the following aspects: dancing, music, sex, dress, drugs and the 'vibe'. He is very upbeat and positive about the clubbing experience – it is painted in a very positive light. Part of the explanation for this enthusiasm is his argument that the experience results in identities and ways of life which are not simply acted out in clubs but also inform other aspects of clubbers' lives. This is significant, as Jackson

Box 6.2   A night of research

Saturday, 22 September 1990. Wonderworld, London W8, 11 p.m.

It's exactly eleven and I'm waiting for Kate. We've never met before, but she knows I'm researching clubs and has promised to show me 'how to have fun'. The 'hardcore techno-house' of the dance floor is just audible from here. Two women police officers patrol on foot. Mostly same-sex groups wear casual clothes and casual expressions; they walk slowly and deliberately until they've got past the door staff, then plunge down the stairs into the club. I feign uninterest because clubbing is the kind of activity that shuns official, parental, constabulary or even 'square' observation. Clubbers often voice antipathy towards the presence of people who don't belong and come to gawk.

A few minutes later, Kate jumps out of a black cab. She's energetic and her immaculately made-up eyes gleam. Her brother runs this club, so she asks the doorwoman to 'sort us out'. The woman takes a pack of cards and hands me a three of diamonds, smiling: 'This will get you all the way.' We descend a flight of steps where a bouncer inspects my card, then ushers us in. The doorwoman insisted that this club, run by ex-rave organizers in rave style, has no door policy – absolutely anyone could come in. Nevertheless, the crowd looks pretty homogenous. They are mostly dressed in a late version of the acid house uniform of T-shirts, baggy jeans and Kickers boots; they're white and working-class. There is also a handful of Afro-Caribbean men hanging out near the door who look as if they might be friends of the entirely black crew of bouncers.

We walk around the club. The venue is early-eighties plush, but it's transformed for tonight's club by large unstretched glow-in-the-dark canvases of surreal landscapes with rising suns and psychedelic snakes. A white boy, wired and talking a mile a minute, stops me in my tracks: 'Want some "E"?' He's referring to 'Ecstasy' and he's eating his words. The volume of the music is such that I can only catch bits of his sales pitch: 'I got burgers and double burgers . . . fifteen quid.' He is a poor advertisement for the effects of his wares. From his aggressive and jumpy delivery, I assume that he is really on some speed concoction or perhaps this is his first night on the job.

We descend some more stairs to the VIP room where another bouncer gestures for my card, then waves us in. No door policy upstairs, but an exacting one down here. This room is so restricted that, at this hour, there is no one here except the barmaid. But it's still early. We get a coke and a mineral water and sit down. It feels private. Kate is very much at home. 'Tell me about your research then.' She's genuinely interested in my work, but also probing into whether I can be trusted. Her brother is one of the original rave organizers, who began by putting on parties in barns and aircraft hangars, then went legit, organizing weekly clubs for ravers in venues around London. As Kate tells it, the police monitored all their parties from the beginning, but as soon as the 'gutter press' were hard up for a front-page story the scene got out of hand: 'Kids, who shouldn't have even known about drugs, read about the raves in the *Sun* and thought, "Cor – Acid. That sounds good. Let's get some", and loads of horrible people starting trying to sell "swag" drugs.'

During our conversation, the VIP room has filled up. Kate suggests I meet her brother who is sitting at the bar with a long blonde and a bottle of Moët et Chandon on ice. He is in his early twenties and wears a thick navy-and-white jumper, something which immediately distinguishes him from those here to dance. Kate tells him that I've never taken Ecstasy ('Can you believe it?') and tells him that we are going to do some tonight. He's not pleased. 'How do you know she won't sell this to the *Daily Mirror*?' he asks. Kate assures me that she's checked me out, that I'm all right. Later, they explain that they want someone to tell the 'true story' of acid house and that they'll help me do it as long as I don't use their names.

Kate pours me a champagne and takes me aside. A friend has given her an MDMA (the pharmaceutical name for Ecstasy) saved from the days of Shoom (the mythic club 'where it all began' in early 1988). We go to the toilets, cram into a cubicle, where Kate opens the capsule and divides the contents. I put my share in my glass and drink. I'm not a personal fan of drugs – I worry about my brain cells. But they're a fact of this youth culture, so I submit myself to the experiment in the name of thorough research (thereby confirming every stereotype of the subcultural sociologist). Notably, there's 'Pure MDMA' for the VIPs and 'double burgers' for the punters. The distinctions of Ecstasy use are not unlike the class connotations of McDonald's and 'no additives' health food.

Source: Thornton 1995: 87–9

differentiates his approach from some of the other academic work on dance culture on this basis. As he says:

> Now I want to examine the ways in which those club experiences move beyond the club space itself and filter out into that everyday world. This has been attempted before, but not altogether successfully because academics have tried to turn clubbing into other forms of knowledge. Redhead (1993) tried to politicise clubbing as a form of resistance, which just doesn't hold up in the long term. Thornton (1995) simply turned it into a field of consumption, which virtually ignores the experience itself. Malbon (1999) focused on the experience but couldn't move beyond the club space. (2004: 115)

Jackson goes on to say: 'My informants were adamant that clubbing had exerted a powerful influence on their lives and that this influence didn't just evaporate once the party was over' (ibid.). He suggests that the club culture experience can move individuals beyond their existing habitus and be a part of the constitution of a new mode of living and identity. He argues that people 'use the social, sensual and emotional knowledge uncovered via clubbing to generate a new bodily posture that re-orientates their relationship to and perspective upon the world that lies beyond clubs' (ibid.: 133). In Jackson's view, this led to a more experimental approach to social life on the part of those who had participated in the experience. He suggests that this has moved them beyond the habitus; however, it could be argued that it had led to a new form of habitus – or way of acting in the world.

It is significant that the two approaches to club or dance culture that have been considered at greatest length in this chapter both deploy (to different degrees, but significantly) the conceptual terms that have been developed by Bourdieu. While it can be seen that they take these terms in rather different directions – Thornton emphasizing the way in which club culture is internally differentiated around sub-cultural capital and Jackson arguing that club culture facilitates a move beyond the established habitus – it is important to note the purchase of this social and cultural theory on dance culture and vice versa.

Other studies have related dance culture to a range of cultural theories even more directly. A good example of this sort of approach can be found in the work of Gilbert and Pearson (1999). In their view, dance culture has gone against some significant and dominant ideas that value particular types of music in Western culture. In broad terms, there has been a privileging of music that makes an appeal to the intellect (rather than being danced to – thus involving the body) and, with particular respect to popular music, is based around the human voice (rather than being around beat). Drawing on feminist and cultural theory, the authors argue how these dominant traditions are gendered and invoke particular pleasures (of meaning) rather than others (of bodily sensation). Thus, their work uses the sorts of distinction discussed by Roland Barthes (see chapter 5).

Gilbert and Pearson contend that, while 'dance music and culture transgress pro-hibitions laid down by powerful western discourses' (1999: 179), their 'threat' in these terms has been countered in Britain by legislation such as the Criminal Justice and Public Order Act of 1994, which 'regulated' raves. However, despite this, they suggest that dance culture has opened the way for new forms of sociality and community.

This section has explored dance and rave culture, as this has been an important episode in the history of popular music. However, the discussion has also furthered the examination of cultural theories that are of relevance to the understanding of popular music, especially the contribution of the French sociologist Pierre Bourdieu. His work and that of other theorists can also be considered in the context of other music-related activity, such as record collecting.

Collecting, masculinity and distinction

The phenomenon of collecting, like other modes of enthusiasm or fandom (see chapters 8 and 9), has often been viewed from two different perspectives. On the one hand, collecting is criticized as being a form of infantile (or 'nerdy') activity: collecting is for children (especially male children) and they should grow out of it, especially if they collect popular cultural artefacts such as comics or football programmes. On the other hand, collecting is seen as a worthwhile cultural pursuit if it is concerned with valued forms such as paintings or sculptures, when it can be seen as an activity more akin to museum curation. As with work on fandom, recent scholarship has moved beyond such simplistic and politically charged representations of collecting (see, for example, the work of Belk 1995 and Pearce 1995). There exist the beginnings of a literature on masculinity and collecting that are relevant to the themes of this chapter on distinction and performance. A good example of this can be found in the work of Straw.

Straw suggests that record collecting has both public and private dimensions: 'Record collections are seen as both public displays of power/knowledge and private refuges from the sexual or social world' (1997: 4). In this sense, collecting is like many other forms of cultural consumption (see Longhurst and Savage 1996). Record collecting is usually seen as a male or masculine activity, and Straw identifies different modes of masculinity that come into play. He distinguishes between three types: the dandy, the nerd and the brute. The dandy, who 'transforms cultivated knowledges into the basis of an ongoing public performance', is sometimes criticized on the basis that 'his persona is frivolous or depthless, reducible to the surface on which this mastery is displayed' (Straw 1997: 8). The nerd is diametrically opposed in the sense that he 'is noted for a mastery of knowledges whose common trait is that they are of little use in navigating the terrains of social intercourse'. The nerd's knowledge is 'a cause of performative social failure, blatantly indexed in the nerd's chaotic and unmonitored self-presentation' (ibid.). The brute is the 'male persona characterised by a pure and uncultivated instinctuality' (ibid.). Straw argues that, while the brute might be thought to be a mode of masculinity associated with popular music, it actually carries the idea of being hip, which has most often been contrasted with the nerd. In this analysis of the hip (see also the discussion of Thornton above), Straw writes: 'Hipness almost always requires a knowledge which is more or less cultivated, but must repress any evidence that this knowledge is easily acquired in the mastery of lists or bookish sources' (ibid.: 9). This stance must seem to be easy and not contrived. Thus, while record collecting can in a number of ways be seen as 'nerdish' – like other forms of male collecting – it also has significant hip aspects and can therefore be part of the performance of a mode of distinction. The interplay of these ideas then informs much representation of male collecting and acquisition. As well as continuing the exploration of distinction and performance, this example has addressed issues of identity. A further example will allow the exploration of other aspects of performance and identity.

Shuker (2010) examines record collecting as a form of social practice, delving into the history and the development of collecting by asking who collects and for what reasons and what type of music is collected. He discusses a number of collecting practices as well as how taste, cultural capital and the canon may determine value of collections and play a part in what is seen as collectable. Shuker's comprehensive study concludes that, instead of seeking to define a typical collector and a set of typical collecting practices, the more useful approach is to consider record collecting as 'a career' during which a collector can move between the different roles and types, such as 'the record collector as cultural preserver, as accumulator and hoarder, as music industry worker, as adventurous hunter, as connoisseur and as digital explorer' (Shuker 2010: 199), or indeed may inhabit two or more of the above positions simultaneously.

Bogdanović's (2009) interviews with a number of working musicians, all of whom were avid record collectors, revealed the collecting to be an essential part of musical enculturation. Together with a number of other practices such as listening to music (recorded or live) and socializing in music spaces, it played a significant part in shaping musical (and gender) identities, as well as establishing hierarchies of status between the musicians. Bogdanović's observations and conversations revealed that there exists a significant pressure for musicians to *know* about music, extending beyond a particular genre or generation to which they belonged. The content of their various collections was frequently foregrounded and served as a departure point for many conversations about music. Age played a significant part in what type of knowledge was communicated. The respondents in their thirties and early forties frequently provided fascinating narratives interspersed by a sense of nostalgia, harking back to some imagined notion of musical authenticity. Younger respondents – those in their early twenties – strived to demonstrate an encyclopaedic knowledge of music, which often incorporated some of the narratives of the older generation but discovered and mediated by music press (which plays a great part in mythologizing certain albums, gigs, musical events, and so on).

On the whole, the respondents were more willing to talk about the music canon, their knowledge of music spaces, and music activities associated with performing than to provide detailed accounts of their collecting practices. In this sense, musicians are similar to women in avoiding the term 'collector'. Unlike women, who are put off by the term 'record collector' on account of 'its possible masculine and even anal connotations' (quoted in Shuker 2010: 36), however, the musicians' avoidance of the term is likely to be governed by principles of musicianship and authenticity: as active producers of music, they are to be distinguished from the collectors, who are merely consumers.

Popular judgements: performance, distinction and identity

So far in this chapter, a number of themes around performance, distinction, identity and the body have been explored. In an influential text, Frith (1996) has brought together a number of these issues. He is particularly concerned with the way in which judgement about music is made in the context of everyday life. He argues that we express our tastes for music very frequently, but that the academic study of popular music has tended to ignore such issues. This book, however, concentrates on the way that music is produced, structured as a text and consumed, rather than on our basis for making a judgement about whether music is good or bad (for an explanation of why this is, see the Introduction). Issues of this kind have come to the fore at several points in this chapter, especially when discussing the work of Pierre Bourdieu.

Frith argues that the basis for making judgements about popular music is no different from that with respect to other art forms. Thus, the grounds for considering whether a piece of popular music is good or bad are in principle no different from those concerning a classical or 'serious' work (in contrast with the theories of Adorno discussed in the Introduction). However, this is not to suggest that judgement of value is straightforward, otherwise discussions of music would either be very short or would consist simply of direct expressions of preference of the type 'I like this, I don't like that', and so on. Frith's argument is sociological in that he seeks to identify the different social contexts as well as the ideas (or discourses) that frame the way in which judgement can be made. He identifies three different forms, or aspects, of the contexts in which judgement operates.

First, there are three key discourses about music that have been in play since the nineteenth century: art, folk and commerce. Despite the difficulties that might exist concerning the definition of these terms, they are all part of the context in which music is discussed. In simple terms, it could be argued that music is artistically worthwhile (for example, it is complex or original), that it is to be valued because it comes from, or expresses, the values of a particular social group (for example, poor black people from the southern states of the USA), or that it is devalued because it is simply produced for commercial gain. These are familiar strands of argument, but what is of most significance about Frith's opinion is that he shows how they apply to a range of different musical forms ('high' and 'popular') at different times and in specific contexts.

Second, Frith demonstrates that such judgements are social in that they are made with reference to 'circumstances' of 'music making, selling and consuming' (1996: 95). Thus musicians express valuations of whether a performance is good or bad, as will the group that Frith terms 'producers' in quite a specific sense – 'to describe the broad range of people whose concern is to turn music and musicians into profitable commodities and to draw attention to the recording studio as the place where the most interesting and influential musical value judgements are made' (ibid.: 59). Furthermore, consumers themselves will make judgements. As Frith notes, with respect to music in everyday life (Crafts et al. 1993; see also chapter 9): 'What is striking about the accumulated voices of people talking about music is the sense that music matters not just because it is (like film) a powerful force for taking one out of oneself, but also because it can take one deep inside' (1996: 73). Music is thus about the body and identity.

Third, Frith points to the importance of genre in the contextualization of judgement. Usefully, he shows that genres are highly variable and are constructed according to a commercial logic of categorization, as well as aspects of the sound, who is playing the music, and so on.

In these ways, Frith demonstrates that there are ideas and practices in society that contextualize the judgements we make about music. In addition, he shows that these judgements are made and deployed in the specific context of more micro-level social interaction. He presents this in a number of ways, but most illuminatingly in an analysis of his own place in a pleasurable evening's debate about taste. It can also be seen that evidence from group discussions can illuminate how taste is deployed. The extract in box 6.3 shows a range of grounds for taste given by participants of the type that Frith analyses. These include genre, that something is 'stupid', that someone has a wide taste, that something is a 'gimmick' and is thus commercial, and so on.

It is important to stress that much musical judgement takes place in this way. A sense of self is being performed in front of an audience (in this case the other participants, but also the researchers who are focusing the discussion). This brings us back to the key themes of this chapter. Music is part of the way in which judgement is performed in everyday life in a number of ways; but, in dimensions that are further considered in chapter 9, as audience members, our identities are partly constituted and reconstituted through the sorts of discourse considered in this section. This leads to the discussion of the important topic of the audience, to be tackled in Part III.

Box 6.3   Extract from focus-group discussion

Male A   I'll listen to anything, if I like it, I like it, whether it be rap, whether it be pop music, chart music, soul, house music, I'll go out and buy tapes that I consider to be like, I've gone out and bought . . . something like that, but at the end I really don't care because I think if I'm secure within myself of what is right and wrong and I'm certainly not going to hide all my tapes that you don't approve of before you come round so.

What about everybody else?
Male B   What?

Do you think A had quite a wide range of music taste? Do you think you have?
Male B   I like anything, if I see a song that's just come out and I like it I'll go and buy the single or wait for the album to see what the rest of the songs are like, I mean if I like then, anyone, Seahorses, anything like that I like it, you know, if I like the sound of it, if it appeals to me.
Female   I've got a particular taste because I don't really like Indie or anything I'm more into like the soul, I like soul.

What sort of soul?
Female   Erm, like Mary Jane B and things like that.
Male B   Oh I can't stand that.
Female   R. Kelly.

Is that R & B?
Female   Yeah.
Male B   Typewriter in it or something.
Female   Typewriter?
Male B   It goes PING!
Female   Everything?
Male B   Yeah stupid song.
Female   It's good!
Male B   Stupid, it's crap. I like Dodgy, Lightning Seeds and Seahorses and Skunk Anansie.

It's not soul though is it?
Female   No it all sounds the same to me, it's just a load of drums, it does!
Male B   I like the Beatles as well.
Female   Oh they are alright.

How do you get to hear it in the first place?
Male B   Just on the radio or friends given it to me or seen it on MTV.
Female   In the charts.
Male A   What's that new song by Cast that's in the charts, I heard that last night, that's beautiful!

Male B   Not heard it.
Male A   I can't really remember what it goes like but that's.
Male B   Like Teletubbies there's a big craze, people say they like the song or they like watching it because it's about nothing and they all go, again, and they can't speak properly, and everyone thinks they are great, it's just another gimmick like the Spice Girls but they've got better voices.

Male A opens this section of the discussion with a significant expression of his variety of likes. He is also at pains to point out that he is 'secure' in this respect and by implication is not affected by others. In this sense, his *identity* is confidently expressed. In response to a general invitation from one of the leaders of the focus group (the authors of this paper), male B expresses a similar view. The female participant who expresses a 'particular taste' for soul and a dislike of Indie disrupts the initial consensus. This leads to a rapid-fire exchange during which male B, who had started from the position of liking 'anything', opines that R. Kelly is 'crap'. In response the female participant takes a shot at Indie music before some level of agreement is re-established around The Beatles. Male A then points to the nature of an aspect of the contemporary mediascape (in this case the role of the Charts) with his comment about Cast, before the discussion turns to the Teletubbies.

Source: Carrabine and Longhurst 1999: 131, 135–6

Summary

This chapter has considered:

- the idea that sex and gender are constructed through performance;
- the social construction of the body and implications for dance;
- a range of different aspects of dance culture;
- identity with respect to record collecting;
- aspects of taste and distinction with respect to popular music.

PART III

AUDIENCE

Part III consists of three chapters and is informed by the production–text–audience thread that runs through the entire book. Although titled 'Audience', it examines a range of relationships and meanings associated with practices within the production and consumption in music, including the production of meaning associated with interaction between audiences and musical texts. It engages with the questions that have been posed in the rest of the book – what is produced, how is it produced, by whom and why, what those musical texts mean and how are they used.

Within this wider context, chapter 7 introduces some of the key debates on the social effects of music through the examination of the relationship between audience and text. Furthermore, it highlights some relevant, earlier work on subcultures rooted in the British cultural studies tradition. Chapter 8 deals more specifically with fans and fandom, introducing the notion of pop fans as productive. Chapter 9 examines a number of more recent texts, debates and re-engagements with the concept and practice of subcultures, before introducing and discussing notions of the scene, the taste and, finally, the place, significance and meanings of music in everyday life.

Organized in this way, Part 3 provides a chronology of development of thinking and writing about popular music audiences, rooted in wider sociological debates about production and consumption of cultural texts, meanings and identities.

7 Effects, Audiences and Subcultures

This chapter begins the examination of the audience for pop music. It falls into three main parts. The analysis begins with a review of some of the different ways in which the relations between texts and audiences have been considered. This entails looking at contemporary debates on the social effects of popular music, and specific examples are fed into this more general discussion. This is followed by an examination of the contemporary consumption of pop music (mainly at this point in terms of the sales of music), which provides a context for the more detailed study of how pop music is actually used in contemporary society. This theme will be addressed through an evaluation of the literature that deals with how music is used within different subcultures, which has been a dominant theme in the consideration of the consumption of popular music. The following chapters in this section develop this theme further.

The relations between texts and audiences

The earliest research on the mass media, in particular on film and radio, argued that there was a straightforward relationship between texts and audiences. The mass media were believed to have great influence over the behaviour of members of the audience. In a commonly used phrase, they were held to act as a hypodermic syringe, injecting messages into the audience (Lewis 1991; Morley 1992; Moores 1993; Abercrombie and Longhurst 1998). The audience would accept such messages, often because they had no alternative sources of opinion, and would be 'brainwashed' by the media. Such a view was developed in the 1930s when fascist and totalitarian governments had come to power in various parts of Europe, partly, it was thought, through the use of propaganda. The earliest work of some of the writers of the Frankfurt School, including that of Adorno considered in the Introduction, adopted a similar perspective. The mass media constituted a form of drug for the masses. Such a view of the media, and television in particular, is often voiced in popular criticism. For example, in the 1990s the Disposable Heroes of Hiphoprisy sang of 'Television, the Drug of the Nation', and in the 1970s the singer Gil Scott-Heron maintained that the revolution would not be televised.

Such characterizations of the relations between texts and audiences often see contemporary society as divided into a very small elite and a large mass. The vast majority of the population, consisting of essentially similar people, form the mass. The creation of such a mass was the result of the rise of industrialism, or industrial capitalism, in the nineteenth century, when people moved from their 'traditional' communities to the new industrial towns. There, they lived apparently uniform lives, working in large factories where they performed largely similar tasks.

Although it is recognized by such theories that the mass is made up of individuals, the latter are not seen to possess true individuality or discrimination. They are 'massified' in that the ties between them have been, or are in the process of being, broken down. Hence, old family or community ties from earlier days were held to be disappearing. It was argued that the development of such a mass society could have important ramifications. First, some writers suggested that the masses might challenge traditional or elite government, leading to its breakdown. This view, which was often expressed by conservatives, held that government by the elite benefited everyone in society and that democracy would result in social breakdown and turmoil. Likewise, it was thought that the masses were calling into question 'good', 'proper' or previous 'folk' cultures. In such accounts, 'traditional' values were seen as threatened and under attack. Second, it was feared that the masses would be manipulated by the mass media, helping the elite to retain its rule and propagate its views. In both these accounts the media are seen to be very powerful in affecting how and what people think and how they behave.

Similar accounts of the power of the media have held that people respond to it in a very direct fashion: the media act as stimuli to particular forms of behaviour. In accord with such a view, there has been a great deal of research into its effects. This has clustered around a number of areas, including the potential effects of representations of sexual activity and different forms of violence; effects on the attitudes and behaviour of children; the effects of media coverage on how voters behave in elections; and the wider ramifications of the usage of stereotypes of race and gender. These sorts of approach have been represented in discussions of the effects of pop music.

In an examination of the case made against heavy metal music along these lines in the United States in the 1980s, Walser (1993) shows how the work of Tipper Gore (wife of ex-Vice-President Al Gore) – who, along with other wives of members of the government, had founded the Parents' Music Resource Center (PMRC) in 1985 – represented 'heavy metal as a threat to youth, enabling her to mobilize parental hysteria while avoiding the adult word censorship. Objecting to eroticism and "lesbian undertones" in popular music, along with sadism and brutality, she conflates sex and violence, which have in common their threat to parental control' (1993: 138). In Walser's account, Gore accepts 'a "hypodermic model" of musical effects; music's meanings are "pounded" or "dumped" into listeners, who are helpless to resist. Young people in particular are thought to be more vulnerable, especially when repetitive listening and headphone use help create "a direct, unfettered freeway straight into the mind"' (ibid.: 141).

Walser argues that such writings are dependent on 'anecdote and insinuation' (1993: 142) and that none of the critics 'is able to connect heavy metal directly with suicide, Satanism or crime' (ibid.: 143). One important case discussed in detail by Walser concerns the lawsuit brought against the heavy metal group Judas Priest, in which it was argued that subliminal messages in the group's music had led to the suicide of two fans called Vance and Belknap. The trial ended with Judas Priest being cleared of the charges, 'for the judge remained unconvinced that the "subliminal" messages on the album were intentionally placed there or were necessary to explain the conduct of Vance and Belknap' (ibid.: 146).

Walser does not argue that there are no representations of violence or, indeed misogyny, in pop music. However, he suggests that it is not possible to establish a direct link between such representations and the behaviour of pop music audience members: '[Critics of heavy metal] imagine that fans are passive, unable to resist the pernicious messages of heavy metal, and thus they themselves commit the sort of dehumanization they ascribe to popular culture. They make the fans into dupes without agency or subjectivity, without social experiences and perceptions that might inform their interactions with mass-mediated texts' (1993: 144). This argument is a particular example of the hypodermic syringe or mass society view. Powerful performers or owners of the media place messages in texts which are accepted by the passive and gullible in the audience. A simple version of such a thesis is relatively easy to criticize. First, it is important to remember that, in the main, people do not live as separated individuals. They are social beings living in groups that mediate media messages. Second, people question media messages: they do not simply accept them. Third, the message people receive from a text is not always the same as the one producers thought that they were putting in to it: we interpret texts in different ways. In sum, such accounts rely on a very narrow and unsophisticated view of the individual.

Attempts to refine such a model included the two-step flow model associated with Katz and Lazarsfeld (Morley 1980). This model adopted a more sophisticated view of the audience than that found in the hypodermic account. Society is seen as consisting of groups, and our opinions, behaviour and attitudes are influenced by the membership of such groups and the relationships between them. We are not just 'bare individuals' but social beings. However, this does not mean that the mass media are unimportant; rather, we are affected by the media in an indirect fashion. Thus, the majority of the audience will be influenced by the views of opinion leaders. For example, in the case of music, we are all familiar with the way in which certain individuals will suggest that we listen to a particular record or go to see a certain band. This sort of approach begins to recognize the complexity of the composition of the media audience and the nature of some of the social relationships between its different members. However, there are criticisms that can be made of it. First, it tends to divide the audience rather strictly between those who are active and those who are passive. Second, it is not clear why there should be only two steps. There might in fact be a whole range of steps, and the relationships between the members of the audience might be extremely complex.

An approach that attempted to shift attention away from the effects of the media was called the 'uses and gratifications' approach. As the name suggests, the focus here is on the way in which the audience use the media to gratify certain needs or wants. It is significant because it takes the everyday life of the audience rather more seriously than earlier approaches. For example, it would be possible to argue that pop music can be used to satisfy a need for excitement or romance, and so on. However, there is a danger of allowing the audience rather too much freedom in the way they employ the media. Thus, the nature of a text will constrain to some extent the uses to which it is put. For example, it would be unusual to satisfy a need to dance in a club with classical music.

Subsequent work argued that it is important to recognize the complex two-way relationship between texts and audiences. A text might be structured in a particular style, but it is liable to be understood or decoded by the audience in ways that are not necessarily determined by the text itself. In a very influential study of the early evening television programme *Nationwide*, David Morley (1980), following the more theoretical work of Stuart Hall (1980), identified three categories of understanding of the programme among the audience. First, there was the dominant reading which followed the common-sense logic of the programme that had previously been identified by Brunsdon and Morley (1978). Audience members go along with and do not question the structure of the programme. Second, there was the negotiated reading. In this case, audience members would accept most of the message in the programme but would negotiate with it to some degree. The message would not be completely accepted: there might be misgivings about some aspects of it. Third, there were those audience members who opposed the programme altogether. They either saw it as a form of ideology, suggesting that it was putting forward a view of the world that suited the dominant class, or they thought that it had no relevance to their lives.

This study was influential for a number of reasons. First, it took audience reactions seriously and maintained that there could be rather different responses to the same programme. Second, these different responses were related to social background; they were not arbitrary or individualistic. Third, before undertaking this project, Morley had, with Brunsdon, carried out a detailed and sophisticated analysis of *Nationwide*. They argued that the programme tended to structure the viewer of the text in particular ways so that it would not always be easy to perform an oppositional reading. The relationship between the text and the audience was therefore a two-way one.

A number of criticisms can and have been made of this influential study, including the relative neglect of how *Nationwide* was produced. The most important criticism for the purposes of the current discussion is that the research was rather artificial: groups of people were brought together to watch particular editions of *Nationwide* and then asked to discuss them afterwards. It can be argued that this is not the way in which we normally watch television. This was a point recognized by Morley, and in subsequent research (for example, 1986) he situated television as a domestic medium and examined the way in which it is watched and viewed in the home. Since the early 1980s, there has developed an extensive literature which attempts to study the actual ways in which television is viewed by audiences (for overviews, see Abercrombie and Longhurst 1998; Staiger 2005). However, there has not been such a corresponding expansion in the study of the audience for pop music, which would situate music use in the home, at concerts or dances, to take just three possible contexts (but see chapter 9 for consideration of some important studies that have investigated these aspects). One still useful study which did examine this topic was carried out by Dorothy Hobson (1980).

Hobson looked at media use by housewives who were at home looking after young children. She found that the majority of those she studied listened to the pop station Radio 1 a great deal, using it as a background to their domestic work and as a way of structuring the routine of their days (see also, more generally, Longhurst et al. 2001). The disc jockey provided 'the missing "company" of another person' (Hobson 1980: 107), linking the women to others in the same position. In a sense, the male disc jockey would construct an 'imagined community' (Anderson 1983) between the women. The way in which daytime DJs address their audience has also been considered by Rosalind Coward, who argues:

> Nowhere is sexual desire more obviously scripted and stage-managed than in the mishmash of music and chat directed at women during the day on popular radio. Sexual desire, attraction and love dominate not just as themes in the music but also

make up a large part of the DJ's chatter. Forthcoming marriages, broken hearts, happy memories – these are the meat of radio discourse; relationships are at the heart of phone-ins; and radio dedications are from lover to lover. Popular music is broadcast into homes and workplaces during the day, presupposing a certain kind of predominantly female audience. The packaging of the music engages the emotions of this female audience, focusing attention on sexual relationships and in particular requiring the listener to think about her own sexual and emotional involvements. (1984: 144)

It is important to note that neither Hobson nor Coward pay much attention to the actual reactions of women to the music on the radio. Further, it is possible to speculate that the nature of daytime radio has changed somewhat since these studies were carried out, especially as daytime television has expanded. However, both these authors do address important issues about how popular music is related to uses in everyday life.

The discussion of Madonna in chapter 3 has already pointed out that different groups respond to her videos in different ways. Other work has examined the way in which young people interpret the lyrics of songs. For example, Prinsky and Rosenbaum (1987) studied the interpretations of song lyrics by teenagers in the context of the concern articulated by parents' pressure groups in the United States in the 1980s, as discussed above. They administered a questionnaire to 266 students (55 per cent male, 45 per cent female), aged between twelve and eighteen, in four high schools in Southern California. In the questionnaire:

> The students surveyed were asked to list their three favourite songs and on the following page they were asked to describe the songs they had selected in about three sentences. Each song description was coded to determine if the interpretation fell into any of the four categories developed by the parents' Music Resource Center: sex, violence, drugs/alcohol, and Satanism. Three additional categories were included to allow for descriptions that were about love without being sexual as well as permitting respondents to find other themes or to say that they did not know what a song was about. These were love/feelings, other, and don't know. (Prinsky and Rosenbaum 1987: 386)

It was found that those respondents who did give descriptions of songs 'appeared to have only a superficial understanding of the lyrics' (ibid.: 387). They were not aware of many of the meanings that pressure groups found in the lyrics. Thus, 'teenage impressions of popular music in general reflect the interests of young people and are somewhat circumscribed by their lack of experience and limited literary abilities' (ibid.: 393). In addition, Prinsky and Rosenbaum show that young people use music in a number of different ways: for relaxation, entertainment, and so on. Furthermore, as was pointed out in chapter 5, lyrics may not be the most important aspect in creating musical meaning anyway. In some ways Prinsky and Rosenbaum's concise research returns us to the emphasis placed upon the uses made of the media in the uses and gratifications approach. More recent approaches, which emphasize the importance of studying media use in the context of everyday life, share some aspects of this (see chapter 9). However, it is important to bear in mind the complex nature of the interaction between what is in a text (as was demonstrated in chapter 5, there are a number of different dimensions to this) and what members of the audience make of it in the context of their social situation.

In making such points, it should not be thought that the role of the media in influencing forms of behaviour and attitudes is being played down. It may be that the media, including pop music, have long-term social effects, and it is important to recognize that the stereotypical ways in which women and black people are represented in pop music may feed into everyday understandings of race and gender, as the discussions of rap and hip-hop (see chapter 4) suggest.

More specifically, the approach known as cultivation analysis has argued that there are long-term effects of the media, maintaining, on the basis of several studies, that, 'the more TV you watch, the more likely you are to have a fearful or distrustful attitude to the world outside' (Lewis 1991: 19). Television is held to influence beliefs and behaviour over extended periods of time.

In recent years, writers interested in audiences have begun to make greater use of the quantitative data produced from within media organizations themselves. Such data can be informative (though, for a critical discussion, see Ang 1991) in helping to build up a clearer picture of what the audience for pop music is like. In the area of music, these data refer in the main to the consumption of different forms of music, and there are issues raised by the concept of consumption itself. These are examined in chapter 8.

Trends in consumption

Until recently, recorded music has been available in five main formats: singles, LPs, cassettes, compact discs and music videos. The introduction of the digital format, downloading, streaming and listening to music on mobile devices such as smart phones have all had a significant impact on trends in consumption. In the UK in 2010 there were 72 licensed digital music services, with 500 million tracks and 50 million albums being sold digitally. Digital's share of music industry's revenue has grown steadily from 0.2 per cent in 2004 to 35.4 per cent in 2011. Table 7.1 shows the breakdown of revenue from physical formats, online, subscriptions, ad-supported, mobile and other digital from 2008 to 2010 (BPI Yearbook 2012: 9). The decreases in physical format sales have meant losses for the music industry which are not yet offset by digital growth, with the revenues from sales falling by 35 per cent since 2004.

According to BPI's data, in 2009 music video sales had risen to 5 million, mainly due to sales from Michael Jackson's catalogue following his death. Sales of music videos dropped to 4.2 million in 2010, while in 2011 they decreased by 2.4 per cent to 4.08 million, thus stabilizing somewhat. This drop in sales may be on account of the growth in popularity of streaming services such as YouTube and Vevo. According to a study by Nielsen (quoted in BPI Yearbook 2011: 57), 57 per cent of 26,644 respondents from fifty-three countries watched music videos online and 23 per cent watched them on their mobile devices. Music video viewing represents 31 per cent of all YouTube traffic, and in February 2010 5.5 billion videos had been viewed online, an increase of 37 per cent on the previous year. In 2011 YouTube retained its popularity, with 4 billion daily streams globally, including all categories. In 2009, Vevo, a joint venture by Universal Music, Sony Music Entertainment and Abu Dhabi Media, opened an office in London as a foothold for their expansion in Central Europe. In addition to showing promo music videos in high definition, Vevo has been developing programming of shows that promote new and emerging acts. Similarly, YouTube has branched into

Table 7.1 *Industry Income (£m)*

		2002	2003	2004	2005	2006	2007	2008	2009	2010	2011	% change
Physical formats	Singles	£97.2	£64.5	£52.8	£43.1	£31.8	£19.0	£10.2	£7.6	£4.9	£3.3	−33.1%
	Albums	£1,089.0	£1,112.0	£1,102.2	£1,057.3	£982.9	£815.6	£749.1	£699.2	£566.4	£484.7	−14.4%
	Music video	£23.5	£46.6	£62.7	£63.3	£49.1	£37.2	£28.5	£33.1	£26.7	£25.8	−3.3%
	Total	**£1,209.7**	**£1,223.1**	**£1,217.7**	**£1,163.7**	**£1,063.8**	**£871.8**	**£787.8**	**£740.0**	**£598.0**	**£513.8**	**−14.1%**
Online	Tracks	–	–	£2,7	£12.4	£25.2	£40.9	£62.5	£91.8	£108.3	£120.5	+11.3%
	Albums	–	–	–	–	–	£30.7	£43.7	£67.3	£82.2	£117.8	+43.2%
	Music video	–	–	–	–	–	–	£4.0	£3.4	£3.0	£2.8	−7.0%
	Total	–	–	**£2.7**	**£12.4**	**£25.2**	**£71.6**	**£110.1**	**£162.6**	**£193.5**	**£241.1**	**+24.6%**
Mobile	Master ringtones	–	–	–	–	–	–	£5.3	£3.7	£3.3	£2.3	−32.0%
	Ringback tunes	–	–	–	–	–	–	£0.8	£0.4	£0.3	£0.2	−14.4%
	Total	–	–	–	–	–	–	**£6.0**	**£4.1**	**£3.6**	**£2.5**	**−30.6%**
Subscriptions		–	–	–	–	–	–	**£8.6**	**£11.8**	**£16.3**	**£23.3**	**+43.2%**
Ad-supported		–	–	–	–	–	–	**£2.4**	**£8.2**	**£10.8**	**£11.4**	**+5.1%**
Other digital music content		–	–	–	–	–	–	**£0.8**	**£2.1**	**£1.6**	**£3.4**	**+105.8%**
	Total	**£1,209.7**	**£1,223.1**	**£1,220.4**	**£1,176.1**	**£1,089.0**	**£943.4**	**£915.6**	**£928.8**	**£823.8**	**£795.4**	**−3.4%**

Note: For the years 2004–2007 digital income was estimated on the basis of Official Charts Company retail volumes. Values are at wholesale, do not include VAT and are net of returns.

Source: BPI Surveys

live broadcasting, providing live streams in 2011 from some of the major US music festivals such as Lollapalooza and Coachella. Audiences for some of the live YouTube streams are impressive, with Coldplay's live stream being watched by 19 million people. Some artists decided to charge for live streams of their shows: to watch the live stream of Florence & the Machine at the Hackney Empire, London, in October 2011, users had to pay £3.99.

An important development in 2011 was the opening of APIs (application programming interfaces) that enable websites to interact with each other. Facebook incorporated open APIs into its business model, allowing its partners to plug into the Facebook platform and thus potentially reach over 800 million users, which meant that by January 2012 over 5 billion songs had been shared through it (BPI Yearbook 2012: 57). EMI launched its own OpenEMI platform, allowing access to its data and the building of new apps based upon it.

It is estimated that music on demand and music anywhere via these multi-platform-enabled services will continue to grow in popularity. A number of locker services, where music can be uploaded to the web and then accessed from computers or mobile devices, have been launched. While providing safe storage and easy access, there are two main factors why such services are still to enter the mainstream: the time it takes to upload entire collections of music and the persisting desire to possess music (albeit in digital format) on one's personal devices. While the sales of smart phones continue to grow, there has been a decline in sales of MP3 players, further pointing in the direction of increased popularity of online, multi-platform services.

With regard to other recent developments, geolocation services and social networking seem to go hand in hand, and these provide some interesting opportunities for both music fans and artists. In an example discussed in the BPI Yearbook 2011, in 'producing' a video for 'We Used to Wait', Arcade Fire utilized Google Maps and Street View to involve the viewer. After entering the address of the place where they grew up, the viewer is taken through a number of windows where a figure can be seen running down the streets of the relevant geographic area. There is also an opportunity to write a letter to a younger self, replay one's film, send a postcard to 'Downtown', share a film, or reply to a postcard sent by somebody else.

'Fan Analytics' or 'Fanalytics' has also entered the popular music vernacular and practice: 'It offers semantic web analysis for musicians and labels so they can assess what is being written about them online' (BPI Yearbook 2011: 63). One such platform is The Echo Nest, which claims to provide 'The Knowledge' through 'large-scale data mining, natural language processing, acoustic analysis and machine learning' (http://the.echonest.com/platform/how-it-works/). The main aim is to help the artist learn about their audience and better understand their motivation and practices. An example of how The Echo Nest works is sentiment analysis of music blogs and review sites, providing the client with information about the sentiment of a review (positive, negative, neutral). Essentially, it is a quantitative measure of 'online "buzz"' – that is, the level of attention an artist is getting across from a variety of online music 'spaces'.

Purchasing music via online outlets amounts to just over 60 per cent of men's overall expenditure on music. At 50.7 per cent, online is the biggest purchasing outlet for women, too, closely followed by supermarkets, which constitute an outlet for 26.6 per cent of women's total expenditure on music. In terms of age, home delivery and online outlets are popular with younger age groups, constituting more than a half of

Table 7.2 *Retailer expenditure by gender and age, 2011*

	Total	Women	Men	13–19	20–24	25–34	35–44	45–54	55–64	65–79
Internet (home delivery & digital)	**57.1**	**50.7**	**60.6**	**66.4**	**68.9**	**62.9**	**55.6**	**52.3**	**43.7**	**45.9**
Amazon	22.4	20.7	23.4	16.3	18.3	21.5	24.8	25.8	23.0	26.8
iTunes	17.9	16.9	18.4	33.0	31.9	24.0	13.7	8.9	7.5	4.7
HMV	3.8	3.3	4.1	5.3	5.5	5.0	3.5	3.2	1.7	2.1
Play.com	3.7	3.6	3.8	2.5	4.2	4.1	4.8	3.9	3.1	2.5
Tesco	1.3	0.9	1.5	1.3	1.1	1.4	1.2	1.9	0.6	0.8
Asda	0.2	0.3	0.2	–	0.1	0.2	0.3	0.3	0.1	0.2
Sainsbury's	0.2	0.1	0.2	0.1	0.1	0.1	0.1	0.3	–	0.1
Other Online	7.6	4.9	9.0	7.9	7.7	6.6	7.2	8.0	7.7	8.7
Music specialists	**20.9**	**20.1**	**21.3**	**24.4**	**19.9**	**18.8**	**20.3**	**20.8**	**24.9**	**14.7**
HMV	19.1	19.0	19.1	23.6	18.6	16.9	18.2	18.8	22.1	13.5
Other music specialist	1.8	1.1	2.2	0.8	1.3	1.9	2.1	2.0	2.8	1.2
Supermarkets	**19.3**	**26.6**	**15.1**	**8.0**	**9.8**	**16.5**	**22.1**	**23.9**	**26.6**	**29.9**
Tesco	7.9	11.2	6.0	4.1	3.6	6.1	9.3	8.8	11.3	13.8
Asda	6.3	9.0	4.7	2.5	3.2	6.6	7.5	7.8	7.6	7.6
Sainsbury's	3.0	4.0	2.5	0.9	1.5	2.1	3.5	4.3	4.8	4.4
Morrisons	2.1	2.4	1.9	0.5	1.5	1.7	1.8	3.0	2.9	4.1
Chains/multiples	**2.1**	**2.1**	**2.1**	**0.8**	**0.6**	**1.4**	**1.4**	**2.6**	**3.7**	**7.4**
Mail order	**0.1**	**0.1**	**0.1**	–	–	–	–	–	**0.2**	**0.6**
Other	**0.6**	**0.3**	**0.7**	**0.5**	**0.7**	**0.4**	**0.4**	**0.4**	**0.8**	**1.5**

Source: BMI Yearbook 2012

Base: All music expenditure excepting music video

Table 7.3 Music Spend by demographic group 2011 (% down)

		Total music	All albums	Physical albums	Artist albums	Compilation albums	Total digital music	Digital singles	Digital albums
Gender	Female	35.7	36.2	38.0	36.9	44.0	30.7	33.0	29.1
	Male	64.3	63.8	62.0	63.1	56.0	69.3	67.0	70.9
Age group	13–19	15.2	13.1	10.5	11.2	6.9	25.6	29.0	23.0
	20–24	9.2	7.9	6.6	6.5	6.9	15.0	17.8	12.9
	25–34	17.7	16.7	15.2	15.3	15.1	23.2	24.0	22.5
	35–44	20.5	21.4	22.5	22.4	23.0	16.2	14.5	17.5
	45–54	18.7	20.1	21.8	21.5	23.1	11.7	9.1	13.7
	55–64	11.7	13.0	14.4	14.1	15.7	5.9	3.6	7.7
	65–79	7.0	7.7	9.0	9.0	9.2	2.4	2.0	2.7
Social group	AB	20.3	20.0	18.3	18.5	17.3	24.6	21.7	26.7
	C1	38.1	38.6	39.3	39.8	36.8	35.6	35.3	35.8
	C2	22.3	22.2	22.6	21.9	25.9	21.8	22.9	21.0
	DE	19.2	19.1	19.8	19.8	20.0	18.0	20.1	16.4

Source: BMI Yearbook 2012

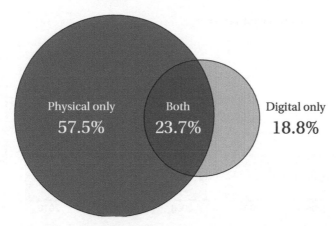

| Physical only | Both | Digital only |
| 57.5% | 23.7% | 18.8% |

Figure 7.1 Digital/physical crossover of music buyers, 2011
Source: BMI Yearbook 2012

Table 7.4 Top 10 international markets, 2011

		Market value (trade income US$m)	*% change from 2010*	*Share of global revenues*
1	USA	4,372.9	−0.1%	26.3%
2	Japan	4,087.7	−7.0%	24.6%
3	Germany	1,473.7	−0.2%	8.9%
4	UK	1,433.7	−3.1%	8.6%
5	France	1,002.2	−3.7%	6.0%
6	Australia	475.2	5.7%	2.9%
7	Canada	434.0	2.6%	2.6%
8	Brazil	262.6	8.6%	1.6%
9	Netherlands	240.2	−12.1%	1.4%
10	Italy	239.9	−6.4%	1.4%

Source: IFPI

their overall spend, while supermarkets tend to be favoured by the oldest groups, who utilize them for about the quarter of all purchases.

With 64.3 per cent of purchases across the entire music market, men still remain the strongest buyers. The trend is repeated within digital purchases, where 69.3 per cent were made by men. Buyers aged thirty-five to forty-four are responsible for the greatest number of overall purchases, while those aged thirteen to nineteen are the biggest buyers of digital music. The greatest number of singles are bought by those in younger age groups.

In the light of the debates about proliferation of digital music and the decrease of sales of physical formats, figure 7.1 is of interest. At 57.5 per cent, and despite the continuing decrease in sales, physical-only format buyers still constitute the largest group, with digital-only format buyers at 18.8 per cent.

Despite 5 per cent growth in the digital sector, overall sales of music globally

Digital's share of global industry revenue

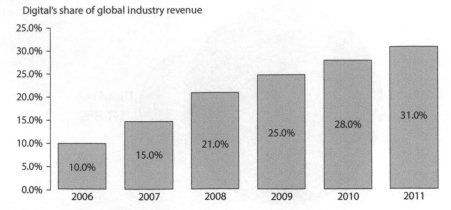

Figure 7.2 Digital share of global industry revenue, 2006–11
Source: BMI Yearbook 2012

declined by 8.4 per cent in 2010, mostly due to a shortfall of $1.8 billion from physical-format sales that could not be offset by the developments and increase in the digital markets. In 2011 the global sales decrease was less significant, with a downturn of 3 per cent. The USA and Japan remain the largest markets, with Germany retaining the third position for the second year in succession. For the first time since 1998, Germany overtook the UK in 2010 to become the third largest international market for music, with 8.9 per cent of global revenue.

As figure 7.2 shows, the digital share of global industry revenue has risen steadily, from 10 per cent in 2006 to 31 per cent in 2011.

Providing us with a context, these figures on consumption are illuminating. However, they still give only a rather broad picture of music use, sometimes leading to audience stereotypes. In order to examine further the ways in which popular music is used in contemporary society, in the sections that follow we turn to the concept of subculture. Subculture frequently features in more ethnographic research examining, for example, the role and meanings of cultural practice of music-making and consumption.

Culture, subculture and music

Most of the research on subculture, which has focused particularly on youth subcultures, draws on two different meanings of culture. In the first, culture refers to the works and practices of artistic and intellectual activity. In this sense, music or a painting are forms of culture, but schoolwork, for example, is not. At times, this version of culture involves a judgement of value. Thus certain forms of music – for example, by Beethoven or Mozart – are held to be proper 'culture', while works by such as Girls Aloud or Kylie Minogue are considered as trash. The second sense of culture is rather different, referring to the idea of culture as a 'way of life'. This more inclusive definition can be found in expressions such as 'the American way of life' or 'British culture'. These definitions both feed into the development of what has increasingly become known as British cultural studies (Turner 1990), and it is from within this context that many of the most important studies of youth subcultures and music have been carried out. The key definition of culture produced within this tradition explains that 'we understand the word culture to refer to that level at which social groups develop distinct patterns of life, and give expressive form to their social and material life experience. Culture is the way, the forms, in which groups "handle" the raw material of their social and material existence' (Clarke et al. 1976: 10). Clarke and his colleagues relate three aspects of social life in this definition: social experience, social groups and patterns of life. In their account, social groups develop distinct patterns of life based on their own social experiences in relation to other social groups and forms of experience. Culture is both a level/an area of society and the forms in which the raw material of social experience is handled.

The approach taken by Clarke et al. was greatly influenced by a paper written in the early 1970s by Cohen (1980), who examined the nature of youth subcultures in the East End of London in the 1960s. He argued that after the Second World War, from the 1950s onwards, the East End working-class community was disrupted by three factors: migration out of the area; the redevelopment of housing involving the building of new tower blocks patterned on a middle-class nuclear family model, which destroyed the forms of communal space and the patterns of female support that had been so important in the area; and a series of economic changes. This led to a 'polarization of the labour force' (Cohen 1980: 80) between more specialized, 'high-tech' and well-paid jobs and more dead-end, unskilled labour.

One outcome of this process of dislocation was the development of youth subcultures, which opposed the working-class parent culture. In Cohen's argument, 'the internal conflicts of the parent culture came to be worked out in terms of generational conflict' (1980: 82). Furthermore, Cohen maintained that youth subcultures 'express and resolve, albeit "magically", the contradictions which remain hidden or unresolved in the parent culture' (ibid.). Subcultures are ways of dealing with the difficulties that structural transformations in society have created in the parent culture to which they belong. Following the pattern of the polarization of the workforce between an upward and a downward social movement, Cohen argued that youth subcultures can express such routes in a variety of different ways. Hence, 'mods, parkas, skinheads, crombies are a succession of subcultures which all correspond to the same parent culture and which attempt to work out, through a system of transformations, the basic problematic or contradiction which is inserted in the subculture by the parent culture' (ibid.: 83). This sort of approach has been represented diagrammatically by Clarke et al. (1976), as shown in figure 7.3.

Cohen argued that there are two main components of the lifestyle of such youth subcultures, which he terms 'plastic' (dress and music) and 'infrastructural' (argot and ritual). Thus, music is an important part of the complex subcultural whole. However, Cohen paid relatively little attention to the detail of the music used by subcultures. Other writers who developed work within the 'Birmingham tradition' of British cultural studies, which was initiated at the Centre for Cultural Studies at the University of Birmingham, placed more emphasis on it. Some of the papers collected in *Resistance through Rituals* (Hall and Jefferson 1976) consider this dimension, but most detail can be found in the work of Paul Willis (1978) and Dick Hebdige (1979).

Willis examined various dimensions of the lives of two youth subcultural groups in the late 1960s: the motor-bike boys and hippies. While these examples are rather dated, it is the nature of the link that Willis makes between music and other aspects of the lifestyle of these groups that resonated through work on subcultures. Willis argued that their musical preferences were intimately connected to the nature of their

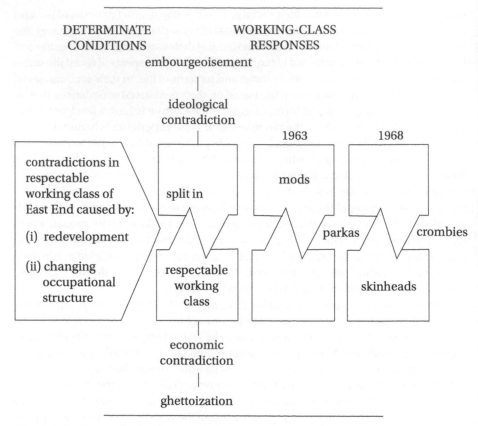

Figure 7.3 Class and subcultures: a version of Cohen's model
Source: Clarke et al. 1976: 34

lives. Thus, the motor-bike boys' preference for early rock 'n' roll in a single format and the hippies' like of album-based progressive rock was no accident. Rock 'n' roll music matched the restlessness and mobility of the motor-bike boys' lives:

> [T]his music allows the return of the body in music, and encourages the development of a culture based on movement and confidence in movement. The classical European tradition has steadily forced the body and dancing out of music, and made it progressively harder to dance to. The absolute ascendancy of the beat in rock 'n' roll firmly establishes the ascendancy of the body over the mind – it reflects the motor-bike boys' culture very closely. The eclipse of tonality and melody in the music is also the eclipse of abstraction in the bike culture. . . . [T]he suppression of structured time in the music, its ability to stop, start and be faded, matches the motor-bike boys' restless concrete life style. As we have seen, it is no accident that the boys preferred singles, nor is it an accident that the rock 'n' roll form is the most suited to singles and its modern technology (fading, etc.). Both the music and its 'singles' form are supremely relevant to the style of the bike culture. (1978: 77)

Willis mounts a similar sort of argument about the homologous relationships between different aspects of a hippie youth subculture (see, especially, 1978: 168–9). In Hebdige's words, this expresses 'the symbolic fit between the values and life-styles of a group, its subjective experience and the musical forms it uses to express or reinforce its focal concerns' (1979: 113). This means that, for Willis, subcultures are structured, as different aspects of the lifestyle of the subculture fit together to form a whole. So, for the hippie subculture, there is a homology or correspondence between an 'alternative value system', 'hallucinogenic drugs' and progressive rock. Subcultures express a response to a set of conditions, and the different aspects of the subculture are tied together into structured relatively coherent wholes. A schematic version of this approach can be seen in the chronology of subcultures reproduced in table 7.5.

Hebdige developed the idea of reading the nature of the style of subcultural groups by means of the structural and semiotic approaches that were introduced in chapter 5. He focused on the different dimensions of the style of subcultural groups. Using the general definition of culture proposed by Clarke and his colleagues, Hebdige argued that the styles expressed by different subcultures are a response to social conditions and experiences. Furthermore, he suggested that such styles often encode an opposition to the dominant or hegemonic forms of culture associated with dominant groups. Such challenges are often indirect and can involve the utilization and transformation of forms of culture that were previously the property of dominant groups. In participating in such practices, subcultural members engage in a process of 'bricolage', responding to the world around them by improvising in a structured fashion, creating meanings that are different from those of the dominant group or groups. As Hebdige says about the style: 'In this way the teddy boy's theft and transformation of the Edwardian style revived in the early 1950s by Savile Row for wealthy young men about town can be construed as act of bricolage' (1979: 104).

Hebdige argues that subcultures generally resist the dominant social order, albeit indirectly and in symbolic ways. However, he also argues that forms of subcultural expression are often incorporated into the dominant social order through two main routes. First, there is the commodity form, which involves 'the conversion of subcultural signs (dress, music, etc.) into mass-produced objects'. Second, there is 'the "labelling" and re-definition of deviant behaviour by dominant groups – the police, the media, the judiciary' (1979: 94) in a process of ideological incorporation.

This account of the ways in which subcultural groups produce new and resistant meanings, which are then bought off or incorporated by the capitalist system, is now relatively familiar. It entails the notion that there is sphere where 'authentic' meanings are produced which is then corrupted. However, as has been pointed out in other parts of this book, this thesis has always been rather difficult to sustain, and that remains the case especially now. Nevertheless, it is also important to note that such characterization of the processes of change in social life is often produced by young music fans themselves.

On the basis of research carried out in 1972, Simon Frith (1983: 205–12) drew a distinction between 'sixth-form culture', based around progressive rock which stressed the individual nature of taste, and 'lower-fifth-form culture', made up of people who 'bought singles and watched *Top of the Pops*, went regularly to youth clubs and discos but rarely to concerts, emphasized beat and sound in their tastes rather than meaning, and identified with specific youth styles' (ibid.: 206). He also identified a group of prospective sixth-formers who had a 'missionary zeal for progressive rock and hatred of commercial pop' (ibid.: 207). This group was very assertive in its views about music and taste. As Frith explains:

Table 7.5 *Chronology of subcultures*

Date	Subculture	Class position	Style	Music	Shifts in post-war hegemony
1953–4	teds	unskilled	drapes	rock 'n' roll	The construction of consensus Macmillanism
1955–6	teds	working class		jazz/folk	
1958–61	beats/CND	middle class	duffle coats, beards	r 'n' b/Tamla	The construction of consensus Social democracy
1963	mods	semi-skilled	scooter of consensus	rock 'n' roll	
1964	rockers	unskilled	motor-bike		
1967–72	hippies	middle class/student	long hair, hallucinogenic drugs	progressive rock	Dissensus Protest and revolution
1967	rude boys	black underclass	hustling	ska	
1968–9	skinheads	unskilled	boots 'n' braces	ska	
1970	glams	working class?	bisexuality	glamrock	The Law and Order Society Authoritarianism and working-class resistance
1970	Rastas	black underclass?	dreadlocks	reggae	
1976–8	punks	working class?	absurdity	punk rock	
1978–81	mod/ted skinhead revivals				
1981	new romantics				
1982	?				

Source: Middleton and Muncie 1981: 90

One of the paradoxes in my survey was that the group which most stress indi-vidual music choice also most stressed the importance of shared musical taste for friendship – music served as the badge of individuality on which friendship choices could be based. One of the ironies was that because music was taken as a symbol of a cluster of values, the most individualistic groups were the ones most thrown by their musical heroes changing direction. This was particularly a problem for the hairies [long-haired followers of progressive rock] because they differentiated themselves from the masses as a self-conscious elite by displaying exclusive musical tastes. Their tastes weren't just a matter of identification; they also reflected a different – more serious, more intense – relationship to music. The hairies thought of themselves not as just another teenage style, but as people who had transcended the trivialities of teenage style. Their music meant something, and when one of their acts 'sold out', became part of mass taste, there was great bitterness. (Ibid.: 208)

Frith tied age and class together, noting that the sixth-formers were more middle class than the more mixed younger groups. He also discussed some important gender dif-ferences, which will be addressed in more detail below. It is important to notice the clear distinction between rock and pop audience tastes which came out of Frith's study and the critique of commercialism expressed by the rock audience. It might be thought that such a division is now rather dated – after all, Frith's study was under-taken more than forty years ago. However, it can be argued that the structure of the division continues to exist even if the contents of rock have changed. For example, it may be that the audience for 'indie' is rather like the one that used to exist for pro-gressive rock, although some evidence suggests that there is also an allegiance to pop music within such subcultures. However, this is not the pop music associated with the top forty charts (Kruse 1993). There certainly seems to be evidence for an 'oppo-sitional' stance in the studies of local music-making by Cohen (1991) and Finnegan (1989), as discussed in chapter 2.

  One of the most important problems with the literature discussed in this section so far is the fact that it concentrated almost entirely on boys or men. This was first challenged by Angela McRobbie in an article co-authored with Jenny Garber in which they asked four main questions. First, 'are girls really absent from the main post-war subculture or are they present but invisible?' Second, where girls were 'present and visible, were their roles the same, but more marginal, than [those of] boys; or were they different?' Third, 'whether marginal or different, is the position of girls specific to the subcultural option, or do their roles reflect the more general social-subordination of women in the central areas of mainstream culture – home, work, school, leisure?' And, 'fourth, if subcultural options are not readily available to girls, what are the dif-ferent but complementary ways in which girls organize their cultural life? And are these, in their own terms, subcultural in form?' (1976: 211).

  In response to the first question, McRobbie and Garber argued that, at least partly because of the male bias of previous investigations, this was very difficult to answer. The men who had studied subcultures had not looked at the possible participation of girls in them, and so their invisibility tended to be a self-fulfilling prophecy. In pursu-ing the second and third questions, McRobbie and Garber looked in more detail at the parts that women have played in three subcultures. First, they examined the rocker, greaser or motor-bike subculture as described by Willis. Here, they saw women as being in a very subordinate position: they were passengers on the motor-bikes – they did not drive them. Second, they considered the mod girls of the early 1960s, whom they saw as prominent within the mod subculture. Third, they examined hippie culture, identifying two particular roles for women: the 'earth mother' and the 'pre-Raphaelite fragile lady'. Furthermore, they suggested that this period saw the development of two particular styles for women in music: the introspection associated with singers/songwriters such as Joni Mitchell and that of the boozy blues singer, as exemplified by Janis Joplin. These roles have continued to be important for women in rock music, where it might be argued that Beth Orton and Martha Wainwright are examples of the former and Courtney Love of the latter.

McRobbie and Garber asserted that the places for women in the subcultures so far described were related to their other roles in life. However, they also suggested that girls tended to organize their cultural lives differently from boys, forming a more home-based, romantic or 'teenybop' culture. McRobbie developed this point and others in a subsequent critique of the male-dominated nature of research on subcultures (McRobbie 1980). She argued that there are two main approaches that can be taken vis-à-vis previous male-dominated writing on subcultures. First, such accounts can be dismissed, or be accepted as applicable only to boys, and attention be placed on the different nature of girls' culture. This extended the point made in the earlier article written with Jenny Garber. Second, previous accounts, such as those by Willis and Hebdige, can be read 'against the grain' to see what they can offer for the analysis of masculinity, both in the nature of the subcultures and in the writing on them.

In developing her points about the different nature of girls' culture, McRobbie contends that the street is a potentially dangerous place for girls and that 'younger girls tend to stay indoors or to congregate in youth clubs; those with literally nowhere else to go but the street frequently become pregnant within a year and disappear back into the home to be absorbed by childcare and domestic labour' (1980: 47). In her view, the use of drink and drugs can induce the same sort of perils: 'it is clear from my recent research, for example, that girls are reluctant to drink precisely because of the sexual dangers of drunkenness' (ibid.).

McRobbie suggested that the working-class girls she studied tended to form a teenybop culture based around romance. These girls spent more time in the home, at least partly because of the dangerous nature of public places such as the street. Frith (1983) added three other aspects to this when he argued, first, that girls are more subject to parental control and discipline than boys and, second, that girls are often expected to carry out domestic duties in a way that boys are not – a point that was illustrated graphically by McRobbie (1978) when she pointed out that girls were expected to perform large amounts of work in the home for very little financial recompense. Frith's third point was that girls spend more time at home getting ready to go out than do boys.

To summarize, this subculture of girls, identified in the 1970s, consisted of the following features:

1 The home, and often the bedroom, is central. Girls tended to get together with other girls and listen to records by their favourite artists in each other's bedrooms.
2 Girls formed a teenybop culture, where there was a romantic attachment to one star or group. There is a history of different stars and groups that have filled such a role.

3   When girls did go out, it was most likely to be to a youth club. Though, as Robins and Cohen (1978) pointed out, youth clubs, such as the one they studied in North London, could be a site of conflict.

4   Dance was important to girls in ways that it was not for boys. McRobbie (1984, 1993) has continued to stress the importance of dance to girls (see also chapter 6).

5   For the girls in McRobbie's study, the relationship with a best friend was very important and was more valued than their relationships with boys.

6   The idea of romance was also very important. Many of the girls, despite at times showing a 'realistic' appreciation of some of the aspects of marriage, placed great stress on the idea of romance and the romantic attachment to one boy. This can be related to the continued existence of a sexual double standard, where girls could easily become known as 'slags' if they went out with several boys.

7   McRobbie argued that the girls she studied stressed some dominant ideas of femininity in an exaggerated fashion. This may form part of a culture which opposed the perceived school ethic of responsibility, hard work and seriousness. The girls spent much time talking about boys and wanted to bend the school rules about dress and make-up in as fashionable a direction as possible. McRobbie maintained that this culture, while it may oppose official culture in some ways, reinforces the culture of romance and the idea of femininity which is a part of this. This parallels the argument advanced by Willis (1977) concerning the way in which the exaggeration of masculinity among working-class boys, in opposition to school norms, suited them for manual labour.

The way in which this teenybop culture of femininity connects with music in more detail is discussed in an article on rock and sexuality by Frith and McRobbie (1990), which was reviewed in chapter 3. Various writers have identified some problems with this idea of the teenybop culture of romance. First, McRobbie may have underestimated the participation and seriousness of the commitment of some girls to subcultural groups. Smith (1978) argued that the 'delinquent' girls she studied were heavily involved in the fighting that took place between subcultural groups. However, she also noted that girls were less committed to the groups in terms of length of time of membership. Second, Cowie and Lees (1981) found that girls had a more realistic appraisal of the potential problems involved with marriage than McRobbie found in her group. Cowie and Lees found far more emphasis on having a good time before marriage. Third, Cowie and Lees suggested that McRobbie's work tended to isolate a discrete female youth subculture, over-integrating and separating it off from the relations between men and women which existed in society more widely. Relatedly, they argued that too much emphasis is placed on the resistance entailed in the culture of femininity. Fourth, McRobbie's work concentrated mainly on white working-class girls, and more evidence is needed about black and middle-class girls for comparison. Furthermore, it might be that some of this work is now rather dated. This point can be considered through an examination of McRobbie's more recent work.

In her earlier publications, McRobbie drew attention to the role of magazines in the culture of romance, demonstrating the difference between contemporary magazines such as *Just Seventeen* and *Jackie*. She argued that romance had drastically declined in importance and that pop and fashion had become central, leading to a greater emphasis on image and the pop star: 'It is pop rather than romance which

Box 7.1   Gender conflict at a junior disco

So the demand for a junior disco was more complex than it first appeared. In fact it concealed two, distinctly antagonistic demands: the girls wanted to start a local chapter of the Donny Osmond Fan Club; the boys wanted a cross between an indoor adventure playground and the North Bank terrace at Arsenal. So when the doors were opened, the organizers found they had *two* distinct clubs which just happened to coincide at the one time and place. The boys swarmed all over the place, swung from the lights, held races across tables and chairs, savaged the football machine and had impromptu bundle fights on the floors, all this interspersed with much North Bank football chanting. They came in scruffy and came out looking – as one mum put it – 'like they've been put in a spin dryer'.

But the girls . . . ! Dressed to the nines in their best party clothes, and the latest teen fashion. Here and there a hint of eye shadow and deft application of mum's Chanel No. 5.

At the first bars of 'Long Haired Lover' they 'took' the dance floor, and remained there for the rest of the evening as if hypnotized, impervious to the boys' bedlam; ten-year-old seductive swaying bottoms, rolling hips – a completely convincing imitation of teenage disco sex. Mostly, the boys ignored them, but from time to time, the chant would go up from the North Bank: 'Donny's a poofta, Donny's a poofta.'* To which the girls would inevitably chorus, 'Charlie's a wanker' (i.e. Charlie George, the footballer).

Osmond-baiting was in fact one of the most familiar weapons used by older brothers in their continuous bickering with their younger sisters. A fourteen-year-old boy told how 'we went by the Rainbow [Theatre] once and we started screaming out the window, "Osmonds are bent, all queers", and they were lobbing everything that come in sight. You see one of them, she's in a state crying over the railing going "you bastards" and the next minute she picked up a bottle and threw it at the bus.'

Source: Robins and Cohen 1978: 52

Reproduced by permission of Penguin Books Ltd.

Copyright © David Robins and Philip Cohen, 1978

now operates as a kind of conceptual umbrella giving a sense of identity to these productions' (1991: 168). In such girls' magazines:

> [T]here is an overwhelming interest in personal information. The magazines increasingly play the role of publicist for the various bands who fall into the teenybopper camp. In return their pages are filled with glossy pictures and they can claim to have a direct line to the stars. This makes for cheap and easy copy. Three pages can be covered in a flash with the help of a transatlantic telephone call, a tape-recorder and a selection of publicity shots often provided by the record company. (Ibid.: 169)

In McRobbie's view, pop music had become more important to girls than it had been in the 1970s. However, girls did not become involved only with pop music of the teenybop type; McRobbie has also drawn attention to their participation in rave culture. She argues that such culture can be connected to drastic changes in femininity over recent years in Britain, suggesting that 'girls both black and white have been "unhinged" from their traditional gender position while the gender and class destiny of their male counterparts has remained more stable' (1993: 408). In an article on rave culture, McRobbie reiterates some of the points already made about the changing nature of girls' magazines but develops her arguments about dance. She points to the continuity of rave culture with earlier cultures in that 'dance is where girls were always found in subcultures. It was their only entitlement.' However, 'in rave it becomes the motivating force for the entire subculture' (ibid.: 419). The centrality of dance allows a far more important place for girls within such contemporary subcultures. In continuity with earlier work, McRobbie still sees the danger of these occasions for girls, even if at this later date it is as a parent rather than as a sociological observer.

At this point it is necessary to consider some of the main points made against the kind of writing on youth subcultures that has been discussed in this section so far. A very useful overall critique has been produced by Gary Clarke (1990), who makes a number of particular criticisms of work emanating from the Birmingham Centre for Contemporary Cultural Studies, such as that by Willis, Hebdige and McRobbie.

1   Much of this writing is imprecise as to the nature both of the 'structural location' of subcultures and of the problem-solving involved in the subculture.
2   There is relatively little explanation of where the different subcultural styles actually come from.
3   There is a rigidity in the analysis, as the subcultures which are identified tend to be 'essentialist and non-contradictory', meaning that there is little attention paid to variations of style and commitment within different subcultures.
4   There is a lack of attention to the way in which individuals move in and out of subcultures. Thus, Clarke argues that 'Cohen, for example, classifies Crombies and parkas as distinct subcultures, but surely the only "problem" which distinguished them from skins and mods respectively was the need to keep warm' (1990: 82–3).
5   There is a tendency for these analyses to start from subcultures and work backwards to class situations and contradictions. This leads to a kind of 'freezing' of distinct subcultures.
6   There is a dichotomy between subcultures and the rest of the young people.

Clarke identifies three important consequences which stem from these criticisms. First, there is the lack of consideration of 'subcultural flux and dynamic nature of styles'. Second, there is the separation of subcultures from the rest of society which is incorporated into a 'consensus' or dominant social relations. Third, there is the point that a 'vague concept of style' is elevated 'to the status of an objective category' (ibid.: 84). Hence, he argues that there is a need to study what all categories of youth are doing, rather than just subcultures: 'It is true that most youths do not enter into subcultures in the elite form described in the literature, but large numbers do draw on particular elements of subcultural style and create their own meanings and uses of them' (ibid.: 92).

Furthermore, Clarke suggests that there are important differences between the early 1980s and the situation described in the 1960s and 1970s by the classic writers from Birmingham. Thus, there was the combination of styles involved in movements such as punk and two-tone, and the argument that 'new wave' broke the 'distinction between "teenyboppers" and youth' based around the distinction between LPs and singles. Thus, Clarke's general conclusion is that 'what is required is an analysis of the activities of all youths to locate continuities and discontinuities in culture and social relations and to discover the meaning these activities have for the youths themselves' (1990: 95). Some recent literature has attempted to take up this challenge and it is reviewed in chapters 8 and 9.

So far, this section has focused on class and gender in relation to youth subcultures and music use. There is also a developing body of literature which considers the ethnic dimensions of subcultures and music. Some general aspects of this have been discussed in chapter 4, and at this point we look at one of the more specific studies of this topic which appeared within the 'Birmingham tradition' of studies of subcultures.

Simon Jones's book *Black Culture, White Youth* (1988) falls into two relatively discrete parts. In the first, he presents an overview of the development of reggae and its connection to forms of culture in Britain and Jamaica. However, it is the second half of the book which is of more interest for present purposes. Jones discusses the formation of identity in a multi-ethnic area of the city of Birmingham in the English Midlands. There, many white boys had adopted a form of culture that would, in more conventional analyses, be seen as black. 'Black' language was used to express opposition to authority on the part of white children (Jones 1988: 149). Reggae was adopted by the young white people growing up in this environment, and Jones shows how different themes from Jamaican music were adapted by young white men and women. He maintains:

> Black music generally and Jamaican music in particular have functioned as transmitters of oppositional values and liberating pleasures to different generations of whites for nearly three decades. They have consistently supplied white youth with the raw material for their own distinctive forms of cultural expression. Through the political discourses of Rastafari, reggae has provided young whites with a collective language and symbolism of rebellion that has proved resonant to their own predicaments and to their experiences of distinct, but related, forms of oppression. (Ibid.: 231)

However, Jones recognizes the contradictions that existed around these modes of appropriation: 'Powerful feelings of attraction to black culture could easily coexist with perceptions of that culture as threatening and with resentment and fear of black people' (ibid.: 216). He suggests that new forms of 'racial' identity are being formed in parts of Birmingham and other inner-city metropolitan areas, and he ends his book with a quotation from one of the people he studied which captures this:

> [In Jo-Jo's] eloquent conclusion is captured both the reality of the new 'England' that is already emerging, as well as the hope that such an England might itself not be 'recognisable as the same nation it has been', or perhaps, one day, 'as a nation at all':
>
>> Its like, I love this place . . . there's no place like home. . . . Balsall Heath is the centre of the melting-pot, man, 'cos all I ever see when I go out is half-Arab, half-Pakistani, half-Jamaican, half-Scottish, half-Irish, I know 'cos I am [half-Scottish-Irish] . . . Who am I? . . . Tell me? Who do I belong to? They criticise me, the good old England. Alright then, where do I belong? . . . you know, I was brought up with blacks, Pakistanis, Africans, Asians, everything, you name it. . . . Who do I belong to? I'm just a broad person. The earth is mine. You

know, 'we was not born in England, we was born not born in Jamaica' . . . we was born here man! It's our right! That's the way I see it. . . . That's the way I deal with it. (Ibid.: 239–40)

Jones's discussion resonates with arguments which suggest that there has been a 'decentring' of our identities in contemporary culture. For example, it has been suggested by a number of writers that we no longer have the same attachments to place as earlier generations did because we now live in a society where, in some respects, it is easier to see what is happening on the other side of the world through television coverage than it is to observe events at the other end of the street. Such themes concerning the study of youth culture were addressed by Steve Redhead.

Redhead (1990) criticized the idea of a neat fit between different elements of youth subcultures and music, which are entailed in the concept of homology used by Willis and Hebdige. He also suggests that it is problematic to see music as the straightforward expression of a subcultural community. For example, it is often difficult to specify what the community is of which music is an expression. This echoes the critique developed by Frith of the realist theory of representation in lyrics which was examined in chapter 5. Furthermore, the subcultures and communities from which music is often held to issue, or which put it to use, do not simply exist but have to be examined within language and communication. They are, in important senses, constructed within writing about them, or, in other terms, discursively constructed.

Redhead considers whether the clear fit between music and subcultural use ever existed in the way identified by the Birmingham writers, or whether there has been a change in the articulation of music with subcultures in the period since punk rock in the late 1970s. In some accounts, postmodernism in pop developed through the 1980s, leading to the break-up of the forms of association identified by earlier writers. However, Redhead argues that in many respects pop music has always possessed some of those features that were held to be characteristic of postmodernism, maintaining that it has broken barriers between high and popular culture at different points. In common with theories of postmodernism, he contends that the best way to understand contemporary pop music is not through some of the conventional 'oppositions' which have often been used to study it, such as those between 'rock and pop', 'authentic and synthetic', 'true and false' and 'high and low, but through the distinction and relationship between the local and the global. Thus, 'world musics' are affecting local music-making in a number of complex and diverse ways.

Redhead's work raises a number of issues about the complex contemporary interaction between forms of cultural production and consumption of contemporary pop music. However, he does not provide, or attempt to provide, a blueprint for how these relationships should actually be studied.

Subsequent work considered different dimensions of contemporary music and youth. Rietveld (1993, 1998) examines a number of different dimensions of rave culture in the north of England in the late 1980s (see also, more generally, chapter 6). The account given of this form of culture is not dissimilar from that of the Birmingham writers. For example, with respect to rave culture, Rietveld argues:

Not only the lack of finance, but also the intensive dancing and the use of the drug Ecstasy determined the style. It makes a person sweat, so baggy cotton clothing is the most comfortable to wear. Make up is useless in those circumstances, because it would simply 'wash' off in a short time. The euphoria caused by the excitement of the rave events, the excessive body movement and drug use all interfere with a person's sense of balance: high heels are therefore definitely 'out of order' from a raver's point of view. (1993: 53)

This is very close to the homology argument used by Willis, which therefore remains influential.

There continues to be a focus on subcultures in the literature on popular music. However, this could be a problem, as the concentration may be both too general and too specific. The general attention paid to subcultures might obscure the very particular uses that are made of music by individuals or even by specific parts of subcultures. This is a problem that is beginning to be addressed in the more sociological literature on fans. The specific focus on subcultures may also be unhelpful in the consideration of how people more widely use or consume music. Both of these themes are picked up in chapter 8.

Summary

This chapter has considered:

- some different theories of the relationship between texts and audiences with particular reference to pop music; this included a discussion of the idea of the 'effects' of pop and the ways in which lyrics are understood;
- some of the different indicators of the consumption of pop music, illuminating patterns of contemporary consumption;
- a number of different studies of the way in which music is a part of youth subcultures; the class, gender and racial patternings of subcultures were addressed.

8 Fans, Production and Consumption

This chapter continues the discussion of audiences begun in chapter 7. Developing the points made at the end of that chapter, it starts with an examination of the ways in which fans have been defined and some of the ways in which audiences as fans have related to different pop stars and groups. This is followed by a review of the general account of fan processes offered by Grossberg (1992a) and leads into consideration of work that has focused on the productive activities of fans. One particular issue is the extent to which social processes associated with fan activities characterize the relationship to the media of other groups. Therefore, the next section in the chapter broadens out to look at the ways in which young people relate to media in general, and pop music in particular. This leads into a more general discussion of the relations between production and consumption in culture. Reference is made back to the studies of local music-making which were introduced in chapter 2.

Fans and pop

The idea of fandom and fan processes can be approached from two broad directions. First, there is a literature on fame and celebrity that starts at a more general level through the examination of processes such as stardom and reputation, often through history or across societies. Second, there is work that starts from the cultural, social and psychological aspects of fan practices themselves. We open this chapter by considering some of the most significant aspects of these literatures for the discussion of popular music.

Fame and celebrity have a long history. In his examination of fame, Braudy (1997) points to a number of the processes involved. For him, 'fame is made up of four elements: a person and an accomplishment, their immediate publicity, and what posterity has thought about them ever since' (1997: 15). He examines the particular processes of fame related to a range of historical people. In particular, it is possible to trace a process whereby fame or celebrity have moved from being 'ascribed' to kings and queens, who were celebrities as a result of a specific place in the social order, to being 'achieved', in that they are dependent on action on the part of the celebrity (Rojek 2001). Two interconnected issues that Braudy introduces and explores are of particular significance: first, the nature of the person and, second, that of the place of the audience.

A paradox of fame for the famous person creates a dilemma of what it means for the self. Thus, the famous person wants to be both celebrated and private. The celebrity has 'the desire to be different but familiar, famous but the kid next door' (Braudy 1997: 585). Second, there is the role of the audience. This is a process that Braudy draws attention to throughout his discussion. However, it has become particularly significant as the mass media have developed in the modern age. It is worth quoting a telling part of his discussion that concerns the Hollywood star Clark Gable:

> As Clark Gable remarked to David Niven on hearing of the mysterious death of the actress Thelma Todd:
>
>> We all have a contract with the public – in us they see themselves or what they would like us to be. . . . They love to put us on a pedestal and worship us. . . . But *they've* read the small print, and most of *us* haven't . . . So, when we get knocked off by gangsters, like Thelma did, or get hooked on booze or dope or . . . just get sold . . . the public feels satisfied. Yeah, it's a good idea to read that small print . . .
>
> Gable's opinion of the implicit contract between public person and audience may be excessively gloomy. But his basic insight remains: modern fame is always compounded of the audience's aspirations and its despair, its need to admire and to find a scapegoat for that need. (Ibid.: 9).

This argument is developed through the course of Braudy's book. He asserts that there is an important interaction between media and audience which promotes fame and celebrity: 'But to be talked about is to be part of a story, and to be part of a story is to be at the mercy of story tellers – the media and their audience' (1997: 592). The pace of development of modern media (including popular music) and consumer culture has had an important role in accelerating and shifting processes of celebrity and fandom (ibid.: 595–6), as 'The media are no longer only what their name implies: intermediaries between events and audiences. Now, a metamedia has come into being, committed to, imprisoned by, and frequently bored to death by its own preoccupation with fame' (ibid.: 600).

Many of these arguments are further conceptualized in the more recent work of Rojek, who discusses 'celebrity as the attribution of glamorous or notorious status to an individual within the public sphere' (2001: 10). He also points to the problem or paradox of the nature of the individual for the celebrity and draws on the distinction drawn by the influential social psychologist George Herbert Mead, 'who argued that the split between the *I* (the "veridical" self) and the *Me* (the self as seen by others) is the human condition, at least since ancient times, in Western society' (ibid.: 11). Thus, a continuing issue for the celebrity, especially compounded in an accelerating media culture, is the nature of the relationship between the I and the me, as, for the celebrity, the me is increasingly subject to extensive media attention. This media attention is critical to the nature of contemporary celebrity, and 'celebrity must be understood as a *modern* phenomenon, a phenomenon of mass-circulation newspapers, TV, radio and film' (ibid.: 16).

As we have partially introduced in a preliminary way above, for Rojek, 'Celebrity status comes in three forms: *ascribed, achieved and attributed*' (2001: 17). 'Ascribed status concerns lineage' (ibid.), 'achieved celebrity derives from the perceived accomplishments of the individual in open competition' (ibid.: 18), and attributed celebrity 'is largely the result of the concentrated representation of an individual as noteworthy or exceptional by cultural intermediaries' (ibid.). Rojek introduces the idea of the 'celetoid' 'as the term for any form of compressed, concentrated, attributed celebrity. I distinguish celetoids from celebrities because, generally, the latter enjoy a more durable career with the public' (ibid.: 20).

Approaches to the study of celebrity, of which Rojek thinks there are three main forms – subjectivism, structuralism and post-structuralism – differ in the extent to which they accord agency and power to the audience. More structuralist accounts tend to emphasize the power of producers to affect the audience (thus celebrities will be sold to an audience), whereas other accounts allow the audience greater power in determining who becomes a celebrity and how enduring they are. In fact, as this book suggests, it is in the interplay between producers and consumers that the most suggestive analysis will be found.

Rojek explores a number of different aspects of contemporary fandom, including how celebrity is potentially a substitute for religion and why and how some celebrities fall out of favour. Moreover, he studies the different ways in which celebrity is constructed in ways that examine the processes that have been introduced by Goodwin (1993) via the idea of the star text. A star text is a form of meta-narrative that comes to constitute an artist's or a band's identity, a non-linear sequence of images and discourses that allow the audience an 'access' to meanings that are communicated through the music video, for example, as well as playing an integral part in the process of branding. However, it is significant that, because it focuses on celebrity and stardom, this approach to celebrity tends to reproduce a view of the fan as perhaps deranged and as a potential serial killer. Those fans that are considered are often those who have committed a criminal act against a star. Despite the many innovations in the book, it is limited by a lack of detailed attention to what fans do.

Another example of this can be found in the very sophisticated analysis by Elliott (1999) of the celebrity status of John Lennon. Again, this work could have figured at several other points in this book, most particularly in a discussion of how stars are constructed and narrated and how pieces of music can be discussed in relation to specific lyrical and musical themes that relate to the nature of the star as author. Elliott's examination of Lennon's track 'Mother', from his album *Plastic Ono Band*, is an excellent example of sustained insight. However, despite the many strengths of this analysis, it is almost inevitable that, because of the murder of John Lennon by Mark Chapman in 1980, a particular version of fandom is deployed by Elliott. His discussion, which starts from a particular interpretation of the process derived from Thompson (1995), centres on an analysis of Chapman. In many respects this is very insightful, as Elliott deploys sociological and psychoanalytical perspectives to good effect. However, a danger in his approach, and the way in which he starts, makes fandom at least potentially a 'problem'.

Fandom, as sociologist John B. Thompson has argued, involves wrapping up a significant part of one's self-identity in an identification with a distant other (the celebrity) and negotiating the necessary shifts between the world of fandom and the practical contexts of everyday social life (Elliott 1999: 136). While Thompson and Elliott (ibid.: 139) both recognize that fandom can have positive aspects, the weight of Elliott's discussion, as with Rojek, tends to suggest otherwise. There has also been a clear tendency for journalistic writing on fans and pop music to suggest that there is something wrong with being a fan. Fans are seen as fanatics (the origin of the term) and deranged (Jenson 1992: 9). Jenson maintains that the literature on fans has produced two models of the 'pathological fan'. First, there is the 'obsessed loner . . . who (under the influence of the media) has entered into an intense fantasy relationship with a celebrity figure. These individuals achieve public notoriety by stalking or threatening or killing the celebrity' (ibid.: 11). Examples might include Mark Chapman. Second, there is the 'frenzied or hysterical member of a crowd' (ibid.), shouting at a rock star or misbehaving at a sports match. Jenson argues that these models of fans relate to general characterizations of the nature of society, similar to the descriptions of mass society or mass culture examined with respect to audiences in chapter 7. As Jenson puts it:

> The literature on fandom, celebrity and media influence tells us that: Fans suffer from psychological inadequacy, and are particularly vulnerable to media influence and crowd contagion. They seek contact with famous people in order to compensate for their own inadequate lives. Because modern life is alienated and atomized, fans develop loyalties to celebrities and sports teams to bask in reflected glory, and attend rock concerts to feel an illusory sense of community. (Ibid.: 18)

Jenson contests this idea that there is something wrong with the fan by contrasting the traits of the fan with those of the high-culture or academic 'aficionado'. Many academics form attachments to their favourite writers or theorists which are just as obsessive as those the fan may feel for the pop star. However, the division of the world into fans and non-fans allows those who define themselves as non-fans to suggest that others are abnormal and thus to constitute themselves as the normal or the safe. For Jenson: 'Defining fandom as a deviant activity allows (individually) a reassuring, self-aggrandizing stance to be adopted. It also supports the celebration of particular values – the rational over the emotional, the educated over the uneducated, the subdued over the passionate, the elite over the popular, the mainstream over the margin, the status quo over the alternative' (1992: 24). She argues that characterizing fans as 'other' in this way blocks analysis and proper understanding of how people actually interact with the media in contemporary society. This means that the exploration of fan activity might have wider benefits in explaining the activities of the audience. For example, Fiske writes 'that fandom is a heightened form of popular culture in industrial societies and that the fan is an "excessive reader" who differs from the "ordinary" one in degree rather than kind' (1992: 46).

Work that has addressed fan response to popular music in a sympathetic manner is potentially illuminating. It has often come from people writing about their own personal experience of being a fan. The first illustrative discussion of this sort to be considered here is by Sheryl Garratt (1984), who uses an examination of her feelings for the Bay City Rollers in the 1970s to ground some general suggestions about the ways young girls relate to male pop stars. She argues that an important part of this phenomenon has little to do with the stars themselves, since what is most important to the girls 'is desire for comradeship' (1984: 144). Thus, what she most remembers from her fan days are the episodes of travelling to the concerts and discussing the band with other fans. She recognizes that there must be some reason why certain idols are chosen over others, and she answers this by suggesting that women are attracted by androgyny: 'men they dress like and identify with, as well as drool over' (ibid.). Moreover, there is an element of opposition in the process, as what is also important is other people's dislike of the teeny group that is the object of the girls' affection. This leads to the defence of the group against attack, as the passage reproduced in chapter 7 (box 7.1) makes clear. Garratt suggests that some aspects of this form of fandom make the girls a 'lucrative market' – 'how exploitable is this urge to collect not only the records, but the posters, tour programmes, fan club specials, books, magazines, and any other product companies wish to foist on them' (ibid.: 147). However, she maintains that the fans may recognize that much of what is written about their idols is fiction, and they are not necessarily 'taken in' by it. In general, she argues that the process of being a fan of the Bay City Rollers had relatively little to do with the Rollers and a great deal to do with the girls themselves.

Sue Wise has further documented the personal nature of the relation to a star. Wise examines her feelings for Elvis Presley in the context of her own development as a feminist. She argues that Elvis has normally been written about, by men, as a kind of 'butch god', whose 'expression of rampant male sexuality' was central to his appeal (1990: 391). This connected to boys' sexual fantasies, as 'his supposed ability to "lay girls" with ease and without consequence' (ibid.: 392) led to the celebration by male writers of the early Elvis. 'Although he had a career of over twenty years, male writers dwell upon only the first couple of these, when they can identify with the super butch sexual hero that they themselves have promoted and lauded' (ibid.). It is after this initial period that Wise's connections with Elvis began. She details how she collected pictures and cuttings and how she created her own space within a crowded household through her immersion in Elvis. He acted as a friend. Wise suggests that her feelings for him were not concerned with sex or romance but rather with those of 'warmth and affection' (ibid.: 395): Elvis was like a 'teddy bear'. One of the general implications of Wise's discussion is that people might have related to Elvis Presley in a variety of ways. She argues that adopting such a 'relativist' view would go some way to overturning the dominant male ways of examining the meaning and audience appropriation of Presley. It is possible to recognize the complexity of these different appropriations and meanings through even a quick inspection of a book such as *Dead Elvis* by Greil Marcus (1992), which identifies the ways in which numerous different images of the star continue to circulate in a variety of media. Furthermore, Presley's death meant that images of him could multiply, since there is no longer a 'real' Elvis who has 'control' over them in any shape or form.

An important analysis of the different meanings of Elvis can be found in Rodman (1996). Rodman thinks that approaches that see the continuing popularity (indeed, perhaps the increased popularity) of Elvis since his death in 1977 as manipulation by the culture industries, as explained by studies of fandom or as a site to deploy versions of postmodern theory do not in themselves account for the Elvis phenomenon, since they throw light only on parts of it and do not account for the specificity of Elvis (ibid.: 18). The argument deployed by Rodman is based in cultural studies, and he approaches his topic from three main directions. First, he examines the way in which Elvis connects to a range of important mythological features of the USA. Second, he explores the way in which Elvis is spatially grounded in ways that make him different from other stars. Third, he discusses a range of features of what he terms 'Elvis culture'. As with many studies that are considered in this book, it is possible to focus only on some aspects of Rodman's sophisticated and wide-ranging discussion – in particular with respect to the idea of myth, which Rodman defines as 'a narrative (or perhaps a cluster of related ideas) that people collectively believe (or believe in) independently of its "truth" or "falsity". The difference here is subtle, but important, insofar as a myth can in fact be partially – or even entirely true' (ibid.: 30–1). 'Thus, it is more than just Elvis's status as a cultural icon that makes him such a ubiquitous presence across the terrain of contemporary US culture; more crucial to Elvis's lingering presence are the range and diversity of cultural myths surrounding him – not only today, but through-out his lifetime – and the multiple, even contradictory ways in which he is articulated to those myths' (ibid.: 41).

In addition to the different aspects of gender that Elvis connects to, as introduced above, Rodman explores the differing views and discourses on Elvis and race and class. Moreover, he points out the interconnections (and contradictions) between these different emphases. He then explores the meanings of Graceland and how Elvis can be theorized in relation to different ideas of culture.

Like Wise, Rodman offers a critique of the idea that women's relation to the pop star is based around sexuality and sexual desire. Several accounts have examined this dimension of the relation between the audience and the performer in more detail. Cline argues that one of the dominant ways of characterizing women rock fans is to see them as 'groupies'. However, 'most girl rock fans never become groupies' in the sense of sleeping with rock stars (1992: 81). Furthermore, Cline suggests that the term 'groupie' is often used as 'a putdown for any woman involved in the industry' (ibid.: 83). She concludes with the warning that 'it's well to keep a sharp watch on how the word "groupie" is bandied about' (ibid.). This is a description that is still applied by some to certain sections of women fans. For example, a number of 'conventional wis-doms' about fans in general and women fans in particular can be found in the article reproduced in box 8.1, which is taken from a 'quality' British Sunday newspaper.

Because of its sexual explicitness, *Starlust: The Secret Life of Fans* (Vermorel and Vermorel 1985) is an unusual collection of confessions and testimonies by fans, gath-ered through interviews, diaries, letters, answerphone messages, dream journals and questionnaires. It gives an insight into fans' most private thoughts and fantasies while at the same time demonstrating the ways in which the fans negotiate and contextual-ize stardom and celebrity within both their social surroundings and everyday life.

A different view of sexuality is expressed by Ehrenreich and her colleagues (1992) in a discussion of Beatles fans in 1964 and 1965 in the United States. They argue that the phenomenon of Beatle hysteria was a form of sexual revolution. It was a protest by young women, if unarticulated, against the confines of the culture in which they were brought up. In their argument, Beatlemania was of a greater intensity than ear-lier female fan movements such as those directed at Frank Sinatra or Elvis Presley. Beatlemania broke out in a middle-class, white culture where gender roles were heavily structured and sex something to be confined to marriage: 'Intercourse was out of the question, so young girls faced the still familiar problem of where to draw the line on a scale of lesser sexual acts, including (in descending order of niceness: kissing, necking, and petting, this last being divided into "light" (through clothes and/or above the waist) and "heavy" (with clothes undone and/or below the waist' (1992: 93).

The authors argue that the appeal of the Beatles was that the young girl would nei-ther marry nor probably even meet one of them: 'Adulation of the male star was a way to express sexual yearnings that would normally be pressed into the service of popu-larity or simply repressed' (Ehrenreich et al. 1992: 97). This mode of sexual repression was one of the factors that made Beatlemania possible. The specific outbreak of fan interaction with these pop stars was fed, in this argument, by the development of a teenage consumer culture in the United States. Rock 'n' roll was at the core of this

Box 8.1   'More sex please, we're groupies – and proud of it'

Eighteen-year-old Jenny ('please don't use my surname') differs from most other fanzine editors in that she is not a shabbily dressed, socially inadequate nerd. Written under her *nom de plume*, Magenta Placenta, her fanzine, *Slapper*, avoids the usual moronic menu of the fan's-eye view of the music world, all pious moralism and verbatim interviews with inarticulate rock stars. *Slapper* is Britain's first 'sexzine'.

Jenny is a student from Slough. She is also a groupie – a rock fan who has sex with her idols. Most male rock musicians and fans despise groupies, and misogynist tales of their humiliations fill rock folklore. Practising groupies are therefore keen to remain anonymous. Jenny has decided it is time for Groupie Liberation, and *Slapper* is the means to that end.

'It started out as a way of getting attention. The first issue was taking the piss out of groupies, I suppose,' she recalls. But then it got serious. Her heroes are The Plaster Casters of Chicago (legendary Sixties groupies who immortalised impressions of their heroes' most vital parts in dental plaster) and Pamela Des Barres, author of the best-selling autobiography *I'm With The Band*.

'I suddenly realised that these were amazing women. They use their initiative, they get things free, they have the most amazing lifestyles. People who think it's degrading are just ignorant.

'Talent is just as good a criterion for choosing sexual partners as any other, isn't it? You have a fantastic time, room service, free booze and great no-strings sex with incredibly talented people. Excuse me, but isn't that what rock's meant to be about? Groupies aren't the pariahs of rock 'n' roll, they're its lifeblood.'

When she was 10, Jenny daydreamed not of princesses or ponies but of 'hanging out' with the American heavy metal band Motley Crüe. Unlike most of her teenage female peers, she has no time for the pretty boys of manufactured chart pop bands such as Take That or Bad Boys Inc. 'I'm not after plastic hunks, I'm after real men, real rock 'n' roll men. Huge, hulking, big, hairy-chested, scowling, tattooed, formidable monsters. Phwooar!'

Jenny is adamant that she has no moral case to answer. 'These are grown men, no one's forcing them into bed are they? They can always say no. Aids? Use a condom, what's the problem?'

Slapper's messianic celebration of the joys of sex with stars contrasts strangely with the wave of fundamentalist feminism that recently swept through non-mainstream rock. The Riot Grrrl movement – represented by bands such as Bikini Kill, Dickless and Huggy Bear – has reinvented the feminist wheel and has no time at all for what it sees as the piggish horrors of 'boy rock'.

But other groupies have greeted *Slapper* with enthusiasm. 'It's a real breath of fresh air,' claims Philippa. 'I mean, the fact that I daren't let you print my real name says it all, really, doesn't it? I shag pop stars – something most men would love to do, if they'd admit it.'

Jill, a university graduate, is typical of the new generation of groupies for whom *Slapper* is written. Espousing a philosophy that struggles to contain strands of bootstrap Thatcherism, feminism and good old-fashioned rock hedonism, she was, she claims, driven towards groupiedom by the effeteness of her male peers.

'Public schoolboys! Ugh! The relief that comes when you realise there's other sorts of men in the world than public schoolboys. Working-class boys know how to handle women and where do you find the best looking working-class boys? In bands. Dead simple really.'

Source: © *The Observer*, 12 September 1993

Box 8.2   Marc Bolan fan

At junior school my desk top was carved in song lyrics, titles and corkscrew-haired doodles! I had 'Marc Bolan' or 'T. Rex' on everything.

The whole village used to save any pictures of Marc they'd find in their papers and pop mags for me so that every inch of my walls was covered in smiling, grinning, frowning and sulking pictures of Marc.

Bolan seemed to mean more and more to me every day. But living in Wales I didn't know any other Bolan fans to share my growing interest and there certainly weren't any clubs that played Bolan music. So the lure of a big city was very strong.

I travelled to Leeds by train with a small suitcase of clothes, make-up(!) and nicknacks, and a huge case full of my Marc Bolan and T. Rex records, pictures and scrapbooks.

There was no way I could leave home without them!

When I moved to Leeds I got in touch with a Bolanite pen-friend I had called Steve who knew of a London Bolanite who wanted to move to Leeds.

The three of us managed to rent a house together.

The house rocked with Bolan: every sound and every picture was Bolan. A nearby metal club played Bolan, so we made it our regular haunt.

The year and a half I lived there holds some of my happiest memories.

Source: Vermorel and Vermorel 1985: 149

consumer culture, which marketed a form of 'hysteria' that could be used subsequently to sell fan goods. The arrival of the Beatles in America was accompanied by press and radio reports of the Beatlemania that had already swept Britain. However, Ehrenreich and her colleagues argue that this consumer culture was double-edged: on the one hand it manipulated the consumer, while on the other hand it structured a teenage culture that was opposed to the adult world and which ran counter to dominant modes of sexuality (ibid.: 98–100). 'For girls, fandom offered a way not only to sublimate romantic and sexual yearnings but to carve out subversive versions of heterosexuality' (ibid.: 100). For these authors, the Beatles expressed a form of playful sexuality, which was shocking in the context of the dominant American codes. This opened the way for the development of alternative roles for women from the 1960s onwards.

This section has so far tended to focus on the relation of fans to one star or group. Some general themes can be derived from these discussions. First, the relationship between fan and performer generated a great deal of emotion. Second, the process had a lot to do with the young women themselves. Third, the fan relationship needs to be interpreted in a social context. An attempt to take these sorts of factor into account in a general account of rock music fandom can be found in the work of Grossberg (for example, 1992a).

Grossberg maintains that the relationship between texts and audiences is an active one and that it cannot be understood as being determined by the nature of either the text or the audience alone, since it is the correlation between them that is important. He conceptualizes this relationship as 'sensibility':

> A sensibility is a particular form of engagement or mode of operation. It identifies the specific sort of effects that the elements within a context can produce; it defines the possible relationships between texts and audiences located within its spaces. The sensibility of a particular cultural context (an 'apparatus') defines how specific texts and practices can be taken up and experienced, how they are able to effect [*sic*] the audience's place in the world, and what sorts of texts can be incorporated into the apparatus. Different apparatuses produce and foreground different sensibilities. (1992a: 54–5)

Grossberg distinguishes between two types of sensibility. The first he calls the 'sensibility of the consumer', which 'operates by producing structures of pleasure' (ibid.: 55). This is the most widespread way of interacting with forms of popular culture, which is based on entertainment and pleasure. The second is engaged in by fans. Grossberg argues:

> The fan's relation to cultural texts operates in the domain of affect or mood. Affect is perhaps the most difficult plane of our lives to define, not merely because it is even less necessarily tied to meaning and pleasure, but also because it is, in some sense, the most mundane aspect of everyday life. Affect is not the same as either emotions or desires. Affect is closely tied to what we often describe as the feeling of life. (Ibid.: 56)

In drawing these distinctions, Grossberg adopts similar arguments to those advanced by Barthes in his discussions of the 'grain of the voice' (see chapter 5), where a distinction is drawn between the pleasure of communication and the feelings produced by the nature of the voice. This is based in turn on the distinction between the 'rational' kinds of pleasure, or *plaisir*, and the explosions of jouissance (see also Gilbert and Pearson 1999: 64–8).

Grossberg argues that affect is very important: it matters to us. Affect helps us to live in contemporary societies. One of the important ways this happens is through the structuring of our identities. The prime way in which this is done is by the construction of differences between ourselves and others:

> [A]s individuals and as members of various social groups, there are many axes along which we register our difference from others – some are physical categories, some are sociological, some are ideological and some are affective. We are women, black, short, middle-class, educated, and so on. Any particular difference, including that marked out by being a rock fan, is always augmented and reshaped by other differences. At different points and places in our lives, we reorder the hierarchical relations among these differences. (1992a: 58)

For the fan, the different dimensions of popular culture matter enormously. Their identities may be most importantly structured by their affect for a particular type of music or a certain performer. According to Grossberg, 'Rock works by offering the fan places where he or she can locate some sense of his or her own identity and power, where he or she can invest his or her self in specific ways' (ibid.: 61). This commitment, or excess of commitment, is then justified or explained by the fan. Thus, rock fans often explain their commitment to particular forms of music through the idea of authenticity.

Grossberg identifies three ways in which authenticity is constructed. First, there is the argument that valued music articulates 'private but common desires, feelings and experiences into a shared public language. The consumption of rock constructs or expresses a "community"' (1992a: 62). Thus the fan may argue that a particular performer expresses his or her feelings and those of others, which bind them together to form a community of those who recognize the profundity of the performer's music. Second, there is the version of authenticity located 'in the construction of a rhythmic and sexual body' (ibid.: 63), which is often associated with black music. The third form of authenticity celebrates artificiality and 'is built on the explicit recognition of and acknowledgment that the difference that rock constructs (and which in turn is assigned back to rock) is always artificially constructed' (ibid.). Thus style and artifice are valued, but some forms of style and artifice are valued more than others by those who recognize the significance of the construction of style.

Grossberg offers an account of how certain forms of music matter to us – through the production of affect – and how we often try to legitimate such affects through arguments. It may be suggested that the distinctions he draws between pleasure and affect are not as clear-cut as he thinks and that the model of legitimation of fandom might not apply to all fans. However, in the notion of affect he has caught something of the way in which members of an audience respond to a valued performer, which might not always be expressible in words. Thus, young children, for example, seem to be particular fans of certain performers, which may have something to do with current fashion, but which also seems to depend in some part on the ability of the performer to affect, or move, them. Of course, this may apply to adults as well. We can be moved by our favourite performers in ways that we find very hard to communicate in language, which never seems adequate to the task; as a result, we justify why someone matters in other terms, using the authenticity sorts of argument identified by Grossberg.

In this section a number of accounts of fans and their different forms of emotional commitment to different pop stars and groups have been considered. The concern has been to examine a variety of the accounts written about this process. To borrow the title of a seminal collection of useful articles on fans, this section has considered the 'adoring audience' (Lewis 1992). This is a clear line of contemporary research on the fans and audiences which has led to the approach of writers, such as Grossberg, who focus on affect (see, for example, Hills 2002; Sandvoss 2005). These writers have considered social, cultural and psychological aspects of fandom, drawing on a number of studies of audience processes that have developed in recent years (see further chapter 9). In general, the suggestion is that audiences are active in their relationship to texts. In no sense are they the rather passive creatures implied by the Frankfurt School approach discussed in the Introduction. Other writers have examined this notion of activity in a rather different direction, through consideration of the idea of the productivity of fans.

Pop fans as productive

Fiske (1992) has argued that fans are semiotically, enunciatively and textually productive. By semiotic productivity, he means that activity which is characteristic of popular culture as a whole. It 'consists of the making of meanings of social identity and of social experience from the semiotic resources of the cultural commodity' (1992: 37). When we make commodities mean something for us, we are engaging in semiotic productivity. When such meanings are communicated to others, enunciative productivity takes place. One of the most important vehicles for enunciation is talk. Thus, according to Fiske, the communication of the meanings that we have made for ourselves to others through talk is an important way in which fans can form communities. However, there are other ways, and Fiske draws attention to the wearing of colours by football fans as another example of enunciative productivity (see also Sandvoss 2003). To take another example from Fiske, the Madonna fans who 'claimed that dressing like Madonna made people take more notice of them as they walked down the street were not only constructing for themselves more empowered identities than those normally available to young adolescent girls but were putting those meanings into social circulation' (1992: 38).

The third category, textual productivity, entails the production of texts for circulation within the fan community itself. A lot of the research on fans has drawn attention to the ways in which they produce texts, such as stories, paintings, songs and videos, about the characters from their favourite television shows (see, for example, Bacon-Smith 1992; Jenkins 1992). Fans write stories which place the characters from different television shows in a variety of contexts and which allow the development of aspects of the original text to which they felt attracted. This may involve placing the characters in different universes or bringing characters from different shows together in one story. Fans also paint pictures of different characters. These activities are discussed at fan conventions and the texts circulate in the fan community.

Music can be very important in fan texts and activities. Fans write and perform songs at gatherings about characters from television shows, not unlike the way in which folk songs are sung in folk clubs. This can be seen in the name of this fan form: filk song. According to Jenkins, filk songs take their cue from commercial culture. They are about the characters from commercial television series, but 'Filk turns commercial culture back into folk culture, existing as a mediator between two musical traditions. Its raw materials come from commercial culture; its logic is from folk culture' (Jenkins 1992: 270). The name of the form came from a typographical error for 'folk music' in a convention programme, and the term then stuck. The nature of a filksing is described in some detail by Jenkins, and an extract from his account can be found in box 8.3.

A further dimension of fan productivity involves the making of music videos. Recent years have seen the growth of participatory cultures enabled by Web 2.0 technologies. A much referenced example is YouTube (see our discussion in chapter 5), a platform where music fans can upload their own content, which can then be rated,

Box 8.3   Extract from a case study of a filksing at Philcon, 1989

A closer examination of one specific evening of filksinging (the Friday night session of Philcon 1989) will allow a more concrete discussion of how a conception of cultural inclusion and social integration has been structured into the filking process. Philcon, held in Philadelphia, is fairly typical of the larger East-Coast cons, featuring role-playing games as well as a mix of literary and media-oriented programing. This particular filksing was scheduled to begin at 11 p.m., actually got under way about half an hour later due to straggling and some confusion about room allocations, and continued until 4 a.m. At its peak, this filksing attracted forty participants, though more typically it maintained a steady population of twenty to thirty fans and sometimes dwindled down to six or seven.

The participants were arranged informally either on the floor or in a somewhat lopsided circle hastily formed by rearranging the chairs in the hotel conference room. The filksing preserves no formal separation between performance space and spectator space. Indeed, the organization of the filksing insures that the center of interest circulates fluidly throughout the floor. This filksing was organized according to the principle of 'Midwest chaos', which simply means that whoever wants to play a song starts whenever there is an empty space in the flow of music. Sometimes, there are gaps when no one is ready to perform; more often, several fans want to sing at once and some negotiation occurs. Eventually, anyone who wants to sing gets a chance (though fan humor abounds with jokes about the sufferings of those waiting for their more aggressive friends to yield the floor). Other filksings are organized as what fans called 'bardic circles', a practice which is also called 'pick, pass, or perform'. Here, each person in the room is, in turn, given a chance to perform a song, request a song to be performed, or simply to pass, insuring an even broader range of participation. At still other conventions, special songbooks are distributed to participants and songleaders conduct the sing as a 'choir practice'.

Music is provided in a haphazard fashion with whoever happens to know a particular tune participating and some songs performed a cappella. A number of participants brought guitars and several performed on the harp. Filk's reliance upon tunes 'borrowed' from other well-known or traditional songs ensures that both musicians and singers typically know much of the music that is performed. Filks, like traditional folk music, also often have repeated choruses, which can be easily mastered even by the most 'neo' of filkers and which, thus, encourage all of those in attendance to participate. Those who don't sing hum or whistle, tap their feet, drum on their chairs with pencils. Some particularly complex or moving songs are performed solo, but at this filksing at least, the tendency was for most of the songs to become collective performances, even if only during the chorus.

While some filkers have polished voices and a few earn money by performing professionally, the climate of the filksing is one of comfortable amateurishness. The singing stops periodically as new guitars are tuned or performers struggle to find the right key. Voices crack or wobble far off tune, and, particularly as the evening wears on, songs grind to a halt as the singer struggles to remember the words. Such snafus are accepted with good humor and vocal expressions of support and acceptance. 'If it ain't tuned now, it never will be', one woman jokes and another responds, 'Put it this way, it's close enough for filking.' A harpist, hesitant about the appropriateness of a traditional folk tune for the occasion, was reassured, 'That doesn't matter. Who do you think we steal our tunes from?'

While some filk songs evoke specialized knowledge either about fan culture or popular texts making them cryptic to the uninitiated, the verbal discourse surrounding the filksing provides new fans with the information needed to appreciate the performed material. 'Does anyone need that last verse explained?' one performer asked after a song particularly heavy with fan slang. The nonprofessionalism and the constant verbal reassurances create a highly supportive climate, encouraging contributions even from fans who have previously displayed little or no musical talent.

Some of the songs were original, written by the performer and 'tried out' for the first time at this session; others were older favorites, either part of the singer's personal repertoire or pulled from filk 'hymnal', remembered from other cons, or fondly associated with particular fan musicians. New songs are often greeted with vocal approval, passed around the room and hastily copied by those who wish to add them to their own notebooks. Several fans played half-finished songs, asking other filkers for advice on their completion.

Source: Jenkins 1992: 255–7

liked, disliked and commented on. Jenkins (2009) argues that this is not a completely new phenomenon, with DIY communities producing DIY media for decades. What has changed is the speed and the ease with which DIY media could become a part of wider participatory networks. In other words, 'communities of practice' were already in existence, ready to embrace the new, easily negotiated platform (ibid.: 110).

Referencing the 'garage bands', Davis (1997) made predictions of 'garage cinema', which, unlike the centrally owned YouTube (purchased by Google for $1.6 billion in 2006), would operate through a decentralized structure. In explaining the idea of DIY participatory cultures, Jenkins draws on the traditions of amateur publishing (e.g. zines), mix tape, home videos and pirate video stations, pointing out that they all have in common low-cost tools of production. And it is not just for music fans: 'YouTube has become the home port for lip-syncers, karaoke singers, trainspotters, birdwatchers, skateboarders, hip hoppers, small time wrestling federations, educators, third wave feminists, churches, proud parents, poetry slammers, gamers, fans, Ron Paul supporters, human rights activists, collectors, hobbyists, and each of these groups has a longer history of media production' (Jenkins 2009: 110).

Similarly, in *Making is Connecting*, Gauntlett (2011) engages with the social meaning of creativity, from handmade physical objects to online production, resulting in and representing the 'making and doing' of culture. He embraces the creative and political potential of both online and offline collaborations, however. In drawing on Lanier's (2011) idea of 'template-driven expressions of identity' (as opposed to a messier, complex and more genuine self-expression) promoted by functionality of Web 2.0 and websites such as Facebook, he calls for some caution amid celebration.

According to Gauntlett, the caution is to be exercised where both the quality of work and the ownership of the means of production are concerned. So, in line with Lanier, Gauntlet suggests that the great works of art or scientific ideas are rarely produced 'through an entirely open and free-for-all method of collaboration' (Gauntlett 2011: 199). Furthermore, we must not forget that most of the free platforms, such as YouTube, Flickr and Blogger, are created and run by commercial companies, which may have significant implications for their future sustainability as well as for the type of content available on them.

The literature considered so far has focused directly on fans (however these are defined), but a similar sort of general perspective has been elaborated by authors who have been associated with the sort of writing on youth subculture and music discussed in the previous chapter. This literature moves away from the discussion of fans to look at young people and is the subject of the next section.

Young people and cultural productivity

Willis and his colleagues (1990) argue that as human beings we are symbolically creative, saying that 'we argue for symbolic creativity as an integral ("ordinary") part of the human condition, not as the inanimate peaks [popular or remote] rising above the mists' (1990: 6). Being symbolically creative involves work which is 'the application of human capacities to and through, on and with symbolic resources and raw materials (collections of signs and symbols – for instance, the language as we inherit it as well as texts, songs, films, images and artefacts of all kinds) to produce meanings' (ibid.: 10). The general structure of this argument can be represented as in figure 8.1. The basic elements of symbolic work are language and the active body, and symbolic creativity involves the 'production of new . . . meanings intrinsically attached to feelings, to energy, to excitement and psychic movement' (ibid.: 11). A number of different products are produced through symbolic work and symbolic creativity, including our own individual identities, the location of those identities in a wider social context, and the notion that we have the capacity to change things in some respect. Thus, in a general sense, Willis et al. argue that:

> In a way the spectacular sub-cultures of the 1950s and '60s prefigured some of the general shifts we are claiming for the contemporary situation. They defined themselves very early and gained their very spectacle from seeking visible identities and styles outside or against work and working respectabilities. Now the idea of a spectacular sub-culture is strictly impossible because all style and taste cultures, to some degree or another, express something of a general trend to find and make identity outside the realm of work. (Ibid.: 16)

The book by Willis and his colleagues explores the symbolic creativity of young people across a number of different dimensions, among them television, video and

human capacities	+	symbolic resources raw materials	=	meanings

Figure 8.1 Symbolic productivity
Source: Constructed from Willis 1990

computer use, relationships to film, advertising, and magazines and engagements with fashion, pub culture, street culture, sport and romance. One of the most important arguments of the chapter on pop music is that consumption is creative and productive of meaning. Five different aspects of 'creative consumption' of music are identified:

1 listening and buying
2 home taping
3 interpreting sounds
4 dance
5 interpreting songs and symbols.

With respect to the first point, it is argued that young people show considerable discrimination in what they buy; they are not simply fed the products of the music industry. This might involve the purchase of old records and the development of extensive knowledge about the history of particular forms of music. Second, it is shown that home taping was extensively used among young people as a means of sharing their favourite music. With the widespread availability of twin cassette decks and the high cost of new tapes and albums, this was an extensive practice, which has now been supplanted by similar processes involving CD copying and file-sharing (Laughey 2006; see also Garofalo 1992b).

Third, the argument is made, which should by now be fairly familiar, that it is often the sound itself, rather than the actual words, that is central to the pleasure derived from the music. Thus, music can be used, and made, to express feelings, as well as to structure everyday life. An example given of the latter is the use of the personal stereo, which was: 'the ultimate artefact in providing a personal soundscape that can be carried around, quite literally, inside the head, while travelling, walking, waiting or negotiating public spaces' (Willis et al. 1990: 64–5). There is further discussion of this topic in chapter 9.

Dance is the fourth dimension to creative consumption (see also chapter 6). The argument is made that, 'Whereas dancing used to be seen as something of a feminine activity by some working-class young men, it has become more acceptable for males to express themselves through body movement. Some of the ties between dance forms and codes of masculinity/femininity have been loosened' (Willis et al. 1990: 68). Finally, it is suggested that there is often a strong identification with the 'lyrical themes, imagery and symbolism of popular music' (ibid.). These forms of creative consumption can often develop into production. Four different aspects of the development of consumption into production are considered by Willis and his colleagues:

1 sound systems
2 black music and oral poetry
3 DIY recording and mixing
4 music-making and performance.

First, there is the sound system, which, as was noted in chapter 4, has been particularly prominent in black musical traditions. This form has also become prominent in rave culture (McRobbie 1993: 421). The sound system was an institution 'where the activities of consumption merge into and become intertwined with more conventional forms of production' (Willis et al. 1990: 72). Furthermore:

> Besides being one of the principal focal points of musical activity within the black community, the sound system also involves a number of primary private production processes, which embrace electronics, sound technology and carpentry. These informal processes are motivated by specifically musical enthusiasms and operate to their own cultural agenda. They often involve the use of independently gained technical knowledge and skills, picked up from electronics magazines. (Ibid.)

Second, connected to the sound system is the form of production engaged in by the DJ, who in the black tradition may draw upon forms of oral poetry. Again, the DJ is important within rave culture. Third, there is the increased importance of DIY recording. Especially with the increased availability of cheaper forms of digital recording equipment (see chapter 2), there have been greater opportunities for the involvement of young people in music-making. 'In this process the hardware and software of consumption have become the instruments and raw materials of a kind of cultural production' (ibid.: 77). Finally, there is the way in which young people develop their interests in music to become involved in the production of music themselves, especially through performance.

This discussion raises a number of issues concerning the nature and relation of production and consumption and how they can be analytically separated. These issues have relevance beyond the cultural activities of young people, and the final section of this chapter explores them in detail and outlines some possible directions for future analysis. It emphasizes the complexity of contemporary musical production and consumption and the importance of social context.

Production, consumption and music-making

Dave Laing has argued:

> It is a commonplace that production and consumption are interdependent. Without production of material or cultural goods, there can be no consumption. Without a demand for, and consumption of, the use-values embodied in these goods, there is no impetus for continuing production. In certain areas of popular culture, the relation between production and consumption has another aspect. There, the producers of today are frequently the consumers of yesterday. Through the experience of consuming music as a listener, many individuals are drawn into producing music of their own. (1990: 186)

There has been research attempting to examine the relationships between production and consumption in more detail. For example, Warde (1992) has argued that discussions of production and consumption are often rather confused, especially between the levels of systems of production and consumption and those of individual production and consumption. He contends that it may be possible to show that there are linkages between mass production and the mass consumption of goods in a factory system. For example, the production of a large number of cars entails the consumption of an equally large number if the firms producing the cars are to survive. However, it cannot be argued that the nature of individual consumption is determined by the fact that a good is mass produced. For example, as shown above, mass-produced Elvis Presley albums or Bay City Rollers pictures and magazines can be consumed in very different ways by particular individuals. This is not to say that there may not be patterns in consumption, but that these are somewhat looser than some theorists have argued. One of the mistakes made by Adorno was to suggest this kind of continuity between the production and consumption of music (see the Introduction).

In an attempt to integrate different current accounts of consumption, Warde develops a conceptual framework which begins with an identification of three different guiding values. These are 'exchange-values, use-values and identity values' (1992: 17). In purchasing a CD, the consumer might be looking to its subsequent value when exchanged. He or she may see it as an investment that may offer a profit at some point in the future. The purchase of a limited-edition record which is then kept in a plastic bag and never played might be said to have been purchased for its exchange value. A CD might be purchased because of the use to which it may be put; it might relax the consumer, make them happy, and so on. Finally, it might be consumed in relation to identity – an idea we have already come across in this chapter – so that the purchase of a particular CD might identify the consumer as a rock fan or someone who can understand and appreciate avant-garde jazz.

Warde further suggests that there are a number of different cycles of production and consumption which occur before a good is finally consumed. He gives the example of food: 'What we eat off our plates typically passes through a number of production processes (the growing, wholesaling, processing, retailing and domestic preparation) and several exchange transactions (some of which are often called consumption) before final enjoyment as a meal' (1992: 18). The complex number of processes that could be involved in the overall production and consumption of a record, for example, or in the production and consumption of a musical performance can immediately be seen. Thus, the work of the sort of 'copy' group described by Bennett (see chapter 2) involves the consumption of a recording already produced by another group as the basis on which they produce their own version of the song. This is then consumed by the audience at the gig at which it was played.

All these separable production and consumption episodes will be carried out in different social contexts. Warde identifies four sorts of social relations which govern different episodes of production and consumption: 'market, state, domestic and communal' (1992: 19). He exemplifies the differences between these social relations through the example of food, though it is possible to apply the same categories to pop music. Thus, we could pay to see the performance of a pop group, we could play a song ourselves at home (provided we had the skill), the state may provide performances (as in former communist countries, or, for example, by a military band playing at a ceremonial occasion) or we can form a band with friends so that we can make music together.

Warde argues that distinct production and consumption 'episodes' should be examined, distinguishing at least four types of phase within an episode: 'the process of production or provision; the conditions of access; the manner of delivery; and the environment or experience of enjoyment' (1992: 20). In the examination of a musical performance, it would be possible to consider the various phases of the episode. Was it by a star band contracted to a transnational company or by a copy group? Was the cost of a ticket over £20 or was the group playing for a small fee at a wedding (MacLeod 1993)? Did the band look as if they were drunk, drugged or having an 'off' night, or were they enthusiastic and communicative? Was the experience a pleasant one, or did someone fall on top of, or spill beer over, you?

1   Values which guide consumption:
- exchange
- use
- identity

2   Social relations which govern production and consumption:
- market
- state
- domestic
- communal

3   Phases in episodes of production/consumption
- process of provision
- conditions of access
- manner of delivery
- environment or experience of enjoyment

Figure 8.2 Framework for the analysis of production/consumption
Source: Adapted from Warde 1992

All these different aspects of the production/consumption episode can be examined separately. Thus, while we might expect a concert costing £50 per ticket to be enjoyable (otherwise it is difficult to understand why we would purchase the ticket), there are no guarantees that this will be the case. Furthermore, we may be pleasantly surprised when we come across a good band playing for nothing in a pub. As Warde maintains, 'There is no simple fit between mode of provision and manner of delivery' (1992: 21). This account, which is summarized in figure 8.2, emphasizes the complexity of the social relationships which are involved in production and consumption.

Other accounts of the relationship between production and consumption have emphasized the changing nature of the relationships between producers and consumers. Abercrombie argues that the power of producers has declined relative to that of consumers. He maintains that, in some respects, this is a loss of authority by the producer 'in determining the form and content of production and consumption; it is no longer possible to say with Henry Ford that consumers can have any colour of car so long as it is black' (Abercrombie 1991: 173). Furthermore, there has been a decline in 'producer culture', which entails the organization of producers 'around the importance of being a producer making something worthwhile' (ibid.: 175). Such producer cultures have been undermined in the culture industries as the focus has moved away from the product itself to the means of selling it. Furthermore, on this argument there has been 'a shift in authority and power in companies from those directly concerned with production to those who are essentially concerned with other aspects of the company' (ibid.: 177). Thus, in the music industry there has been an increased emphasis on those concerned with the production of image rather than with music per se and by the staff who control the finance, so that it is sometimes contended that these are the people who make the important decisions (see chapters 1 and 2).

This argument suggests that consumers are growing increasingly more powerful. Furthermore, as they become more 'enterprising', they come to be more involved in 'enthusiasms' (see chapter 9). By enthusiasm, Abercrombie means 'the dedication of leisure time to the intense involvement in some activity, whether it is gardening or fishing, swimming or collecting antiques, model building or body building' (1991: 179). Within these enthusiasms, there may be a variety of relationships between production and consumption. One way of considering the complexity of these social relations is to return to the discussions of local music-making summarized earlier in chapter 2.

In *The Hidden Musicians*, Finnegan (1989) explores the often drawn distinction between professional and amateur musicians. In common-sense terms, it might be thought that the professional is more of a producer and the amateur more a consumer. This issue is important to Finnegan, as her book is concerned with everyday, local music-making (in Milton Keynes). However, she argues that the distinction between amateur and professional is in practice very difficult to draw:

> The term 'professional' . . . at first appears unambiguous. A 'professional' musician earns his or her living by working full time in some musical role, in contrast to the 'amateur', who does it 'for love' and whose source of livelihood lies elsewhere. But complications arise as soon as one tries to apply this to actual cases on the ground. Some lie in ambiguities in the concept of 'earning one's living', others in differing interpretations about what is meant by working in 'music', and others again – perhaps the most powerful of all – in the emotive overtones of the term 'professional' as used by the participants themselves. (Finnegan 1989: 13)

Therefore, Finnegan maintains that the relationship between amateur and professional can best be seen as a continuum, with most of the musicians playing in Milton Keynes working at some points in the middle of that continuum. In many respects, the key term used to describe the musicians studied by Finnegan is 'performer'. This catches some important distinctions that can be drawn in the areas of production and consumption and fandom. Thus, Finnegan writes:

> [My research] leads me further to query once again not only the still fashionable view that human beings somehow gain their central social reality from their economic involvement in society (usually based on the 'man as paid worker' model) but even the richer and, in my opinion, more realistic 'man as symboliser' approach (current in some social science, specially anthropology) with its overtones of an ideational and ultimately linguistically modelled view of humanity. It is surely equally valid to picture human beings essentially as practitioners and performers: [as] artistic and moral enactors rather than as symbolic perceivers or paid workers. (1989: 341)

It is important to take all these different dimensions into account in considering the activities of fans and the complex sets of relationships between producers and consumers, production and consumption. In accord with the suggestions of Finnegan, these relations should be seen as continua. Thus, it is possible to argue that there is a continuum of creativity in musical production. Copying a CD for a friend involves the production of a text in a domestic environment, structured by use value (with the hope that the friend will enjoy it) and identity value (it may cement our common identity as jazz fans), but is relatively low in creativity. By contrast, the recording of a piece of music is far more complex and may involve much greater levels of creativity. It may stem from all the forms of value identified by Warde, and aspects (or episodes) of the process are governed by different social relations.

Furthermore, it is possible to trace a process by which someone who begins as a relatively passive consumer of pop music becomes a communal producer. As the music affects them, they become more interested in particular types of music. They may then define themselves (or be defined by others) as a fan, and begin to use arguments about authenticity to defend their tastes in arguments concerning music with other people. They may be enthusiastic enough to form their own band with other like-minded people. This band might rehearse in facilities that are partly sponsored by the local state as part of an attempt to use cultural production to stimulate the local economy (Frith 1993; Street 1993). This might lead to the production of new records, which are then sold locally or on the international market, thus moving into the commercial sector.

Employing an ethnographic approach, Bogdanović (2009) found that this was indeed the case with the large majority of professional and semi-professional musicians with whom she interacted and whom she interviewed. Before forming a band there had been a strong tendency among all to take active part in a range of extra-musical activities – listening to music, collecting and sharing recordings, publishing music fanzines (offline and online), participating in online music forums, attending gigs, and generally socializing in real life and online music spaces. Only three out of twenty interviewees had some degree of formal music education, with the rest embarking on their musical pathways as fans of certain groups and musical styles, which they then often proceeded to emulate in their own creative endeavours.

Many of these individuals remained involved in such extra-musical activities, which are an essential part of music enculturation, during their professional careers, although their priorities naturally changed as they moved down their various paths. Once established, the musicians were dedicating significantly more time to creative processes such as practising/rehearsing, writing, recording and performing, though they still continued with many fan practices such as 'collecting' music knowledge and artefacts and attending live gigs.

This discussion shows the complexity of the social relations involved in production and consumption. For ease of exposition, this book has analytically bracketed dimensions of production, textual structure and audience consumption. This concluding analysis shows that such analytical bracketing should not blind the student or the researcher to the complexity of cultural relations. Likewise, it should be reiterated that general theories which suggest simple relations between the dimensions of production, textual structure and consumption are likely to prove increasingly unhelpful in a future of greater cultural complexity and fragmentation. These issues will be considered further in the next chapter in the context of the development of studies of audience consumption and productivity.

Summary

This chapter has considered:

- ideas of fame and celebrity;
- discussions of fans which argue that they should not be seen in a pejorative light;
- some accounts of fan relationships vis-à-vis different pop stars and groups;

- the general theory of fandom produced by Grossberg;
- accounts and theories of the productive nature of fans;
- studies of the productive consumption of pop music by young people;
- work that has attempted to reformulate the understanding of the relations between production and consumption.

9 Beyond Subcultures and Fans: New Audiences, Scenes and Everyday Life

The last two chapters have examined a number of aspects of the audience processes for popular music. This chapter takes this narrative forward in a number of ways. First, it considers discussions that suggest that, because of the many problems with the theorization of and empirical research on youth subcultures and popular music, a new terminology should be deployed to characterize these links and this field. Second, building on this discussion, some recent studies of young people and popular music are examined to illustrate the way that contemporary research has continued to debate and, indeed, deploy the concept of subculture. Third, specific attention will be paid to the concept of scene that has been used to examine the particular role of music in giving meaning to local (and increasingly translocal and virtual) production and consumption of music. Fourth, returning to themes concerning the nature of wider audience processes beyond young people, some recent studies that examine the thesis that middle-class people have become more omnivorous in their musical tastes will be discussed. In the fifth section of the chapter, it will be suggested that another potentially fruitful way of considering audiences and popular music is to look in some depth at how music is a significant part of the processes of everyday life.

Post-subcultures: conceptual innovation

In addressing a number of the issues that have arisen in the theorization and empirical use of the concepts of subculture and the audience that were considered in chapters 7 and 8, a number of writers have argued that the concept of subculture should no longer be used and that the 'space' that it fills in the examination of the culture of young people should be replaced by another concept (see also Hesmondhalgh 2005). The reasons given by these writers vary in their emphases, but key points are that social and cultural life has fragmented so that it is no longer possible to find clearly isolatable forms of subculture and that, as discussed by writers such as Willis et al. (1990), the spectacular processes deployed by youth subcultures have become more generalized. Thus clear subcultural groupings cannot be located and identified either. Both of these aspects are discussed by Chaney, who suggests that 'The idea of subculture is redundant because the type of investment that the notion of subculture labelled is becoming more general, and therefore the varieties of modes of symbolization and involvement are more common in everyday life' (2004: 37). A clear opinion in this respect is represented by the work of Andy Bennett (e.g. 1999), who argues that the idea of subculture is 'deeply problematic in that it imposes rigid lines of division over forms of sociation which may, in effect, be rather more fleeting, and in many cases more arbitrary than the concept of subculture, with its connotations of coherence and solidarity allows for' (1999: 603).

This line of argument, which emphasizes fragmentation, fluidity and the increasing lack of distinctiveness of what were often seen as separable subcultural groups, has sometimes been supplemented by another form of thinking. This maintains that a key problem of the Birmingham approach to subcultures (see chapter 7) was that it became concerned more with the decoding of the meaning of subcultures as texts and less with the voices and views of those who make them up (see, for example, Widdicombe and Wooffitt 1995; Muggleton 2000). These general concerns have led to a range of arguments and concepts that are able potentially to supersede that of subculture.

In this debate there are three broad positions:

1   that which argues that the concept of subculture is redundant and that it needs to be replaced;
2   that which wishes to retain some aspects of the subculture concept but to consider the way in which subcultures have in some sense been 'postmodernized';
3   that which suggests that the term 'subculture' can be deployed but only in reference to groups that retain some of the key features of subcultures as examined by writers such as those associated with the Birmingham Centre for Contemporary Cultural Studies.

While these positions often shade into each other, it is possible to see how studies discussed in the subsequent parts of this chapter represent them.

The idea that the concept of subculture needs to be replaced has led to the formulation and deployment of several related concepts (see Hodkinson 2002: 19–24; Bennett and Kahn-Harris 2004: 11–14). The key ideas to have been suggested and deployed here are tribe and neo-tribe, lifestyle (Miles 2000) and scene. The idea of tribe is, in the main, derived from the work of the French sociologist Michel Maffesoli (1996). This emphasizes that, in an increasingly consumerist society, groupings are related through consumerist practices. Groups may therefore exist that are more fluid, in the sense that their commitment may shift depending on consumer choices and consumer change. This concept is related to that of lifestyle, which has become popularized into the everyday as depicting in some sense the way in which a series of choices become crystallized into a form of living that has some consistency and which can be related to some social basis (even if it is only those who share a particular postcode). As Hodkinson (2002) points out, another related term – *Bunde* – was introduced into this conceptual space by Hetherington (1992), who follows many of these emphases, while suggesting that groups may have more solidity and substance. In many ways these concepts recognize the significance of the social changes concerning consumerism, fluidity of commitment, and the fragmentation of society into numerous niches that are the hallmarks of the ideas that have been grouped under the heading of postmodernist thinking. A slightly different approach has picked up on the idea of scene as used in everyday speech to examine the production and consumption of music (initially) in a specific locality. This will be further considered in a later section of this chapter.

The second broad trend in contemporary subcultural thinking also picks up on some key aspects of this position, though it seeks to retain rather more of the subculture heritage than the writing associated with the first position. Thus, in arguing for a post-subcultural or postmodern subcultural position, Muggleton examines the extent

MODERN	POSTMODERN
Group identity	Fragmented identity
Stylistic homogeneity	Stylistic heterogeneity
Strong boundary maintenance	Boundary maintenance weak
Subcultural provides main identity	Multiple stylistic identities
High degree of commitment	Low degree of commitment
Membership perceived as permanent	Transient attachment expressed
Low rates of subcultural mobility	High rates of subcultural mobility
Stress on belief and values	Fascination with style and image
Political gesture of resistance	Apolitical sentiments
Anti-media sentiments	Positive attitude towards media
Self-perception as authentic	Celebration of the inauthentic

Figure 9.1 Ideal-typical traits of modern and postmodern subculturalists
Source: Muggleton 2000: 52

to which 'subculturalists may be expected to display a number of "postmodern" characteristics, some of which have an affinity with certain countercultural sensibilities' (2000: 52). The broad set of 'ideal-typical traits' identified by Muggleton are represented in figure 9.1. In the rest of his book (see next section), Muggleton discusses the extent to which the (post-)subculturalists whom he examines exhibit the features that he has described in these postmodernist ways. In so doing, he perhaps retains more ways of thinking about subcultures than he might have expected to do and which might be represented by the first strand of thinking discussed above.

The third strand of thinking continues to deploy the idea of subculture while restricting its use to particular subcultures that deploy (relatively) the forms of coherence that approximate those discussed in the earlier Birmingham literature. Hodkinson's (2002) examination of Goth is a very good example of this.

While, therefore, there are different positions advanced here, and, as Muggleton and Weinzerel (2003: 6) point out, 'some of this confusion can . . . be alleviated if we recognize that different concepts can be used to abstract different aspects of social reality', it is important to examine in more detail the findings of different studies which, in various ways, have sought to advance the debate on subculture and music.

Subcultures and music: some key studies

In many ways, the study of subcultures and music was revitalized by the development of dance and rave culture. Key aspects of this have already been examined in chapter 6, where the Bourdieu-influenced work of Thornton (1995) was considered. However, Thornton's book was also important in prompting new thought and work on youth subcultures and music. She makes a number of points, only some key aspects of which will be picked up for the present discussion. First, she points out that the definition of and approach represented by the Birmingham Centre is empirically unworkable. This is important, as it suggests the need for more empirical work on youth and music. As has been suggested above, as it developed, the Birmingham approach was concerned more with the reading of subcultures as texts than with in-depth investigation of the views of the participants themselves. However, it is significant that these views are often relatively neglected in Thornton's study, and it is only in more recent work (e.g. Muggleton 2000; Hodkinson 2002) that they have been represented in more detail.

Second, Thornton points to the role of key divisions within the working of the subculture rather than focusing on the relationship between the subculture and the dominant culture, or on the youth subculture and the 'parent' culture. This means that she can examine the way in which cultural hierarchies or oppositions work within the subcultural group. These distinctions are complex but revolve around issues such as the authentic versus the phoney, the hip versus the mainstream, and the underground versus the mass media.

Third, and relatedly, Thornton points out that the club culture worked around the possession and deployment of what (following Bourdieu) she terms 'subcultural capital', which is represented through the idea of being 'hip' – that is, culturally aware and on the cutting edge of developments and knowledge that are prized within the subculture – which may be valueless outside it. Different forms of media are critical to the circulation of subcultural capital. These might be flyers for particular events or the fanzines produced by those who are particularly committed to the subculture. In this way, Thornton developed the idea that media are critical to subcultures. Thus, in a world where various forms of media have become increasingly important (Abercrombie and Longhurst 1998; Longhurst 2007), there are still forms of subculture, but they have become increasingly mediatized.

Thornton examined the relationships within the broad area of dance culture and pointed to its media-centred nature, but also to its internal divisions. Different aspects of these developments have been picked up by further studies.

Muggleton (2000) has sought to evaluate the extent to which subcultural adherents had been affected by the development of forms of postmodernist culture, in accordance with the points made in the first section of this chapter. Given the focus of this book on popular music rather than on subculture per se, the details of Muggleton's findings with respect to this overall thesis can be summarized fairly briefly, in the sense that he finds that the subculturalists had not moved completely to the postmodern position. As he says:

> We can, I feel, grant a qualified acknowledgement of a postmodern sensibility. Subculturalists are postmodern in that they demonstrate a fragmented, heterogeneous and individualistic stylistic identification. This is a liminal sensibility that manifests itself as an expression of freedom from structure, control and restraint, ensuring that stasis is rejected in favour of movement and fluidity. Yet there is no evidence here of some of the more excessive postmodern claims. Informants did not rapidly discard a whole series of discrete styles. Nor did they regard themselves as an ironic parody, celebrating their own lack of authenticity and the superficiality of an image saturated culture. (2000: 158)

In many ways, Muggleton draws attention to the way in which the subculturalists whom he studied wished to retain (and promote) key aspects of their individuality, partly through music, while also expressing some aspects of commitment to belonging to a recognizable group. However, although it runs through his book in a number of ways, the actual detailed discussion of music in the subcultures is relatively slight. Yet some significant themes do arise: thus, when asked about their tastes in music, even those who are committed to a subculture tend to express a preference for a range of different forms of music (see, for example, Muggleton 2000: 74, 112–13). If this is the case, as Muggleton points out, it raises, at the least, some doubts as to how important the idea of subculture is for the understanding of audience processes for music. This is discussed further below.

In another detailed piece of research, Hodkinson (2002) has examined the Goth subculture in late 1990s Britain, in which he argues for the continuing value of the concept of subculture as applied to those groups that exhibit the relative coherence of features such as those combined in Goth. Thus, although there is significant internal variation in, for example, modes of dress within the subculture (as clearly shown by Hodkinson), there are also clear commonalities and patterns. In reworking the idea of subculture, Hodkinson shows how it can be retained 'to capture the relatively substantive, clearly bounded form taken by certain elective cultural groupings' (2002: 9). He considers the criteria of 'identity, commitment, consistent distinctiveness and autonomy' and argues that 'each of them should be regarded as a contributory feature which, taken cumulatively with the others, increases the appropriateness of the term subculture' (ibid.: 29). Music is a part of this subculture, and Hodkinson discusses its importance in a number of places. It remains an important aspect of the subcultural package.

Keith Kahn-Harris (2007) examines extreme metal – a multifaceted, cross-national and controversial genre on account of its associations with violence, the occult, death, neo-fascism, Satanism, and so on. Based on fieldwork research in the UK, the USA, Israel and Sweden, and informed by Kahn-Harris's participation as both 'critical insider' and 'sympathetic outsider', and also his involvement with the British extreme metal magazine *Terrorizer*, the book examines the definitions and meanings of extreme metal. Kahn-Harris takes a look at the inside of the scene, tackling issues of hierarchy and power, as well as examining its location and its creation of forms of 'subcultural capital'. His participants construct the meaning of the scene in several ways: to denote something specific such as space where musical action enfolds (e.g. a gig), something more vague, such as 'the underground' or 'good scene' (2007: 14), something much larger, such as 'musical scene', or even understanding that there is the distinction between 'a musical side' and 'a commercial side' of a music scene.

For Kahn-Harris, extreme metal is global yet constituted as a confederation of local scenes and networks, which themselves can encompass a variety of metal subgenres: 'The extreme metal scene is a global music scene that contains local scenes within it. It also contains other scenes based on the production and consumption of particular forms of extreme metal genres, such as black metal and death metal' (Kahn-Harris 2007: 22).

In a different piece of writing Kahn-Harris (2004) points out that the global extreme metal scene is non-essentialist and opaque, meaning that it is difficult to pinpoint specific values and characteristics that define it. Different participants may use the genre in different ways, and to different purpose, or negotiate both scenic and non-scenic worlds simultaneously, maintaining friendships and familial relationships outside the scene, as well as engaging with the worlds of education and employment. This, however, does not result in a fluid and fragmented membership but rather facilitates continuity and stability. According to Kahn-Harris, extreme metal fits neither within the subcultural paradigm of the Centre for Contemporary Cultural Studies nor within a post-subcultural paradigm characterized by fragmentation, fluidity, transiency and a low level of commitment.

Andy Bennett's (2000) work represents another study that has considered in some detail a number of groupings with more focus on music itself. After developing the sort of critique of the Birmingham approach to subculture considered in the opening section of this chapter, Bennett argues that it is important to examine the way in which the experience of popular music is largely local. This can be seen as connected to themes that were considered at the end of chapters 1 and 8 of this book. The local is a space where different forms of culture are brought together and new syntheses created that involve creativity on the ground. This does not mean that the culture (or subculture) is locally bounded, but that, facilitated by the increasing availability of computers and the Internet, it is lived out in localities that are connected both to other places and to translocal processes (as is also discussed at some length by Hodkinson 2002).

Bennett includes four case studies in his book that show the significance of the processing of different influences in particular contexts: dance music; Bhangra; hip-hop in Newcastle in the northeast of England and Frankfurt in Germany; and the live music of the Pink Floyd tribute band the Benwell Floyd, again in Newcastle. These studies bring out the further significance of the local interaction of music production and consumption that have been discussed in chapters 2 and 8. Bennett's conclusion is important in that he argues that 'Aspects of popular culture, such as music and style, in addition to being understood as global cultural forms, assume particularised "everyday" meanings which respond to the differing local contexts in which they are appropriated and which frame their incorporation into forms of social action' (2000: 197). This is significant in two ways: first, because it suggests the importance of the local consumption of global products and, second, because it links music to other forms of popular culture. Thus, while subculture remains a useful concept in some respects (especially in analyses such as those of Muggleton and Hodkinson), it directs attention to wider production and consumption processes and how they are lived out. An important concept in this respect which has been developed via the study of popular music is 'scene'.

Popular music scenes

In recent years, the concept of scene has been increasingly used to refer to sites of (predominantly) local music production and consumption. In some respects this has built on common-sense understandings of the idea as represented in formulations such as the New York scene or the Manchester scene. Furthermore, at times, the term has been used in conjunction with that of subculture – for example, in the work of Hodkinson (2002) and Kahn-Harris (2004, 2007) discussed in the previous section. There is much overlap in the literature in the use of the term, although there has more often been an attempt to separate the two meanings. As discussed in the previous chapter, the work of Finnegan (1989) is an important resource in the rethinking of these relationships in local contexts. A key study that has advanced this research is that on Austin, Texas, by Barry Shank (1994), which builds upon earlier work by Shank himself and the sort of influential theorization produced by Will Straw, who argues that the musical scene can be defined as:

> that cultural space in which a range of musical practices co-exist, interacting with each other within a variety of processes of differentiation, and according to widely varying trajectories of change and cross-fertilization. The sense of purpose

articulated within a musical community normally depends on an affective link between two terms: contemporary musical practices, on the one hand, and the musical heritage which is seen to render this contemporary activity appropriate to a given context, on the other. Within a music scene, that same sense of purpose is articulated within those forms of communication through which the building of musical alliances and the drawing of musical boundaries take place. The manner in which musical practices within the scene tie themselves to processes of historical change occurring within a larger international musical culture will also be a significant basis of the way in which such forms are positioned within a scene at a local level. (1991: 373)

Shank traces the development of the music scene in Austin in some detail – filling in the way in which the different influences have come together to produce a changing musical patchwork. In more theoretical terms, he argues that the boundaries between producers and consumers break down in the sort of scene that is represented in Austin. As he argues: 'within the fluid stream of potential meanings, the audience and the musicians together participate in a nonverbal dialogue about the significance of music and the construction of their selves' (1994: 125). To develop and summarize this idea, he suggests that '[s]pectators become fans, fans become musicians, musicians are always already fans, all constructing the nonobjects of identification through their performances as subjects of enunciation – becoming and disseminating the subject-in-process of the signifying practice of rock 'n' roll music' (ibid.: 131). This captures the way in which the participants in a scene can take on a number of different roles or can change their roles within it. This sort of change is also captured by Hodkinson (2002), where he shows how the Goth subculture can involve the promotion of gigs, tape-swapping, the sale and purchase of clothing, and so on – suggesting the sort of fluidity and complexity of the construction of meaning theorized by Shank. It is illustrative that, in this context, Hodkinson often refers to the Goth scene.

Building on this sort of approach, where the idea of scene 'has increasingly been used as a model for academic research on the production, performance, and reception of popular music' (Peterson and Bennett 2004: 3), Peterson and Bennett argue that three broad types of scene can be identified: local, translocal and virtual.

Local scenes are those based around a particular place; this has been the most common use made of the term, notably in the work of Cohen (1991), examined in chapter 2, and that of Shank (1994), considered above. A local scene is:

> a focused social activity that takes place in a delimited space and over a specific span of time in which clusters of producers, musicians, and fans realize their common musical taste, collectively distinguishing themselves from others by using music and other cultural signs often appropriated from other places, but recombined and developed in ways that come to represent the local scene. The focused activity we are interested in here, of course, centers on a particular style of music, but such music scenes characteristically involve other diverse lifestyle elements as well. These usually include a distinctive style of dancing, a particular range of psychoactive drugs, style of dress, politics and the like. (Peterson and Bennett 2004: 8)

The translocal scene involves the communication between local scenes and refers to 'widely scattered local scenes drawn into regular communication around a distinctive form of music and lifestyle' (Peterson and Bennett 2004: 6). Examples of this are alternative rock in the 1980s, as examined by Kruse (1993), and the way in which hip-hop has diffused across the world but taken on specific local forms. Another phenomenon discussed under this heading is the so-called music carnival that existed around the American band the Grateful Dead, where 'a band's fans regularly follow their favorite musicians around the country from tour date to tour date and energize local devotees of the music and lifestyle' (Peterson and Bennett 2004: 10). The virtual scene 'is a newly emergent formation in which people scattered across great physical spaces create the sense of scene via fanzines and, increasingly, through the internet' (ibid.: 6–7).

As technologies such as the Internet develop, it can be expected that there might be more virtual scenes developing. In their edited collection, Peterson and Bennett include a range of studies that they locate under these headings of local, translocal and virtual. Among studies of local scenes are Chicago blues (Grazian 2004), rave in a city near Detroit (Spring 2004) and Salsa in London (Urquia 2004), translocal scenes considered include Schilt (2004) on Riot Grrrl and Hodkinson (2004) on Goth, while examples of virtual scenes are Bennett (2004) on the Canterbury scene and Vroomen (2004) on Kate Bush.

One of the issues raised by this expansion of the conceptualization of the idea of scene to include the translocal and the virtual is that it may reduce the specificity of the concept itself and make it descriptive rather than analytical. Thus, while it may be useful to point out that scenes have translocal and virtual dimensions, it is important to retain the idea that a scene involves some measure of co-present interaction.

When writing about independent music, Kruse (2010) suggests, that despite the changing landscape of musical interaction, local scenes, together with local, interlocal and translocal practices, persist. She argues that the ubiquity of the Internet and the emergence of so-called 'virtual scenes' does not lead to the local scenes disappearing, but rather that virtual and offline (conventional) scenes complement each other, with online often enabling face-to-face interaction: 'For musicians, fans, and other participants in indie music who have internet access, the technology helps, for example, to enable embodied social interaction between and among geographically proximal participants, in more or less organized ways' (Kruse 2010: 636). The concepts of locality and located-ness, Kruse maintains, retain their importance, with updates of mobile communication devices (e.g. via tweets or Facebook) increasingly incorporating the physical location of the participants through geolocation technologies that can easily be enabled. It is suggested that such features facilitate and promote more efficient face-to-face interaction among scene participants.

It seems increasingly likely that those who are enthusiastic about a form of music and a mode of dress will engage, to varying degrees, with others who live locally and who are involved, as well as hoping to meet up with yet others who are involved but who live elsewhere. Hodkinson's discussion of Goth (2002) illuminates the differential interaction of these processes very well. In addition, Grazian's (2004) study of the blues scene in Chicago discusses the role of tourists in affecting the continuing existence of blues clubs, and so on. There is some danger here of a loss of specificity and purchase once the concept of scene is generalized, unless the particular features to which it draws attention – the aspect of interaction around some degree of performance, the role of place in acting as a node of communication – are recognized. This also takes us back to the idea, discussed from Muggleton and Weinzerel (2003), that different concepts may have purchase in different contexts and may refer to different parts of reality. This will be further developed in the final part of this chapter, where a particular typology for different audience positions will be considered (see also Abercrombie and Longhurst 1998). However, it is important first to examine some other related aspects of audience activity.

Omnivorous audiences

As was discussed above with respect to work on subcultures, Muggleton, in his examination of youth subculturalists, found that, in several respects, some of his respondents sought to convey the variety of their musical tastes and that their tastes had changed in quite significant ways over a period of time. In a study of the patterns of middle-class culture in and around Manchester in the northwest of England, Savage, Bagnall and Longhurst point to the way in which, when asked about musical tastes, people usually respond with a statement along the lines of 'I like all sorts of things', or 'I have a wide taste in music' (2005: 168–70; see also Carrabine and Longhurst 1999). And this is despite the fact that, when this sort of statement is investigated further or qualified, the range of taste that is being referred to is generally actually relatively narrow. It appears that a socially accepted way of characterizing musical taste is both to admit to liking something and to suggest that one's taste is wide. There is a clear contrast here with the way in which individuals responded in the same study to a similar question about television. In this case, they were usually defensive in the sense that they sought to downplay the amount of television they watched, or to suggest that they only watched particular selected programmes such as news and documentaries (Savage et al. 2005: 157–68). This can be seen as some evidence for the idea that (in particular) the middle classes in societies such as the UK and the USA have become more omnivorous in their musical tastes.

This idea has been developed by (for example) Peterson and Kern (1996), who argue that in the United States there has been a shift from a division between the elite and the mass in culture. In particular, they maintain that middle-class groups have become more expansive in taste. This means that they engage with a wider range of cultural forms than was the case in previous historical periods. So, for example, whereas in the past educated middle-class people might have restricted themselves to classical literature and music, they are now likely also to read detective novels, watch soap operas on TV and listen to popular music from around the world. In this sense, they are omnivores, since they consume both high and popular culture. As Peterson and Simkus argue:

> There is mounting evidence that high-status groups not only participate more than do others in high-cultural activities but also tend to participate more often in most kinds of leisure activities. In effect, elite taste is no longer defined as an expressed appreciation of the high art forms (and a moral distain or bemused tolerance for all other aesthetic expressions). Now it is being redefined as an appreciation of the aesthetics of every distinctive form along with an appreciation of the high arts. Because status is gained by knowing about and participating in (that is to say, by consuming) all forms, the term *omnivore* seems appropriate. (1992: 169)

Further, according to this thesis, those at the bottom of the social scale are univores, in that their cultural consumption is more restricted and constrained by material factors (Bryson 1997). Evidence for the omnivore thesis was initially produced with respect to the consumption of music in the USA and has now been subject to empirical investigation and theoretical refinement in a number of other countries (see Peterson and Anand 2004). This has suggested that the patterns of omnivorous taste may vary according to the medium being considered.

Although there may be debate about the effects or spread of these forms of taste, it is significant that, when they discuss their musical tastes, younger people often do so using omnivorous statements. For example, in research on the musical preferences of those aged seventeen to eighteen living in a relatively affluent suburb of Greater Manchester, Carrabine and Longhurst found that 'the most common way of express- ing musical taste is *not* to appear to be exclusive. On the contrary, it is important for these young relatively affluent, late teenagers to display a fluid and wide range of musical likes' (1999: 131). While there is some variation in the confidence with which such pluralistic inclinations are held and expressed, as Carrabine and Longhurst (ibid.: 131–6), deploying focus group evidence, suggest, it does seem important to recognize that a range of musical taste (or the expression that this is the case) is common, and that this is further evidence for the idea that it is difficult consistently to tie musical preferences to the nature of subcultural taste and practice (see chapter 6, box 6.3). Again, this raises the point that it is important to consider the range of dif- ferent aspects or forms of audience experience that exist, perhaps suggesting that this entails significant attention to the idea of the place of music in everyday life.

Music and everyday life

It is possible to see how significant music can be in everyday life through the follow- ing quotation, taken from research based on interviews where respondents were able freely to comment on the meaning of music for them (Crafts et al. 1993: 109):

Q: What does music mean to you?
A: Music is just part of life, like air. You live with it all the time, so it's tough to judge what it means to you. For some people, it's a deep emotional thing, for some people, it's casual. I turn on the radio and it's there in the morning; it's there when I drive; it's there when I go out.
Q: If it isn't there, do you miss it?
A: No.
Q: So you're not really aware that it is there?
A: It's like a companion, or a back-up noise. Just something in the background. A lot of people turn the radio on and they're not listening to it for the most part, but it's there to keep them company, it's background noise. It's like the TV; they leave the TV on all the time, although it never gets watched. But it's background, people use it just to feel comfortable with.

More recent research has continued to explore such themes and ideas in theoreti- cal and empirical terms. A good example of this approach can be found in the work of DeNora (2000). She adopts a stance that has its roots in the premises of interaction- ist sociology – that is, she seeks to explore how music plays a role in the interactions between people and in the constitution of those people themselves. Who we are and how we engage with other people are processes that are brought about significantly by interaction. DeNora points out that some of the subcultural literature explored in chapter 7 went quite a long way towards looking at how music was a part of such pro- cesses. In her view, therefore, a strength of this approach was its 'focus not on what can be said about cultural forms, but on what the appropriation of cultural materials achieves *in action*, what culture "does" for its consumers within the contexts of their lives' (2000: 6). In seeking to add some theoretical context to the relatively descriptive approach adopted by authors such as Crafts and her colleagues, DeNora explores three main dimensions of music's place in everyday life: its place in the constitution of our senses of self, or what might also be termed identity; its role in the construction of the body and the physical self (see also chapter 6); and its function in the 'ordering' of social relationships.

With respect to the first of these, DeNora shows, through a number of examples, how music is involved in the construction of feelings, as well as preventing the onset of moods and feelings that are not wished for. Thus, for DeNora, 'Music is not simply used to express some internal emotional state. Indeed, that music is part of the reflexive constitution of that state; it is a resource for the identification work of "knowing how one feels" – a building material of "subjectivity"' (2000: 37). DeNora discusses a number of examples of this process and argues that 'In none of these examples . . . does music simply *act upon* individuals, like a stimulus. Rather, music's "effects" come from the ways in which individuals orient to it, how they interpret it and how they place it within their personal musical maps, within the semiotic web of music and extra-musical associations' (ibid.: 61).

The interaction between music and the body has already been considered in chapter 6. DeNora shows in some detail how some of the themes explored there play out in practice. A good example of this is her discussion of the role of music in an aerobics class. On one level, music 'defines the components of a session through its tempo changes (for example, music for warm up, core and cool down) and it also profiles the bodily movements associated with each of these components' (2000: 92). However, on another level, the music is also part of structuring how the body is to be deployed in the course of the particular movements of aerobics. Music is not just the background for those movements; it is a part of how those movements are defined. As DeNora puts it: 'Following aerobics' musical changes and the ways in which real bodies interact with prescribed musical bodily changes, bodily changes allow us to examine the body, moment by moment, as it interacts with, and is configured in relation to, music' (ibid.: 93). The aerobic body is (partly) constituted through the interaction with music, which is just a specific example of how '[m]usic is, or rather can serve as, a constitutive property of bodily being' (ibid.: 99).

In a third broad theme, DeNora considers the way in which music is involved in the production and reproduction of ordered social life. Such social order is not simply imposed; rather, it is itself produced through a process of 'ordering'. As the extract in box 9.1 shows, music can be part of the ordering and reordering of close relationships.

To take another example, music is also used in the ordering of the consumption practices involved in shopping, and this is discussed in empirical research by DeNora and Belcher (2000). Yet another important study that addresses the role of music in everyday life in a different way was written by Bull (2000), who deploys a detailed consideration of the role of personal stereos in the everyday lives of listeners, with a conceptualization of everyday life that draws on aspects of the work of the Frankfurt School (see the Introduction).

Bull explores a number of different aspects of personal stereo use, only the most significant of which can be considered here. First, he points out how users deploy the

Box 9.1   Music and the ordering of relationships

[Let us] consider how music is used not only to reinforce but also to undermine particular relations between friends and intimates. Here, for example, Lesley describes how a shift in music listening habits and tastes at home was associated with the deterioration of her relationship with her partner.

> Lesley: In the '80s I sort of got distanced from music. My [children] were little and my husband didn't really like a lot of the music going on – he wasn't particularly keen on the radio being on all the time, probably – I suppose the bands I didn't identify with at the time were Dire Straits – those sort of bands. I liked some of the things they did but I think it was more excitable and so my ex-husband liked them and didn't mind them being put on, whereas some of the other music I'd put on he thought would upset the [children] and of course then they got to identify with some of the things I liked with being morose, like the Leonard Cohen. So it tended to be more popular jiggly music. . . . Normally if I listened to Leonard Cohen I wanted to be in my own space listening and of course so normally I would have been in a bit of a strange mood in comparison to how I would be, and I suppose he picked upon that and maybe the [children] did as well. . . . When we first got married we used to listen to the radio a lot, and within nine months I was listening to Radio 4 rather than Radio 1 because he didn't like Radio 1 at all. When the boys were young, babies, occasionally I'd put something on raucous or heavy metal or something and his attitude was that he definitely didn't want it on because it was too noisy. But I think the [children] picked up on that as well because if I put anything on that was a bit loud – [here she gestures that they would act up] . . . during the '80s I didn't really bother with music because I thought it would cause friction – be upsetting or whatever – so I stopped . . . The late '80s I started listening to Beehive and the Thompson Twins, which of course my husband didn't identify with at all . . .

Lesley describes how she began to make a deliberate musical move away from her relationship, replacing the 'popular jiggly' music that she perceived as within the bounds of the relationship – for example, Dire Straits – and also the more, as she perceived it, 'intellectual' mode of Radio 4, with music that her husband disliked and viewed with disapproval. Lesley goes on to describe how, near the end of her relationship with her ex-husband, she would sometimes, when she was angry, play a Soft Cell song entitled, 'Say hello, wave goodbye' (from an album called *Erotic Cabaret*). She would play the track at high volume so that it would be audible from any room in the house. As she puts it, 'It was a hint really', but admits she is not sure her husband understood ('He didn't say anything').

Lesley used music to convey a message (perhaps about her evolving aesthetic and stylistic stance) that she had not yet formulated in words – she was formulating a sense of how she was 'different' from her partner, thinking through musical practice about leaving that partner. Via music, Lesley may also have been undermining the aesthetic basis of their relationship, preparing the aesthetic ground for her departure, creating an aesthetic trajectory for the agency of her departure.

Source: DeNora 2000: 126–7

music that they listen to in order to give pleasure to an otherwise dull routine. Second, personal stereos are used in a related way to 'escape' from aspects of everyday life, but in addition to go into 'dream worlds', which Bull compares to films that the users construct, drawing on bodily and visual experiences. In a sense the personal stereo provides a soundtrack to the filmic transformation of everyday life on the part of the user. Bull uses these insights to argue that music should be seen as a more important part of daily life, as it often was in the past when the emphasis was more on the visual. Bull maintains similar arguments about personalization of public spaces through music when writing about the iPod, where users 'create their own soundworlds' (Bull 2005: 347). In addition, with such MP3 players they have access to much greater choice of songs that can reflect or accompany their mood, and thus greater control in managing both the mood and the urban space through which they move. Similarly, in his study of out-of-home listening, Bull focuses on experiences of people who listen to music in their cars while navigating usually urban spaces. His interviewees described the car as a refuge where, facilitated by sound, a great degree of thinking, planning and solitary reflection takes place: 'Automobiles thus become spaces of temporary respite from demands of the "other" while the driver is often sitting in gridlocked unison with all the other drivers who are in illusionary control of their environment' (Bull 2004: 249). Referring to Adorno's notion of 'an illusion of immediacy in a totally mediated world', Bull concludes that mobile technologies allow the user to transform the public (e.g. urban) space into an intimate, 'domestic' space (ibid.: 255).

Bull's earlier (2000) study was carried out when tape-based personal stereos were still relatively common. Since then, CD players and even MP3 players such as iPods have been decreasing in popularity, while smart phones with integrated music players and music streaming are gaining ground. Such transformations no doubt have an influence on audience processes. In the view of Kusek and Leonhard:

> Along with the utterly astounding growth of the Internet has come a new, networked mobility exemplified by the explosion of the digital music player and cell phone usage, particularly in Europe and Asia. Today's kids are 'always on', natural digeratis, constantly networking, plugged-in and communicating with each other in many unprecedented ways. They are the *screenagers* – and are rapidly changing the way that music is discovered and that business is conducted. (2005: 99)

In an exploratory study of adult MP3 users (those who have listened to music in other formats), Gerber (2011) asks in which ways the new audio technology impacts on our listening experience. Some earlier studies signalled that the listeners were focused on 'experiential peripherals' – that is, 'experiences connected to but not directly involved with the listening function of audio consumption' – including the brand (coolness, hipness and associated status), ease of use (acquisition, sharing and portability), and psychological manipulation (e.g. shuffle). Although she utilized an extremely small sample (three male participants aged thirty and above), Gerber's study results did not support earlier assertions that experiential peripherals play a more relevant part in MP3 consumption compared to earlier technologies such as vinyl, cassette tape and CD. Gerber concludes that 'MP3 still just simply means listening to audio, or in particular, to music.'

Recent years have seen an abundance of debates about the transformative capacities of new digital technologies. Frequently, the distinction is drawn between younger generations of consumers/audience – so-called digital natives – and everybody else's experiences and practices of consumption. As was discussed in chapter 1, the suggestion here is that the music business is having to take account of the desires of this group or 'generation'. It has been argued that, with respect to younger people in societies such as the UK and the USA, 'Their way of communicating with their friends is profoundly different than that of previous generations. Instant messaging and e-mail have eclipsed many prior means of socializing; for some, online networking has become as popular as actual dating. This generation is far more into interactivity than into passive consumption – couch potatoes have become cyber-networkers' (Kusek and Leonhard 2005: 99). At the same time, the desire to maintain tactile dimensions of digital media 'alive', albeit in their visual form, has resulted in smart phone applications such as Hipstamatic, Instagram and Super8, selling the vintage 'look' of both camera cases and photographic images. In terms of musical consumption, periods of resurgence of interest in the vinyl and labels issuing material exclusively on tape could be seen as a form of 'resistance' to new digital technologies. However, unlike large, commercial and mainstream take-up of Instagram, for example, the vinyl and tape markets remain relatively small and niche.

It is important to recognize that these potential shifts are occurring in the context of wider audience changes. Thus, in broad terms the attention to the role of music in everyday life paid by DeNora and Bull, and the speculation of Kusek and Leonhard, need to be seen as part of a more general understanding of audience processes.

In *Audiences*, Abercrombie and Longhurst (1998) argue that, while the move towards greater research attention to everyday audiences is important, future work will be weakened unless it takes account of the changing nature of audience processes and the way in which such processes are conceptualized. They argue that the two most significant ways of conceptualizing the audience, which they term the behavioural paradigm and the incorporation/resistance paradigm, are deficient in crucial respects. The behavioural paradigm tends to consider the audience as individuals in two ways. On the one hand, individuals in social contexts are affected by the media (often in a pernicious way) – for example, by some forms of pop music, as discussed in the first section of chapter 7. On the other hand, as also considered in chapter 7, individuals are seen to sue the media to satisfy certain wants and needs (in the 'uses and gratifications' approach). There are significant difficulties with this approach, such as its relatively restricted understanding of social life and its lack of attention to both power relations and the textual nature of media products. Furthermore, it was severely criticized by what has been called a critical approach to the study of the media (Hall 1980), or what Abercrombie and Longhurst called the incorporation/resistance paradigm (see figure 9.2).

The incorporation/resistance paradigm, reflecting its Marxist origins, takes the operation of power in society seriously. It pays particular attention to the way in which society is structured, especially in the earlier work done within its parameters in terms of class, but, subsequently, with respect to gender, race and age. Its key research problem concerns the extent to which such social structuring and social location influence particular modes of decoding of media texts (rather than media messages or stimuli in the behavioural approach) in ideological terms. As mentioned in chapter 7, this approach considers the extent to which audiences resist or are incorporated by media texts (see, for example, Morley 1980). The classic studies

	1 **Behavioural**	2 **Incorporation/Resistance**	3 **Spectacle/Performance**
Audience	Individuals (in social context)	Socially structured (e.g. by class, gender, race)	Socially constructed and reconstructed especially by spectacle and narcissism
Medium	Stimulus (message)	Text	Mediascape(s)
Social consequence(s)	Functions/ dysfunctions, propaganda, influence, use, effects	Ideological incorporation and resistance	Identity formation and reformation in everyday life
Representative studies and approaches	'Effects' literature, uses and gratifications	Encoding and decoding, Morley (1980), Radway (1987), fan studies	Silverstone (1994), Hermes (1995), Gillespie (1995)

Figure 9.2 The three paradigms
Source: Abercrombie and Longhurst 1998: 37

	Simple	**Mass**	**Diffused**
Communication	Direct	Mediated	Fused
Local/Global	Local	Global	Universal
Ceremony	High	Medium	Low
Public/Private	Public	Private	Public and Private
Distance	High	Very high	Low
Attention	High	Variable	Civil inattention

Figure 9.3 Modes of audience experience
Source: Abercrombie and Longhurst 1998: 44

showed that resistance, while hugely significant, needed to be examined in the context of ideological incorporation into the dominant structures of society. Thus much of the work with respect to youth subcultures looked at in chapter 7 and in the earlier parts of this chapter is at least partly concerned with how such groups resist, to some extent, the dominant order. However, this approach tended to overemphasize the coherence of the response to different texts, often in line with one of the social bases identified above, or to conflate an active response to media with a critical one. In this context, Abercrombie and Longhurst speculated that such problems could only be rectified through the formulation of a new paradigm for audience research.

The argument for the spectacle/performance paradigm (SPP) rests on the recognition that both audiences themselves and conceptualizations of audiences were changing. Abercrombie and Longhurst propose that three different types of audience currently co-exist: simple, mass and diffused (see figure 9.3). A simple audience, as represented, for example, by an audience at a pop music concert, involves relatively direct communication from performers to audience; the performance takes place in a confined locale, tends to be highly ceremonial in the sense that it is a special event and the space of performance is ritualistic, and the site has a high level of meaning for participants. The performance and the audience response take place in public and the performers are separated from the audience by clear boundaries. The attention level of the audience with respect to the performance is high.

The development of mass audiences reflects the growth of more mediated forms of communication. An example of this would be listening to a CD at home. Here, communication is highly mediated in that performance takes place a long way from the audience spatially and is normally recorded at an earlier time and place. The relatively direct connection between 'live' performance and audience is broken. As has been discussed at several points in this book, the texts of the music industry are globally available and are not restricted to a one-off performance in time and space. The ritual aspects of the simple audience decline as the mass audience becomes used to texts and media being part of everyday life. Much CD listening is done while other things are going on. The mass audience tends to exist in private rather than public spaces. CD listening takes place in the home or in the car. Likewise, the attention of the audience can vary from highly engaged, focused viewing to complete distraction. Finally, the distance in spatial and time dimensions of the audience from the performance is high.

Key to Abercrombie and Longhurst's argument is the development of what is termed the diffused audience:

> The essential feature of this audience-experience is that, in contemporary society, everyone becomes an audience all the time. Being a member of an audience is no longer an exceptional event, nor even an everyday event. Rather it is constitutive of everyday life. This is not a claim that simple audiences or mass audiences no longer exist, quite the contrary. These experiences are as common as ever, but they take place against the background of the diffused audience. (1998: 68–9)

Several social processes are related to the development of the diffused audience. First, people spend more and more time in media consumption. Second, such consumption is increasingly woven into the fabric of everyday life, as explored by writers such as DeNora (2000). Third, Western societies have become more performative in the broadest sense (see chapter 6).

Abercrombie and Longhurst argue that, in studying audience processes, it is crucially important to consider the interaction between simple, mass and diffused audiences – for example, the relationship between the seemingly increasing importance of attending live performances and festivals (Kusek and Leonhard 2005: 114), which, on one level, are simple audience experiences. However, these can also be relayed via the mass media, as at Glastonbury, and therefore become mass televisual experiences, and diffused as aspects of identity work in everyday life. Abercrombie and Longhurst identified that the previous two paradigms (the behavioural and the incorporation/resistance paradigms) were not up to studying these relationships, and so proposed that the spectacle/performance paradigm provided the more adequate account of audience processes. This approach pays greater attention to how the audience is socially constructed and reconstructed (rather than being determined or structured). Attention would focus on the way in which media interact to form as

---

Consumer—Fan—Cultist—Enthusiast—Petty Producer

Figure 9.4 The audience continuum
Source: Abercrombie and Longhurst 1998: 141

mediascape (Appadurai 1990) rather than on media messages or texts per se. Instead of considering the effects, functions or ideological operations of the media, the SPP focuses on the interaction between everyday life, audience processes and identity formation and reformation.

In elaborating the SPP, Abercrombie and Longhurst argued that there were a number of potential positions that audience members could occupy (see figure 9.4; for further elaboration and critique, see Hills 2002; Crawford 2003; Longhurst 2007). At one end of this audience continuum was the consumer, who interacted with the media in a relatively generalized and unfocused fashion. It is important to stress that the term 'consumer' here is not intended to have pejorative connotations. The next step along the continuum is that of the fan (again without any intended pejorative connotations), who becomes particularly attached to certain programmes or stars within the context of relatively high media usage. At the next point are the cultists, who build on such attachments to focus their media and audience activities around certain key programmes. Cultists also tend to interact more directly with those who have similar tastes. Enthusiasts tend to be involved more in the actual production of artefacts connected to their fan and cultic activities. Classic studies, such as those of *Star Trek* fandom, point to the writing of stories and the making of videos and paintings (see, for example, Bacon-Smith 1992; Jenkins 1992; Penley 1992). The final point on the continuum is that of the petty producer, who is reaching the point where enthusiasm is becoming professionalized into a full-time activity (see Moorhouse 1991). The identification of this continuum allows further differentiation in contemporary audience positions than had hitherto been the case (see also chapter 8). These positions can be considered in the context of popular music.

In his discussion of Goth, Hodkinson (2002) shows how this 'subculture' contains several of the positions identified by Abercrombie and Longhurst. Some of those who engage with Goth may be fanlike in that they are particularly attached to Goth bands, but they may be relatively unengaged with other forms of the culture; cultists become more engaged and may dress in a Goth way; others may move more into the enthusiast position if, for example, they become an author of a fanzine. Those who run shops specializing in Goth records or clothes as a full-time occupation have moved into the final category. These positions would contrast with someone who might be said to be a consumer of Goth or Goth-related music – someone who owned one of the records that have been defined as part of Goth.

This approach can also be used to capture the fluidity of the way in which people relate to music (Williams 2001). For example, in a study of young people and music, Laughey (2006) demonstrates the way in which ideas of different audience positions and of everyday life can be combined to excellent effect. He demonstrates how fluidity of commitment to different forms of music is played out in personal terms as well as in a range of public performances. This surely captures the way in which music flows through contemporary life in a number of interacting ways.

Summary

This chapter has considered:

- current debates on the idea of youth subcultures and music;
- recent work that has continued to deploy the idea of subculture;
- the idea of scene;
- the theory of the omnivore with respect to music;
- the place of music in everyday life, including the implications of digitization;
- recent theories of audiences and performance.

Conclusion

Chapters 8 and 9 of this book suggested that the relationships between the production and consumption of contemporary popular music are very complex. Consequently, it is worth stressing again that the division of this book into discussions of production, text and audience, as well as reflecting how the field of popular music studies has developed, is meant to facilitate the presentation and understanding of different aspects of popular music and society. These aspects are not completely separate, nor can they be related in a simple fashion. This, in many ways, is the major problem with the sort of account offered by Adorno and the rationalization approach outlined in the Introduction. Here, clear linkages are hypothesized between the nature of production, the form and content of texts and their understanding by audiences. However, as was suggested in the critiques of these approaches, such accounts are deficient in not realizing the complexity of the different dimensions of production, text and audience and the complicated relationships between them. The claim of this book is that an analytic separation of these dimensions facilitates more detailed examination of their nature and the relations between them.

This approach is similar to that outlined by Richard Johnson (1986), who maintains that cultural studies need to consider the production of texts, the nature of texts themselves, the 'readings' that have and can be made of such texts, and the way in which such readings take place in the context of the 'lived cultures' of everyday social relations.

This book has followed through the five sets of issues or questions outlined towards the end of the Introduction. These were:

1   What is meant by production and producers?
2   How does production take place?
3   How are texts structured and what meanings do they contain?
4   What is an audience?
5   How are texts consumed by an audience?

A full understanding of popular music requires consideration of all these dimensions. Thus, for example, Frith (1990), in his criticism of his earlier work with McRobbie, noted how they had tended to overvalue production and downplay the importance of consumption in the creation of musical meaning. To take another example, the full understanding of the advent of rock and roll would need to combine the emphasis laid on production by Peterson with the attention to textual nuance and meaning given by writers such as Middleton or Brackett and the reconstruction of the meaning of this form for its audience in a way similar to the discussion of The Beatles in chapter 8.

The complexity of some of these issues can be shown through the example of the fan music video texts, also considered in chapter 8. These are texts whose source material was originally produced within large companies for transmission on broadcast television and for mass circulation as music. The television texts and music were structured as realist narratives with the aim of appealing to mass audiences. However, such television programmes became exceptionally popular with groups of fans who formed subcultures that met at conventions and located different meanings in the texts from those perhaps intended by the producers. One of the things these audience members then did was to make videos, using music to foreground their own favourite meanings. The texts produced by multinational corporations in the pursuit of profit were understood and used by distinct groups for their own ends, and new meanings and texts were created. One way of understanding this is to say that these fans were actually producing new texts and new meanings and that they had therefore moved away from being consumers of the texts in question. Contemporary rap and hip-hop music involve similar processes of transformation and relocation of meaning. What remains to be further investigated is the extent to which such active understandings and relocations of texts are going on in other sectors of the population, as well as the specific transformations that are occurring as a consequence. Despite the many advances made in the study of fans and audiences (see, for example, Hills 2002; Sandvoss 2005; Staiger 2005), there remains much to be done. An exemplar with respect to young people and popular music can be found in the work of Laughey (2006).

As discussed in chapter 5 and in relation to YouTube, DIY fan culture is not a new phenomenon. However, Web 2.0 continues to facilitate an expansion of participatory cultures across all fields, including popular music. User-generated content, frequently co-created by collaborative networks of music fans, has led to the theorizing of the convergence of production and consumption. Leadbeater (2009) writes about the 'principle of *with*' that marks all Web activity, while Gauntlett (2011) suggests there is a political dimension to engaged communities who understand that happiness and fulfilment come from creation and not purely from the consumption of media, art and culture, and thus may represent a threat to big businesses. Amid celebrations of the functionality provided by Web 2.0, some commentators such as Lanier (2011) call for a consideration of the limits and dangers of 'template identities' facilitated by new platforms such as Facebook.

The analyst should be wary of making judgements of political worth and aesthetic value simply on the creativity involved in the sorts of transformation carried out in the production of fan music video and rap music. Our suggestion is that cultural forms should be evaluated in their social context and that, even once this has been done, it may be possible to say that some aspects of music are progressive while others are less so. For example, consider again the Madonna phenomenon. In the earlier stages of her career, Madonna may have been an empowering figure for some young women, but she may also have been used as a pin-up for young men, replacing pornographic images. More recently she has been debated as a role model for the older woman. This could also be the case with many other female pop stars.

In general, our view is that even what seem to be the most commodified products of the culture industry need to be examined in their social contexts of production and consumption before any judgements of value can begin to be made. We are suspicious of accounts that 'write off' whole forms of music because they do not seem to conform to traditional standards of high art. If this sounds like a call for appreciation of the relativity of worth and the suspension of critical judgement in the interest of sustained empirical enquiry informed by theoretical innovation, then so much the better.

A key strength of a framework that considers production, text and audience and which resists premature critical or celebratory judgements is that it provides a solid base on which to examine not only what has been achieved in the study of popular music, but also how it can respond to changes in technology, society and culture. It seems clear that technological shifts around digitization and the convergence of technologies have changed the production, textual nature and consumption of popular music greatly. While the prevalence of downloading and file-sharing can still be overestimated, there is no doubt that there are some potential major changes at play. The detailed research evidence on the social and cultural aspects of these shifts is beginning to appear. It shows some significant changes in consumption practices. Being able to carry a large collection of music (and images) in tiny devices and stream services to a mobile phone has implications. However, it is important to recognize that there are some ongoing issues that continue to be significant even in the context of major technological change. Thus, digitization raises important issues about the ownership of rights and brings these even more to the fore in debate. However, as a topic, this in itself is not new, as the research considered in this book demonstrates. The future of music production and consumption will therefore take important and in many ways unanticipated turns, but they can be studied on the basis of what has been found out already. Many other shifts can be thought about in the same way. The studies that have been accumulated during the progress of the development of popular music, media and cultural studies (even if, on the face of it, they may seem dated) therefore have much to offer in helping new directions and practices to be evaluated. It is easy to believe that we always stand on the verge of major shifts. Indeed, while the greater mobility of music and other media is a fundamental change, we must not forget that other changes have been thought of in similar terms in the past. Thus, the introduction of portable transistor radios was much debated in technological social and cultural terms in Britain in the 1960s, as were 'ghetto blasters' in the 1980s. This is not in any way to downplay current shifts, which are major. It does mean taking a deliberate approach to them on the basis of evidence (of the sort of different kinds considered here) and the theoretical frameworks that have been introduced in this book. For example, to what extent will large companies succeed in protecting their positions? What will happen to the way in which musicians work? What do we mean by a musician? Will there be new rights regimes? Will new texts develop? What will be their implications for politics, globalization and sexuality? By whom will the texts be consumed? What technologies are likely to be popular with consumers? These are all questions that the research examined here can begin to allow us to address.

It is clear that work on popular music (and in cultural and media studies in general) has advanced significantly in the period since the first edition of this book was written. One of the pleasures of doing a second and now a third edition has been to reflect as much of this as space allows, but this has still meant leaving much out, especially where research papers published in journals such as *Popular Music* and *Popular Music and Society* are concerned. Some of this research has been addressed, but there is still much more out there for the student, researcher and fan to explore. This is a very positive development, and we hope that it continues, so that the field can continue to expand and take further account of contemporary changes.

Further Reading

A number of the most important books and articles on pop music are discussed in the individual chapters of this book. The reference list that follows provides full bibliographical details for these and other cited texts. In this section, we comment briefly on the key books in this field, primarily as an initial further guide for students to move beyond this text. This is not meant to be exhaustive.

There are two excellent edited collections on the sociological study of popular music. These are *The Popular Music Studies Reader* (2006), by Bennett, Shank and Toynbee, and Frith and Goodwin's collection *On Record* (1990). These are very impressive and useful books which stand comparison with the best of readers. We think that both can be consulted profitably by a student, as the latter provides a base that the former updates and develops in a number of ways. Other introductory books that can be consulted with profit are Negus (1996), Shuker (2012) and Bennett (2001). Also helpful as a companion is Shuker (2011).

Simon Frith has been a key figure in the development of the sociological study of popular music, and any of his work is worth study. His *Performing Rites* (1996) is excellent. Middleton's *Studying Popular Music* (1990) is a thought-provoking musicological discussion of a number of issues arising in the study of popular music. It can be hard going in places, but the considerations of Adorno, folk culture and subculture are particularly rewarding. Relatively little attention has been given in the current book to the more philosophically based studies of the role of music in society and the ways in which society is structured through music. The work of John Shepherd – see his collection *Music as Social Text* (1991) – is central here. Peter Martin's *Sounds and Society* (1995) is also useful. There are now many texts in critical musicology. The Popular and Folk Music Series published by Ashgate and edited by Derek B. Scott contains many examples.

The Music Business and Recording Industry, by Hull, Hutchison and Strasser (3rd edn, 2011), is a comprehensive introduction. It situates the business of music within the wider entertainment industry, thus providing a context that is sometimes missing in other introductory texts. The book utilizes the structure of three income streams (music publishing, live entertainment, recorded music) which we have adapted and used at various points in this edition of *Popular Music and Society*. It includes and addresses the changes brought about by the digital era, as well as their impact on production, marketing, consumption and the legal dimensions of the business such as copyright. For students, it provides interesting case studies, helpful questions for review, DIY activities, a glossary and illustrative figures. Wikström's (2009) *The Music Industry* examines the impact of 'the digital revolution' and, in so doing, provides a practical overview of the industry's traditional structures before exploring the most significant transformations brought about by digitization. Wikström engages with 'music in the cloud' and new business models, roles and related processes, including an examination of practices of both the musicians and audiences/fans. Ogg's (2009) *Independence Days: The Story of UK Independent Record Labels* is based on over 160 interviews with important figures from the UK independent record labels from 1970s onwards, such as Rough Trade, 4AD, Factory, Mute, Beggars Banquet, and so on. It is somewhat 'undisciplined' and has no index, though the advantage of such structure is that it can be picked up and read in a non-linear fashion. Through the combination of summaries and primary data gathered in interviews, Ogg provides an engaging and detailed account of the dynamics and practices within many of the main UK independents. More generally, Hesmondhalgh's *The Cultural Industries* (2012) is very useful in locating the music industry in wider developments. The detail of who owns what changes, so such books can always be supplemented for these matters by the quality daily press and current affairs magazines, as well as their websites.

Works dealing with Web 2.0 and associated music practices are starting to emerge. However, the following more general accounts of audience creativity and participatory cultures will provide helpful introductions to some of the most pertinent issues: Burgess and Green's *YouTube* (2009); Gauntlett's *Making is Connecting: The Social Meaning of Creativity, from DIY and Knitting to YouTube and Web 2.0* (2011); Leadbeater's *We-Think* (2009); and Lanier's *You Are Not a Gadget* (2011).

The work of Marshall (2005) is excellent on copyright. Much of the literature on musicians and local music-making can appear dated, but the general issues that it explores are still important. Cohen's *Rock Culture in Liverpool* (1991) is particularly good on masculinity and gender, and only small parts of Finnegan's admirable *The Hidden Musicians* (1989) have been reported on here. Bayton's *Frock Rock* (1998) is very readable and addresses a number of issues concerning gender. Toynbee's excellent *Making Popular Music* (2000) covers a wide range of issues, including musicians and creativity. As with the work of Finnegan, only limited aspects of his work have been considered in this book.

Histories of pop abound, as do its different genres. Gillett's *The Sound of the City* (1983) is the classic source on the origins of rock. Bradley's *Understanding Rock 'n' Roll* (1992) is useful, as is Chambers's *Urban Rhythms* (1985). An extended examination of the politics of pop can be found in Street's *Music and Politics* (2012). Book-length examinations of punk include Laing's *One Chord Wonders* (1985), Savage's *England's Dreaming* (1991), which focuses on McLaren and the Sex Pistols, and Heylin's *From the Velvets to the Voidoids* (1993), which concentrates on the USA. Sheila Whiteley's edited collection *Sexing the Groove* (1997) is useful on gender. A good, if more journalistic, read is Reynolds and Press (1995). The best collection on the early stages of the over-examined Madonna phenomenon is *The Madonna Connection* (1993), edited by Schwichtenberg.

Oliver's edited collection *Black Music in Britain* (1990) is a useful overview of a number of different dimensions of this topic. Hatch and Millward's *From Blues to Rock* (1987) is informative and relatively neglected. Gilroy argues for a political definition of black music in *There Ain't No Black in the Union Jack* (1987) and again in his *The Black Atlantic* (1993). His work is of ongoing importance. Some of the debates around black music have been brought into sharp focus by the popularity of rap. The reader edited by Forman and Neal entitled *That's the Joint!* (2012) is comprehensive. Rose's *Black Noise* (1994) is still influential. Good discussions of reggae can be found in Clarke's *Jah Music* (1980) and Hebdige's *Cut 'n' Mix* (1987). However, all these genres are now well served by an extensive critical literature.

Machin's (2010) *Analysing Popular Music: Image, Sound, Text* approaches music as discourse, utilizing a semiotic approach to demonstrate how words (lyrics), sound (music) and visuals (album sleeves, video) can be used in the 'decoding' of meaning. The book is concise and accessible, and it features a variety of examples and exercises that go a long way towards demystifying the process of textual analysis. A useful discussion of musical meaning is contained in Moore's *Rock: The Primary Text* (1993). Also excellent is Brackett's *Interpreting Popular Music* (1995). A good collection of popular musicology is Middleton's edited volume *Reading Pop* (2000). Much of the discussion of this topic is best found in studies of specific musical forms. Walser's examination of heavy metal in *Running with the Devil* (1993) is most interesting, and Whiteley has discussed progressive rock in *The Space between the Notes* (1992). Her subsequent books contain analyses of the work of a number of different musicians in the context of cultural theory: see her *Women and Popular Music* (2000) and *Too Much Too Young* (2005). The most important and complete discussion of music video can be found in Goodwin's *Dancing in the Distraction Factory* (1993). Many of Goodwin's other writings can also be consulted with profit. A collection of articles on music video is in the edited collection by Frith, Goodwin and Grossberg, *Sound and Vision: The Music Video Reader* (1993), and an overview of music and the visual in Mundy's *Popular Music on Screen* (1999).

Salih's (2002) excellent commentary is a good way into the work of Judith Butler. Helen Thomas has written much on dance and the body, which has only been touched on in this book, in her *The Body, Dance and Cultural Theory* (2003). The main texts on dance culture are reviewed in chapters 7 and 9 above. Thornton's *Club Cultures* (1995) has been much discussed and set new terms for discussion for subcultural theory. As with other genres, there is now a large literature on dance culture.

Much recent work on audiences has been based around television. In addition to arguing for a new approach to the study of audiences, Abercrombie and Longhurst also summarize the literature in *Audiences* (1998); see also Staiger's *Media Reception Studies* (2005). The most well-known discussion of subculture and music is Hebdige's influential *Subculture* (1979). The best place to start for an overview of the literature is Gelder and Thornton's *The Subcultures Reader* (2005). Other case studies are present in Hall and Jefferson's seminal edited collection *Resistance through Rituals* (1976). Jones's *Black Culture, White Youth* (1988) contains an interesting ethnography. The feminist critique of work from the Birmingham Centre for Contemporary Cultural Studies is collected in McRobbie's *Feminism and Youth Culture* (1991). More recent edited collections on subcultures and subcultural debate include Muggleton and Weinzierl's *The Post-Subcultures Reader* (2003) and Bennett and Kahn-Harris's *After Subculture* (2004). Useful additions to the subcultural literature can be found in Muggleton's *Inside Subculture* (2000) and Hodkinson's *Goth* (2002).

An excellent edited collection on fans is Lewis's *The Adoring Audience* (1992), which contains interesting theoretical and substantive material. Again, much of the most interesting work on fans has been concerned with television – for example, by Jenkins in *Textual Poachers* (1992) and Bacon-Smith in *Enterprising Women* (1992) – though music does figure in these accounts in several places. The literature on fans has grown significantly in recent years. Useful discussions can be found in Hills's

Fan Cultures (2002) and Sandvoss's *Fans: The Mirror of Consumption* (2005). Music and everyday life is explored to excellent effect in DeNora's *Music in Everyday Life* (2000), and Laughey's *Music and Youth Culture* (2006) points the way forward on youth, music and everyday life. A useful edited collection on scenes is Bennett and Peterson's *Music Scenes* (2004), and Shank's ground-breaking examination of the scene in Austin, Texas, *Dissonant Identities* (1994), is worth close study.

The leading academic journals on popular music are *Popular Music* and *Popular Music and Society*. They are both interdisciplinary and contain many useful articles.

In our view, the tip of the icebergs of rock journalism and history can be found in the works of both Marcus and Guralnick. All their books are worth reading. Heylin's *The Penguin Book of Rock & Roll Writing* (1993) also contains much of the best of the rock era's journalism. Simon Reynolds's work is always thought-provoking, as is that of John Harris. The Rough Guide series of books and CDs are also very informative on almost any genre that could be explored, and there are a number of useful websites, in particular:

The Wire (the website has a lot of extra material not published in the magazine) – www.thewire.co.uk

The Quietus – http://thequietus.com

Pitchfork – http://pitchfork.com

Stylus (now defunct, but there are some great articles in the archive) – www.stylusmagazine.com

Sound on Sound (an online version of the sound engineering/production magazine, with lots of interviews with producers, etc.) – www.soundonsound.com

Tape Op – www.tapeop.com

www.rocksbackpages.com

http://the.echonest.com

References

Abercrombie, N. (1990) Popular culture and ideological effects. In N. Abercrombie, S. Hill and B. Turner (eds), *Dominant Ideologies*, London: Unwin Hyman, pp. 199–228.

Abercrombie, N. (1991) The privilege of the producer. In R. Keat and N. Abercrombie (eds), *Enterprise Culture*, London: Routledge, pp. 171–85.

Abercrombie, N., and Longhurst, B. (1998) *Audiences: A Sociological Theory of Performance and Imagination*, London: Sage.

Abercrombie, N., Lash, S., and Longhurst, B. (1992) Popular representation: recasting realism. In S. Lash and J. Friedman (eds), *Modernity and Identity*, Oxford: Blackwell, pp. 115–40.

Adorno, T. (1990) On popular music. In S. Frith and A. Goodwin (eds), *On Record: Rock, Pop, and the Written Word*, London: Routledge, pp. 301–14.

Adorno, T., and Horkheimer, M. (1977) The culture industry: enlightenment as mass deception. In J. Curran, M. Gurevitch and J. Woollacott (eds), *Mass Communication and Society*, London: Edward Arnold, in association with the Open University Press, pp. 349–83.

Alfino, M., Caputo, J. S., and Wynyard, R. (eds) (1998) *McDonaldization Revisited: Critical Essays on Consumer Culture*, Westport, CT: Praeger.

Anderson, B. (1983) *Imagined Communities*, London: Verso.

Ang, I. (1986) *Watching 'Dallas': Soap Opera and the Melodramatic Imagination*, London: Methuen.

Ang, I. (1991) *Desperately Seeking the Audience*, London: Routledge.

Angelou, M. (1985) *Singin' and Swingin' and Gettin' Merry Like Christmas*, London: Virago.

Appadurai, A. (1990) Disjuncture and difference in the global cultural economy. *Theory, Culture and Society*, 7: 295–310.

Appadurai, A. (1996) *Modernity at Large*, Minneapolis and London: University of Minnesota Press.

Auslander, P. (2006) Liveness: performance and the anxiety of simulation. In A. Bennett, B. Shank and J. Toynbee (eds), *The Popular Music Studies Reader*, London and New York: Routledge.

Azzerad, M. (2001) *Our Band Could Be Your Life: Scenes from the American Indie Underground 1981–1991*, London: Little, Brown.

Bacon-Smith, C. (1992) *Enterprising Women: Television Fandom and the Creation of Popular Myth*, Philadelphia: University of Pennsylvania Press.

Bagguley, P. (1991) Post-Fordism and enterprise culture: flexibility, autonomy and changes in economic organization. In R. Keat and N. Abercrombie (eds), *Enterprise Culture*, London: Routledge, pp. 151–68.

Ball, M. S., and Smith, G. W. H. (1992) *Analyzing Visual Data*, London: Sage.

Banerji, S., and Baumann, G. (1990) Bhangra 1984–8: fusion and professionalization in a genre of South Asian dance music. In P. Oliver (ed.), *Black Music in Britain: Essays on the Afro-Asian Contribution to Popular Music*, Milton Keynes: Open University Press, pp. 137–52.

Bannister, M. (2006) *White Boys, White Noise: Masculinities and 1980s Indie Guitar Rock*, Aldershot: Ashgate.

Barber-Kersovan, A. (2003) German Nazi bands: between provocation and repression. In M. Cloonan and R. Garofalo (eds), *Policing Pop*, Philadelphia: Temple University Press, pp. 186–204.

Barker, H., and Taylor, Y. (2007) *Faking It: The Quest for Authenticity in Popular Music*, London and New York: Faber & Faber.

Barnard, S. (2000) *Studying Radio*, London: Edward Arnold.

Barnes, K. (1990) Top 40 radio: a fragment of the imagination. In S. Frith (ed.), *Facing the Music: Essays on Pop, Rock and Culture*, London: Mandarin, pp. 8–50.

Barthes, R. (1976) *Mythologies*, St Albans: Granada.

Barthes, R. (1990) The grain of the voice. In S. Frith and A. Goodwin (eds), *On Record: Rock, Pop, and the Written Word*, London: Routledge, pp. 293–300.

Bayton, M. (1990) How women become musicians. In S. Frith and A. Goodwin (eds), *On Record: Rock, Pop, and the Written Word*, London: Routledge, pp. 238–57.

Bayton, M. (1992) Out on the margins: feminism and the study of popular music. *Women: A Cultural Review*, 3: 51–9.

Bayton, M. (1993) Feminist musical practice: problems and contradictions. In T. Bennett, S. Frith, L. Grossberg, J. Shepherd, and G. Turner (eds), *Rock and Popular Music: Politics, Policies, Institutions*, London: Routledge, pp. 177–92.

Bayton, M. (1998) *Frock Rock: Women Performing Popular Music*, Oxford: Oxford University Press.

Becker, H. (1963) *Outsiders: Studies in the Sociology of Deviance*, New York: Free Press.

Behind the music (2009) Behind the music: unlimited downloading is a risk worth taking, www.guardian.co.uk/music/musicblog/2009/dec/17/unlimited-downloading-file-sharing/print.

Belk, R. (1995) *Collecting in a Consumer Society*, London: Routledge.

Bell, V. (1999a) Historical memory, global movements and violence: Paul Gilroy and Arjun Appadurai in conversation. In V. Bell (ed.), *Performativity and Belonging*, London: Sage, pp. 21–40.

Bell, V. (1999b) Performativity and belonging: an introduction. In V. Bell (ed.), *Performativity and Belonging*, London: Sage, pp. 1–10.

Bennett, A. (1999) Subcultures or neo-tribes? Rethinking the relationship between youth, style and musical taste. *Sociology*, 33: 599–617.

Bennett, A. (2000) *Popular Music and Youth Culture: Music, Identity and Place*. Basingstoke: Macmillan.

Bennett, A. (2001) *Cultures of Popular Music*, Milton Keynes: Open University Press.

Bennett, A. (2004) New tales from Canterbury: the making of a virtual scene. In A. Bennett and R. A. Peterson (eds), *Music Scenes: Local, Translocal, and Virtual*. Nashville: Vanderbilt University Press, pp. 205–20.

Bennett, A., and Kahn-Harris, K. (2004) Introduction. In A. Bennett and K. Kahn-Harris (eds), *After Subculture: Critical Studies in Contemporary Youth Culture*, Basingstoke: Palgrave Macmillan, pp. 1–18.

Bennett, A., and Peterson, R. A. (eds) (2004) *Music Scenes: Local, Translocal, and Virtual*. Nashville: Vanderbilt University Press.

Bennett, A., Shank, B., and Toynbee, J. (2006) *The Popular Music Studies Reader*, London: Routledge.

Bennett, H. S. (1980) *On Becoming a Rock Musician*, Amherst: University of Massachusetts Press.

Bishop, J. (2005) Building international empires of sound: concentrations of power and property in the 'global' music market. *Popular Music and Society*, 28: 443–71.

Björnberg, A. (2000) Structural relationships of music and images in music video. In R. Middleton (ed.), *Reading Pop: Approaches to Textual Analysis in Popular Music*, Oxford: Oxford University Press, pp. 347–78.

Blair, M. E. (2004) Commercialization of the rap music youth subculture. In M. Forman and M. A. Neal (eds), *That's the Joint! The Hip-Hop Studies Reader*, London: Routledge, pp. 497–504.

Bogdanović, D. (2009) Men Doing Bands: Making, Shaping and Performing Masculinities through Popular Music, PhD dissertation, University of Salford.

Boulaire, C., Hervet, G., and Graf, R. (2010) Creativity chains and playing in the crossfire on the video-sharing site YouTube, *Journal of Research in Interactive Marketing*, 4: 111–41.

Bourdieu, P. (1984) *Distinction: A Social Critique of the Judgement of Taste*, London: Routledge & Kegan Paul.

boyd, d. (2007) Why youth (heart) social network sites: the role of networked publics in teenage social life. In D. Buckingham (ed.), *Youth, Identity and Digital Media*, Cambridge, MA: MIT Press. Available at: www.danah.org/papers/WhyYouthHeart.pdf (accessed 19 June 2012).

BPI (British Phonographic Industry) (2005) *Statistical Handbook 2005*, London: BPI.

BPI Yearbook (2011) *Recorded Music in the UK: Facts, Figures and Analysis*, London: BPI.

BPI Yearbook (2012) *Recorded Music in the UK: Facts, Figures and Analysis*, London: BPI.

Brackett, D. (1995) *Interpreting Popular Music*, Berkeley: University of California Press.

Bradby, B. (1990) Do-talk and don't-talk: the division of the subject in girl-group music. In S. Frith and A. Goodwin (eds), *On Record: Rock, Pop, and the Written Word*, London: Routledge, pp. 341–68.

Bradby, B. (1992) Like a virgin-mother? Materialism and maternalism in the songs of Madonna. *Cultural Studies*, 6: 73–96.

Bradby, B., and Torode, B. (2000) Pity Peggy Sue. In R. Middleton (ed.), *Reading Pop: Approaches to Textual Analysis in Popular Music*, Oxford: Oxford University Press, pp. 203–27.

Bradley, D. (1992) *Understanding Rock 'n' Roll: Popular Music in Britain 1955–1964*, Buckingham: Open University Press.

Braudy, L. (1997) *The Frenzy of Renown: Fame and its History*, New York: Vintage.

Breen, M., and Forde, E. (2004) The music industry, technology and utopia – an exchange between Marcus Breen and Eamonn Forde, *Popular Music*, 3(1): 79–89.

Brett, P., Wood, E., and Thomas, G. C. (eds) (1994) *Queering the Pitch: The New Gay and Lesbian Musicology*, London: Routledge.

Browne, M. E., and Fiske, J. (1987) Romancing the rock: romance and representation in popular music videos. *OneTwoThreeFour*, 5.

Brunsdon, C., and Morley, D. (1978) *Everyday Television: 'Nationwide'*, London: British Film Institute.

Bryson, B (1997) 'What about the univores? Musical dislikes and group-based identity construction among Americans with low levels of education. *Poetics*, 25: 141–56.

Bull, M. (2000) *Sounding Out the City: Personal Stereos and the Management of Everyday Life*, Oxford: Berg.

Bull, M. (2004) Automobility and the power of sound. *Theory, Culture and Society*, 21: 243–59.

Bull, M. (2005) No dead air! The iPod and the culture of mobile listening. *Leisure Studies*, 24: 343–55.

Burchill, J., and Parsons, T. (1978) *'The Boy Looked at Johnny': The Obituary of Rock and Roll*, London: Pluto Press.

Burgess, J., and Green, J. (2009) *YouTube: Online Video and Participatory Culture*, Cambridge: Polity.

Burkart, P. (2005) Loose integration in the music industry. *Popular Music and Society*, 28: 489–500.

Burnett, R. (1996) *The Global Jukebox: The International Music Industry*, London: Routledge.

Burt, R. (2007) *The Male Dancer: Bodies, Spectacle, Sexualities*, London: Routledge.

Butler, J. (1990) *Gender Trouble: Feminism and the Subversion of Identity*, London: Routledge.

Butler, J. (1993) *Bodies that Matter: On the Discursive Limits of Sex*, London: Routledge.

Butler, J. (1997) *Excitable Speech: A Politics of the Performative*, London: Routledge.

Butler, J. (1999) *Gender Trouble: Feminism and the Subversion of Identity*, 10th anniversary edn, London: Routledge.

Carr, I. (1999) *Miles Davis: The Definitive Biography*, London: Harper Collins.

Carrabine, E., and Longhurst, B. (1997) What difference does a course make? Music, education and everyday life. *Journal of Popular Music Studies*, 9–10: 79–91.

Carrabine, E., and Longhurst, B. (1999) Mosaics of omnivorousness: middle-class youth and popular culture. *New Formations*, 38: 125–40.

Chambers, I. (1985) *Urban Rhythms: Pop Music and Popular Culture*. Basingstoke: Macmillan.

Chaney, D. (2004) Fragmented culture and subcultures. In A. Bennett and K. Kahn-Harris (eds), *After Subculture: Critical Studies in Contemporary Youth Culture*, Basingstoke: Palgrave Macmillan, pp. 36–48.

Chapman, R. (1992) *Selling the Sixties: The Pirates and Pop Music Radio*, London: Routledge.

Chester, A. (1990) Second thoughts on a rock aesthetic: The Band. In S. Frith and A. Goodwin (eds), *On Record: Rock, Pop and the Written Word*, London: Routledge, pp. 315–19.

Christian, H. (1987) Convention and constraint among British semi-professional jazz musicians. In A. L. White (ed.), *Lost in Music: Culture, Style and the Musical Event*, London: Routledge & Kegan Paul, pp. 220–40.

Clarke, G. (1990) Defending ski-jumpers: a critique of theories of youth subcultures. In S. Frith and A. Goodwin (eds), *On Record: Rock, Pop, and the Written Word*, London: Routledge, pp. 81–96.

Clarke, J., Hall, S., Jefferson, T., and Roberts, B. (1976) Subcultures, cultures and class: a theoretical overview. In S. Hall and T. Jefferson (eds), *Resistance through Rituals: Youth Subcultures in Post-War Britain*, London: Hutchinson, pp. 9–79.

Clarke, M. (1982) *The Politics of Pop Festivals*, London: Junction Books.

Clarke, S. (1980) *Jah Music: The Evolution of the Popular Jamaican Song*, London: Heinemann.

Cline, C. (1992) Essays from *Bitch*: the women's newsletter with bite. In L. Lewis (ed.), *The Adoring Audience: Fan Culture and Popular Media*, London: Routledge, pp. 69–83.

Cloonan, M., and Garafalo, R. (2003) Introduction. In M. Cloonan and R. Garofalo (eds), *Policing Pop*, Philadelphia: Temple University Press, pp. 1–9.

Cohen, P. (1980) Subcultural conflict and working-class community. In S. Hall et al. (eds), *Culture, Media, Language: Working Papers in Cultural Studies, 1972–79*, London: Hutchinson, pp. 78–87.

Cohen, S. (1991) *Rock Culture in Liverpool: Popular Music in the Making*, Oxford: Clarendon Press.

Cohodas, N. (2000) *Spinning Blues into Gold: Chess Records: The Label that Launched the Blues*, London: Aurum Press.

Cole, B. (2001) *John Coltrane*, New York: Da Capo Press.

Collins, Jim (1989) *Uncommon Cultures: Popular Culture and Post-Modernism*, London: Routledge.

Collins, John (1992) Some anti-hegemonic aspects of African popular music. In R. Garofalo (ed.), *Rockin' the Boat: Mass Music and Mass Movements*, Boston: South End Press, pp. 185–94.

Connell, R. W. (1987) *Gender and Power: Society, the Person and Sexual Politics*, Cambridge: Polity.

Connell, R. W., and Messerschmidt, J. W. (2005) Hegemonic masculinity: rethinking the concept. *Gender and Society*, 19: 829–59.

Cook, N. (1998) *Music: A Very Short Introduction*, Oxford: Oxford University Press.

Coppa, F. (2009) A fannish taxonomy of hotness. *Cinema Journal* 48: 107–13.

Coupland, D. (1992) *Generation X*, London: Abacus.

Coward, R. (1984) *Female Desire: Women's Sexuality Today*, London: Paladin.

Cowie, C., and Lees, S. (1981) Slags or drags. *Feminist Review*, 9: 17–31.

Crafts, S. D., Cavicchi, D., and Keil, C. (1993) *My Music*, Hanover, NH, and London: Wesleyan University Press and University Press of New England.

Cranny-Francis, A. (1995) *The Body in the Text*, Carlton South: Melbourne University Press.

Crawford, G. (2003) The career of the sport supporter: the case of the Manchester storm. *Sociology*, 37: 219–37.

Crisell, A. (1994) *Understanding Radio*, London: Routledge.

Cross, B. (1993) *It's Not about a Salary . . . Rap, Race and Resistance in Los Angeles*, London: Verso.

Cubitt, S. (2000) 'Maybellene': meaning and the listening subject. In R. Middleton (ed.), *Reading Pop: Approaches to Textual Analysis in Popular Music*, Oxford: Oxford University Press, pp. 141–59.

Cultural Trends (1993) The music industry, 5(19): 45–66.

Davis, M. (1997) Garage cinema and the future of media technology. *Communications of the ACM*, 40: 42–8.

Davis, M., with Troupe, Q. (1990) *Miles: The Autobiography*, London: Picador.

Davis, S. (1984) *Bob Marley: The Biography*, London: Panther.

De Kloet, J. (2003) Confusing Confucius: rock in contemporary China. In M. Cloonan and R. Garafalo (eds), *Policing Pop*, Philadelphia: Temple University Press, pp. 166–85.

DeNora, T. (2000) *Music in Everyday Life*, Cambridge: Cambridge University Press.

DeNora, T., and Belcher, S. (2000) 'When you're trying something on you picture yourself in a place where they are playing this kind of music': musically sponsored agency in the British clothing retail sector. *Sociological Review*, 48: 80–101.

Dery, M. (2004) Public enemy confrontation. In M. Forman and M. A. Neal (eds), *That's the Joint! The Hip-Hop Studies Reader*, London: Routledge, pp. 407–20.

DeVeaux, S. (1997) *The Birth of Bebop: A Social and Musical History*, Berkeley: University of California Press.

Dredge, S. (2012) MTV Under The Thumb app will stream shows with 'co-viewing' social features, *The Guardian*, www.guardian.co.uk/technology/appsblog/2012/feb/28/mtv-under-the-thumb-app, 28 February.

Drew, R. (2001) *Karaoke Nights: An Ethnographic Rhapsody*, Lanham, MD: AltaMira Press.

Drewett, M. (2003) Music in the struggle to end Apartheid: South Africa. In M. Cloonan and R. Garafalo (eds), *Policing Pop*, Philadelphia: Temple University Press, pp. 153–65.

Ehrenreich, B., Hess, E., and Jacobs, G. (1992) Beatlemania: girls just want to have fun. In L. Lewis (ed.), *The Adoring Audience: Fan Culture and Popular Media*, London: Routledge, pp. 84–106.

Elliott, A. (1999) *The Mourning of John Lennon*, Berkeley: University of California Press.

Fairley, J. (2001) The 'local' and 'global' in popular music. In S. Frith, W. Straw and J. Street (eds), *The Cambridge Companion to Pop and Rock*, Cambridge: Cambridge University Press, pp. 272–89.

Featherstone, M. (1988) In pursuit of the postmodern: an introduction. *Theory, Culture and Society*, 5: 195–215.

Finnegan, R. (1989) *The Hidden Musicians: Music-Making in an English Town*, Cambridge: Cambridge University Press.

Fischer, P. D. (2003) Challenging music as expression in the United States. In M. Cloonan and R. Garofalo (eds), *Policing Pop*, Philadelphia: Temple University Press, pp. 221–37.

Fiske, J. (1987) *Television Culture*, London: Methuen.

Fiske, J. (1992) The cultural economy of fandom. In L. Lewis (ed.), *The Adoring Audience: Fan Culture and Popular Media*, London: Routledge, pp. 30–49.

Fiske, J., and Hartley, J. (1978) *Reading Television*, London: Methuen.

Fonarow, W. (2006) *Empire of Dirt: The Aesthetics and Rituals of British Indie Music*, Middletown, CT: Wesleyan University Press.

Forman, M. (2002) *The Hood Comes First: Race, Space and Place in Rap and Hip-Hop*, Middletown, CT: Wesleyan University Press.

Forman, M. (2012) Ain't no love in the heart of the city: hip-hop, space and place. In M. Forman and M. A. Neal (eds), *That's the Joint! The Hip-Hop Studies Reader*, 2nd edn, London: Routledge, pp. 255–7.

Forman, M., and Neal. M. A. (eds) (2004) *That's the Joint! The Hip-Hop Studies Reader*, London: Routledge.

Forman, M., and Neal, M. A. (eds) (2012) *That's the Joint! The Hip-Hop Studies Reader*, 2nd edn, New York and Abingdon: Routledge.

Fornäs, J., Lindberg, U., and Sernhede, O. (1995) *In Garageland: Rock, Youth and Modernity*, London: Routledge.

Fouz-Hernández, S., and Jarman-Ivens, F. (2004) *Madonna's Drowned Worlds: New Approaches to her Cultural Transformations, 1983–2003*, Aldershot: Ashgate.

Fowler, B. (2000) Introduction. In B. Fowler (ed.), *Reading Bourdieu on Society and Culture*, Oxford: Blackwell/Sociological Review, pp. 1–21.

Freeman, P. (2005) *Running the Voodoo Down: The Electric Music of Miles Davis*, San Francisco: Backbeat.

Frith, S. (1983) *Sound Effects: Youth, Leisure, and the Politics of Rock*, London: Constable.

Frith, S. (1987) Copyright and the music business. *Popular Music*, 7: 57–75.

Frith, S. (1988a) Afterword: making sense of video: pop into the nineties. In S. Frith, *Music for Pleasure: Essays in the Sociology of Pop*, Cambridge: Polity, pp. 205–25.

Frith, S. (1988b) Why do songs have words? In S. Frith, *Music for Pleasure: Essays in the Sociology of Pop*, Cambridge: Polity, pp. 105–28.

Frith, S. (1990) Afterthoughts. In S. Frith and A. Goodwin (eds), *On Record: Rock, Pop, and the Written Word*, London: Routledge, pp. 419–24.

Frith, S. (1992) The industrialization of popular music. In J. Lull (ed.), *Popular Music and Communication*, 2nd edn, Newbury Park, CA: Sage, pp. 49–74.

Frith, S. (1993) Popular music and the local state. In T. Bennett, S. Frith, L. Grossberg, J. Shepherd and G. Turner (eds), *Rock and Popular Music: Politics, Policies, Institutions*, London: Routledge, pp. 14–24.

Frith, S. (1996) *Performing Rites: Evaluating Popular Music*, Oxford: Oxford University Press.

Frith, S. (2001) The popular music industry. In S. Frith, W. Straw and J. Street (eds), *The Cambridge Companion to Pop and Rock*, Cambridge: Cambridge University Press.

Frith, S. (2002) Look! Hear! The uneasy relationship of music and television. *Popular Music*, 21: 277–90.

Frith, S., and Goodwin, A. (eds) (1990) *On Record: Rock, Pop, and the Written Word*, London: Routledge.

Frith, S., and Horne, H. (1987) *Art into Pop*, London: Routledge.

Frith, S., and McRobbie, A. (1990) Rock and sexuality. In S. Frith and A. Goodwin (eds.), *On Record: Rock, Pop, and the Written Word*, London: Routledge, pp. 371–89.

Frith, S., and Street, J. (1992) Rock Against Racism and Red Wedge: from music to politics, from politics to music. In R. Garofalo (ed.), *Rockin' the Boat: Mass Music and Mass Movements*, Boston: South End Press, pp. 67–80.

Frith, S., Goodwin, A., and Grossberg, L. (eds) (1993) *Sound and Vision: The Music Video Reader*, London: Routledge.

Furgason, A. (2008) Afraid of technology? Major label response to advancements in digital technology. *Popular Music History*, 3: 149–70.

Garofalo, R. (1992a) Introduction. In R. Garofalo (ed.), *Rockin' the Boat: Mass Music and Mass Movements*, Boston: South End Press, pp. 1–13.

Garofalo, R. (ed.) (1992b) *Rockin' the Boat: Mass Music and Mass Movements*, Boston: South End Press.

Garofalo, R. (1992c) Understanding mega-events: if we are the world, then how do we change it? In R. Garofalo (ed.), *Rockin' the Boat: Mass Music and Mass Movements*, Boston: South End Press, pp. 15–35.

Garratt, S. (1984) All of us love all of you. In S. Steward and S. Garratt, *Signed, Sealed and Delivered: True Life Stories of Women in Pop*, London: Pluto Press, pp. 138–51.

Gauntlett, D. (2011) *Making is Connecting: The Social Meaning of Creativity, from DIY and Knitting to YouTube and Web 2.0*, Cambridge: Polity.

Gelder, K., and Thornton, S. (eds) (1997) *The Subcultures Reader*, London: Routledge.

Gendron, B. (1986) Theodore Adorno meets the Cadillacs. In T. Modleski (ed.), *Studies in Entertainment: Critical Approaches to Mass Culture*, Bloomington: Indiana University Press, pp. 272–308.

Gerber, H. (2011) Adult MP3 users' perspectives on past and present consumer audio technology: does the music still matter? *Journal on the Art of Record Production*, no. 5.

Gilbert, J., and Pearson, E. (1999) *Discographies: Dance Music, Culture and the Politics of Sound*, London: Routledge.

Gillett, C. (1983) *The Sound of the City: The Rise of Rock and Roll*, London: Souvenir Press.

Gillett, C. (1988) *Making Tracks: The Story of Atlantic Records*, London: Souvenir Press.

Gilroy, P. (1987) *'There Ain't No Black in the Union Jack': The Cultural Politics of Race and Nation*, London: Hutchinson.

Gilroy, P. (1993) *The Black Atlantic: Modernity and Double Consciousness*, London: Verso.

Goodwin, A. (1991) Popular music and postmodern theory. *Cultural Studies*, 5: 174–90.

Goodwin, A. (1992) Rationalization and democratization in the new technologies of popular music. In J. Lull (ed.), *Popular Music and Communication*, 2nd edn, Newbury Park, CA: Sage, pp. 75–100.

Goodwin, A. (1993) *Dancing in the Distraction Factory: Music Television and Popular Culture*, London: Routledge.

Gordon, R. (1995) *It Came from Memphis*, London: Secker & Warburg.

Grazian, D. (2004) The symbolic economy of authenticity in the Chicago blues scene. In A. Bennett and R. A. Peterson (eds), *Music Scenes: Local, Translocal, and Virtual*. Nashville: Vanderbilt University Press, pp. 31–47.

Griffiths, D. (1999) The high analysis of low music. *Music Analysis*, 18: 389–435.

Griffiths, D. (2000) Three tributaries of 'The River'. In R. Middleton (ed.), *Reading Pop: Approaches to Textual Analysis in Popular Music*, Oxford: Oxford University Press, pp. 192–202.

Grossberg, L. (1983) The politics of youth culture: some observations on rock and roll in American culture. *Social Text*, 8: 104–26.

Grossberg, L. (1992a) Is there a fan in the house? The affective sensibility of fandom. In L. Lewis (ed.), *The Adoring Audience: Fan Culture and Popular Media*, London: Routledge, pp. 50–65.

Grossberg, L. (1992b) *We Gotta Get Out of This Place*, London: Routledge.

Gruzelier, J. (2007) Moshpit menace and masculine mayhem. In F. Jarman-Ivens (ed.), *Oh Boy! Masculinities and Popular Music*, London and New York: Routledge.

Guilbert, Georges-Claude (2002) *Madonna as Postmodern Myth: How One Star's Self-Construction Rewrites Sex, Gender, Hollywood and the American Dream*, Jefferson, NC: McFarland.

Guralnick, P. (1991) *Sweet Soul Music: Rhythm and Blues and the Southern Dream of Freedom*, London: Penguin.

Guralnick, P. (1992) *Feel Like Going Home: Portraits in Blues and Rock 'n' Roll*, London: Penguin.

Guralnick, P. (1995) *Last Train to Memphis: The Rise of Elvis Presley*, London: Abacus.

Hall, S. (1980) Encoding/decoding. In S. Hall et al. (eds), *Culture, Media, Language: Working Papers in Cultural Studies, 1972–79*, London: Hutchinson, pp. 128–38.

Hall, S. (1992) The question of cultural identity. In S. Hall, D. Held and T. McGrew (eds), *Modernity and its Futures*, Cambridge: Polity, in association with the Open University, pp. 273–325.

Hall, S., and Jefferson, T. (eds) (1976) *Resistance through Rituals: Youth Subcultures in Post-War Britain*, London: Hutchinson.

Haridakis, P., and Hanson, G. (2009) Social interaction and co-viewing with YouTube: blending mass communication reception and social connection, *Journal of Broadcasting & Electronic Media*, 53: 317–35.

Harker, D. (1980) *One for the Money: Politics and Popular Song*, London: Hutchinson.

Harris, J. (2003) *The Last Party: Britpop, Blair and the Demise of English Rock*, London: Harper Perennial.

Haslam, D. (2000) *Manchester, England: The Story of the Pop Cult City*, London: Fourth Estate.

Hatch, D., and Millward, S. (1987) *From Blues to Rock: An Analytical History of Pop Music*, Manchester: Manchester University Press.

Hawkins, S. (2000) Prince: harmonic analysis of 'Anna Stesia'. In R. Middleton (ed.), *Reading Pop: Approaches to Textual Analysis in Popular Music*, Oxford: Oxford University Press, pp. 58–70.

Hebdige, D. (1979) *Subculture: The Meaning of Style*, London: Methuen.

Hebdige, D. (1987) *Cut 'n' Mix: Culture, Identity and Caribbean Music*, London: Methuen.

Hebdige, D. (1988) *Hiding in the Light*, London: Comedia.

Heble, A. (2000) *Landing on the Wrong Note: Jazz, Dissonance and Critical Practice*, London: Routledge.

Held, D. (1980) *Introduction to Critical Theory: Horkheimer to Habermas*, London: Hutchinson.

Hendy, D. (2000) *Radio and the Global Age*, Cambridge: Polity.

Hesmondhalgh, D. (1997) Post-punk's attempt to democratise the music industry: the success and failure of Rough Trade. *Popular Music*, 16: 255–74.

Hesmondhalgh, D. (1998) The British dance music industry: a case study in independent cultural production. *British Journal of Sociology*, 49: 234–51.

Hesmondhalgh, D. (2002) *The Cultural Industries*, London: Sage.

Hesmondhalgh, D. (2005) Subcultures, scenes or tribes? None of the above. *Journal of Youth Studies*, 8: 21–40.

Hesmondhalgh, D. (2012) *The Cultural Industries*, 3rd edn, London: Sage.

Hess, M. (2012) The rap career. In M. Forman and M. A. Neal (eds), *That's the Joint! The Hip-Hop Studies Reader*, 2nd edn, New York and Abingdon: Routledge, pp. 634–54.

Hetherington, K. (1992) Stonehenge and its festival: spaces of consumption. In R. Shields (ed.), *Lifestyle Shopping: The Subject of Consumption*, London: Routledge.

Heylin, C. (1993) *From the Velvets to the Voidoids: A Pre-Punk History for a Post-Punk World*, London: Penguin.

Hills, M. (2002) *Fan Cultures*, London: Routledge.

Ho, W.-C. (2003) Between globalisation and localisation: a case study of Hong Kong popular music. *Popular Music*, 22: 143–57.

Hobson, D. (1980) Housewives and the mass media. In S. Hall et al. (eds), *Culture, Media, Language: Working Papers in Cultural Studies, 1972–79*, London: Hutchinson, pp. 105–14.

Hodkinson, P. (2002) *Goth: Identity, Style and Subculture*, Oxford: Berg.

Hodkinson, P. (2004) Translocal connections in the Goth scene. In A. Bennett and R. A. Peterson (eds), *Music Scenes: Local, Translocal, and Virtual*. Nashville: Vanderbilt University Press, pp. 131–48.

Hoggart, R. (1958) *The Uses of Literacy*. Harmondsworth: Penguin.

Holmes Smith, C. (2012) 'I don't like to dream about getting paid': representation of social mobility and the emergence of the hip-hop mogul. In M. Forman and M. A. Neal (eds), *That's the Joint! The Hip-Hop Studies Reader*, 2nd edn, New York and Abingdon: Routledge, pp. 672–89.

Hugill, A. (2008) *The Digital Musician: Creating Music with Digital Technology*, New York: Routledge.

Hull, G. P., Hutchison, T., and Strasser, R. (2011) *The Music Business and Recording Industry*, London: Routledge.

Hung, M., and Morencos, E. G. (1990) *World Record Sales: 1969–1990*, London: International Federation of the Phonographic Industry.

IFPI (International Federation of the Phonographic Industry) (1990) *World Sales 1989*, London: IFPI.

IFPI (2012) Digital Music Report 2012: Expanding Choice – Going Global. London: IFPI; www.ifpi.org/content/library/DMR2012.pdf.

Irving, K. (1993) 'I want your hands on me': building equivalences through rap music. *Popular Music*, 12: 105–21.

Jackson, P. (2004) *Inside Clubbing: Sensual Experiments in the Art of Being Human*, Oxford: Berg.

Jay, M. (1973) *The Dialectical Imagination: A History of the Frankfurt School and the Institute of Social Research 1923–1950*, London: Heinemann.

Jenkins, H. (1992) *Textual Poachers: Television Fans and Participatory Culture*, London: Routledge.

Jenkins, H. (2009) What happened before YouTube. In J. Burgess and J. Green, *YouTube: Online Video and Participatory Culture*, Cambridge: Polity.

Jenkins, H., with Purushotma, R., Clinton, K., Weigel, M., and Robison, A. J. (2006) *Confronting the Challenges of Participatory Culture: Media Education for the 21st Century*, Chicago: MacArthur Foundation.

Jenson, J. (1992) Fandom as pathology: the consequences of characterization. In L. Lewis (ed.), *The Adoring Audience: Fan Culture and Popular Media*, London: Routledge, pp. 9–29.

Johnson, R. (1986–7) What is cultural studies anyway? *Social Text*, 16: 38–80.

Jones, Simon (1988) *Black Culture, White Youth: The Reggae Tradition from JA to UK*, Basingstoke: Macmillan.

Jones, Steve (1992) *Rock Formation: Music, Technology and Mass Communication*, Newbury Park, CA: Sage.

Kahn-Harris, K. (2000) 'Roots'? The relationship between the global and the local within the extreme metal scene. *Popular Music*, 19(1): 13–30.

Kahn-Harris, K. (2003) Death metal and the limits of musical expression. In M. Cloonan and R. Garofalo (eds), *Policing Pop*, Philadelphia: Temple University Press, pp. 81–99.

Kahn-Harris, K. (2004) Unspectacular subculture? Transgression and mundanity in the global extreme metal scene. In A. Bennett and K. Kahn-Harris (eds), *After Subculture: Critical Studies in Contemporary Youth Culture*, Basingstoke: Palgrave Macmillan, pp. 107–18.

Kahn-Harris, K. (2007) *Extreme Metal: Music and Culture on the Edge*, Oxford and New York: Berg.

Kaplan, E. A. (1987) *Rocking Around the Clock: Music Television, Postmodernism, and Consumer Culture*, London: Routledge.

Kealy, E. (1990) From craft to art: the case of sound mixers and popular music. In S. Frith and A. Goodwin (eds), *On Record: Rock, Pop, and the Written Word*, London: Routledge, pp. 207–20.

Keat, R., and Urry, J. (1975) *Social Theory as Science*, London: Routledge & Kegan Paul.

Kelly, K. (2005) 'We are the web', *Wired*, www.wired.com/wired/archive/13.08/tech.html (accessed 19 June 2012).

Kitwana, B. (2004) The challenge of rap music from cultural movement to political power. In M. Forman and M. A. Neal (eds), *That's the Joint: The Hip-Hop Studies Reader*, London: Routledge, pp. 341–62.

Knopper, S. (2009) *Appetite for Self-Destruction: The Spectacular Crash of the Record Industry in the Digital Age*, London: Simon & Schuster.

Kruse, H. (1993) Subcultural identity in alternative music. *Popular Music*, 12: 33–41.

Kruse, H. (2010) Local identity and independent music scenes, online and off. *Popular Music and Society*, 33: 625–39.

Kusek, D., and Leonhard, G. (2005) *The Future of Music: Manifesto for the Digital Music Revolution*, Boston: Berklee Press.

Laing, D. (1985) *One Chord Wonders: Power and Meaning in Punk Rock*, Milton Keynes: Open University Press.

Laing, D. (1990) Making popular music: the consumer as producer. In A. Tomlinson (ed.), *Consumption, Identity and Style: Marketing, Meanings, and the Packaging of Pleasure*, London: Routledge.

Laing, D. (2008) World music and the global music industry: flows, corporations and networks. *Popular Music History*, 3: 213–31.

Lange P. G. (2007) Publicly private and privately public: social networking on YouTube, *Journal of Computer-Mediated Communication*, 13(1): 361–80.

Lanier, J. (2011) *You Are Not a Gadget*, London: Penguin.

Laughey, D. (2006) *Music and Youth Culture*. Edinburgh: Edinburgh University Press.

Leach, E. E. (2001) Vicars of 'wannabe': authenticity and the Spice Girls. *Popular Music*, 20: 143–67.

Leadbeater, C. (2009) *We-Think: Mass Innovation, Not Mass Production*, London: Profile Books.

Lee, S. (1995) Re-examining the concept of the 'independent' record company: the case of Wax Trax! Records. *Popular Music*, 14: 13–31.

Lewis, J. (1991) *The Ideological Octopus: An Exploration of Television and its Audience*, London: Routledge.

Lewis, L. (ed.) (1992) *The Adoring Audience: Fan Culture and Popular Media*, London: Routledge.

Lewis, L. (1993) Being discovered: the emergence of female address on MTV. In S. Frith, A. Goodwin and L. Grossberg (eds), *Sound and Vision: The Music Video Reader*, London: Routledge, pp. 129–51.

Lin, N. (2001) *Social Capital: A Theory of Social Structure and Action*, Cambridge: Cambridge University Press.

Lindvall, Helienne (2009) Behind the music: the real reason why the major labels love Spotify, 17 August, www.guardian.co.uk/music/musicblog/2009/aug/17/major-labels-spotify.

Longhurst, B. (2007) *Cultural Change and Ordinary Life*, Maidenhead: Open University Press.

Longhurst, B., and Savage, M. (1996) Social class, consumption and the influence of Bourdieu: some critical issues. In S. Edgell, K. Hetherington and A. Warde (eds), *Consumption Matters: The Production and Experience of Consumption*, Oxford: Blackwell, pp. 274–301.

Longhurst, B., Bagnall, G., and Savage, M. (2001) Ordinary consumption and personal identity: radio and the middle classes in the north west of England. In J. Gronow and A. Warde (eds), *Ordinary Consumption*, London: Routledge, pp. 125–41.

Longhurst, B., Smith, G., Bagnall, G., Crawford, G., and Ogborn, M., with Baldwin, E., and McCracken, S. (2008) *Introducing Cultural Studies*, 2nd edn, Harlow: Pearson Education.

Lury, C. (1993) *Cultural Rights: Technology, Legality and Personality*, London: Routledge.

McClary, S., and Walser, R. (1990) Start making sense: musicology wrestles with rock. In S. Frith and A. Goodwin (eds), *On Record: Rock, Pop, and the Written Word*, London: Routledge, pp. 277–92.

McGuigan, J. (1992) *Cultural Populism*, London: Routledge.

Machin, D. (2010) *Analysing Popular Music: Image, Sound, Text*, London: Sage.

McKay, G. (1996) *Senseless Acts of Beauty: Cultures of Resistance since the Sixties*, London: Verso.

McKay, G. (2005) *Circular Breathing: The Cultural Politics of Jazz in Britain*, Durham, NC, and London: Duke University Press.

MacKenzie, D., and Wajcman, J. (1985) Introduction. In D. MacKenzie and J Wajcman (eds), *The Social Shaping of Technology: How the Refrigerator Got its Hum*, Milton Keynes: Open University Press.

MacLeod, B. (1993) *Club Date Musicians: Playing the New York Party Circuit*, Urbana and Chicago: University of Illinois Press.

McRobbie, A. (1978) Working class girls and the culture of femininity. In Women's Studies Group, Centre for Contemporary Cultural Studies, University of Birmingham, *Women Take Issue: Aspects of Women's Subordination*, London: Hutchinson, pp. 96–108.

McRobbie, A. (1980) Settling accounts with subcultures: a feminist critique. *Screen Education*, 34: 37–49.

McRobbie, A. (1984) Dance and social fantasy. In A. McRobbie and M. Nava (eds), *Gender and Generation*, Basingstoke: Macmillan, pp. 130–61.

McRobbie, A. (1991) *Jackie* and *Just Seventeen*: girls' comics and magazines in the 1980s. In A. McRobbie, *Feminism and Youth Culture: From 'Jackie' to 'Just Seventeen'*, Basingstoke: Macmillan, pp. 135–88.

McRobbie, A. (1993) Shut up and dance: youth culture and changing modes of femininity. *Cultural Studies*, 7: 406–26.

McRobbie, A., and Garber, J. (1976) Girls and subcultures: an exploration. In S. Hall and T. Jefferson (eds), *Resistance through Rituals: Youth Subcultures In Post-War Britain*, London: Hutchinson, pp. 209–22.

Maffesoli, M. (1996) *The Time of the Tribes: The Decline of Individualism in Mass Society*, London: Sage.

Mahajan, S. (2006) Concentration ratios for businesses by industry in 2004. *Economic Trends*, 635: 25–47.

Malbon, B. (1999) *Clubbing: Dancing, Ecstasy and Vitality*, London: Routledge.

Mandel, H. (2008) *Miles, Ornette, Cecil: Jazz Beyond Jazz*, London and New York: Routledge.

Marcus, G. (1992) *Dead Elvis: A Chronicle of a Cultural Obsession*, London: Penguin.

Marcus, G. (1993) *Lipstick Traces: A Secret History of the Twentieth Century*, London: Penguin.

Marshall, G. (1990) *The Two Tone Story*, Dunoon, Argyll: S. T. Publishing.

Marshall, L. (2005) *Bootlegging: Romanticism and Copyright in the Music Industry*, London: Sage.

Martin, P. J. (1995) *Sounds and Society: Themes in the Sociology of Music*. Manchester: Manchester University Press.

Martindale, D., and Reidel, J. (1958) Introduction: Max Weber's sociology of music. In M. Weber, *The Rational and Social Foundations of Music*, Carbondale: Southern Illinois University Press.

Masuch, Hartwig (2011) BMG boss predicts death of A&R. *MusicWeek*, 25 January, www.musicweek. com/story.asp?storyCode=1044011&sectioncode=1.

Middles, M. (2009) *Factory: The Story of the Record Label*, London: Virgin.

Middleton, R. (1990) *Studying Popular Music*. Milton Keynes: Open University Press.

Middleton, R. (1993) Popular music analysis and musicology: bridging the gap. *Popular Music*, 12: 177–90.

Middleton, R. (2000) Introduction: locating the popular music text. In R. Middleton (ed.), *Reading Pop: Approaches to Textual Analysis in Popular Music*, Oxford: Oxford University Press, pp. 1–19.

Miles, S. (2000) *Youth Lifestyles in a Changing World*. Buckingham: Open University Press.

Miller, M. (2012) Rap's dirty south: from subculture to pop culture. In M. Forman and M. A. Neal (eds), *That's the Joint! The Hip-Hop Studies Reader*, 2nd edn, New York and Abingdon: Routledge, pp. 228–47.

Moore, A. F. (1993) *Rock: The Primary Text*, Buckingham: Open University Press.

Moore, J. (2000) 'The hieroglyphics of love': the torch singers and interpretation. In R. Middleton (ed.), *Reading Pop: Approaches to Textual Analysis in Popular Music*, Oxford: Oxford University Press, pp. 262–96.

Moores, S. (1993) *Interpreting Audiences*, London: Sage.

Moorhouse, H. F. (1991) *Driving Ambitions: An Analysis of the American Hot Rod Enthusiasm*, Manchester: Manchester University Press.

Morley, D. (1980) *The 'Nationwide' Audience*, London: British Film Institute.

Morley, D. (1986) *Family Television: Cultural Power and Domestic Leisure*, London: Comedia.

Morley, D. (1992) *Television Audiences and Cultural Studies*, London: Routledge.

Muggleton, D. (2000) *Inside Subculture: The Postmodern Meaning of Style*, Oxford: Berg.

Muggleton, D., and Weinzierl, R. (eds) (2003) *The Post-Subcultures Reader*, Oxford: Berg.

Mundy, J. (1999) *Popular Music on Screen: From Hollywood Musical to Music Video*, Manchester: Manchester University Press.

Murdock, G., and Golding, P. (1977) Capitalism, communications and class relations. In J. Curran, M. Gurevitch and J. Woollacott (eds), *Mass Communication and Society*, London: Edward Arnold, in association with the Open University Press, pp. 12–43.

Napoli, P. M. (1998) Evolutionary theories of media institutions and their responses to new technologies. In L. C. Lederman (ed.), *Communication Theory: A Reader*, Dubuque, IA: Kendall/Hunt, pp. 317–329.

Neal, M. A. (1999) *What the Music Said: Black Popular Music and Black Public Culture*, London: Routledge.

Neal, M. A. (2012) I used to love H.E.R.: hip-hop in/and the culture industries. In M. Forman and M. A. Neal (eds), *That's the Joint: The Hip-Hop Studies Reader*, 2nd edn, New York and Abingdon: Routledge, pp. 631–3.

Negus, K. (1992) *Producing Pop: Culture and Conflict in the Popular Music Industry*, London: Edward Arnold.

Negus, K. (1996) *Popular Music in Theory*, Cambridge: Polity.

Negus, K. (1999) *Music Genres and Corporate Cultures*, London: Routledge.

Ogg, A. (2009) *Independence Days: The Story of UK Independent Record Labels*, London: Cherry Red Books.

Oliver, P. (ed.) (1990) *Black Music in Britain: Essays on the Afro-Asian Contribution to Popular Music*, Milton Keynes: Open University Press.

Owens, J. (1979) *Dread: The Rastafarians of Jamaica*, London: Heinemann.

Palmer, R. (1981) *Deep Blues*, London: Macmillan.

Pearce, S. (1995) *On Collecting: An Investigation into Collecting in the European Tradition*, London: Routledge.

Pekacz, J. A. (1964) Did rock smash the wall? The role of rock in political transition. *Popular Music*, 13: 41–9.

Penley, C. (1992) Feminism, psychoanalysis and the study of popular culture. In L. Grossberg, C. Nelson and P. Treichler (eds), *Cultural Studies*, London: Routledge.

Perry, M. D. (2012) Global black self-fashionings: hip-hop as diasporic space. In M. Forman and M. A. Neal (eds), *That's the Joint! The Hip-Hop Studies Reader*, 2nd edn, New York and Abingdon: Routledge, pp. 294–315.

Perullo, A. (2012) Hooligans and heroes: youth identity and hip-hop in Dar es Salaam, Tanzania. In M. Forman and M. A. Neal (eds), *That's the Joint! The Hip-Hop Studies Reader*, 2nd edn, New York and Abingdon: Routledge, pp. 315–36.

Peterson, R. A. (1972) A process model of the folk, pop and fine art phases of jazz. In C. Nanry (ed.), *American Music: From Storyville to Woodstock*, New Brunswick, NJ: Transaction Books, pp. 135–50.

Peterson, R. A. (1990) Why 1955? Explaining the advent of rock music. *Popular Music*, 9: 97–116.

Peterson, R. A. (2005) In Search of Authenticity, *Journal of Management Studies*, 42: 1083–98.

Peterson, R. A., and Anand, N. (2004) The production of culture perspective. *Annual Review of Sociology*, 30: 311–34.

Peterson, R. A., and Bennett, A. (2004) Introducing music scenes. In A. Bennett and R. A. Peterson (eds), *Music Scenes: Local, Translocal, and Virtual*, Nashville: Vanderbilt University Press, pp. 1–15.

Peterson, R. A., and Berger, D. G. (1990) Cycles in symbol production: the case of popular music. In S. Frith and A. Goodwin (eds), *On Record: Rock, Pop, and the Written Word*, London: Routledge, pp. 140–59.

Peterson, R. A., and Kern, R. M. (1996) Changing highbrow taste: from snob to omnivore. *American Sociological Review*, 61: 900–7.

Peterson, R. A., and Simkus, A. (1992) How musical taste groups mark occupational status groups. In M. Lamont and M. Fournier (eds), *Cultivating Differences: Symbolic Boundaries and the Making of Inequality*, Chicago: University of Chicago Press.

Pinard, A., and Jacobs, S. (2006) Building a virtual diaspora: hip-hop in cyberspace. In M. D. Ayers (ed.), *Cybersounds: Essays on Virtual Music Culture*, New York: Peter Lang, pp. 83–105.

Pini, M. (2001) *Club Cultures and Female Subjectivity: The Move from Home to House*. Basingstoke: Palgrave Macmillan.

Plotkin, F. (2003) *Classical Music Unbuttoned: A Complete Guide to Learning and Loving Classical Music*, London: Aurum Press.

Popular Music (2002) Music and Television, 21(3) [special issue].

Prinsky, L. E., and Rosenbaum, J. L. (1987) 'Leer-ics' or lyrics: teenage impressions of rock 'n' roll. *Youth and Society*, 18: 384–97.

Railton, D., and Watson, P. (2011) *Music Video and the Politics of Representation*, Edinburgh: Edinburgh University Press.

Rayna, T., and Striukova, L. (2009) Monometapoly, or the economics of the music industry. *Prometheus*, 27: 211–22.

Redhead, S. (1990) *The End-of-the-Century Party: Youth and Pop Towards 2000*, Manchester: Manchester University Press.

Redhead, S. (ed.) (1993) *Rave Off: Politics and Deviance in Contemporary Youth Culture*, Aldershot: Avebury.

Reynolds, S. (1998) *Energy Flash: A Journey through Rave Music and Dance Culture*, London: Picador.

Reynolds, S. (2005) *Rip it Up and Start Again: Postpunk 1978–1984*, London: Faber & Faber.

Reynolds, S., and Press, J. (1995) *The Sex Revolts: Gender, Rebellion and Rock 'n' Roll*, London: Serpent's Tail.

Rietveld, H. (1993) Living the dream. In S. Redhead (ed.), *Rave Off: Politics and Deviance in Contemporary Youth Culture*, Aldershot: Avebury.

Rietveld, H. (1998) *This is Our House: House Music, Cultural Spaces and Technologies*. Aldershot: Ashgate.

Ritzer, G. (1993) *The McDonaldization of Society: An Investigation into the Changing Character of Contemporary Social Life*, Thousand Oaks, CA: Pine Forge Press.

Ritzer, G. (ed.) (2002a) *McDonaldization: The Reader*, Thousand Oaks, CA: Pine Forge Press.

Ritzer, G. (2000b) Some thoughts on the future of McDonaldization. In G. Ritzer (ed.), *McDonaldization: The Reader*, Thousand Oaks, CA: Pine Forge Press, pp. 255–66.

Ritzer, G. (2004) *The McDonaldization of Society: An Investigation into the Changing Character of American Life*, rev. edn, Thousand Oaks, VA: Pine Forge Press.

Robertson, R. (1995) Glocalisation: time–space and homogeneity–heterogeneity. In M. Featherstone, S. Lash and R. Robertson (eds), *Global Modernities*, London: Sage.

Robertson, R., and White, K. E. (2005) Globalization: sociology and cross-disciplinarity. In C. Calhoun, C. Rojek and B. Turner (eds), *The Sage Handbook of Sociology*, London: Sage, pp. 345–66.

Robins, P., and Cohen, P. (1978) *Knuckle Sandwich: Growing up in the Working Class City*. Harmondsworth: Penguin.

Robinson, J. Bradford (1994) The jazz essays of Theodor Adorno: some thoughts on jazz reception in Weimar Germany. *Popular Music*, 13: 1–25.

Rodman, G. B. (1996) *Elvis after Elvis: The Posthumous Career of a Living Legend*, London: Routledge.

Rogan, J. (1993) *Morrissey & Marr: The Severed Alliance*, London: Omnibus.

Rojek, C. (2001) *Celebrity*, London: Reaktion Books.

Rose, T. (1994) *Black Noise: Rap Music and Black Culture in Contemporary America*, Hanover, NH, and London: Wesleyan University Press and University Press of New England.

Ross, P. G. (2005) Cycles in symbol production research: foundations, applications, and future directions. *Popular Music and Society*, 28: 473–87.

Salih, S. (2002) *Judith Butler*, London: Routledge.

Sandvoss, C. (2003) *A Game of Two Halves: Football, Television and Globalization*, London: Comedia.

Sandvoss, C. (2005) *Fans: The Mirror of Consumption*, Cambridge: Polity.

Savage, J. (1991) *England's Dreaming: Sex Pistols and Punk Rock*, London: Faber & Faber.

Savage, M., Bagnall, G., and Longhurst, B. (2005) *Globalization and Belonging*, London: Sage.

Schilt, K. (2004) 'Riot Grrrl is . . .': contestation over meaning in a music scene. In A. Bennett and R. A. Peterson (eds), *Music Scenes: Local, Translocal, and Virtual*. Nashville: Vanderbilt University Press, pp. 115–30.

Schloss, J. G. (2004) *Making Beats: The Art of Sample-Based Hip-Hop*. Middletown, CT: Wesleyan University Press.

Schulze, L., Barton White, A., and Brown, J. D. (1993) 'A sacred monster in her prime': audience construction of Madonna as low-other. In C. Schwichtenberg (ed.), *The Madonna Connection:*

Representational Politics, Subcultural Identities, and Cultural Theory, Oxford: Westview Press, pp. 15–37.

Schwichtenberg, C. (ed.) (1993) *The Madonna Connection: Representational Politics, Subcultural Identities and Cultural Theory*, Oxford: Westview Press.

Shank, B. (1994) *Dissonant Identities: The Rock 'n' Roll Scene in Austin, Texas*, Hanover, NH: Wesleyan University Press and University Press of New England.

Sharma, S., Hutnyk, J., and Sharma, A. (eds) (1996) *Dis-orienting Rhythms: The Politics of the New Asian Dance Music*, London: Zed Books.

Shepherd, J. (1991) *Music as Social Text*, Cambridge: Polity.

Shuker, R. (2010) *Wax Trash and Vinyl Treasures: Record Collecting as a Social Practice*, Farnham: Ashgate.

Shuker, R. (2011) *Popular Music: The Key Concepts*, 3rd edn, London: Routledge.

Shuker, R. (2012) *Understanding Popular Music Culture*, London: Routledge.

Simon, B. S. (1997) Entering the pit: slam-dancing and modernity. *Journal of Popular Culture*, 31: 149–76.

Skeggs, B. (2001) The toilet paper: femininity, class and mis-recognition. *Women's Studies International Forum*, 24: 295–307.

Smith, L. S. (1978) Sexist assumptions and female delinquency: an empirical investigation. In C. Smart and B. Smart (eds), *Women, Sexuality and Social Control*, London: Routledge & Kegan Paul, pp. 74–88.

Spring, K. (2004) Behind the rave: structure and agency in a rave scene. In A. Bennett and R. A. Peterson (eds), *Music Scenes: Local, Translocal, and Virtual*. Nashville: Vanderbilt University Press, pp. 48–63.

Stahl, M. (2002) Authentic boy bands on TV? Performers and impresarios in *The Monkees* and *Making the Band*. *Popular Music*, 21: 307–29.

Staiger, J. (2005) *Media Reception Studies*, New York: New York University Press.

Starkey, G. (2004) *Radio in Context*, Basingstoke: Palgrave Macmillan.

Starkey, G. (2011) *Local Radio, Going Global*, Basingstoke: Palgrave Macmillan.

Stephens, G. (1992) Interracial dialogue in rap music: call-and-response in a multicultural style. *New Formations*, 16: 62–79.

Steward, S., and Garratt, S. (1984) *Signed, Sealed, and Delivered: True Life Stories of Women in Pop*, London: Pluto Press.

Straw, W. (1991) Systems of articulation, logics of change: communities and scenes in popular music. *Cultural Studies*, 15: 368–88.

Straw, W. (1997) Sizing up record collections: gender and connoisseurship in rock music culture. In S. Whiteley (ed.), *Sexing the Groove: Popular Music and Gender*, London: Routledge, pp. 3–16.

Street, J. (1986) *Rebel Rock: The Politics of Popular Music*, Oxford: Blackwell.

Street, J. (1993) Local differences? Popular music and the local state. *Popular Music*, 12: 43–55.

Street, J. (2001) Rock, pop and politics. In S. Frith, W. Straw and J. Street (eds), *The Cambridge Companion to Pop and Rock*, Cambridge: Cambridge University Press, pp. 243–55.

Street, J. (2012) *Music and Politics*, Cambridge: Polity.

Struthers, S. (1987) Technology in the art of recording. In A. L. White (ed.), *Lost in Music: Culture, Style and the Musical Event*, London: Routledge & Kegan Paul, pp. 241–58.

Swendenberg, T. (1992) Homies in the hood: rap's commodification of insubordination. *New Formations*, 18: 53–66.

Tagg, P. (1989) Open letter: 'black music', 'Afro-American music' and 'European music'. *Popular Music*, 8: 285–98.

Tagg, P. (2000) Analysing popular music: theory, method, and practice. In R. Middleton (ed.), *Reading Pop: Approaches to Textual Analysis in Popular Music*, Oxford: Oxford University Press, pp. 71–103.

Tagg, P. (2011) Caught on the back foot: epistemic inertia and visible music. *Journal of the International Association for the Study of Popular Music*, 2: 4–18.

Taylor, S. (2003) *False Prophet: Field Notes from the Punk Underground*, Middletown, CT: Wesleyan University Press.

Taylor, T. (1997) *Global Pop: World Music, World Markets*, London: Routledge.

Taylor, T. (2000) His name was in lights: Chuck Berry's 'Johnny B. Goode.' In R. Middleton (ed.), *Reading Pop: Approaches to Textual Analysis in Popular Music*, Oxford: Oxford University Press, pp. 165–82.

Théberge, P. (1989) The 'sound' of music: technological rationalization and the production of popular music. *New Formations*, 8: 99–111.

Théberge, P. (1997) *Any Sound You Can Imagine: Making Music/Consuming Technology*, Hanover, NH, and London: Wesleyan University Press and University Press of New England.

Thomas, H. (2003) *The Body, Dance and Cultural Theory*, Basingstoke: Palgrave Macmillan.

Thornton, S. (1995) *Club Cultures: Music, Media and Subcultural Capital*, Cambridge: Polity.

Tingen, P. (2001) *Miles Beyond: The Electric Explorations of Miles Davis, 1967–1991*, New York: Billboard.

Tomlinson, J. (1999) *Globalization and Culture*, Cambridge: Polity.

Toop, D. (1984) *The Rap Attack: African Jive to New York Hip Hop*, London: Pluto Press.

Toynbee, J. (2000) *Making Popular Music: Musicians, Creativity and Institutions*, London: Edward Arnold.

Tsitsos, W. (1999) Rules of rebellion: slamdancing, moshing, and the American alternative scene. *Popular Music* 18: 397–414.

Turner, G. (1990) *British Cultural Studies*, London: Unwin Hyman.

Urquia, N. (2004) 'Doin' it right': contested authenticity in London's salsa scene. In A. Bennett and R. A. Peterson (eds), *Music Scenes: Local, Translocal, and Virtual*. Nashville: Vanderbilt University Press, pp. 96–112.

Véran, C., et al. (2012) Native tongues: a roundtable on hip-hop's global indigenous movement. In M. Forman and M. A. Neal (eds), *That's the Joint! The Hip-Hop Studies Reader*, 2nd edn, New York and Abingdon: Routledge, pp. 336–45.

Vermorel, F., and Vermorel, J. (1985) *Starlust: The Secret Life of Fans*, London: W. H. Allen.

Vroomen, L. (2004) Kate Bush: teen pop and older female fans. In A. Bennett and R. A. Peterson (eds.), *Music Scenes: Local, Translocal, and Virtual*. Nashville: Vanderbilt University Press, pp. 238–53.

Wallis, R. and Malm, K. (1990) Patterns of change. In S. Frith and A. Goodwin (eds), *On Record: Rock, Pop, and the Written Word*, London: Routledge, pp. 160–80.

Walser, R. (1993) *Running with the Devil: Power, Gender, and Madness in Heavy Metal Music*, Hanover, NH: Wesleyan University Press and University Press of New England.

Warde, A. (1992) Notes on the relationship between production and consumption. In R. Burrows and C. Marsh (eds), *Consumption and Class: Divisions and Change*, Basingstoke: Macmillan, pp. 15–31.

Weber, M. (1958) *The Rational and Social Foundations of Music*, Carbondale: Southern Illinois University Press.

Weinstein, D. (1991) *Heavy Metal: A Cultural Sociology*, New York: Lexington Books.

Wernick, A. (1991) *Promotional Culture: Advertising, Ideology and Symbolic Expression*, London: Sage.

White, A. L. (1987) A professional jazz group. In A. L. White (ed.), *Lost in Music: Culture, Style and the Musical Event*, London: Routledge & Kegan Paul, pp. 191–219.

White, T. (1984) *Catch a Fire: The Life of Bob Marley*, London: Corgi.

Whiteley, S. (1992) *The Space between the Notes: Rock and the Counter-Culture*, London: Routledge.

Whiteley, S. (ed.) (1997) *Sexing the Groove: Popular Music and Gender*, London: Routledge.

Whiteley, S. (2000a) Progressive rock and psychedelic coding in the work of Jimi Hendrix. In R. Middleton (ed.), *Reading Pop: Approaches to Textual Analysis in Popular Music*, Oxford: Oxford University Press, pp. 235–61.

Whiteley, S. (2000b) *Women and Popular Music: Sexuality, Identity and Subjectivity*, London: Routledge.

Whiteley, S. (2005) *Too Much Too Young: Popular Music, Age and Gender*, London: Routledge.

Wicke, P. (1992a) The role of rock music in the political disintegration of East Germany. In J. Lull (ed.), *Popular Music and Communication*, 2nd edn, Newbury Park, CA: Sage, pp. 196–206.

Wicke, P. (1992b) The times they are a-changin': rock music and political change in East Germany.

In R. Garofalo (ed.), *Rockin' the Boat: Mass Music and Mass Movements*, Boston: South End Press, pp. 81–92.

Wicke, P., and Shepherd, J. (1993) 'The cabaret is dead': rock culture as state enterprise – the political organization of rock in East Germany. In T. Bennett, S. Frith, L. Grossberg, J. Shepherd and G. Turner (eds), *Rock and Popular Music: Politics, Policies, Institutions*, London: Routledge, pp. 25–36.

Widdicombe, S., and Wooffitt, R. (1995) *The Language of Youth Subcultures*. Hemel Hempstead: Harvester Wheatsheaf.

Widgery, D. (1986) *Beating Time*, London: Chatto & Windus.

Wikström, P. (2009) *The Music Industry: Music in the Cloud*, Cambridge: Polity.

Williams, C. (2001) Does it really matter? Young people and popular music. *Popular Music*, 20: 223–42.

Williams, R. (1973) Base and superstructure in Marxist cultural theory. *New Left Review*, 82: 3–16; repr., with alterations, in Williams, *Problems in Materialism and Culture*, London: Verso, 1980, pp. 31–49.

Williams, R. (1983) *Towards 2000*, London: Chatto & Windus.

Williams, R. (1989) *The Politics of Modernism: Against the New Conformists*, London: Verso.

Williams, S. F. (2007) 'A walking open wound': emo rock and the 'crisis' of masculinity in America. In F. Jarman-Ivens (ed.), *Oh Boy! Masculinities and Popular Music*, London and New York: Routledge.

Willis, P. (1977) *Learning to Labour: How Working Class Kids Get Working Class Jobs*, Farnborough: Saxon House.

Willis, P. (1978) *Profane Culture*, London: Routledge & Kegan Paul.

Willis, P., with Jones, S., Canaan, J., and Hurd, G. (1990) *Common Culture: Symbolic Work at Play in the Everyday Cultures of the Young*, Milton Keynes: Open University Press.

Winkler, P. (2000) Randy Newman's Americana. In R. Middleton (ed.), *Reading Pop: Approaches to Textual Analysis in Popular Music*, Oxford: Oxford University Press, pp. 27–57.

Wise, S. (1990) Sexing Elvis. In S. Frith and A. Goodwin (eds), *On Record: Rock, Pop, and the Written Word*, London: Routledge, pp. 390–8.

Young, S., and Collins, S. (2010) A view from the trenches of Music 2.0. *Popular Music and Society*, 33: 339–55.

Index